D0027346

The Year of the
ANGLER
and
The Year of the
TROUT

Tales of Fly Fishing, Rivers,
the Environment, and Life

Steve Raymond

THE LYONS PRESS
Guilford, Connecticut
An imprint of The Globe Pequot Press

Dedicated to my mother, Grace A. Raymond,
and also to Joan, Stephanie, and Randy —
for sharing all the seasons.

To buy books in quantity for corporate use
or incentives, call **(800) 962–0973, ext. 4551,**
or e-mail **premiums@GlobePequot.com.**

Copyright © 1995 by Steve Raymond

First Lyons Press edition, 2005

The Year of the Angler originally published in 1973 by Winchester Press. *The Year of the Trout* originally published in 1985 by Winchester Press. Both editions published and distributed by Sasquatch books in1995. Distributed in Canada by Raincoast Books Ltd.

ALL RIGHTS RESERVED. No part of this book may be reproduced or transmitted in any form by any means, electronic or mechanical, including photocopying and recording, or by any information storage and retrieval system, except as may be expressly permitted in writing from the publisher. Requests for permission should be addressed to The Lyons Press, Attn: Rights and Permissions Department, P.O. Box 480, Guilford, CT 06437.

The Lyons Press is an imprint of The Globe Pequot Press.

10 9 8 7 6 5 4 3 2 1

Printed in the United States of America

Interior illustrations by Dave Whitlock

ISBN 1-59228-598-8

Library of Congress Cataloging-in-Publication Data is available on file.

CONTENTS

PART Two: *The Year of the Trout* • 241

INTRODUCTION

to the 2005 Edition

Now at last they are together. I have always believed these two books belonged under a single cover; although they were written a dozen years apart, one followed the other in a natural progression, like a brace of trout taken back-to-back on the fly.

Much has changed since they were first published. It could hardly be otherwise, for change is the natural order of things. Some things inevitably have changed for the worse—some, but not all. In at least a few instances the fishing is better now than when these books were written.

Let's take stock of some of those changes, beginning with *The Year of the Angler:*

The "Hoh," which we will fish together in the first chapter, still runs free, protected in its upper reaches by Olympic National Park. A friend just caught his first-ever steelhead in the Hoh, which proves it is still a generous river on occasion.

"The Quality of Courage," described in the second chapter, remains perpetually strong in both people and wild creatures. Anglers still wade boldly into swift waters, pursuing the sport they love even when the hour is late and shadows are gathering.

The sea-run cutthroat fishing around "Belfair" in Hood Canal is better than ever, thanks to catch-and-release regulations implemented after years of lobbying by anglers. The sea-run is among the Northwest's last wild trout, so such regulations are both appropriate and necessary.

Unfortunately, Hood Canal itself has not fared as well. Too many homes have been built along its scenic shores and runoff from septic systems has polluted this great natural fjord, leaving its depths almost devoid of oxygen during summer. This has caused the death of many bottom fish, but the shallower waters, where cutthroat and salmon dwell, have not been affected—so far.

Fly fishing has become much more popular as "A Choice of Method" since the chapter bearing that title was written, and this is both good and bad—good because most ardent fly fishers become conservationists, bad because they now crowd waters set aside for their use.

Fly fishing also is now more of a year-round sport than it used to be, so anglers are no longer anxiously for "Waiting for Winter's End." Many of the mail-order fly-fishing businesses mentioned in this chapter have passed into oblivion while others have moved onto other and not necessarily better things. In their place we now see a proliferation of fly-fishing businesses on the Internet.

If I were return to Pass Lake these days—as I still do occasionally—I would no longer expect to find a "Trout Under

the Cedar Limb." The lake still holds large trout, but a burgeoning scrap-fish population has changed the character of
the fishing. Now it is usually necessary to work a fly slowly
and deeply, a method for which I have little enthusiasm.

I would also not expect to find the same quality of shad
fishing if I spent another "Day on the Yuba." Bill McGrath,
my Yuba River fishing partner, has long since gone to fish in
uncharted waters, but other California angling friends tell
me the Yuba's shad fishing is no longer as reliable as it was.

I don't fish "After Dark" as often as I once did. Perhaps
I've just had enough of that experience, though I still re-
member some wild times battling big fish in total darkness.
They always seem bigger when you can't see them.

"Spring in British Columbia" is still on my fishing
agenda, but no longer as regularly as before. New highways
have made the fishing altogether too easy to reach, and
many of my once-favorite spots have been overrun by hordes
of anglers. Strict angling regulations have preserved some
waters, however, and that's enough to keep me going back,
if not as frequently as before.

Quail Lake, the little pond where I once found "Basin
Browns," was later treated to remove an exploding population of sunfish. After that it was stocked with rainbow trout,
then later with Atlantic salmon, and now again holds only
rainbows. But brown trout have been stocked in other Columbia Basin waters and I still catch one now and then—
most larger than any I ever caught in Quail Lake.

I haven't been to "The Firehole" recently, but other
fishermen tell me it's still just as hauntingly beautiful as
ever—and just as enigmatic.

If my old friend Lloyd Frese were still around, he would-
n't worry any longer that heaven might not be as good as
Oregon's "Hosmer" Lake. Hosmer has fallen on hard times.
(More about that later when we turn to the chapter in *The
Year of the Trout* that deals in part with Hosmer.)

Since my "First Encounter" with a steelhead that turned out so disappointingly, I have had many more that turned out favorably. In fact, I have been seduced by summer steelhead. (More about that also in *The Year of the Trout*.)

The Hanford Reach of the Columbia River, described in "Once There Was a River," has thankfully been preserved, but the Columbia's general health has continued to decline until now its runs of salmon and steelhead are in grave peril. State and federal governments continue throwing dollars at the problem but so far have lacked the resolve to face up to the real solution, which is to breach some of the fish-killing dams.

There are still plenty of "Brook Trout in the West," although probably not as many as before. Fisheries managers have decided that "exotic" species—those not native to the region—should no longer be stocked. Brook trout, however, can spawn successfully in many waters where indigenous rainbow and cutthroat can't spawn at all, so brookies won't go away quickly. As for Leech Lake, where I once caught so many, it still hosts a plentiful population of brook trout, augmented now by some larger triploid (sterilized) rainbow trout.

I have added many chapters to my "North Fork Diary" since *The Year of the Angler* was written. One of those chapters found its way into *The Year of the Trout*. We'll peruse it there.

Even after all these years I'm still asked occasionally about the location of "Mystery Lake." All I will say is that nobody has guessed it yet.

"The Plastic Flags" no longer fly over that wonderful little brook-trout pond I discovered on a long-ago October day. The pond is now surrounded by an ugly subdivision. Enough said.

The salmon fishing described in "Duwamish Episode" also is a thing of the past, at least for me. Large runs of salmon still ascend the Duwamish, but thanks to federal court decisions most fishing in the lower river is now done with Indian nets. That section is also so crowded with shipping traffic that I wouldn't want to fish there again in any case.

The experiment described in "A Lady Named Lenice" failed to produce the desired results. Kamloops trout stocked in the lake did not live as long or grow as large in their new environment as had been hoped, but the good news is that Lenice Lake still provides fine fishing for sizable trout, thanks to continued restrictive angling regulations.

The mysterious ways of the sea-run cutthroat chronicled in "The Track of a Trout" inspired me to conduct a one-man research program that continued for an astonishing eighteen years (the results are reported in another book, *The Estuary Flyfisher*). During that time I was able to discern several patterns in the behavior of sea-runs, but I'd be first to admit there is still a great deal more to learn.

The reasons people fish, enumerated in "The End of the Year," remain as valid today as when the chapter was written. After decades more angling experience, I also remain convinced that the very best friendships are those made along rivers.

It's also worth noting that the English language has changed appreciably since *The Year of the Angler* was written. In those days it was customary to use masculine pronouns to describe groups ranging from the whole human race down to a couple of anglers or trout whose gender was not established. Such pronouns now seem like quaint artifacts, and properly so. I hope women readers will overlook them.

Now let's turn the pages to *The Year of the Trout*:

The steelhead's "Upstream Journey," described in the opening chapter, remains one of the great wonders of nature, but the numbers of fish making that journey have declined over the years. Nevertheless, I continue to pursue them—

and remain grateful that my own journey has led me along the shores of rivers.

I have many fond memories of "The Land of the Long White Cloud." Friends who have been there recently describe big changes in that faraway country, but the fishing seems as good as ever—if one has the necessary patience and persistence.

Books are still "The Next Best Thing" to fishing, and I hope these two will prove the point again. Despite a firm intention to resist becoming a serious collector of fishing books, I seem to have become one anyway, and half a wall of my office is now lined from floor to ceiling with shelves of fishing books. Aside from the great pleasure they have given me, I know that somewhere in all those volumes is the answer to any angling question I could ever think to ask.

The saga chronicled in "Steelhead Blues" is still playing out. Happily, much of the bitterness between competing fishing interests has subsided, but the bottom line remains the same: Anglers have been left with only a small fraction of the number of steelhead they used to catch, and the steelhead itself remains without protection as a game fish. But more enlightened management by state governments and some Indian tribes have helped sustain or even enhance steelhead runs in a few rivers. Despite these limited successes, the overall future of Northwest steelhead runs remains clouded.

I don't know what the fishing is like now in "Cutthroat Slough"—I haven't been there in a long time—but I still remember the bitterly cold day when that mysterious canoe materialized out of the swirling snow, carrying a passenger who was soon to become my friend.

My son, Randy, whom you will meet in "Like Father, Like Son," has grown to manhood and now works too hard and fishes too little. That first trout that took his fly in a little side channel of the North Fork of the Stillaguamish truly did set the hook; fly fishing is now and always will be an important part of his life. He is my favorite fishing partner.

The story of the ice age "Dawn Trout," uncovered in the ancient sediments of Miocene Clarkia Lake, remains an unusual chapter in the history of trout evolution. Those sediments have yielded other discoveries, but none so important to fishery biologists.

The trout's "Family Tree" has undergone a thorough shake-up since *The Year of the Trout* made its first appearance. Rainbow, steelhead, and cutthroat trout and their near relatives have been reclassified from the genus *Salmo* to the genus *Oncorhynchus,* which includes the Pacific salmon. Rainbow and steelhead went from *Salmo gairdneri* to *Oncorhynchus mykiss* and the cutthroat in all its varied forms is no longer *Salmo clarkii* but *Oncorhynchus clarkii.* Taxonomists made the change because research indicated the dividing line between Western trout and Pacific salmon was not as distinct as previously thought. I think the jury is still out on this question, however, and it would not surprise me to see further changes.

Hanging on the wall of my home office is a photograph of an unnamed river, taken when I was "Fishing the Misty Fjords." The photo does no justice to the beauty of the spot— nothing could—but it reminds me of one of the most magical places I've ever seen. Whenever I look at it I think of that river and wonder if it's still there, still untouched and unnamed. I hope so, even if I never have a chance to return and find out.

The Atlantic salmon described in "A Well-Traveled Fish" continue their nomadic ways. Thousands are now being raised commercially in saltwater pens in Puget Sound and around Vancouver Island. Many have escaped and some of these fugitives have established apparently viable spawning runs in Vancouver Island rivers; others have been caught by anglers in Puget Sound and some of its tributary rivers. This isn't necessarily good because there is great fear these fish could spread diseases to which the native Pacific salmon and steelhead have no immunity.

Meanwhile, the landlocked Atlantic salmon planted in Oregon's Hosmer Lake, replacing the original strain of sea-run fish, have turned out to be a disappointment. They do not live as long or grow as large as their predecessors nor do they rise as well to dry flies. Worse yet, they don't seem to know how a hooked game fish is supposed to behave. The breathtaking scenery around Hosmer Lake also has been severely compromised by heavy-handed and incredibly inept mismanagement by the Forest Service. The future of the lake and its fishery are both highly uncertain.

It has been a few years since I last fished "Price's Lake." Thanks to advancing age and a couple of serious back injuries, the steep trail to the lake, crisscrossed by many large deadfalls, has become a little more than I can manage with a boat on wheels. I suppose I could fish the lake from a float tube or pontoon boat, but I don't like the restricted visibility available from such low-slung craft. I still have friends who fish the lake, however, and they tell me it is as enigmatic as ever, generous sometimes, frustrating at others.

I haven't had a "Birthday Fish" in a while, so it's about time I had another. I expect to spend my next birthday on the North Fork, as I usually do, and maybe once again the river will remember.

I keep adding pages to my "Trout Fisherman's Diary," but I don't ever expect to record another experience like that day in 1980 when the sky literally fell at Dry Falls Lake. That day the sky also fell on "The Once and Future River," but the volcano-damaged little Green has managed to recover more quickly than I ever expected and anglers are catching steelhead there again. The North Fork of the Stillaguamish now commands nearly all my summer steelhead fishing time, however, so I haven't gone back to see what the reincarnated Green is like.

The fish described in "Hello Dolly!" has enjoyed something of a rehabilitation. No longer considered such a voracious threat to other fish, the Dolly is now sought by many anglers as a worthwhile quarry in its own right. Fisheries scientists also have determined that some fish formerly identified as Dolly Varden are really members of a separate species, to which they have given the unromantic name of Bull Trout.

If my old friend and mentor Enos Bradner is looking down from some fishing Valhalla, he's no doubt pleased to see that hardly anything has changed at "Bucktail Camp." The river has chiseled away some of the bank and the wind has toppled some trees, but everything else is pretty much the same as when Bucktail Camp was Bradner's steelhead fishing headquarters, as it now is mine.

The river itself has not fared as well. The great Deer Creek slide was stabilized years ago, but the North Fork of the Stillaguamish remains choked with silt and a series of floods has wiped out much of the best fishing water. Despite these problems, there has been a slow but steady increase in the number of steelhead returning to Deer Creek and its tributaries, and a similar increase in their progeny. The fishing will never again be the same as it was in the river's glory days, but at least now the trend seems to be moving slowly in the right direction.

"Blackberry Run" has disappeared under an avalanche of gravel brought by winter floods, and I now pass it by in favor of more productive water. But who knows? Given a few more winters and a few more floods, maybe it will be worth fishing again.

I've caught other "Lahontans" since the trip to Grimes Lake described in these pages, but the Lahontan's reluctance to rise to dry flies has kept it from becoming one of my favorite fish. Still, the large average size of these fish has made them popular with many anglers and the Lahontan has definitely established itself as an important part of the regional angling scene.

I've already touched on New Zealand fishing, sea-run cutthroat and steelhead, so there's no need to say more about those chapters in the "Fall" section of *The Year of the Trout*; they pretty much speak for themselves anyway.

As for the last-trip syndrome described in "The End of the Year," I still can't escape it—even though such fishing remains as uncertain as ever. But the trout are still there, somewhere below the surface of the silent winter streams.

Looking back on all this, I think it's fair to say we haven't done too badly since these books were first published. True, some fishing has been lost, but some also has been gained and other fisheries have at least held their own. Of course it's also true there are now many more fishermen chasing fewer fish in fewer waters, but even that has had an unexpected benefit: It has forced all of us to sharpen our fly-fishing skills in order to remain in the game, and there's certainly nothing wrong in that.

I remain grateful for the good fishing I have had and for that which still exists, and dare hope there may be yet more to come. The magic of fishing, which inspired these books to begin with, remains as strong for me as ever, and I still expect that my very next cast, or perhaps the one thereafter, will bring the electric throb of another strong trout.

So *The Year of the Angler and the Year of the Trout* is not about history; it is simply a waypoint along a continuing angling journey—yours and mine.

—Steve Raymond

PART ONE

The Year of the
ANGLER

INTRODUCTION

to the 1995 Edition

How quickly now the seasons pass, laying down their lessons amid the fallen leaves of time. Defying time, restless rivers still challenge the limits of their courses, and bright salmon and steelhead are still drawn into them to push upstream against their stubborn flow. Each spring the lakes and ponds again are dimpled with the rising rings of hungry trout, and each fall the eagles feed as they have always fed on the dashed-out corpses of the salmon. Anglers still come and go, leaving brief glimpses of themselves or their ideas, and everything in their world is as it was. Yet everything has changed.

This book was born into a world more innocent than the one we know now, and in the many seasons since its first appearance there have been countless changes to the fish and fishing it describes. Now, on the eve of a new edition, it seems a good time to take stock of some of those changes.

First the rivers: The Hoh, which is the first river you will meet in this book, remains protected in its upper reaches by Olympic National Park, and still runs with the same cold, gray strength as always. Bright steelhead still come to it in winter, and anglers still pursue them there.

The Duwamish, on the other hand, has fared far less well. The farms and meadows that once lined its middle reaches have given way to strip malls, subdivisions and huge industrial parks, and the river now is too busy and dirty to be worth fishing in the way that I once fished it.

The North Fork of the Stillaguamish, about which I have written extensively here and elsewhere, has also fallen on harder times, mostly a result of the savage logging of its watershed, and although there are a few small signs of recovery, it will be at least another human generation, if ever, before it once again resembles the productive river of the past.

The Hanford Reach of the Columbia is still free and unfettered by dams and apparently will remain so, but now there is great uncertainty about the future of the land on either side of the river—and exploitation or "development" of those wild lands would destroy the river as surely as a dam.

It has been a long while since I fished the Yuba or the Firehole, but I am told the shad fishing in the Yuba is now largely a thing of the past—although there is other good shad fishing in the same vicinity. Happily, the Firehole—safe within the confines of Yellowstone Park—remains the same wonderful, challenging, productive stream as always.

Next the lakes: Pass Lake, where years ago I found the fat trout feeding under the cedar limb, still holds trout. Their numbers are fewer but their average size is much larger now than it was then. Yet the lake now is also infested with shiners and the fishing has changed; the once-lively top-water angling has been replaced mostly by slow, bottom-dredging techniques with large nymphs or shiner imitations, a kind of fishing I dislike.

The brown trout have vanished from that little Columbia Basin pond that once favored me with so many of them, but browns have been stocked in enough other local waters that they are no longer quite the novelty they used to be.

The results of the Lenice Lake experiment described in these pages unfortunately fell short of expectations. Kamloops trout planted in the lake did not live as long or grow as large as expected, and anglers' hopes for a genuine trophy fishery went unrealized—although Lenice still provides worthwhile fishing from time to time.

Hosmer Lake still retains its serene beauty, but the sea-run Atlantic salmon are gone, victims of predation, wanderlust, neglectful management, and their own genetic weakness. They have been replaced by true landlocked salmon which have never shown the same capacity for sport as their late, lamented predecessors.

Then the fish: After years of decline, the sea-run cutthroat have made a remarkable comeback in the waters of Hood Canal. Most likely their recovery is due to a belated change in regulations that restricts both the size and number of fish anglers may keep; in any case, they are back, and the fishing is as good or better than ever. But my old friend Ed Foss, who introduced me to the sea-run, is gone now, and for me the fishing will never be quite the same.

Elsewhere, the great runs of salmon and steelhead that once returned to Northwest rivers have dwindled alarmingly nearly everywhere, for a whole host of unhappy reasons, until now many are being considered for endangered-species classification. There are signs the public may finally be recognizing the value of this vanishing resource, but the steps necessary to restore the runs are difficult and expensive and I do not think it is realistic to expect they will ever be returned to their historic abundance.

Finally the anglers: There are many more now than there were twenty years ago. Waters I once fished in near solitude are now often crowded, and I find myself avoiding them for that reason. But the legions of new anglers also have lent support to the causes of fisheries conservation and enhancement, so their increase has been a mixed blessing.

The years also have brought many changes to my own angling habits. Rarely now do I fish after dark, a concession to advancing age that often reminds me that eight hours in the daylight is enough fishing for one day. The names and dressings of the flies I now tie are mostly quite different from those of 20 years ago, and so are the ways I fish them. The Skykomish Sunrise, which I said then was my favorite steelhead fly, no longer occupies that status; it is still a grand fly, one of the truly great steelhead wet-fly patterns, but now I fish almost exclusively with dry flies for steelhead in summer and with other patterns in winter.

During idle winter hours I still enjoy thumbing through the pages of mail-order fly-fishing catalogs, but many of the old favorites have disappeared—Herter's, William Mills & Son and the Wretched Mess Gift Catalog, to mention a few. Some of the old-timers—Orvis, L. L. Bean and others—still come faithfully, however, and there are so many new ones that snowbound winter anglers will never lack for reading material.

So the changes have been many—and yet some things are still the same. The quality of courage that has always fueled the will to survive among wild creatures, and among humans, still seems as noble and strong as ever. The reasons why people fish are the same reasons why people have always fished, and the pleasures and satisfactions they derive from fishing also are still the same. *The Year of the Angler* still offers many gifts, and each new season still brings a rich full measure of rewards.

At least it is so for me. I hope it will always be the same for you.

—*Steve Raymond*

PREFACE

to the First Edition

Enos Bradner, Roderick Haig-Brown, Ben Hur Lampman . . . so begins the roll-call of Legend, as the subject of Western fishing comes up, which it does more and more often. It does because the preponderance of American quality angling has been moving steadily westward for now very nearly half a century. The great days of the storied Eastern streams had peaked by 1925, and by midcentury mid-Pennsylvania had become the last Eastern redoubt of the kind of fishing from which Legend is engendered. There on the rivers that served as the nearest American equivalent of those chalk streams that bracket the English Channel from Hampshire and from Normandy, the mantle of glory-cloud-stuff that had earlier enveloped Gordon, Hewitt and La Branche began to weave itself around the figures of Fox, Grove and

Marinaro, the masters of the minutiae, and even the prodigiously gifted young Schwiebert, who had come among them, precocious as a grisle invading the redds of spawning salmon, so far ahead of his normally allotted season.

History, with its peculiar propensity for repeating itself, now appears to be restaging the same play of Legend for the West Coast, complete even down to this latter detail of the casting, for we clearly discern, right beside the three venerable figures first mentioned, a fourth who is a much younger man but already stands tall among them.

Bradner, after all, is in his eighties, like Charlie Ritz, and even among such longevity-prone people as anglers, that has to be regarded as an obvious length of tooth; and as far back as 1965, when *A Leaf from French Eddy* first appeared, Lampman was already enshrined in a memorial edition; and as for the peerless Haig-Brown, he has retired, after many a long year, from the magistrate's bench, and as everyone knows, judges constitute a separate category of those who practically have to be born old; and now front and center in such company appears Steve Raymond, who is by contrast a mere stripling. It's only a couple of years ago that he took over the editorial reins of *The Flyfisher*, the official journal of the Federation of Fly Fishermen, and that virtually at the moment of the publication of *Kamloops*, his first book.

But he came on the scene full-armed, like Minerva from the brain of Jove, and not Methuselah himself could have found the time to do a more exhaustive job than he did in that brilliant book on the one unique fish, the Kamloops trout. All it left some of us asking was what could he possibly do for an encore? Well, we needn't have wasted any time wondering. Here, in *The Year of the Angler*, we have the answer, and it's stunning. This book is as clearly in a class by itself as its predecessor, yet the contrast between two books couldn't be more complete. Where that one stuck with single-minded and even dogged devotion to every possible ramification of only one subject, this one ranges over a veritable smorgasbord of subject matter, with a diversity of topic and treatment that would be bewildering in its variety if it were not endowed with homogeneity by the strict discipline of its yearbook form. It is a rich compound of nature-study, philosophy, history, ecology and environmental activism, demographics and social studies, aphorism and anecdote and—no, I'm not going to shy away from this one—sheer poetry. The fishing encompasses both summer and winter steelhead, both Pacific and Atlantic salmon—the former in a busy industrial district and the latter in a lake formerly known as Mud!—and both kinds of trout fishing, seagoing and, I nearly said, sedentary (which of course the non-migratory variety, at least as practiced here, is anything but), and there's even one excursion into cutthroat fishing by electronic tracking. Also thrown in at no apparent extra charge is a full-fledged mystery story, as well as the best trip to the Firehole that I for one have as yet encountered in print. What an angling menu!—and all within the Western region. It's enough to account for the greening of anglers' faces from some three-quarters to seven-eighths of the rest of America.

After reading *Kamloops* and now after reading this I can only echo the sporting poet John Gay in a thought he expressed for his own epitaph. The way he put it was:

> *Life is a jest, and all things show it.*
> *I thought so once, and now I know it.*

That's how I felt, then and now, about the promise and the performance of Steve Raymond, as an angling author.

—*Arnold Gingrich*

FOREWORD

to the 1983 Edition

The reader may notice that Arnold Gingrich never used the word "classic" in his Preface to the original 1973 edition of this book. With all the praise that he lavished upon both author and book, it certainly would have been easy to use that word. He refused to do so because he felt that no one man should label a book a classic; by his definition, a book could qualify as a classic only after years of appreciation.

Now, more than ten years after the original edition appeared, *The Year of the Angler* is being republished because it has been appreciated by a diverse fly-fishing audience. This is one of those rare books not bound by place or time. Anglers everywhere will share the thoughts and feelings expressed in these essays and stories of Northwestern fly fishing. If in truth it takes more than one generation to judge a book a classic then this reprint represents a giant step for *The Year of the Angler*.

There were compelling reasons for bringing this book back into print. It became evident that many fly fishermen wanted a copy of *The Year of the Angler* for their libraries. Antiquarian booksellers reported a brisk trade for used copies of the first edition at escalating prices.

The book's reputation was established immediately by the many fine reviews. The honors it received guaranteed that the reputation would grow through the years. It won the Governor's Award at the Washington State Festival of the Arts, and it was chosen by the American Booksellers Association as one of the select list of books presented to the President of the United States for the White House library.

Steve Raymond, of course, continued writing after the appearance of *The Year of the Angler*. He has contributed chapters to almost every estimable fly-fishing anthology published since 1973 (including *Fishing Moments of Truth*, *The Masters on the Dry Fly*, *The Masters on the Nymph*, *Stillwater Trout*, and *Waters Swift and Still*). His magazine articles, especially a series of short, insightful pieces in *Sports Illustrated*, have won him new devotees and satisfied old ones. The publication in 1980 of a revised edition of his first book, *Kamloops* (1971), verified both the worth of that well-researched work and the lasting popularity of the author.

A demand for *The Year of the Angler* made this new edition possible; the unique quality of the book made it necessary. All other fly-fishing books before or since have never quite filled the same niche in our literature, because Steve Raymond shared with the reader a view of an uncommon world—his own. By revealing something of himself in his stories, he colored each of them with his own feelings.

What makes *The Year of the Angler* such an excellent book? It is beautifully written, thoughtful, and at the same time entertaining. It is not a collection of rollicking humor, although there are moments of piercing wit. Overall, there is a gentle mixture of hope (chiefly with the discoveries of new waters) and despair (chiefly with the loss of favorite fisheries); by the end of the book, the feelings of melancholy balance with the joy. *The Year of the Angler* is an admirable fishing book because it is about more than fishing.

As William Humphrey cogently observed in *My Moby Dick*, instructional books can be produced by fishermen who write, whereas "devotional books" must be produced by writers who fish. Of course, good writers who are also sufficiently good fishermen may produce either or both, and both have value. The works that have no value, or at least hold no interest for many of us, are the superficial fish stories to be found on too many shelves. Especially in the devotional literature—those works categorized as "mood" books—the author has an obligation to formulate a philosophy as well as describe an experience. There is always the danger that the ideas may be trivial, or the philosophy too pedantically expressed. In these instances the mood book fails for angler and non-angler alike. Steve Raymond is too intelligent an angler, too gifted a writer ever to be guilty of such failure.

At its best, mood writing describes not only fish caught or fish lost but also a way of viewing life. As with any novel, the telling of a rapping-good story grabs the reader; the piece expresses the author's philosophy only in an unobtrusive way, almost subliminally. The ideas that ran like a barely noticed current in a trout stream linger sweetly when the story is finished.

Many angling books are so appealing that they are read by people who have no intention of ever chasing a fish. Perhaps no other sport can boast of such a rich literature. Examples range from *The Compleat Angler* by Izaak Walton to *The Old Man and the Sea* by Ernest Hemingway (which are so very different in manner and content but which both celebrate the nobility of the fisherman).

The aforementioned *My Moby Dick* is another masterful example of an angling story that can be thoroughly appreciated by a far wider audience than those who fish. It was reviewed in *Newsweek* and sold exceptionally well not only in bookstores but in supermarkets, where one expects to encounter mysteries and romances but hardly a book about fly fishing. (And it can be argued that in our culture, success in the supermarket may well be the ultimate symbol of public acceptance.)

The Year of the Angler is a mood book infused with similar grace, intelligence, and broad appeal. There is a recurrent theme in Steve Raymond's writing: "In his searching, the angler sees many things. Often he is the first to notice change, because change always has meaning for an angler." In this book, the author marks time by the changing seasons. Each season has its own angling rituals. Somehow a sense of ritual can give order to one's life. A sadder theme in *The Year of the Angler* seems to be that personal rituals have no effect on the destructive changes assailing our world.

In his Preface, Arnold Gingrich compares Steve Raymond with other legendary writers of the Northwest; here let me simply add that he belongs to a select group of modern angling authors. He has the ability as a storyteller to bring the reader with him on the emotional roller-coaster ride, and at the end he lets us, as fly fishermen, celebrate our own nobility. *The Year of the Angler* definitely deserves its broad audience, for it does one thing more: it makes the angling life a bit more understandable to nonfishermen as well as fishermen.

—Gary LaFontaine

WINTER

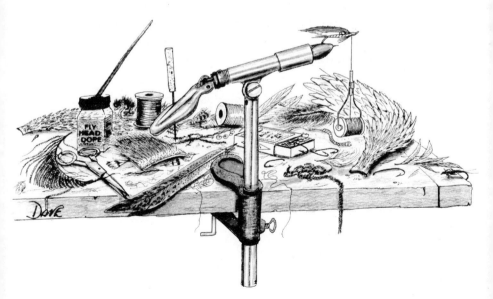

The first fish of a new year is special in a way that all the rest are not. It may be a great, shining steelhead, taken on a cold, short January day from a pool surrounded by barren alders framed in ice, or a husky cutthroat, grown fat on humpback fry in a minor estuary in March, or a chunky rainbow from a landlocked lake in April.

Regardless of where and when it is taken, the details of the catch remain fresh in the mind, remembered after many other catches are forgotten. The first fish of a new year ends a subconscious suspense in the mind of a fisherman and becomes an omen that somehow sets the pattern for the remainder of the year.

The quest begins in winter, at the beginning of the year. And it seems strange that the year should be born then. It is a time when there is more darkness than light, more death than life, more silence than sound. In winter, the earth seems to draw into itself, resting from the business of having sustained life through the other seasons. The leaves are long gone from the forest limbs, the geese have flown in ragged arrows to the south and the roar of rivers is lost in drifts of snow along their banks.

Yet the rivers still harbor life, even in the frozen days of January. The last spawned-out salmon still thrash in the river shallows, while beneath the gravel the seeds of a new generation are growing. Steelhead, still bright from the sea, move upstream cautiously against the winter flow to seek their own spawning grounds. Close behind are the mysterious cutthroat in their own private, small tributaries.

Even so, winter ordinarily is not considered a time for angling. The gentleman trout fisherman hangs up his waders and his wicker creel and stores his fly lines in loose coils so they will be ready when the ice is gone and resident trout rise again in April or in May. His thoughts are of spring streams and summer rivers, and for him winter is merely a wait that must be endured before the changing of the season.

But there are other anglers who begin seeking their first fish of the new year on the first day, who wade the winter rivers and search them with a fly for steelhead. It is a long and sometimes painful search, and sometimes it goes on in vain until there is no longer a chance of finding fish in the river. It is a succession of long and fruitless hours spent in the rhythmic motions of cast and retrieve, of following the bright glimmer of the fly into the winter depths, of cheeks stinging in the cold and clots of ice forming in the rod guides.

The reward for all this effort sometimes never comes, because winter steelhead fishing with a fly is difficult indeed. But when and if it comes, it is dramatic and sudden: a quick, strong pull, the fleet feeling of helplessness as a heavy fish begins a long run or a high, shaking leap that somehow magnifies its size and strength. In a flashing moment, all the hours of effort and discomfort are forgotten in the sudden exhilaration of the strike, and total concentration is spent on the movement of the fish and the countermove of the angler.

That is winter steelheading: long hours of cold, interminable work, punctuated with breathless moments of high excitement. And if I were offered a choice of circumstances in which to take the first fish of a new year, I should prefer that it come in just that way.

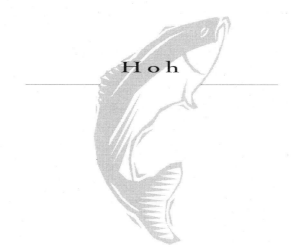

Hoh

January had come and gone and half of February had slipped away and there had been little opportunity for fishing. I had spent only a single day fishing in January, at a river close to home. It had been a bitter winter day, a day when it was necessary to wade through a thin layer of ice to reach the pools—a strange experience like punching one's way through a plate-glass window, taking care not to tear the waders on the splintered shards. It had been a day of hard work and no fish, and here in the middle of February I was still seeking my first fish of the year.

It was a cold, blustery morning when I left the city to

drive to the Olympic Peninsula. A southwester swept in ragged shreds of dirty cloud heavy with the promise of rain, and whitecaps slapped at the sides of the ferry as it crossed Puget Sound. It was still early in the day when I reached the Hoh.

Born in the Olympic snows, fed by the Pacific rains, the Hoh hurries down to the sea. In its high-mountain head-waters, the river is a precocious infant, skirting the base of glaciers, then growing as it absorbs the product of a hundred springs and tributaries, the rain forest runoff and the amber-stained water of the cedar swamps.

Hardly more than a brook at first, it grows quickly in size and strength and rumbles out of the mountains a full-fledged river with great sound and vigor and passes into the hushed canyons of the Hoh Rain Forest. From the forest it flows on to the brief coastal plain, dropping more gently now, restless in its passage, sprawling out and drawing in, seeking new channels as it passes through land scarred from logging. A short river as rivers go, it moves quickly from its source to where it meets the tide and is lost suddenly in the Pacific breakers.

In the summer the river carries the gray silt of its parent glacier, bleeding from the sun's wounds, and it never is without a trace of color from its source. The silt camouflages the quick movement of steelhead and salmon fry in the shallows. Deer slip silently from the forest to drink from the pools and eagles wheel in eccentric orbits overhead. When the fall rains come the river bustles with the life of returning salmon and cutthroat and the first bold vanguard of the steelhead run. It is a wild river, free and unrestrained, quick and exuberant and forever in hurried movement.

Winter comes slowly and subtly to the rain forest along the river. The first frosts leave a crimson rust on the vine maples, and the following wind sends dead leaves spiraling down to be swallowed up in the river.

One morning the higher hills are crowned with early snow, and as the days grow shorter and colder the snow creeps down to fill the higher valleys and the swamps are layered with ice. The lower valleys are hidden in a drenching gloom, coming down to settle in the forest itself, washing the tops of the highest firs and spruce.

The first big run of steelhead bursts into the river in December, struggling past the Indian nets at the river's mouth. They briefly rest in the quiet pools and pockets to restore themselves for the next frantic dash against the flow. The anglers know this, and seek them there, tempting them with strips of salmon roe or small bits of fiery yarn made fast to a hook; with bright nickel spoons and strangely shaped plugs and bobbers.

The fishermen wade out into the current or along the bars and cast with awkward grace, sending their unlikely offerings far out to be seized in the flow and sucked down, tumbled across the gravel and swept before the thrusting current, clumsily searching the places where resting steelhead lie.

The steelheaders come from everywhere, many with the river guides from the peninsula town of Forks. They bring their boats, stout McKenzies and sturdy Rogues, and trundle them down over the river rocks in the raining dawn. There is a sodden freshness to the morning that reaches through clothing and sets a man shivering, and the men talk in low voices in deference to the roar of the river.

The promise of rain had been fulfilled by the time I came to the river. The trees dripped moss and the moss dripped rain and the droplets formed rings on the river before the current snatched them away. It was still cold and the upper hills still held the snow so that the river was low and had only a trace of color.

The Hoh is a fisherman's river. There are pools and runs, pockets and slots throughout its length. Here a lone angler was plunking from the bank with a heavy bait rig, and there a pair of anglers fished from a boat in midstream. Fish were in the river and the river was right and it was a day in which a fisherman could feel confident that he would find fish if he looked long and hard enough.

I chose a spot where the river slowed and entered a broad bend, pausing midway to accept a small tributary, then broke in a riffle down to a large deep pool formed by an ancient log jam at its lower end.

There followed the familiar ritual of rigging up with all the accouterments that are a necessary part of the winter steelheader's uniform: the heavy wool socks, drawn up over the pair already being worn, and the whipcord trousers tucked in so there would be no bare expanse of skin between trousers and socks to touch the cold rubber of the waders. The waders themselves, chest-high, were cinched tight with a belt over a flannel shirt, a sweater and a heavy jacket.

And finally the vest, its many pockets sagging with fly boxes and all the other things an angler carries with him to the stream. And then the rod, a sturdy 8½-footer with a heavy, weight-forward, high-density fly line and a big reel filled with 150 yards of backing to follow the run of a strong fish; the leader, short and stout and testing at eight pounds; and finally the fly, a big one, size 1/0, with bright fluorescent chenille and a polar wing.

Thus equipped, I scrambled down a steep bank to the river's edge and worked upstream along the shore to the spot I had chosen to begin. It was hard going along a narrow path in the face of a cliff that dropped off sharply to deep water, then wading across the mouth of the tributary that had carved a respectably deep hole for itself where it entered the river. Finally I was able to walk out onto the shallow bar at the head of the drift and strip line off the reel for the first cast.

There is always a certain air of expectation about the first cast of a day of fishing. On rare occasions it is the very first cast that brings a smashing strike and wild excitement. And so

I was slightly tensed and slightly braced as I always am when I sent the first cast angling downstream. The fly floated momentarily and then disappeared as the current drew it under and swept it down into the deep water, and I saw it there in my mind's eye, the hackles swimming as it tumbled over and down and straightened out below me.

The current drew the line taut and the fly hung in the water, searching and seeking. After a proper wait, I drew it back, satisfied that this was not one of those days when the first cast would produce a rise.

I fished the water carefully, wading far out on the underwater bar until the waves lapped dangerously close to the wader tops. There was deep satisfaction in the graceful feel of the long rod, a sense of pleasure in watching the line roll far out, carrying with it the tuft of bright color that seemed so out of place in the darkening sky.

Nothing moved to the fly, and when I had covered all the water I could reach, I retreated from the bar and made my way downstream along the same hard path to the lower end of the river's bend, just above the riffle that carried down into the pool.

The water here was faster, pressing firmly against the waders until the cold could not be ignored. The sky dripped sporadically and the cry of a gull caused me to look up into the gathering rain. The river whispered and talked in a soft, low voice and seemed suspended in time and space, rushing out of the mist, flowing past and disappearing back into it. It was a time for thought, a time when the trained reflexes of the angler lead him to go on fishing while his mind turns to other things.

My mind was on the river, unique in some ways yet similar in others to all rivers. It was doing the things that all rivers do, moving the earth in tiny fragments, wearing down the hills, keeping the earth in a constant state of motion too slow for the human eye to see.

A river is like a man's life. It starts as a tiny, noisy thing, full of unchanneled strength and energy, a thing of unending movement. As it grows older and stronger it slows down a bit and begins to do important things, using its strength to dig canyons and fertilize flood plains with its silt. A few rivers, like a few men, do great things, carving monuments that are a wonder to the world. And also like some men, a few rivers create sorrow and disaster, bursting out of their channels with vicious strength to flood the fragile dwellings of men. But most rivers, like most men, pass quickly and are forgotten, having barely scratched the surface in their brief moment of time.

In their old age, rivers—again like men—grow ponderous and portly, spreading out and slowing down, always moving but somehow more reluctant now to go to their destiny. But finally the river flows across the last bar and is swallowed in the sea, quickly lost in all the waters that have gone before.

The fragments of matter the river has brought with it are scattered among the salts and minerals and flotsam of a thousand other rivers, and together they are mixed, separated and mixed again, driven by currents and carried by the wind to far shores. They are washed onto beaches in strange harbors, frozen into icebergs, drowned in the pollution of the coastal cities, and they are carried to the seven seas and the shores of all the continents. Water from all the rivers is drawn up by the sun's rays to condense and fall as rain on some distant watershed, there to seep into some distant river and begin the long cycle again.

Rivers breed legends, and the Hoh has one that seems appropriate for a river of its size and strength, a story about an extraordinary man who won for himself the name of the Iron Man of the Hoh. His real name was John Huelsdonk, a German immigrant who homesteaded on the river in the 1890s, and his great feats of strength as a logger, hunter and trapper quickly won him local fame. He was said to have killed more than a hundred cougars, including one huge, legendary cat known as Big Foot, and his great strength was attributed to the supposition that he ate the meat of the cougars he had killed. Huelsdonk survived a hand-to-hand fight with a black bear, an episode that made local headlines in the 1930s, and it was said he would pack 175 to 200 pounds of supplies on his back in order to earn two men's pay.

But perhaps the most appealing of all the stories about the Iron Man is one told by a forest ranger who said he encountered Huelsdonk packing a cook stove on his back down a forest trail.

"That must be quite a load," the ranger said.

"Well," the Iron Man replied, "the stove isn't so bad, but there's a sack of flour in the oven that keeps shifting around."

The Iron Man of the Hoh now is long dead, but there are other legends that linger on about the river. The Hoh flows into the sea between two great rocks that loom like monuments to its passage, and local Indian lore has it that these rocks once were animals that lived along the riverbanks. When they were told by the gods that humans were destined to come to the river, they chose to turn to stone, and there they remain as silent sentinels at the river's mouth.

The river now bears the name of a band of Indians that lived along its shores, but earlier in its history it was known as the Destruction River, so named by the captain of a ship who lost part of his crew in an Indian massacre at the river's mouth in 1787.

So the Hoh is a river rich in history and lore, and it is easy to understand how such tales were born and grew among the Indians and the early settlers who made their way through the dark and ghostly corridors of the great rain forest through which the river flows.

While my mind had been busy with these thoughts, I had fished down through the riffle to the point where it broke into the pool and cut its way far under the edge of the log jam, and there a sudden movement brought my attention back to the business at hand.

Deep in the pool there had been a quick flash near my fly, a fleeting image that had passed almost too quickly to discern. But it could have been a fish, and so I drew the fly back swiftly and cast again to the spot.

The current here was slow, and the fly was visible for a long time as it sank leisurely in the pool and was drawn toward the shadows of the overhanging logs, finally disappearing in the depths. And then came a hard jolt that pulled the rod tip down to the water, and slack line was whistling out through the guides until the line was taut to the reel and the sound of the reel's noisy ratchet echoed from the rocky banks.

Ignoring the refuge of the log jam, the fish moved quickly into the pool, heading downstream where the slack water of the pool was sucked out into a stretch of fast water. Once the fish reached that water it would be impossible to climb around the log jam to follow it, and so I tightened the drag on the reel and swung the rod around in an effort to turn the fish.

The fish broke water in a flash of gunmetal and silver, then turned and charged upstream through the pool. Now it was a matter of reeling quickly to recover the sudden belly of slack line forming below the fish. It ran past me and jumped again in the tail of the upstream riffle before the line was taut again against the reel. It was not an especially large fish, but it was strong and active and I wanted it badly.

Now it was back in the pool, twisting and shaking its head, and I could see the glint of its turning sides. Two short runs toward the tail of the pool set the reel buzzing again, and then the fish began edging toward the log jam where it had been hooked. The rod formed a tight bow against the raining sky as I put on as much pressure as I dared and kept the fish swimming parallel to the jam, away from its threatening snags.

And in a few moments more it was over and I edged the

fish carefully onto the gravel. It lay quivering on the wet
stones, the fly stuck firmly in its lower jaw and a bright spot of
blood on its lip. It was a fresh-run buck of seven pounds or
better, clean and silver and strong, a classic example of a
noble race, the brightest thing in the gray-painted day.

I crouched over it and twisted the fly free, then grasped
the fish carefully and slipped it back into the pool, holding it
upright until a throb of life returned and it swam slowly away,
down and out of sight. It had given me all I wanted from it,
and I had no good reason to take anything more.

I fished on without seeing another fish, and as the
afternoon spent itself the drizzle ceased, the low clouds lifted
to reveal the mountains overhead, and it grew colder. Finally,
when it was time to go, my face was flushed with the cold and
I felt an honest weariness.

As the truck rolled down the still-wet pavement, the sun
broke through a higher overcast to paint the bold Olympics in
changing pinks and golds, and the higher peaks became bright
beacons to ships passing far out, a last soft sight of the dying
day. I knew that behind that vast wall of mountains, two
million lights soon would flicker on in the cities man has built
on the banks of Puget Sound, signs flashing atop the great
structures he has built to touch the low Pacific skies. All these
works of man seem small and pale next to the silent majesty of
the Olympics, the great thrusting shoulder of the continent,
father of rivers, mysterious and unattainable even with great
cities close at hand.

I leaned back in the seat of the truck and sighed with
satisfaction. I had taken the year's first fish, taken it in just the
way I would have wished, and it was bound to be a good year.

The Quality of Courage

Frozen patches of old snow lay here and there along the path leading down to the river. The day was cold and very still, and beyond the ragged tops of the surrounding firs and alders the sky had the strange white look that promised a new fall of snow.

I came out of the woods onto a broad gravel bar. On the far side of it flowed the river, dark and lazy in the cold gray light. I was hoping for a steelhead from the river, but as I started toward it a sudden movement caught my eye.

For a moment I was uncertain what I had seen. Looking around, I saw nothing except a small pool of water in the gravel at the edge of the woods, a pool that had been formed when last the river was in flood. The floor of the pool was lined with a soft carpet of decaying leaves, and a pair of downed alders lay across its surface. Beyond that there was only the gray and dun-colored gravel, the dusky green forest and the frozen sky.

And then I saw the fish. She was an old, spawned-out chum salmon, her once-handsome body now thin and scarred with fungus, and she had been hopelessly trapped in the little pool left behind by the flood. There was no telling how long she had been trapped there, and soon she would surely die as all Pacific salmon do after spawning. But she was still alert, and she had seen me coming, and it had been her quick movement of response that I in turn had seen. Now she was lying absolutely still in the shelter of the alder logs, and I had to look long and hard to distinguish her outline in the clear water.

I admired the fish. She had survived at sea and returned to find her native river, braved the pollution from the city on its banks, fought the freshets and floods to find this tributary, and finally she had spawned and fulfilled her duty to her race. And now she was trapped and dying in a lonely little pool, her courage and will to live intact to the very last.

I fished through the day, but stopped again at the little pool on the way back. The fish was there, still lying in the shelter of the log. For a moment I thought she was dead, but then I saw the slow movement of her gills and knew that she was not. I watched her for a while, and she watched me, and then I left, wondering if she would see the light of another morning. And I thought about the courage that had brought her so far and sustained her so long.

There is a great deal of courage in nature. A strong will to live is necessary for the species to survive, and each day wild creatures are tested anew in the cruel, efficient process of natural selection. The challenge of winter is met by different species in different ways. Some migrate to warmer places and new feeding grounds, some hibernate, and some change their habits to conform with the rigors of the season. The salmon survive in still a different way, the adults dying early in the winter after having laid eggs that will hatch in the spring to perpetuate the species.

The will to live extends to even the smallest creatures, the tiny mayfly nymphs clinging tenaciously to the undersides of rocks in the river's swiftest flow, the microscopic creatures of the plankton, breeding and dying, consuming and being consumed with the same determination to survive that is inherent in all the larger forms of life. The determination to live is so natural, so inbred, that usually it is accepted as a part of the natural scheme of things and only occasionally do we see it on display.

Once on a fall day when I was fishing a small lake in the Columbia Basin I saw such a display. It was a week after the opening of the hunting season and the surrounding hills resounded with the shots of duck and pheasant hunters. Three hunters had taken position in the cattails at the far end of the lake, and when an unwary mallard passed over all three stood and fired.

The mallard was hit and tumbled sharply in a shower of feathers, then caught itself and struggled gamely upward in erratic flight. It flew the length of the lake, but could go no farther and splashed lamely in the water close by, then swam ashore and dragged itself up into the grass.

All this had been visible to the hunters, but they made no move to retrieve the wounded duck. And when it became apparent they did not intend to do so, I went ashore and looked for it.

I found it, huddled and quivering in the bunch grass. There was no outward sign of injury, but when I picked it up the ground beneath was streaked with blood and I could see there were half a dozen holes in its belly. I stood there a moment, not really sure what I was going to do, and then the frightened mallard gave a sudden lurch and wrenched free. It stumbled to the water and made an awkward takeoff, struggling up from the water into clumsy flight. I watched its halting progress until it vanished over the next ridge. Surely it would not survive, but its will to go on living would be strong as long as life could last.

The determination to survive plays an important role in fishing. It is the will of the fish to live that causes it to struggle with all its strength against the restraining force of the angler. Fishing may be a matter of pleasure to the angler, and we think of it as such, but to the fish itself it is no less than a question of life or death.

Nearly every game fish that is in reasonably good condition will struggle valiantly for its freedom, but occasionally an angler will hook a fish that is unaccountably more violent than all the rest. Such fish test the angler's skill to its absolute limits, and regardless of the outcome the memory of the struggle remains vivid and clear.

One afternoon on a wilderness lake I hooked three such fish in succession. The day was well spent and I had taken many fish, but nothing had prepared me for the violence that followed. I covered a nearby rise and twitched the fly once and a trout had it. What followed was a stunning blur of motion: immediately the trout leaped, high and twisting, and was off and running almost before it hit the water. It was not an especially big fish—sixteen or seventeen inches—but it took yard after yard of line, then leaped high again and fell back on the leader, breaking it with an audible snap. The whole affair had taken only seconds and left me breathless and shaking.

I tied on a new fly and cast to the same spot. Another

trout, a twin of the first, took the fly and vaulted high in the air, shaking spray from its flanks. Six or eight times in succession it leaped with wild, reckless violence until the fly was wrenched loose from its fragile purchase in the fish's jaw.

Having lost two good fish in succession, I was now thoroughly rattled and spent a long moment in a conscious effort to calm myself, and to resolve that I would not lose the next fish if one was there. Two or three casts later another fish struck hard, and it too was wild, tearing long lengths of line from the reel, flinging itself out of the water in a series of twisting, inverted U's. I used every trick I knew to wear it down, and after a long fight it came in grudgingly until it was close enough to land. But as I reached for the net, the fish found strength enough to make a final, savage leap, shaking so violently that again the tiny hook tore out.

All this had occurred in less than ten minutes, but then the flurry ended. I was left with the knowledge that I had been beaten thoroughly by three splendid trout, wild things that deserved their freedom.

A defiant struggle for freedom and life is not the exclusive property of wild creatures. It belongs to men, too, though usually it shows itself in different ways.

I remember an old man I met once on a river, wading deep. His old frame looked too frail to stem the river's flow, but he waded boldly into the current, standing ramrod straight. His hair was white with age and his face leathered and burnt from countless days in the open, but his casts were swift and sure and he covered the water well. I admired him, much as I had admired the salmon in the pool, for his strength and courage had brought him a long way and he was not about to give up the sport he so obviously loved. Thinking of him now, I still see him standing in the river with such an air of quiet determination that I would not be surprised to return and find him standing there still.

There is no monopoly on courage. It is the quality of courage found in fish that leads men to fish for them. And it is something of the same quality in man himself that keeps him wading bravely through swift waters even when the hour is late and shadows are closing in around him.

Bright Fly, Dark Fly

This was a happy river. It chuckled and talked as it spilled its way over shelves and ledges and broke into deep laughter as it slid into a turn at the foot of a steep cut bank. It was an exuberant river, rushing downhill quickly from its source as if anxious to reach a larger river and finally to reach the sea.

It was the best of winter days, and the air was clear and deeply cold, with a deceptively bright sun floating in a sky the color of a robin's egg. The sun painted shadows on the gravel bars along the river, using naked alders as its brush. The cold had kept the snow fastened to the hills so that the river was as low and clear as it would be again in late summer. Where the water level had dropped along the banks it had left a gallery of frozen art, with icy stalactites hanging from the lower limbs of the adjoining forest. These too were struck by the sun, and the light was fractured into a thousand rays of color. It was a fresh day, a frozen day, a day when old storms were forgotten and future storms seemed distant.

On such days the world stands out in bold relief. There are no grays; only blacks and whites, brightness and darkness. The river rippled out of sunlight into dark shadow, drove itself into foam over the shallow, rocky stretches and resolved itself into dark and quiet glides in the slower sections.

Even at low water, it was a fast river, and today the water was very cold. There were steelhead in the river, but the low water and strong light promised that the fishing would be difficult and slow.

What fly to use? The bright, clear water seemed to call for a bright fly. The cold water meant that the fish would be deep and probably would be unwilling to move far to accept a fly. These factors and the strength of the heavy current made it mandatory that the fly be one large and heavy enough to be fished well down. And so the choice was a bright pattern with sufficient size and weight to search the depths of the faster runs and pockets.

But what of the shadowed pools? Strangely it seemed as if the sun were shining only on the fast water and the slower stretches were bathed in deep shadow by the surrounding forest. Here, perhaps, a darker pattern was called for, but again the water temperature—and, in this case, the greater depth—called for a fly that would sink even further. And so the choice here would be a fly with a dark wing and a layer of fuse wire around the body to carry it down.

Having made these decisions, I tied on the bright fly first and waded in. The strong current curled around the waders and built a wave on the upstream side, and I felt the familiar pressure as the water compressed the air trapped inside the waders.

Every feature of the stream bottom was plainly visible in the strong light, and it was easy wading, even in the swiftest part of the flow. Here and there among the rocks I could see bright bits of yarn and broken bobbers, relics left by the bait and lure fishermen who had come earlier when the river was high. It was a small river, not the kind one thinks of as a steelhead river. There was no need here for the long cast, the double haul or the heavy rod. This was a roll-cast river, where the brush grew down close to the bank and it was but twenty careful paces through the current from one bank to the other.

The snow had come earlier, driven hard by the wind, clinging to the alders, gathering in the hollows, filling the network of crevices between the round rocks on the river bars. Then rain had followed, washing the snow from the limbs, and the runoff had come spilling out of the forest into the river in a thousand places. And then suddenly it had turned cold and the whole process had been frozen in a moment, and now the whole earth seemed still except for the river.

I started in at a spot where a mound of gravel split the river's flow, diverting a small part of it to one side and the larger part to the other. Where the larger flow skirted the edge of the opposite bank, it was busy gnawing its way into the network of roots and soil that marked the beginning of the forest.

And here it had made casualties of several maples and alders, whose dead limbs had fallen into the river. The run along the bank was deep, and the dead limbs provided an extra measure of cover. It was a natural place for steelhead.

Making short, careful roll casts, I dropped the fly in the small openings between the limbs and let it drift until another limb threatened, and in this unusual way I fished half the length of the run without result. And then I saw a fish, an old cock fish, working his way up from the lower end. He kept to the deepest water nearest the bank, moving up against the current a few feet at a time, pausing to rest under the protective cover of each downed limb, and it occurred to me that he was moving upstream in much the same way that I was fishing down.

I could see him clearly in the bright water. His belly and flanks were dark and there was a pronounced hook to his lower jaw. He was near to his spawning, less cautious than he otherwise would be, and I knew that had he still been a fresh fish I probably would not have seen him. My bright fly was swimming in a pocket above him, and I withdrew it to let him pass. It was doubtful he would have taken it at this stage of his migration, and in any case he needed his strength for another purpose and I had no need of him.

I left the fish to his difficult task, with a silent wish that he would be successful in his spawning and leave the river with a host of his progeny, and moved down to fish the water below.

I fished through a fast, deep run below a huge boulder, casting upstream to let the line sink and carry the fly deep through the hole, then fished through the tail of the run where hidden rocks revealed their presence by sudden boils in the current. Still nothing.

And then I entered the shadows and immediately it was colder. I changed then to the darker pattern, roll-casting to drop it near the far bank where the water slowed in a deep, mysterious pool. Half a dozen casts produced nothing, and then a hidden root deep in the pool seized the fly and held it so that finally it was necessary to break it free. I tied on another of the same pattern and moved downstream, where another deep run tailed off into a large pool, dark with shadow.

The first part of the run produced nothing, but midway through there came the sudden electric thrill of a strike and a large steelhead leaped, high and twisting, from the current. And in a split-second image that engraved itself on my memory I saw the fish, suspended in the spray of its leap, and the fly as it sailed clear of the steelhead's jaw. And in another second everything was just as it had been before, the current unbroken, the pool quiet, the line slack, as if nothing had happened.

No other fish came to the fly that day, and I hiked through the frosty thickets back to the car, thinking over the day's events. The bright fly in bright water had produced nothing, which was not surprising, because steelhead often seem reluctant to take under such circumstances.

The dark fly fished in the shadows had at least yielded a momentary connection with a fish. But had my choice of fly been made on valid premises? I had considered that the bright pattern would be easily visible in the strong light, but not so visible in the shadow. The darker pattern, I had reasoned, would show its silhouette in the shadow and thus be more readily visible there. A logical conclusion, no doubt, but with one important flaw: I had forgotten that fish are not necessarily logical animals, and they do not necessarily see or interpret things as humans do.

So many factors determine whether the fish takes the fly, and light is only one of them. Perhaps I had fallen into the old trap of following the traditional approach at the cost of trying something new that might have been more fruitful.

Bright fly, dark fly. So many theories surround the use of one or the other, and when the angler stops to consider them all, he begins to realize how little he really knows.

Belfair

The sea trout of the Pacific Coast is the cutthroat, a nomadic wanderer of the estuaries. From the Alaska Panhandle to the Oregon shores, he moves in mysterious local patterns, probing now and then into the coastal streams, straying again into salt water, but never moving far from the mouth of a river.

Fishing the estuaries offers a change from the sound and swift movement of the rivers. In the estuaries, movement is slower and more subtle; the tide eases gently in and out, first touching, then covering the banks of eelgrass along the shore, then dropping quickly to reveal dark mudflats, mottled banks of gravel and crowded oyster colonies. In the estuaries there is nearly always a wind from the sea, a soft, sighing wind usually, sometimes gusting, and the graceful, dirty-white gulls balance on it and soar where it takes them, drifting as free and clear of the earth as a man's dream. The wind carries the scent of far places, of fish and kelp, of salt and distant rain, and it presses gently on the limbs of the windward timber, bending them into strange surrealistic shapes.

In all of nature, there is no place so rich in life as an estuary. The rivers bring a cargo of nutrients from the hills to mix with the abundant salts and minerals of the sea, and the tides flow back and forth in a great broth that breeds and sustains an infinite variety of life. The estuaries are plankton gardens, flashing with phosphorescent life by night, hosting the countless larvae of fish, crabs, barnacles and other creatures. Sticklebacks move in migratory swarms along with candlefish and herring and ugly sculpin in the shallows.

Steelhead and salmon move in and out, singly or in schools, searching for a familiar river, waiting for a freshet to bring water enough for them to make an ascent to their spawning grounds. Herons fish with quiet dignity along the shores; black brant and buffleheads make annual stops along their migratory routes; and occasionally harbor seals may be seen resting on the isolated, windswept spits. And in the midst of it all is the cutthroat, wearing the dark green of the forests on his back and the olive of the meadows on his sides.

Any good fisherman knows that it does not make good sense to seek the cutthroat in salt water. Finding him there is a very uncertain thing, because he literally has an ocean in which to lose himself. It is far more intelligent to fish for cutthroat in rivers, where they are confined to the limits of the river itself. Nevertheless, there is a strange attraction to fishing in salt water, because the search is an added challenge and when fish are found the pleasure is therefore greater.

There are many theories about where and when the cutthroat may be found and caught in salt water, and nearly all of them may be proved one day and disproved the next. The truth is that there is no pattern to the movements of cutthroat. They may come surging in schools when the rising tide comes boiling into the shallows, then linger long after the tide has ebbed; and then again they may not.

Cutthroats may follow the salmon into the rivers, trailing the spawning runs of cohos, pinks and chums, and indeed sometimes they do; but sometimes they do not. One school of thought holds that it is wise to look for cutthroats over oyster beds, and indeed often they are found there; and again, often they are not.

There is even uncertainty about the spawning time of cutthroats. Some say they spawn in November, others say in the winter; and a third group maintains they spawn in the spring. About all that may be said with certainty is that they do spawn, sometime, crowding into the little jump-across streams that run into the saltwater bays and sounds. And once having spawned, they may leave; and then again they may not.

Even in winter, when at least some fish are spawning, there are still bright fish along the beaches and in the bays, foraging for winter food. If the angler finds them, they will come willingly to the fly, and though they never reach extremely large size—four pounds would be exceptional—they are tough, stubborn fighters. Characteristically, the cutthroat fights in a series of strong, short rushes, taking maximum advantage of any underwater obstacle close at hand. And though they are not known as jumping fish, the only fish I have ever seen leap higher than my head was a sea-run cutthroat.

So this was the quarry that took five of us to Belfair on a rainy January day.

Belfair is a small town near the end of Hood Canal, a giant natural arm of salt water that runs north-south, dividing Washington's Kitsap and Olympic peninsulas, then doubles back in a deep stab of water pointed northeast toward Seattle. A dozen small streams run down out of the logged-off hills on the north shore of the canal, and it is a natural place for cutthroat.

A steady rain struck the water with a heavy hiss as we put up our rods and donned rain-repellent gear. Ed and Walt and I had brought cartop boats to explore the beaches; Doc and Syd were clad in waders to search the shallows off the creek mouths. The wind was only a faint stir, and the tide was sneaking in, reaching up for the driftwood scattered along the high-water line. It was the kind of day on which cutthroat seem to prowl.

Often we have found the cutthroat close to shore, in water so shallow it scarcely covers them. And so on this day we rigged up with floating lines in order to search the shallows without fear of hanging up on the eelgrass or the debris swept in by the tide. Each of us chose a bright fly, in keeping with the cutthroat's usual preference, and each of us tied on a light tippet to match the clear winter water.

The fishing technique is a simple one. One searches thoroughly, always watching for a telltale rise that may indicate the presence of a whole pod, or school, of fish.

And while searching, one also casts repeatedly, covering all the water around on the chance of hooking fish that may not have shown themselves. Anglers in boats follow the shoreline, casting in. Fishermen wading in the shallows also follow the shoreline, casting out.

So we set out to find the fish, Walt and I with our boats in the twin bays where creeks flowed in, Ed heading farther down the distant beach, and Doc and Syd wading along the shore. The canal was a broad expanse of dark water more than a mile wide, empty except for the black shapes of buffleheads rafted up far out. At the mouth of the nearest creek a swarm of gulls fed on the flesh of spawned-out salmon carcasses washed down from above.

We fished through the morning without seeing a single rise or sign of trout, indeed no sign of life at all except for an occasional grebe bobbing in the shallows. The rain never ceased, and soon it was necessary to pull the boats ashore and dump out the accumulated rainwater.

After noon, Walt and I broke for lunch, still fishless, and sprawled in the back of his wagon on the beach to eat our sandwiches. Ed still was out of sight, and Doc and Syd still waded, coming now and then into view through the swirling rain and gathering mist. The tide was almost at its height, sucking at the sand along the shore, reaching out for the row of flotsam left by the last high water.

We had nearly finished lunch when we heard Doc exclaim and looked up to see his rod bent sharply, the tip plunging in response to the frantic struggle of a fish. In a few moments, Doc had a handsome cutthroat on the gravel, a bright fish of about fourteen inches. "That, gentlemen, is what we came for," he said.

Encouraged, Walt and I returned to the boats and began searching the same water we had covered earlier. Still, there was no result, no sign of fish, and after a time our casts became mechanical and we had no real hope that a strike would be forthcoming. The tide was now at its highest, flooding up into the streams themselves so that their own identity was briefly lost in the intermingling waters.

And then there was a sudden rise in the small bay where we had fished so long and hard without seeing a prior sign of life. I cast toward the rise, and immediately there was a bulge near my fly, and I struck hard. There was a momentary resistance, and then nothing. Almost at the same moment came Walt's exclamation as he too missed a fish.

I cast again to the same spot, and this time there was no doubt. The fish took the fly firmly along the edge of the eelgrass, and I steered it toward open water as it struggled and turned. It fought with twice the vigor of a landlocked cutthroat, twisting and shaking and showing first one side and then the other, until I had it in the net, a twin of the trout Doc had taken earlier. And on the very next cast another fish took the fly boldly and struggled gamely before it came to the net.

But that was all. We fished the rest of the day without seeing another rise or fish. The tide and the day began their retreat simultaneously, the light ebbing along with the water. Ed returned from his trip along the beach with three small cutthroat on the seat beside him. We shed our drenched rain gear and packed up our rods, and Doc, Syd and Walt left for home while Ed and I went to dry out before the great stone fireplace at the nearby inn.

For most of the day the five of us had fished through the downpour, and we had only six trout between us. All the accumulated years of our angling experience, all the craft we had put into our flies, all the skill we could bring to bear had produced only six trout.

But that is the way of the sea-run cutthroat, a mysterious fish that moves in secrecy and silence along the beaches and the bays, vulnerable only to the most diligent searcher.

Belfair Revisited

I have written of a typical day of sea-run cutthroat fishing, a cold, gray, wet day when the fish were few. Indeed, an angler has good reason to feel fortunate if he is able to take more than a few of these unpredictable trout in a day's fishing. Yet, even with the enigmatic cutthroat, there occurs an occasional, rare, red-letter day when all goes well, when the fish come quickly and easily, even though conditions do not seem completely right.

I have fished often near Belfair, but only one such day has come to me there. There was nothing about it to set it apart from many other days in the estuaries, except that on this particular day the trout seemed to lack their usual cautious ways and accepted eagerly any fly I offered them.

Less than a week earlier the canal had been frozen solid enough for a man to walk across it. The fresh water draining down from the creeks and small rivers had frozen in a layer upon the salt water, and it had stayed that way until warming temperatures and a strong wind had broken it up with splitting sounds like pistol shots. The wind had carried away the broken shards of ice, and the ice had taken with it many of the docks and floats built by cabin owners along the shore.

The ice was gone when Ed Foss and I reached the canal, but frozen drifts of snow were still in evidence along the shore. A steady south breeze sent waves sliding up the gravel beach, and rain mixed with snow spattered on the hoods of our rain parkas.

The tide was rushing in, piling up over the eelgrass and the oyster beds, slapping against the concrete seawall by the old house on the point. Smoke rose from the fireplace chimneys of a dozen cabins, but the beaches and the water were empty except for the usual buffleheads and gulls.

We unloaded our boats from Ed's truck and carried them down the beach to the water's edge, then rigged up our rods and lines. It was nine a.m. when we started fishing, obeying the old adage that the best time to fish for sea-run cutthroat is just before the high tide, which was at ten. We fished along the shore of the first shallow bay, a place where we had seldom failed to find at least a few scattered cutthroat, but at this hour there were none in evidence. Slowly we worked our way to the tip of the far point, where a small stream runs into the canal. We reached it at high tide, when the salt water reached far into the creek mouth, and cast over the oyster beds at its mouth. Still, there was no sign of fish. We had been fishing more than an hour, and it was beginning to appear as if we were in for another day of long searching and few trout.

A great bald eagle suddenly broke cover from the brush

near the old house on the point and took flight on long, graceful wings. We watched as it flew more than a mile distant, still plainly visible, until it settled in the top limbs of the tallest tree on the next point.

Now the tide was changing, and the wind and the tide were at war with one another. The waves swept in by the breeze fought the outgoing tide, setting up a tidal rip along the edge of the point. Sometimes the cutthroat will come to feed in the rips, searching out the food organisms tossed about by the contending waters, but Ed fished through the rip carefully and there was no response.

Then we separated, and Ed headed farther up the beach while I elected to return to the bay we had fished earlier. The water was as clear as I had ever seen it, and each oyster shell and colored rock stood out boldly on the bottom. I cast into the beach where the water scarcely covered the gravel, then cast outward into pockets sometimes five or six feet deep. But there was not a single rise, nor any sign of fish.

At one time there had been two old pilings standing in the bay, and it seemed as if there always were cutthroat somewhere around them. But then the pilings had disappeared, pulled out, I suppose, by the landowner whose property they fronted. After they were gone the fishing became much less certain, but still I searched the old area thoroughly, casting in and out, working the fly shallow and deep, fast and slow. And still there was no response.

I moved farther back into the bay and stopped at a place where a small stream carried the runoff from the melting snow down over the gravel beach, through a patch of eelgrass and into the canal. It was such a tiny flow as to hardly qualify as a stream, scarcely enough water to wet one's boots.

Casting in, I probed the area along the beach where the streamlet flowed in. It was nearly eleven o'clock, and in two hours of fishing I had not seen a sign of trout. But then, without any forewarning, there was a strong take, and I was fast to a good cutthroat. He plunged and turned and sought the bottom, and I tried to steer him into deeper water. Even as I did so, there came a rise near the spot where I had hooked him, followed closely by a second rise nearby, and I knew I had found a school of feeding cutthroat.

I netted the first fish as quickly as I could, anxious now to make another cast before the school moved on. The first trout was bright and fat, about one and a half pounds, with deep crimson slashes underneath its jaws and an iridescent olive gleam to its flanks.

I removed the fly and cast again toward the rises and immediately hooked a second fish, followed quickly by another on the next cast. In years of cutthroat fishing, I have learned never to expect to take more than two or three fish from a school before it moves on, so I hurried my casts, hooking fish, playing them and releasing them as quickly as I could. The tide was dropping rapidly and I felt sure that the school would move out into deep water.

Yet strangely, it stayed where it was, the rises continued, and I continued to catch fish. I looked for Ed, but he was still far off down the beach, out of hailing distance.

I did not know what food had brought the cutthroat to this place, but they responded willingly to my fly. It was an old pattern called an Omnibus, with a body of peacock herl, a red-and-yellow hackle and a bucktail wing. It was the invention of Lendall Hunton, a banker who developed the pattern in the estuaries of Willapa Bay, and it was a proven taker of cutthroat. But I had only two of them in my fly box, and soon the cutthroat chewed them both to shreds. So I switched to another pattern, and it made no difference.

Now the trout were rising almost as if a mayfly hatch were on the water, and one fish jumped clear of the surface to fall upon my fly. It was the type of fishing I have come to know and expect in lakes when a heavy hatch is on, but it was completely unexpected on a winter day in salt water.

Ed now was rowing toward me and I hailed him and told him to come alongside. He anchored his boat nearby and began fishing. Ed is a veteran cutthroat angler who fishes with great skill; he also was using an Omnibus, casting to the same spot, retrieving in the same way. But as sometimes happens, all the luck was with me that day, and none with him. I continued to hook cutthroat, but the trout ignored his fly. Finally he had a strike, fought the fish and landed it—and it turned out not to be a cutthroat, but a small silver salmon.

For two hours the trout rose in the same spot and we fished for them there until the tide dropped so far down it seemed our boats soon would go aground. When we quit fishing and started rowing back to Ed's truck parked on the beach, I had caught more than twenty cutthroat, all of them strong, bright and unusually heavy fish. Nearly all of them had been returned to the water, but I had kept a few in order to examine their stomach contents.

That night I did so, digging out preservative formula, collection bottles, identification keys and a strong magnifying glass. The trout stomachs were filled with several species of shrimp and with aquatic sow bugs. Scale samples, studied under the microscope, indicated the fish all were entering their third year of life, and I assumed that their larger brethren had been busy with spawning on this February day.

Since then I have fished at Belfair other times, and the fishing always has been what it was before that memorable day—long hours of casting and searching, with only a few trout to remember at the end of the day. But since that one occasion when the trout came so frequently and well, I always go there with the hope that there will be another such day. And someday, I know, there will be.

A Choice of Method

I should like to know something about the man who first thought of luring a fish with an artificial fly. I should like to know something of his motives, and of what he felt in that exciting moment when his grand experiment was successful.

I would like to think that he was a visionary man, and that in the moment of success he had some inkling of the significance of the event, some glimmer of knowledge that one day many thousands of anglers would fish in the tradition he established on some long-forgotten river.

Whoever this man was, he must have been a keen student of the life of rivers to have perceived the subtle relationship between the fish and the fly. I wonder if his knowledge went beyond that, and whether he also knew something of the relationship between the sun, the wind and the water, the plants of the river and the insects that feed upon them, and of the relationship between the fish and man himself. If he knew all this, then he truly was a perceptive man, because even today there are few who know it.

Most anglers regard their relationship with the fish as a competitive one, and when they succeed in outwitting the fish they consider they have won the competition. This is a false view of the way things really are. Whether man realizes it or not, the true nature of the man-fish relationship is one of cooperation, not competition. The man is dependent upon the fish and the fish is dependent upon the man, just as all life is interdependent.

What this means in the modern context is that the angler must give up the old idea that trout or salmon are crops to be harvested. With so many fishermen and so many fewer fish, there is a danger that soon there will be nothing more to harvest.

Modern technology has addressed the problem in a different way. If runs of fish are endangered by overfishing, by pollution or by dams, technology's answer has been to raise them artifically in hatcheries so the numbers of fish may be maintained or even increased.

But this is not a solution. There is very little natural selection in a hatchery. The weak survive as well as the strong, and the whole race suffers as a result. The genetic qualities that have made each strain of fish uniquely suited to its native river are quickly erased in hatcheries. Evolution always has been been a trend from the random to the specific, but this trend is reversed in the hatchery.

Hatchery fish may still provide a quality of sport sometimes equal to their wild counterparts. But there will be subtle differences in their behavior—in the time of their return to the river in which they were stocked, in the time spent ascending the river, in their response to temperatures and flow, in other ways. They are not fully in harmony with their environment, as a native fish would be. And that is one reason why wild, native trout and salmon are today so valuable, and why the angler has little right to remove them and their precious source of genetic material.

This is not to say that an angler has no right to keep or kill his catch. Some strains of fish have overpopulated, and in such cases the fisherman does the whole race a favor when he keeps his catch. And the hatchery fish are meant to be harvested; in fact, are considered in terms of economic crops by the agencies which produce them. But the angler should be careful when he is fishing for wild fish, lest he assist in the destruction of something that, once gone, never will be seen again.

Man is so used to the idea that he enjoys complete dominion over the earth that only recently has he given much thought to the consequences of some of his actions. Still, in the literature of angling, there is evidence that from time to time some fishermen have questioned the wisdom of removing trout or salmon from their native waters, and some have gone so far as to construct elaborate justifications for it. Perhaps the most imaginative and amusing of them all is that set forth by William Scrope in *Days and Nights of Salmon-Fishing in the Tweed* in 1843. Scrope says:

"Let us see how the case stands. I take a little wool and feather and tying it in a particular manner upon a hook make an imitation of a fly; then I throw it across the river and let it sweep around the stream with a lively motion. This I have an undoubted right to do, for the river belongs to me or my friend, but mark what follows. Up starts a monster fish with his murderous jaws. It makes a dash at my little Andromeda. Thus he is the aggressor, not I; his intention is evidently to commit murder."

And so, if Scrope may be taken seriously, he would have us believe that it is the fish who is at fault, and the poor angler is merely defending himself. But there were a good many more salmon in the English waters of Scrope's day than there are now, and one wonders what his attitude would be now.

The next logical question for the reader to ask is, what is the use of fishing if one should not always keep or kill his catch? The answer to that, as many anglers have found, is that there is much more to fishing than merely catching fish. There is more excitement and more accomplishment in the stealthy approach, the careful cast, the gentle float of the fly and the slashing rise of the fish than there is in killing the fish after it has been subdued and may no longer struggle for its freedom. Indeed, killing the fish is an incongruous act after all the preparation and effort that has gone into the deceiving and the hooking of it.

That is why fly fishing is so important, and it is one reason why I have adopted fly fishing as my own method. The experienced fly fisherman knows that the method is more important than the result. And if the result is successful, as it often is, then he has the option of returning his catch to the river with little risk of injury.

There is nothing sacred about fly fishing, although so much has been said and written about it that it has acquired nearly the status of a religion. There is really nothing important that sets it apart from other methods except the attitude of the practitioner. Indeed, fly fishing is more nearly defined as a philosophy than a method, and the philosophy should include tolerance of other methods, so long as they do not endanger the resource held in common by all anglers.

But it is very difficult to explain this philosophy to people who fish with the sole objective of bringing home their catch. They do not understand that it is possible to measure success in other ways.

I have mentioned the difficulty of taking winter steelhead on a fly. The winter fly fisherman knows that his chances of success are small, that the odds are stacked against him. And yet there are many who fish through the winter with nothing but a fly.

Why do they do it? Obviously there is something more involved than a simple desire to catch fish. The winter fly fisherman may measure success in terms of the sights and sounds of a winter river, or the sense of pleasure he receives from sending his fly on a long cast across the swirling current to a steelhead lie on the distant side of the river. Or it may be nothing more than the chance to breathe the clean, cold air of winter, to feel the rush of current against his waders and the solid feel of gravel underfoot. The angler may come home fishless after a long day on the river and still feel he has been denied nothing.

Admittedly, this is still an uncommon attitude, but it is growing in the face of reality. There is slow acceptance of the idea that if a man does not practice conservation in sport, he is not likely to practice it in other ways, and when the equation is carried out to the very end he finds that it is really his own habitat that he is trying to conserve.

And so the lesson is that man and the fish must co-exist, that the angler should use the resource but not use it up, that success need not be measured by the number of the kill, and that every care should be taken to guard the wild heritage of salmon and trout so that these best examples of nature's work shall not vanish from the earth. And fly fishing, with all its other inherent pleasures, is the method—and the philosophy—most consistent with this noble purpose.

Waiting for Winter's End

Winter ebbs in March. The crackling cold of January and the February frosts are past, and the earth shrugs and begins to awake from the long night of winter.

The southwesters begin sweeping up the Narrows, piling smoky surf on the beach in front of the house, driving the rain hard against the windows like fistfuls of buckshot. The nights still are long and often stormy, but the days are warmer and there is an imperceptible stirring of life in the forests and the fields.

The steelhead are fewer now, and though March may be a prime month for cutthroat, the weather often is inhospitable to fishermen. There is a raw violence to the storms that mark the changing of the season, the labor pains of the renewal of life.

When March arrives, the opening of the trout season is not far away and there always is much to be done to prepare for it. And so in March I fish less often, preferring to spend the blustery evenings next to the warmth of a blazing hearth, tying leaders and flies, wrapping rods, looking after the equipment that soon will be used to test the trout in the lowland lakes.

It always is necessary to tie new leaders, and a couple of evenings are spent with tape measure and micrometer and spools of material in various diameters. And usually it is time to replace the guides on a favorite rod, and out comes the winding silk and varnish until the job is done. But most of all, there is a need to tie flies, to replenish the supply that dwindled in the last season when flies were left on overhanging limbs or underwater snags, given away to other fishermen or left in the jaws of fish that would not be restrained.

A fly tier is an artist. The pelts of exotic birds and animals are his paints and the hook is his palette. He uses a vast and varied assortment of materials—steel hooks forged in England or Norway, fur from the belly of a red fox or a hare, hackles from the neck of an Indian gamecock—and binds them all together with natural silk to create his impression of a living insect. His work is subjected to an eye far more critical than that of any human reviewer—the sharp, wary eye of the trout.

The number of fly patterns is infinite. Usually the novice tier develops his skill on old and tested patterns, then moves quickly on to his own designs. And, just as each artist has a different view of the world, so each fly tier sees things in his own special way. The result is many different patterns, even though the number of insect types on which trout are known to feed is relatively small.

The concern of the trout fisherman must be with those

patterns that imitate the nymphs, larvae and pupae of aquatic insects or their winged adult stages, plus the many and varied terrestrial insects that live along the shores of rivers. But the fly-tying trout fisherman has gone beyond that to create imitations of small forage fish and minnows and a host of "attractor" patterns that bear no resemblance to anything in nature. And there are still other patterns, created especially for a single species, such as the delicate, beautiful Atlantic salmon flies, the gaudy patterns used for sea-run cutthroat and steelhead and the new generation of flies for saltwater species.

Many anglers have a few favorite flies they will fish with confidence under any circumstances. In fact, looking back over my own records, I see that I have taken more trout on a nondescript nymph pattern than on any other single fly. Though the pattern never was meant to imitate a specific insect, it seems to have something that makes it appealing to trout. Looking further, I see that it has been about equally effective for rainbow and brook trout, but almost a total failure for Kamloops trout—for reasons I cannot fathom.

I have taken many cutthroat on a fly with a body of hot-orange chenille, suggestive of nothing found in nature but in keeping with the strange preference cutthroat seem to have for bright and gaudy colors. And although my box of steelhead flies is filled with a grand assortment of patterns, the old Skykomish Sunrise overshadows all the rest in effectiveness.

It is all very well for an angler to have favorite flies, but he must always fish with an open mind and be willing to try the untried if he is to be a consistently effective fisherman. Sooner or later he will encounter a hatch or some set of conditions in which his old favorites will prove to be of little value, and then he must be willing to depart from established procedure. This seems obvious, but anglers—especially fly fishermen—are a strangely conservative lot and often they insist that the fish meet them on their own terms, an attitude which is not likely to result in many fruitful days.

Though I try to tie enough flies in winter to last through

the trout season, I discovered long ago that on extended trips it is wise policy to take along at least a minimum amount of fly-tying gear in case a new pattern is needed to match local hatches or conditions. Some of my most effective patterns were first tied under such circumstances.

In particular I remember an occasion at Leighton Lake in British Columbia. It had been an unseasonably warm spring and when we arrived late in May the fish already had been driven deep by the heat. Leighton is one of the richest of the British Columbia lakes, with a vast abundance of shrimp, snails, chironomids, sedges and nymphs of damsel and dragonflies. But despite the heat, the hatches still were sparse and it was impossible to tell what the trout were seeking in their deep feeding. Neither I nor other anglers could find a consistent fly.

Finally I took a decent trout and examined its stomach contents. It had been feeding very selectively on damselfly nymphs of a pale translucent green, unlike anything I had in my fly box. So I mounted a tying vise on the seat of my boat and went to work, experimenting with silks and feathers and furs until I had devised an imitation that seemed reasonably close in color and shape. Armed with a pair of the new flies, I returned to fishing and took six Kamloops trout in the next hour, all bright, strong and wonderfully active fish. And in the ensuing years that pattern first tied on the shore of Leighton Lake has proved to be one of the most effective I have used whenever damselfly nymphs are active in the spring.

Over the years, I have kept rather careful records of the effectiveness of the fly patterns I have used, a practice which has yielded valuable information and more than a small share of pleasure. The figures and the names of the patterns and places transform themselves into memories of spring or autumn days, of far-flung lakes and rivers, of Colorado's Roaring Fork surrounded by the mantle of the season's first snow and the slow, sweet water of Silver Creek amid the bare hills of Idaho. One notation reminds me of the incredible hatch on the Henry's Fork, another of the day the flying ants flew in clouds over Hihium Lake. Here is the record of my first salmon, and there the one for the first wily brown enticed from the Madison.

October always has been my favorite month for fishing, and it always seems to me that I do best then, but my own figures prove me wrong. The record shows that September actually has been the best, and July, surprisingly, is second. October is only third, and I suspect it is because October fish are larger and more difficult and I remember them better that October always seems the best.

There are other things to do in the dying days of winter besides tying flies and mending rods. Perhaps the most enjoyable pastime of all is looking through the many tackle and fly-tying catalogs that come in the mail. It seems they come in every month of the year, and pile up unopened until there is time in the winter to leaf through them and take note of the old, the new and the unusual.

Of them all, one of my favorites is the little book from Rogan of Donegal, Ballyshannon, County Donegal, Ireland. It isn't much as catalogs go—lists of flies printed on only one side of thin, tissuelike pages. But the name itself has a good, Irish richness to it, and somehow it always makes me think of a steaming mug of thick Irish coffee on a frosty morning.

But the name is not the only unusual thing about this little catalog. It is the only one I know that offers only hand-tied flies—flies tied without the aid of a vise. This method is a difficult and dying art in which the tier holds the hook between his thumb and index finger throughout the tying process.

As the catalog itself states, "This method of tying which was developed and perfected by three generations . . . ensures the correct tension on the tying silk, eliminates local stress on the hook caused when using a bench vise, and produces a uniform fly of great durability."

I can't testify for the durability of Rogan's flies, but I can vouch for their beauty and perfection. I first saw the catalog when I was given a copy by Doc Musgrove, who then was president of the fly-fishing club in the Seattle suburb of Edmonds where I had gone to give a talk. It seems he had made a wager with a friend that it was impossible to tie a fly smaller than size 16 without using a vise. Doc had seen an advertisement for the hand-tied flies of Rogan and had written to the firm in hopes that it could provide evidence to settle the wager in his favor. Back came a small package with a size-18 Royal Coachman and a letter advising that the fly indeed had been tied without the aid of a vise. Not only that, but the tier apologized for the fact that he had been out of size-22 hooks or he would have sent a hand-tied fly in that size.

I examined the fly under a magnifying glass and found it perfect in every detail, at least the equal of any fly I have ever seen come out of a vise. Doc lost his wager, but he introduced a number of us to Rogan's quaint catalog.

Another favorite is the catalog from E. Veniard Ltd., which includes perhaps the most complete list of fly-tying materials available anywhere.

As John Veniard wrote in the introduction to the 1970 catalog, ". . . our aim is to supply the needs of the amateur fly-tyer at a reasonable cost commensurate with the highest standard of quality and service, and although in some instances our prices may seem to be a little high, this is amply compensated by the fact that everything purchased by our clients is usable. In other words, all 'rubbish' is excluded. . . ."

Veniard's well-illustrated book is indexed so that one may quickly turn to the item he is searching for. It has the most complete line of tying vises I have seen anywhere, including a hand-held model. And I don't know of another place where one could order such items as "the 'Peter Deane' Fly Tyers' Bottle Stand," the "Hills Patent Cast Carrier" or a "fluorescence detector."

Of the many American catalogs, my first choice is that of William Mills & Son. It offers nothing but fishing tackle and accessories and doesn't clutter its pages with extraneous items aimed at catching the eye of a fisherman's wife. And, of course, it features the great H. L. Leonard rod, along with an illustrated explanation of how the rod is made.

The Orvis Co. catalog probably is the most colorful of all, and though it advertises many items that have little interest for anglers, the publishers have had the good sense to put their fine bamboo rods right up in front. And there also are large selections of flies, fly-tying materials and books for window-shoppers such as I.

Then there is the Abercrombie & Fitch catalog with its Bogdan, Seamaster and Fin-Nor reels and its fine mahogany tackle boxes; and Anglersmail with its wide selection of rods—R. H. Woods, Sharpes of Aberdeen, and Leonard—and of British and American flies and books.

Less known but just as interesting is the newspaperlike catalog of the Brule River Tackle Supply. It offers nothing out of the ordinary in the way of tackle, but has a complete selection of snowshoes, along with some unusual items such as Steen's Pure Ribbon Cane Syrup and Black Duck Wild Rice.

And there are so many others—the Rangeley Sport Shop; Bud Lilly's; Arthur L. Walker & Son Fly Reels; Vince Cummings Rods; Harrington & Richardson, with its line of Hardy rods and reels; L. L. Bean, Inc.; Eddie Bauer, and on and on, each one a separate treasure trove of tackle and accessories. Among them are two that deserve special mention—the Wretched Mess Gift Catalog, and Herter's.

The first of these offers a strange assortment of odds and ends compiled by Dave Bascom, better known as Milford (Stanley) Poltroon. Poltroon has gained a dubious sort of fame with his zany magazine, *The Wretched Mess News*, a "piscato-rial periodical" devoted to satire and slapstick about fish and fishing.

It's probably safe to say there is no other catalog that offers, in addition to rods and flies, a book entitled *How to Conquer Stupidity*; a Venus flytrap plant; or dog, cat and husband tags. It's also probably the only catalog that allows the customer to buy everything in it for one lump sum.

Herter's is notable because it's the largest outdoor catalog, and also because of its old-fashioned text and endorsements from satisfied customers. There are a lot of unusual items in Herter's catalog, but perhaps the strangest of all is "Herter's Ancient Passenger Pigeon Decoys." They must have been effective, because the passenger pigeon long ago was rendered extinct by overhunting as well as by destruction of its habitat. As the catalog says: "Not too long ago the passenger pigeons were very plentiful. A few passenger pigeon decoys hung up in a tree would bring flock after flock. The Herter women would go to the decoy tree and pick up the dead pigeons in their aprons and walk back to the house to clean them. Passenger pigeons were nothing special to eat as they were dark fleshed and a little livery. But well flavored with onions they were not too bad, especially if you had a lot of children to feed."

Perusing catalogs is an entertaining pastime, but it doesn't compare with angling. And when the last catalog is closed, the last fly is tied, and the last winter storm has blown itself out, it is time for Opening Day—time to go fishing again.

SPRING

In the spring, the rainbow and Kamloops trout spawn, and always it is exciting to watch this ritual in the small tributary streams. The larger rivers are often in freshet with runoff from the winter snows, and the steelhead and salmon fingerlings ride to sea on the wings of the flood. The forests and fields bloom with fresh life, and in the heat of the day the insects hatch and the trout in the lowland lakes begin to rise. The mornings are cool and fine, the evenings grow long with gentle, dying light, and everywhere there is new life and renewed life.

I have seen many seasons pass since that first spring trout

took my fly, but I still remember it well. My father had come home from the war and together we made the long, exciting trip into the British Columbia interior, a strenuous journey in those days. Finally we turned off what then was the main road and started up a pair of ruts into a grove of tall aspens. The silver leaves twinkled where the sunlight caught them until finally we were above them and into a stand of lodgepole pine. Here and there we passed cleared fields rimmed with split-rail fences where white-faced Herefords grazed. And then at last we came to a tiny tributary stream that flowed into the lake that was our destination.

The stream was hardly two feet wide, with an even flow of cold springwater over a fine gravel bottom. It was jammed with spawning Kamloops trout, some longer than the stream was wide, some so thick the water scarcely covered them.

It was the first time I had seen spawning fish, and we lingered at the stream to watch as the scarred males fought one another for supremacy and the females thrust their tails into the gravel to make nests for their spawn. Perhaps it was then that I first realized what hardships a trout must overcome to be born in the river gravel, to survive and grow, to return and spawn, and what a miracle it is that they are able to overcome them.

Then we went on to the lake, and the next morning it was bordered with thin ice before the sun was full upon the water. The sky was a brilliant blue, and beyond the dark pine forest on the far side of the lake the mountains still were crowned with snow. It was a scene of bright beauty and freshness that made the whole earth seem new and clean. And then came the fragrance of burning alder as fires were started in the cookstoves, and soon the aroma of frying bacon was mixed with the warm, pleasant scent of the alder smoke.

After breakfast we started out on the lake, and my father handed me a fly rod and showed me how to trail the fly behind the boat. Soon I felt the sudden wrench of a hard strike, a feeling that was to become familiar over the years, but one which still never fails to generate something of the same excitement I felt in the moment of that first violent pull.

The trout was not a large one, but it leaped gamely and I quickly thrust the rod into my father's hands so that he could play and land it. Even so, I thought of it as "my" trout, my very first, because I had been the one who had hooked it.

A good many years have passed since that event, but the bright visions of those early days are with me still, and I am grateful for them. And each April, when the trout begin to rise again, I go out with something of the same feeling, and I suspect that no matter what his age, each fisherman becomes a small boy again in the spring.

The Trout Under the Cedar Limb

It was a day typical of April, bright but cool, with a stiff breeze sweeping in through the timber from the south, riffling the water of Pass Lake. A late snowstorm in the mountains had forced the cancellation of a planned trip east, so at the last moment I had decided to return to Pass Lake, where only the previous weekend the members of the Washington Fly Fishing Club had gathered for their annual Opening Day celebration.

Pass Lake is perched on the high shoulder of Fidalgo Island in Puget Sound, overlooking the great chasm of Deception Pass where saltwater tides rip in and out with awesome speed and force. The lake itself is surrounded by tall timber and lush pasture, kept that way by conservationists who waged a long fight to save it from a massive real-estate development. The lake is shallow and rich and restricted to fishing with the artificial fly. It is kept heavily stocked with rainbow trout so that no angler, even the most clumsy, need go home empty-handed. Usually there are more trout than the lake can comfortably support, so that the average size is not large. But each year there are a few fish that survive until the next season, and of that number there are again a few that hold out for a third year and grow to a respectable size. Two-pounders are not really uncommon and occasionally a lucky angler will hook a really heavy fish of four pounds or better.

But on this particular day, Pass Lake was not eager to yield its trout. The water was cold from a winter that had held on more persistently than most, and the angling pressure during the season's first week had been heavy so that the trout were both sluggish and wary.

I fished in all the usual spots with all the usual flies and released several small fish and a single dark two-pounder, but the action was slow compared to the usual standard. And then, as I let my boat drift down the lake on the gathering breeze, I noticed a cautious rise close to shore, followed quickly by another. It was not a place where I usually fished; in fact, it was a place that most anglers seemed to ignore. But on such a day as this, when the trout were not coming easily, nothing could be overlooked.

Maneuvering close to shore, I watched and waited to see what had prompted the rises I had seen. And there it was: the pupal shuck of a small chironomid bobbing to the surface, the adult fly struggling to free itself, then drying its wings in the open air as the wavelets carried it away. Studying the water, I noticed others hatching, so I traded the sinking line and nymph pattern I had been using for a floating line and a dry fly tied to imitate the chironomid adults.

On the first cast the fly cocked nicely and rode up one side of a small wave and down the other before it disappeared quickly in a swirl. I raised the rod and was fast to a fish, but it was not a large one. I brought it in quickly, twisted the fly free from its jaw and watched it dart away. Two others quickly followed, but neither was large and I was hoping for some bigger game.

And then I saw a quiet rise far back under the overhanging limb of an old cedar growing at the edge of the lake. The limb sagged under its own weight, the foliage dragging in the water. There was no way to cast directly to the spot without hanging the fly in the foliage. I dried my fly and studied the situation, trying to think of a way to reach the trout. The rise had left me with the impression that this might be a bigger fish, and there was confirmation in the well-sheltered spot chosen by the trout as its feeding station.

As I watched, I saw another chironomid pop to the surface and begin to struggle out of its pupal shuck, and as it did so the breeze carried it slowly back under the cedar limb, where it disappeared in a careful rise that was a duplicate of the first one I had seen.

Perhaps, I thought, I could use the wind in the same way, letting it carry my artificial to the trout. I cast ahead of the limb and threw extra slack line on the water, then waited while the breeze slowly carried the fly back into the shadows beneath the cedar limb. But the cast had not been long enough and the fly swung around short of the spot I was aiming for. A second cast, with more line, and another wait, and this time the wind carried the fly precisely to the spot. There was a rise, the fly disappeared, and I raised the rod gently to set the hook. The water erupted and a fine trout leaped, shaking itself and nearly striking the limb overhead. Just as quickly, the line went slack as the fly pulled out. It was easily the largest trout I had ever hooked in Pass Lake, and, as it turned out, the last large fish I was to hook that day.

A week later I went back to try again. The conditions were much different; this time the sky had the iron-gray look of a battleship's side and the wind came from the north in sporadic, blustery puffs. Only an occasional scattered rise was visible and the trout were even more reluctant than they had been the week before. I fished slowly and carefully through the afternoon, but still had nothing to show for my efforts by the time I came again to the old cedar with the sagging limb.

Again the chironomids were hatching, but they were fewer this time and there were no rises. There was no sign of life under the limb. Knowing that trout in lakes tend to cruise about and change position rapidly, I had no thought or expectation that the trout I had hooked the week before would still be there. Nonetheless, the dark water under the cedar limb seemed as likely a spot as any other and I decided to try it once again.

This time it was necessary to maneuver to the opposite side of the limb to take advantage of the north breeze. As before, I dropped the fly above the limb and waited while it drifted underneath. Suddenly the fly was gone and there was a single large bubble floating in its place. I raised the rod and a large trout thrashed the surface.

This time, I thought, I've hooked him solidly. But just in the moment it took to think so, the fly came away. I drew it back and examined it; the tiny, fine-wire hook had been straightened by the heavy fish. And I was certain it was the same fish I had hooked the week before.

Another two weeks went by before my next visit to Pass Lake. This time I headed directly for the overhanging limb. But this time someone was there ahead of me, a young man wading along the shoreline, casting a dry fly. I hailed him and we exchanged greetings, and then I asked him whether he had yet cast under the cedar limb.

"Yes," he replied with excitement. "I hooked a big fish that jumped and broke my leader."

I knew then that I would not get another chance at the fish that day, and I was glad somehow that it had kept its freedom.

It was late in the fall before I spent another day on Pass Lake. By then the water level had fallen, and the sagging cedar limb was over dry land. I wondered if the big trout had survived the summer to find another feeding station in the lake, or whether some other angler, luckier or more skilled than I, had found his hiding place and captured him.

I have mentioned this experience because there are two things about it that seemed unusual. One was that it is rare for trout in lakes to remain in the same place, though the extraordinary cover provided by the sagging cedar limb would help to explain it. The other was that it is not often that anglers on the Pacific Slope find a trout so willing to rise consistently to a floating fly—especially in a lake.

Many Western rivers, especially those of the Northwest, are large, fast, brawling streams. They fall rapidly and flood frequently and they are freestone streams with only relatively sparse fly life.

There are notable exceptions, of course, especially on the inland streams—the food-rich Montana rivers, Henry's Fork and Silver Creek in Idaho, Oregon's Deschutes and Williamson, and others. But in many Western rivers, a good, sustained hatch is something of a rarity, and in some of them the primary fishery is for anadromous fish that do not come into the rivers to feed.

That is why so much trout fishing is done on lakes in the Western states and provinces. But even in the richest lakes, there is so much subsurface food that a really good rise to flies on the surface comes only infrequently. Again, there are exceptions—the great mayfly and sedge hatches on Oregon's Hosmer Lake, the mayfly on Davis Lake in the same state, the sedge hatches on the better lakes of the British Columbia interior. But more often than not, the trout will be feeding below the surface on freshwater shrimp or the nymphs and pupae of aquatic insects, and sometimes they range deep and feed mostly on snails.

Still, there are occasions—such as the one on Pass Lake—when rises come often enough to make the dry fly worthwhile. But it is not dry-fly fishing in the classic sense because the angler does not have to cope with currents and eddies and drag.

As a beginning angler, I used the dry fly often. And surprisingly, I caught many trout at first. In particular I remember a sunny April day when I came upon a heavy mayfly hatch in the shallows of Bay Lake, near Tacoma.

It was a windy day and the flies were hatching thickly over the weedbeds, with big rainbow trout rising to them eagerly. It was an afternoon of furious excitement and I ended it with one trout over three pounds and several over two, and I began to wonder why more anglers did not use the dry fly.

Further experience taught me why: In Western fishing, the wet fly and nymph are effective far more often than the dry fly. Looking back over the journals I have kept throughout the years, I see now that I have used dry flies only 10 to 20 percent of the time. And even that, I suspect, is more often than most anglers who fish the majority of their time on Northwest streams and lakes.

The literature of angling is filled with many great works of entomology, most of them dealing with the mayfly, and whole schools of angling tactics and fly dressing have grown up around the imitation of this single insect family. Dry-fly tactics based on imitation of the mayfly flowered in England under the development of Halford and Marryat, and Theodore Gordon revamped their thinking to suit the requirements of America's Catskill streams. Gordon's work was further developed by Hewitt, LaBranche and Jennings, and more recently by Marinaro, Schwiebert and Flick. Their books constitute the backbone of dry-fly theory and practice in America.

But for all the years spent in the development of this knowledge, it remains largely irrelevant in the West. Perhaps it is because of the great variety of fish and insect species and conditions present on Western waters that a coherent "Western school" of angling theory has yet to be devised.

Or perhaps it is because the sport is still developing in the West, and the bold thinkers and innovators who will write the definitive treatises on Western angling have yet to arrive on the scene.

In any case, it is clear that there are vast differences between the traditional approaches employed on Eastern waters with their surface and terrestrial hatches, and the tactics used on the broad, swift rivers and windblown lakes of the West.

Several years ago, an Eastern firm that was compiling data for a calendar of hatches wrote the game department in my state seeking information on local emergences, and the department sent the letter on to me in hopes that I could answer it. I suspect the authors of the calendar were a little surprised at my reply that we did not have any hatches worth cataloging. There has been little research on Western hatches, and their relative sparsity discourages anyone who might set out to do the job.

But good hatches sometimes do occur, even on the majority of waters that are not known for them. Mostly they are of short duration, and always they are unpredictable because of the rapidly changing conditions present on most waters. And sometimes they take place where the angler least expects to find them.

One day I waded up a small tributary of a major river, hoping to find cutthroat that had come in early from the sea. At one time the creek had carried a substantial flow of water through the year, winding down from the hills through a thick forest that kept the water cool and clear. But then loggers had attacked the upper watershed and raped it (there is no better word), and now the stream pours in a thick, brown flood through the spring runoff and then subsides quickly to a trickle of water, naked and open to the sun. And so it was on this day, when only a small stream of water—hardly enough to flow over the feet of my waders—spilled its way down through the piles of shattered gravel heaped up earlier by the floods. I had not seen the stream since it had been devastated, and I quickly lost any hope of finding fish within its reaches, or of seeing any insect life.

But I was wrong on both counts. A hatch began over the shallow riffles, with dozens of tiny mayflies riding down the weakened current and then taking to the air. Soon there were hundreds of them, and then still more, until everywhere I looked the air was filled with the motion of gossamer insects in gentle flight. It seemed impossible that such a hatch could occur in a stream that had been so sadly abused, but there it was. Still, there were no trout to rise to the hatching flies. There was no cover for them in the sun-drenched shallows of the little stream.

But then, on the way back, I explored a side channel carved by the spring floods and found a place where a small spring bubbled out of the ground and flowed in above a great old stump. The springwater had worn a large, deep hole under the stump, and ferns growing on the stump itself kept the water shaded from the sun. I watched the hole, looking for a rise, but there was none, and finally I made a short roll cast and let the gentle current carry a small nymph down to the spot, where an eddy sucked it out of sight. I felt a sudden pull and struck back, and there was a flash of gold as a large cutthroat came tumbling out from under the stump. It ran strongly downstream, where a strand of barbed wire from an old fence sagged into the water, and quickly took my leader around the wire. It left me the fly and the task of untangling the leader.

Good hatches—and good rises—occur so haphazardly on Western waters that I never go out with the expectation of finding them. But they happen just often enough that I always go prepared to deal with them if they should occur. And on those rare occasions when everything goes just right—when the new flies are thick on the water, and the trout come eagerly and fast to naturals and imitations alike—it provides a sense of satisfaction that one seldom receives from using the wet fly or the nymph. Perhaps that is why good hatches on Western waters are so often discussed, so well remembered and so much appreciated.

A Day on the Yuba

Each year in the spring, the shad seek out the fog-shrouded entrance of the Golden Gate and pass quickly through it to the filth and traffic of San Francisco Bay. In unnumbered thousands they find they way through the silt and shifting currents of the great bay to the muddy mouth of the Sacramento River.

Still unseen, the silver hordes enter the river and pass upstream beyond the busy docks and the freeway bridges, swimming up against the river's broad flow and into the hot, dry-grass country of the Sacramento Valley. And there they seek the mouths of their native tributaries—the Feather, the Yuba and the American.

Far to the north, another great run comes back to the Columbia, crossing the great, stormswept bar at the river's mouth. They struggle upstream past the Portland waterfront, dividing at the entrance of Camas Slough where thousands turn aside to spawn at the Washougal River's mouth. The remainder of the run continues up the main stem until it is caught in the violence of the Bonneville tailrace, and there the fish mill in confusion until they find the gentler flow of the fish ladders at the dam. The shad ascend the ladders and disappear on their way to still undiscovered spawning grounds in the upper Columbia and the Snake.

The shad is not native to the West. It was brought from its native Eastern rivers and stocked in the Sacramento and the Columbia in the 1870s. In the hundred years since, the runs have built themselves to major proportions, spilling over into other rivers as they did so.

The shad is a member of the herring family, and it looks very much like a giant herring. It has a large, tender mouth and heavy gill rakers used to trap the plankton that is its primary food during its years at sea. When the shad matures and returns to its native river to spawn, its dime-sized scales are silver-bright and gleam with a mother-of-pearl luster in the sun. Shad are streamlined, deep-bodied fish, and when hooked their favorite maneuver is to turn their broad sides against the current and use its leverage against the angler.

Female shad grow larger than males. The average is three to four pounds, but individuals of seven or eight pounds have been caught. The shad runs well and jumps well, and though its fight pales in comparison to that of a fresh-run steelhead, it still is a strong, lively, fly-rod fish.

In California, the anglers flock to the Sacramento tributaries when the shad are in, and the shad fishery has become an important one. Yet, strangely, anglers have been slow to take advantage of the big Columbia River run. A few fishermen who have discovered the sporting qualities of shad journey faithfully to the Washougal's mouth or the Bonneville tailwaters to fish for them, but the great majority of the Columbia River shad never see an angler's lure.

Perhaps one reason is that the fishing is difficult and the surroundings far from pleasing. The Columbia is far too large and dangerous to wade at Camas and at Bonneville. At Camas, a boat is necessary to reach the main schools of fish, and anglers must hazard the obnoxious fumes from a huge pulp mill. Sometimes the air becomes so foul it is difficult to ' breathe and nearly impossible to see the far bank of the river. Even when the wind carries the fumes away, the landscape is ugly with clusters of high-tension power poles and heaps of refuse from the mill.

At Bonneville, the river is too swift for any but the largest, strongest boats, and anglers who try to fish from shore confront a steep, stone bank that leaves little room for backcasts. To make matters more difficult, the prevailing wind sweeps in against the shore and limits the range of even the finest casters.

The scenery along the Sacramento tributaries is not much better: flat, dry fields and scrub willows along the riverbanks, with little shade from the sun. But here at least the angler can wade the cool, shallow rivers and often see his quarry before he casts.

The Yuba River is especially popular, and anglers from all over California and beyond gather there each Memorial Day to catch the shad spawning run at its peak.

Memorial Day was just past and so was the peak of the run when I made my first visit to the Yuba. Still, the fish were there in great numbers, and so were the fishermen.

Bill McGrath and I rendezvoused in the dawn and set out in his car for the long drive out of the traffic-clogged Bay Area suburbs, north through onion-scented Vacaville and into the open spaces and smaller towns of the Sacramento Valley. Bill had fished the Yuba many times and knew the route well.

East of Marysville we turned off the highway onto a rutted dirt road that led down to the river, flushing huge jackrabbits from the high grass as we passed. Where we came to the river it was surrounded by high banks of gravel, dredged and sifted and dredged again by generations of gold seekers until literally every stone along the river had been prodded and poked, examined and re-examined. A bewildering array of high-tension lines crossed the river at half a dozen points with no apparent coherence to their patterns, and jet aircraft rumbled and throbbed overhead on the approach to a nearby air base.

We parked among the gravel mounds, put up our rods and walked down to the river. It was midmorning and warm, but a strong wind was blowing up the river between the twin walls of rubble left by the gold dredges. The drift that Bill had chosen for us to fish already was crowded with anglers, most of them fly fishermen, and they told us the fishing had been slow.

We waded out onto the smooth, gently sloping gravel of the river bottom and began casting toward the far bank where the water was faster and deeper.

I was using a fast-sinking fly line, standard equipment for the big, swift water of the Columbia, but the Yuba was low and some of the other anglers were fishing with floating lines—the first time I had seen them used for shad. As I watched one of the other casters, there was a quick swirl behind his line; he struck, and was fast to a shad.

Moments later I heard a shout from Bill and turned to see his rod bent in a tight arc. His reel buzzed as the fish took line, but he recovered it quickly, and after a spirited struggle he eased the fish into the shallows and discovered that his fly had foul-hooked the shad in its head. Bill twisted the fly free and returned the fish to the river.

After that there was little action for a long while, and the crowd along the drift began to thin as anglers left for other parts of the river. We moved upstream to what appeared to be more desirable water, a fast run breaking down over a rocky chute and fanning out into a deeper drift below.

The wind had subsided to an occasional, gentle gust that rattled the scrub-willow leaves. The sun was tall in the sky and hot, and scattered, chiming birds competed with the grumble and whine of insects and the slow, sullen sound of the river. Here and there crows picked at the rotting remains of spawned-out shad, and a big blue heron flew along the crest of a mountain of gold tailings. I cast into the faster water and let the current take the fly in a sweeping semicircle until the long line was straight below me.

Then came the sudden, jolting strike so characteristic of a shad, and the heavy Beaudex reel sang a baritone growl that rose quickly to a tenor's pitch. The shad took a long length of line downstream, then veered quickly toward the bank and took the line right around the feet of another angler.

The other fisherman sensed the strange pressure on his waders and glanced down to see the cause of it. He saw the line through the clear water and stepped back so that it came free and once again was taut to the fish.

Thwarted there, the shad turned back into the current, shifting and turning its broad body to take full advantage of the faster water. Then it jumped in the peculiar way shad have of jumping, coming out in a flat trajectory, coming down to slap the water with its side.

Slowly the fish tired and I recovered the line it had taken. And finally it was resting on the gravel at my feet, a bright female gleaming in the sun. The fly came easily from the soft jaw and I eased the fish gently back into the river, holding it erect until its strength returned.

Now there was a flurry of activity. Quickly I landed two other fish and lost a third. Bill hooked another and had a hard fight with it in the fast water, discovering when he landed it that it, too, had been foul-hooked. But then the flurry subsided as quickly as it had come. We fished on for a while, then drove into Marysville to eat lunch and browse through the tackle shops.

In the afternoon we returned to the river, at a point farther downstream. We fished there an hour, seeing no fish and hooking none. It was late in the day when we returned to Bill's car and headed upriver again, stopping this time just below a small irrigation dam. The water slid smoothly over the round face of the dam and broke into a large, oblong pool at the bottom. It moved in curious, indecisive eddies through the pool, then gathered itself together and spilled down a narrow, shallow chute to the head of a second, smaller pool below. It was the second pool we chose to fish.

I waded deep into the upstream end of the pool and cast out and down, watching the line swing and sink in the current. The sun was low in the sky, with fierce light glinting obliquely off the moving surface of the pool, but I could make out the massive, ghostly shapes of boulders rearing up beneath the water. I thought to myself that it would make fine holding water for steelhead, and looking deep into the pool I conjured up a mental image of the shadowy form of a fresh summer-run steelhead swaying in a gentle eddy behind a boulder.

And then the image moved.

The light had shifted just a little, just enough to show that what I had thought was only a figment of imagination was in reality a fish. And it was quickly joined by another, and then another, and suddenly it seemed as if a thousand silver leaves were drifting through the pool, turning slowly in the current, glinting with dull flashes as the light caught their shifting sides. But they were not steelhead, nor were they leaves—they were shad!

A great school of fish was in the pool, and as I watched it

slowly circled, moving first to the head of the pool where the fast water flowed into it, then turning back and passing out of sight on the far side, only to reappear at the foot of the pool and begin the circuit once again.

I watched the progress of the school and cast so that the current would sweep my fly into the head of it as it came around again. Suddenly there came a solid strike, and a shad leaped near the foot of the pool. It made the characteristic run, then turned and came back, and I fought it in close until only the leader showed beyond my rod tip. The fish was turning and fighting right in the center of the school, now so close that shad were nearly brushing against my waders, but the other fish paid no attention to the struggles of their brother. I backed out of the pool onto the high, rocky bank and eased the fish ashore. After releasing it, I waded out and cast again, and soon another fish came, and then another, and the action grew even faster as the light dwindled and evening came on.

Bill, fishing just upstream, had several strikes, but could not seem to get a solid hook-up. Then, moving to a new spot, he slipped on a rock and sat down hard in the river. He emerged, dripping and profane, and headed back to his car to change clothes. I stayed on, fishing until the last light drained out of the day and mosquitoes came out of the brush to settle eagerly on my hands and face.

Finally I released a last fish and climbed back over the gravel bank to where Bill was waiting in the car. It had not been one of Bill's better days, but soon he would get another chance at the river. For me, it had been a pleasant and unusual change from fishing in the ugly, roaring violence of the Columbia, a chance to wade a small river and to see what I was fishing for.

I found myself wishing that the Columbia offered similar sport. Perhaps one day it will, if more Northwest anglers begin to fish for shad and ferret out the upstream spawning grounds, and if nitrogen poisoning does not kill the shad as it has most of the native salmon and steelhead of the Columbia.

And if the Columbia does not develop such sport, then perhaps it will come later in some other, smaller river, where even now the shad may be building up a run that so far has escaped the attention of anglers. And even if it never comes at all, it is not really so very far to the Yuba and her sister rivers—where men once searched for gold and anglers now search happily for silver.

After Dark

James Chetham, writing in *The Angler's Vade Mecum* (1681), called night fishing an "unwholesome, unpleasant and very ungenteel" sport, and a practice "to be used by none but idle poaching fellows."

Without doubt there is more than a grain of truth in what he says, and certainly the literature of angling is replete with tales of poachers and perpetrators of other foul angling deeds who committed their crimes under cover of darkness.

But if it is true that the darkest hours bring out the worst in men, it also is true that they bring out the best of trout. Great trout, quiescent by day, begin to prowl and feed at night, and hidden hatches set off explosive rises from fish the daytime angler never sees. For those anglers whose intentions are honorable and above reproach, the hours of darkness may provide angling of an exciting, different sort.

I am not a night fisherman by regular habit, but occasionally when the day is warm and the wind gentle I will stay on the water long after the last light fades, and try to tempt the larger trout that come forth to feed at night. And occasionally, when I become aware of the presence of a large trout that will not take my fly by day, I make a special trip to try for him by night. More often than not these expeditions are successful, but successful or not they never fail to generate high excitement.

Night angling has a special quality. As the last light steals from the day, the earth changes suddenly in a confusing movement of dark and growing shadows. Familiar landmarks grow or shrink, become magnified in total size as individual details disappear, or dwindle into obscure and hidden shadows. A well-known place becomes suddenly mysterious and strange, forbidding and forbidden, and as total darkness descends all reference points slowly disappear until only the tops of the tallest ridges remain silhouetted dimly against the sky.

The stars begin their slow, silent climb to the zenith, and perhaps there is a pale moon with light enough to cast cold, silver shadows across the meadows or the mesas. The familiar life of day is gone and the creatures of the night take over. The rings from rising fish gleam briefly like spreading circles of molten steel in the ghostly evening light, and the swallows that fed on the daylight hatches are replaced by silent, plunging bats.

The night fisherman knows a different world. Normal daytime sounds subside so that one may hear the soft, close rush of wings from a bird in hidden flight. The bullfrogs talk to one another more freely than by day, and the loud slap of a beaver's tail echoes through the wild. The moon trades its cold light with the clouds, and occasionally meteors flash overhead with a last quick burst of dying flame. The stars wheel in their silent orbits—bright Rigel and mysterious Betelgeuse, and the Arab mourners plodding eternally after a casket traced in stars.

It is a time to pause, to look up in awe and wonder about the nature of things; a time that teaches humility in the face of evidence that the angler is only a small fisherman on a small water, an infinitesimal fragment of life hurtling through the void from an unknown source to an uncharted destination, with only his fragile faith to guide him.

But if it is a time for contemplation, it also is a time for action. There comes the sudden sound of a heavy rise, and the angler wheels blindly toward the sound and casts into the night. His fly rides an invisible wave and tensely he waits for the sound of a take or the sudden jolt that will tell him the trout has seen what he cannot see.

And then follows the struggle with an invisible opponent, a silent battle between a man who cannot see his quarry and a trout robbed of the sanctuary of familiar obstacles now hidden in the dark. And when it is over the angler is either flushed and trembling with the excitement of victory or filled with the pangs of defeat and wonder at the size of the unseen thing that defeated him.

My first real try at night fishing came on a warm September evening in central British Columbia. We were camped in the bottom of a great granite canyon with ancient Indian pictographs painted on its walls. The canyon held a pair of lakes, twin jewels of sparkling clear water with shallow, sandy shoals that sloped off into unknown turquoise depths.

I had spent the day fishing one of them, and in the shallow water behind a large weedbed I had found trout rising freely to a hatch. I had taken and released many on a dry fly, but most of them were small and I was frustrated because I could see much larger fish moving in and out of the shallows to feed. The larger fish refused everything I tried, wet fly, or dry, and so I waited to fish the evening rise in hopes they would be less cautious then.

The light went quickly off the water in the deep canyon, and the sky changed from blue to deep purple. But there was no hatch and no rise, and I watched and waited as the last light disappeared without seeing a single ring on the placid surface of the lake. The next day we would have to leave and return to the city, and I badly wanted at least one more good fish before we left, so I determined to wait even until after total darkness had fallen. I had with me a small flashlight to aid in changing flies or leaders, and I settled down to wait.

It was quiet in the darkness, except for a gentle stir of breeze that set the tules rubbing against one another and pushed small wavelets at my boat that made a tiny lap-lap sound as they struck its windward side. And then, far back in the weeds, came the heavy splash of a feeding trout. It was far beyond casting range, and hopelessly hidden in the weeds, and so I waited further. Far off came the sound of another splashing rise and I sensed rather than saw the great, mothlike sedges that were beginning to flutter awkwardly from the surface of the lake.

Another heavy splash, this one close by, just at the edge of the weedbed from the sound of it. I cast quickly toward the sound, and as I felt the line strike the water in the darkness there was another explosive rise, and I struck instinctively. There was immediate, furious resistance from a fish so strong I thought for a moment I could not hold it on the light tackle. It ran along the edge of the weedbed and my reel screamed in angry protest. I felt the backing splice slide out through the guides and heard a great crash in the darkness as the fish leaped and fell back into the water.

Then it was a long and silent struggle as the fish turned and plunged and vainly sought the sanctuaries it used by day.

It was confused in the darkness and turned away from the weedbed where it would have broken me off quickly, and I held it as firmly as I could so that it would not stray again out of the deeper water into which it had blundered.

Time passes quickly in the darkness, and it seemed a very long time indeed before all the line was back on the reel and only the leader extended beyond the tip of the rod. The trout circled the boat once, then again, and in the starlight I caught a glimpse of silver and stabbed at it with the net. The surface erupted as the net closed around the trout and I lifted it clear, struggling and twisting in the mesh. And then it lay quivering in the bottom of my boat, illuminated by the wavering beam of my flashlight, a great old trout of many summers, with broad silver flanks that bounced the light back into my eyes.

It had been as exciting a fight as I had ever had with a fish, and though I had waited for darkness with some reservations about the ethics of it all, I felt now that no trout ever had been more honestly taken or had struggled more nobly than this one. And as for the ethics of the matter, if the trout was somewhat handicapped by the darkness, the angler had been handicapped even more, and is not the taking of fish under difficult circumstances indeed the essence of the sport?

For me, the answer was affirmative, and with that question having been resolved my path has led to other nighttime waters.

I suspect all anglers are night fishermen in their hearts. Who among us has ever fished who did not look forward to the evening, the long, drawn-out death of the day when, as every angler knows, the trout grow less cautious and the fishing more rewarding? When does evening end and night begin? What is less honorable about fishing when the darkness is nearly total than fishing when a little light remains? What separates the night fisherman from the man who stays to fish the "evening rise"?

It is, of course, a matter of definition, and each angler has his own idea of the best time to fish and the best time to quit fishing, whether it be at five o'clock or midnight. Perhaps the most eloquent answer was that given by the great angling pioneer Thaddeus Norris, who said:

"Of all places, commend me, in the still of the evening, to the long placid pool, shallow on one side, with deeper water and an abrupt overhanging bank opposite. Where the sun has shone all day, and legions of ephemera sported in its declining rays; the bloom of the rye or clover scenting the air from the adjoining field! Now light a fresh pipe, and put on a pale Ginger Hackle for your tail-fly, and a little white-winged Coachman for your dropper. Then wade in cautiously—move like a shadow—don't make a ripple. Cast, slowly, long, light; let your stretcher sink a little. There, he has taken the Ginger—lead him around gently to the shallow side as you reel him in, but don't move from your position—let him tug awhile, put your net under him, break his neck, and slip him into your creel. Draw your line through the rings—cast again; another and another—keep on until you can see only the ripple made by your fly; or know when it falls, by the slight tremor it imparts through the whole line down to your hand—until the whippoorwill beings his evening song, and the little frog tweets in the grass close by;—not till then is it time to go home."

And so it is, in the sweet of the evening.

Three springs ago, I spent an evening among the rushes at Dry Falls Lake, at the head of the great coulee where eons ago the Columbia River plunged over in a mighty falls many times the height and width of Niagara. Now there is nothing left but the huge, silent, eroding walls of stone, and the rich lake that fills the old catchbasin where once the river fell.

It had been a bright, hot day, with the temperature well up in the 80s and the sun peering brightly into the depths. The fishing had been poor, as it usually is under such circumstances, and now I was waiting for the light to die beyond the coulee rim.

The light was a long time fading from the water, but slowly it did so and the great rocks reached out with shadows to replace the brilliance of the day. And as the shadows deepened, the trout began to move into the shallows to feed, with a steady march of rises to the shore.

I cast toward the rises and strained in the gathering darkness to see my fly. It was hopeless; my eyes were not keen enough to pick out the tiny dark pattern and separate it from the dark water on which it rode. So, holding the fine point of the leader up to the twilight in order to see what I was about, I tied on a larger pattern with hackle fore-and-aft and cast it out. This one I could see, with its dark bulk riding on stiff hackles as it waited for a trout to notice it was there.

I teased the fly with my rod tip so that it crept across the surface, and quickly it was gone, swallowed up in a rising wave by a trout which had it and was quickly away. There was no need to lift the rod; the tension came immediately as the fish began a powerful run. My reel on this occasion was an especially noisy one, and the echo of its ratchet rattled off the coulee walls as the trout took all the line and the backing quickly followed. He jumped, sixty yards out, and when I thought of the fine, 6X tippet on the leader, I had no hope that I would ever have him.

The trout turned and came back a little way, and once again I had some line on the reel. But then it was off again on another run, this one perpendicular to the first, and took the line around a clump of tules growing in the shallows. I slacked off to keep tension from the line and avoid a break in the leader.

For a long moment, nothing happened, and I stood there holding slack line. And then I saw the tip of my floating white line in the faint light beyond the tules, moving slowly through the shadows. The trout was still on. There was only one way I would ever get him out of the spot where he had gone, and risky as it was I had to try it. I threw a great loop in the line, almost as if I were mending an upstream cast. The loop cleared the tops of the tules and fell in open water on the other side. I reeled in, tightened, and once again felt the resistance of the fish.

From then on it was a long, slow, delicate fight, the trout tired from its two long runs and I afraid to be heavy-handed because of the light leader tripper. Finally the trout was kicking feebly in the shallows and I had my net under it. It was a rainbow, one of the prettiest I have seen, clean and bright with a sharp dividing line between the silver of its sides and the gunmetal gray of its back. I removed the hook from the gristle of its jaw and eased it back into the water, holding it for a long time until it regained strength enough to swim slowly away.

It was pitch dark when I started back, and I heard the faint call of the vanguard of a flock of Canada geese, winging their way north after a winter spent on the flats of Tulelake in California's northern hills, or in the grain-rich fields of the Sacramento Valley. Soon the flock was directly overhead, and though the great birds were invisible against the night, their haunting calls filled the great stone amphitheater with sound, echoing and re-echoing long after the flock itself had passed. It had been a satisfying day, rich with sensations of sight and sound and feel.

I have spent nights on many waters, gazing up at the Southern Cross while the gentle trade wind rippled at my shirt, or watching the silent flicker of the Northern Lights play across the horizon of a Canadian lake. I have fought a losing match with a great brown trout that took my fly on the darkest of all nights, and a winning contest with a giant rainbow that fell upon my fly in the middle of a night hatch where hordes of insects swayed and brushed lightly against my face and hands, all unseen. I have thrilled to the cry of a cougar and the lost, lonely call of a loon, the wildest sound in all of nature; and I have fought silent battles with unseen trout while coyotes howled in the hills.

The night is not to be feared; it is to be felt, touched, sampled and explored. It is filled with exciting secrets forever hidden from the day. It is a frontier, to be tried and tested and won, and I commend it to all anglers.

Spring in British Columbia

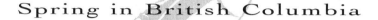

Once I made to myself a vow that I would never again fish in British Columbia in the spring. So many spring trips had been miserable, with freezing cold and snow at night, hard rain and sleet by day, with vicious muddy roads and fishing that was terrible at least as often as it was good.

But of course I made the vow at the end of a trip during which the weather had been particularly mean, and I forgot it almost as quickly as it was made. And now at least once each spring I head north into the interior, fully aware that my chances for success hinge on the fickle vagaries of weather, but also aware that some of my most pleasant memories have come from these spring expeditions.

There was, for instance, the year when we arrived at Hihium Lake on the 15th of May, the first anglers to visit the lake that year. Four inches of snow had fallen the night before our arrival, and at night it was so cold that we bundled up in heavy clothing and slept as close to the big wood stove as we could get. The days were cold, too, but the trout were eager and hungry and rose willingly to the first chironomid hatches, and we caught them by the dozen on dry flies.

There was a warm, bright spring afternoon when I drove to a small lake near Merritt and launched my boat. I had never fished it so early in the season and the lake was far higher than I had ever seen it.

But everything else about it was familiar; the thick stand of timber growing down to its southern shore, the waving green fields of grass stretching away to the north. A pair of stately loons glided on its clear water and an equally handsome pair of ospreys looked down from a tall pine. A badger scampered along the bank and disappeared in the timber, and a gentle breeze sent wavelets sliding in against the rocky beach. I felt a warm, happy feeling such as one has when greeting an old, dear friend after a long absence.

I rowed out into the lake, empty except for me, and anchored in a favorite spot. I stood up in the boat and stripped line from the reel for the first cast, and even as I did so I saw a fish dimple cautiously close by. I cast toward the spot and dropped the little shrimp fly where the rise had been, then began the slow, deliberate retrieve. Suddenly there was a vicious strike and a great trout shot straight upward, its bright sides flashing in the sun. The trout was off and running hard, and a sudden gust of wind dislodged my anchor and sent the boar drifting out into deep water, making it that much more difficult to cope with the determined trout. The little Hardy reel screamed until I feared for its bearings, and the trout seemed to be all over the lake at once, jumping, tail-walking, twisting, shaking and wrapping itself in the leader. It was a long struggle, made more difficult by the gusting wind and the drifting boat, but at last I led the trout alongside, thrust the net under it, and lifted it—dripping and squirming—into the boat. There I quickly weighed and measured it—twenty-four inches and six and a half pounds—and then gently slipped it back into the lake.

And that was only the start. In the hours before darkness, I took two other fish, nearly as large, and lost three others that broke water in silver bursts in the gathering dusk and then shook themselves free. Every pine on the far hill was traced in vivid silhouette against a sky of dark flame when I left the lake, deeply satisfied with the day, and a solitary coyote barked a greeting to a rising full moon as I took my leave.

But those were pleasant times. There was also the time on the road to Derry Lake when the Jeep skidded on a rock in the middle of a bottomless gumbo mudhole and became stuck so deeply that water was running in through the tailgate. I shoveled and jacked and pushed and strained for half an hour trying to free it, but gained not a single inch. Then another fisherman came along in a pickup truck and, in trying to pull me out, got himself stuck too. But he had a hand winch which he used to pull himself free and which we then used to free the Jeep. A crust of dried gumbo covered me from head to foot, and my respect for this peculiarly thick, viscous type of mud grew another notch.

On one trip I quickly became convinced that a storm had become attached to me and was bound to follow wherever I went—a fate similar to that of the unfortunate character in Al Capp's comic strip who was born with a black cloud over his head that follows and rains on him wherever he goes.

His was a small cloud compared to mine, however—mine was a towering collection of clouds that stretched darkly from one horizon to the other and reached out occasionally with bright bolts of lightning and freezing rain and sleet, followed sometimes by bursts of wet snow. And though I went to half a dozen widely scattered lakes, it followed me to every one, and lashed the surfaces of them all with high winds and rain and hail.

I worked my way west and finally stopped at Tunkwa Lake, but the storm was only a couple of hours behind me. No sooner had I begun fishing than the first telltale gust of wind stirred the surface and the familiar dark thunderheads rolled in across the pinetops and exploded in violence. Fierce blue lightning flashes reached into the forest, followed by a roll of thunder like all the cannons of history firing together. The waves quickly built themselves into whitecaps, splashing up over the sides of the boat and spilling water into it, and then—almost before I could struggle into my rain gear—the rain came, a thick gray veil sweeping down the hills, heralding its approach with a few large, spattering drops. And then it was upon the lake with a dull roar of water, a great, drenching sheet of drops, and I began the long row back into the teeth of the wind.

Reaching shore, I quickly packed my gear and headed down the road to Six Mile Lake. It was at a much lower elevation and I thought perhaps it would escape the storm.

The sky was dark and unpromising when I arrived, but the surface of the lake was calm and here and there were the rings of trout rising to a hatch. I quickly launched and rowed out among them. They proved to be discerning trout and it took some experimentation to find a pattern they would take. But soon I found one that did the job, and in a moment I was playing my first fish. I landed it and released it, then stood up to make another cast. The air was quiet and still, and then there came a distant cannonroll of thunder and scattered drops of rain hit the surface around me. Little williwaws of wind suddenly chased themselves across the surface, stirring dark riffles that collided with one another. One of them spun my boat around and threw a belly into the floating line, and before I could retrieve it the storm struck with all its strength. The forest moaned as a hundred thousand pines bent before an invisible wall of wind, and the scattered drops of rain turned into a stinging fusillade of hail. Lightning spat from the dark sky and dirty whitecaps raced across the lake, and I was drenched and shivering before I could get into my still-wet poncho.

That was the last straw, and I decided it was time to head for home. The storm raged all around as I hauled the boat up through the mud and loaded it onto the truck, quickly changed into some dry clothes and started to drive out, with the truck's windshield wipers trying vainly to clear away the wall of mixed rain, snow and sleet that now was falling.

Lightning strikes straddled the road and the truck shook from the concussion of thunder as I started alone from the lake. I had gone a mile and had driven to the top of a steep rise when suddenly I came upon a sight that made me stop in awe.

All around the pine forest was hidden in dark, shifting waves of rain and hail, broken momentarily by splintered lines of lightning, but in front of me a shaft of deep golden afternoon light poured through an opening in the clouds and illuminated a brillilant green meadow in the pines, and beyond it was a rainbow so vivid that the colors hurt the eye. I got out of the truck and stood in the moisture-laden air, heavy with ozone, while the earth trembled from the thunder and the lightning cast weird, split-second shadows, and gazed on the splendid sight, so perfect in its beauty it seemed as if the very gates of heaven had opened before my eyes. When I think of the interior country, a land that I love deeply, I think of that sight.

Spring fishing in the British Columbia interior can change at a moment's notice. I remember another day on Tunkwa Lake when an incredible hatch of chironomids was in progress. The insects came off the water by the thousands, in all sizes, and each puff of wind blew them like sleet into the faces of the anglers. They were in our ears and eyes and their empty cases were so numerous that they floated in windrows on the surface and hung, two or three at a time, from each leader knot at the end of every retrieve.

For days the trout had gorged themselves on the great hatch and would take nothing. For nine long hours I fished, without a single strike, trying every chironomid imitation I had and fishing in every reasonable way I could think of. But then, in the last hour of the day, the rise began, with big fish cruising in a steady line across the mouth of a shallow bay. And in that brief, exciting hour before final darkness, I hooked ten fish, and the long, fruitless hours of the day were soon forgotten.

Each spring, when the Americans celebrate Memorial Day, the fly-fishing clubs of the Northwest gather at Peter-hope Lake in British Columbia to compete for the Totem Trophy. The trophy consists of a reel and a line dryer once owned by the late angling artist Tommy Brayshaw, whose name still is deeply revered by Northwest anglers. The reel and dryer, polished to a fine glow, are handsomely mounted in a glass case with brass plates engraved with the names of the winning clubs. While winning the trophy is considered an honor, the competition is second to the fellowship that ensues when anglers gather to renew friendships that transcend state lines and international borders. At night the lakeside flickers with campfires and the sound of bagpipes and song, and many a tall tale and angling secret is passed back and forth over the flaming embers in the spring night. The fishing never seems particularly good at that time, and perhaps that in itself is good because it makes the contest a more truthful test of angling skill.

When the contest is over and the trophy has been awarded to the winning club for the coming year, the anglers quickly break camp and head for home or for other fishing waters. And so it was one year that when the festivities were done I elected to set out for nearby Blue Lake, which I had heard described as a beautiful lake containing some very large trout.

Phil Aigner had been there the day before, and I asked him for directions to find my way through the maze of logging roads that run near the lake.

"It's easy to find," he said. "Just take the main logging road to the Mile 11 sign, then take the left-hand fork to the lake."

Easy enough, I thought, and so I took the main logging road and sure enough, right at the Mile 11 sign the road forked. I took the left-hand fork and began to look around for the lake. Phil had said it was about five miles beyond Peterhope, but the odometer on my truck soon showed that I had gone more than seven miles, and there was no sign of any lake. In addition, the road was getting worse, with some bad mudholes. I was getting a long way from anyone, and I was getting worried. Finally the road became a pair of deep, soft ruts, disappearing here and there into a quagmire of mud, and I had some bad moments as the truck slewed around while I gunned it through the mudholes. I had nearly decided to turn around and go back when the road came to an end. Driving back through the muck, I came again to the Mile 11 sign and got out to see if I could find where I had gone wrong.

And then I discovered that Phil had neglected to tell me there were *two* left-hand forks, and I had driven past the one I should have taken.

I started down the other fork, confident I would soon be at Blue Lake. But before I had driven a hundred yards I heard a whistle and a shout. Back behind me on a side road was a four-wheel-drive truck, stuck deeply in a gumbo mudhole. I recognized the driver as Pete Caverhill, a fisherman from Vancouver whom I had met several times before.

Pete explained that he also had been looking for Blue

Lake and had taken a wrong turn. The road suddenly had given way under his heavy truck and camper, which now was stuck hopelessly. Pete's wife had gone ahead on foot, hoping to find someone at the lake who could help.

I had a small hand winch or "come-along" in my truck, but I told Pete I doubted it had sufficient strength to pull his heavy truck. But I also had a long length of cable, and I offered to try to tow him out with my truck. We looked over the road, and then Pete said, "I don't think you should try. I'm afraid you'll bugger up your own truck."

We stood there a moment, discussing various things we might do to free his truck, when we heard the sound of another truck back on the main road. We yelled and waved and the truck stopped. It was an old pickup, filled with Indians. There were at least eight of them, maybe ten, ranging in age from twelve or fourteen up to fifty or so. One of the older Indians seemed to be the leader, a thick, muscled man with iron-gray hair and a face lined by a life in the sun.

The Indians swarmed around Pete's truck and immediately assumed control of the situation as if they had been rehearsing for just such an occasion. From the back of their pickup they produced a tow chain and hooked one end to Pete's truck and the other to their pickup. Then, with one of the Indians at the wheel of the pickup and Pete in the driver's seat of his own truck, the rest of us got behind the camper and pushed while both drivers applied power. The camper edged forward slowly, its rear wheels spinning wildly in the muck, until it looked as if it would pop free. Then the chain broke.

The leader of the Indians swore. Then he sent the others scurrying over the logged-off landscape until one of them found a discarded piece of timber about twelve feet long. Another hooked my cable to what was left of the broken tow chain. The free end of the cable was made fast around a big stump and the end of the chain was fastened to Pete's truck. Then it became clear that the Indians planned to try to pull the truck out with a "Spanish windlass," an old wilderness trick which I had heard of but never had seen.

The slack part of the chain was doubled around one end of the timber. Then, while Pete urged the engine of his truck, several of the Indians and I walked the timber around in a circle, twisting the chain around it and tightening it link-by-link. As the pressure increased on the chain, it became more and more difficult to turn the timber, and the cable bit deeply into the wood of the stump to which it was fastened. But, little by little, Pete's truck inched forward until once again it looked as if it would come free. Then, once again, the chain broke.

The Indians swore. The sun was hot and all of us were sweating and panting. Mosquitoes came out of the timber and hovered around us in vicious, whining clouds. But the leader of the Indians seemed undismayed. He sent his crew to work with a shovel, and a large hole was dug under the rear of the camper truck. A log was thrown across this, and another timber was placed across the log with the short end under the rear of the camper. Using this as a lever, five or six of us pulled down on the long end, lifting up the back of the camper. The other Indians jammed more timbers underneath, so that for the first time the truck's frame was clear of the mud.

A similar operation was performed on the truck's right rear wheel, which was stuck deepest, and a two-by-six plank from the Indians' pickup was jammed under the tire. Then, with all of us pushing, Pete gunned the engine of his truck. It lurched, the wheels spun and mud flew, and then the truck broke free and drove out onto firm ground. We all sighed in relief and mopped the sweat dripping from our brows.

Pete thanked the Indians and gave them a spare jack in payment for their assistance, and they all piled back into the old pickup and disappeared into the woods.

All this had taken several hours. Now it was late in the day and I was wondering if I would ever get to Blue Lake.

Pete's wife had returned, saying she had not found the lake and that the road ahead had more dangerous mudholes in it.

Pete and I nevertheless decided to try to find the lake together. Because of his wife's warning, we decided to walk ahead to see if the road was passable. Together we walked down a hill and into the welcome shade of the uncut woods, scouting ahead for perhaps a quarter of a mile. There was some mud, but nothing which looked too formidable, and we decided we would try to go ahead. Then, walking back to the place we had left the trucks, we heard a strange noise ahead. An old, incredibly battered Chrysler sedan came into view, bucking and lurching hesitantly over the rough road, and wheezed to a stop in front of us. It was filled with Indian teenagers.

The driver, a lad of eighteen or twenty years, leaped out.

"What's that noise?" he asked. "Is something wrong with my car?"

I looked at the ancient vehicle. It had no front bumper or grille. It was dented and scraped. Several of the windows had spiderweb patterns of broken glass in them. It looked as if it had a lot of things wrong with it.

The car kept edging forward down the hill in six-inch jerks until one of the other passengers jumped out and kicked rocks under the rear wheels.

"We hit something on the way up and broke the brake line," he said. "All the brake fluid ran out, but we filled it up with water and it works pretty good. Except downhill."

Pete and I exchanged glances.

"Why don't you raise the hood and we'll listen to that noise?" I suggested to the driver. He agreed, and one of his companions lifted the hood and held it up with one hand while the driver started the engine and gunned it. There was an explosive rumble and a sound like a washing machine starting up after ten years of inactivity. Blue flame erupted from the rear of the engine.

"Your exhaust manifold is gone," I told the driver. "It's rusted away. That's what's causing the noise."

"Oh, I knew that," he said. "That's not the noise I meant. I mean the funny, high-pitched noise."

We listened a moment and quickly diagnosed the source of the latter noise as a loose fan belt. So loose, in fact, that it wobbled. We showed the driver how to loosen the bolts holding the generator in place and move it until the belt was tight.

"I'll look to see if I have a wrench," the driver said. His friend took away the arm that had been holding up the hood and it fell where our heads had been a moment earlier, landing with a dangerous crash.

The driver untied a length of rubber that was being used to hold the car's trunk shut. He lifted the trunk and looked inside. "I don't have a wrench," he said.

Pete had one in his camper. He went to get it, and the car's hood was propped up with a tree limb so the Indians could work on the generator.

"Where were you guys headed?" Pete asked while they worked.

"Down to the creek at the bottom of the hill," the driver answered. "Goin' to do some fishing."

"Fishing?" Are there fish in the creek?"

"Sure," the Indian said. "Trout. Big ones."

"Are they spawning?"

Suddenly the Indian's face wore a wary look. "Well, yes, I suppose some of them are," he said.

I looked in the back seat of the car. There were three big dip nets and a large burlap bag.

"Don't you know it's illegal to net spawning fish?" Pete asked.

The Indian feigned surprise. "No!" he said. "Really?" It was a masterful performance.

Pete and I assured him that, yes, it really was illegal to

net spawning trout, and furthermore Blue Lake was one of the
local game warden's favorite spots (which was true) and that
he traveled this road frequently and surely would arrest the
driver and his friends if he found them netting spawners from
the stream at the bottom of the hill. The Indian nodded
solemnly and said that now he and his friends had this
knowledge they certainly would not try to net the trout
spawning in the stream.

Meanwhile, the Indian working under the hood had
stripped the threads on the bolt holding the generator in place
so that it was impossible to loosen it.

We told the Indians there was nothing more we could do
and they would simply have to make the best of it with a loose
fan belt.

The tree limb was removed and the hood fell with
another crash. Most of the Indians piled back inside the aged
vehicle. Two remained outside; one kicked the rocks out from
under the wheels and then both got behind the car and began
to push. The car lurched forward down the hill; the engine
gurgled, then spluttered into explosive life. The two pushers
caught up with the car and jumped in, and with an occasional
hiccough the car disappeared into the forest, leaving a heavy
scent of burned oil in its wake.

I looked at my wristwatch. It was nearly six o'clock, and I
had promised to be back at the Peterhope camp in time for
dinner. Still, I decided to go along with Pete and at least have
a look at Blue Lake. Pete and his wife planned to spend the
night there.

We followed the road for another couple of miles,
crossing the creek the Indians had spoken of and spying their
car, still filled with its passengers, parked on a spur road
waiting for us to pass. And then, finally, shining through the
trees was the sparkling surface of Blue Lake.

It was, indeed, a beautiful lake, lying in what appeared to
be an old lava vent. Shallow pumice shoals ran around its

edge, then disappeared into deep, mysterious depths in the center of the lake. The water was air-clear, and large fish could be seen cruising along the edge of the drop-off.

It would be a challenging place to fish, and under normal circumstances I would have been eager with the anticipation of exploring an untried water. But the exertions of the afternoon had left me tired, and the day was fast drawing to a close. After a few halfhearted casts, I started alone on the return to Peterhope.

The trip back was without incident. But in camp that night, I heard from other fishermen who had come over the same road that a group of young Indians had been seen netting spawning trout from the creek at the bottom of the hill during the time I had been at Blue Lake. I didn't need to ask whether the Indians had been driving a battered old Chrysler.

Such are the adventures one has while fishing in British Columbia in the spring. Sometimes the fishing is slow, and sometimes it is not, but I can't remember a single time when it ever was dull. And I wouldn't miss it for the world.

Basin Browns

A long search, and there it was—a thin sheet of water glinting through a dip between the hills.

Of course, I still was not certain it was the place I was seeking. My informant had been a little vague, perhaps deliberately so as he realized his indiscretion in giving up what he obviously considered a valuable secret.

Yet if he had been a little uncertain about the location, there was no doubt about the rest of what he had said: "The lake is filled with brown trout, good ones, and they take a dry fly well."

That was enough to stir my interest, because brown trout

are relatively rare in the far Northwest. Their reputation as cannibals, deserved or not, has kept management authorities from planting them where they might get into anadromous rivers and swallow up the fry of steelhead and salmon. A few of them have been stocked here and there in lakes with rainbow trout, but to my knowledge nowhere within five hundred miles was there another lake that held brown trout alone.

And so I had searched through the desert and the dunes of the Columbia Basin until I topped a rise above a large and well-known lake and looked beyond it through that little dip and saw more water. From the map, I could not tell with any certainty whether this was, indeed, the right lake because it was surrounded by numerous other lakes and ponds. But, of course, I would find out.

It was a lonely spot. The fierce wind that blows through the basin came in ugly gusts, kicking up little spirals of sand, carrying them along, discarding them at its whim. It blew choppy riffles across the lake below me and built little waves that shattered themselves against the basalt outcrops.

The surrounding landscape appeared flat, with clumps of sage and bitterbrush and occasional thrusting basalt blocks. But it was not flat; it was crisscrossed with ancient coulees, deep cuts in the earth's surface, some of them so abrupt that one could pass within a few feet of them without knowing they were there. Some of them are filled with water, new lakes created by irrigation drainage; others are dry washes, filled with runoff only when visited by infrequent rains, dry the remainder of the time; and some look as if they had always been dry and always will be.

It is rattlesnake country, and deermouse, jackrabbit, lizard and darkling-beetle country. It also is great bird country—waterfowl and pheasant, hawk and magpie, meadowlark and cliff swallow, yellowhead and redwing blackbird country. And usually it is alive with the myriad songs of its residents, but not today. Even the cattails along the water, a favorite haunt of birds, were silent, bending and bowing in the breeze. A high, thin overcast reduced the sun to a fuzzy patch of light, and there was only the muted thunder of the wind and the rattle of dry bush.

It would be a long hike overland to the little lake beyond the far shore, but it looked to be an easy portage between the two. And so I went back to my truck and steered it gingerly between the rocks, the sandholes and the sage and parked it on a steep bluff overlooking the larger lake. It was difficult getting the cartop boat down the steep bank to the water, and the wind tried to hold me back as I rowed across to the far side. I pulled the boat ashore and hiked about a hundred yards up a gentle, sandy slope and finally stood on the shore of the little lake.

The lake was nestled in a coulee with steeply rising sides in three directions. Only the end from which I had approached was open, and I marveled at how well hidden it was. If I had gone twenty feet in either direction when I was searching I never would have seen its water gleaming through the draw.

Well-sheltered from the wind, the surface of the lake showed only the suggestion of a riffle. I studied it for long moments, hoping for a rise that would indicate it was the lake I was seeking, but there was none. I knelt at the shoreline, turned over a stone and watched freshwater shrimp dart away in confusion. It was a lake obviously rich in aquatic life, shallow, with sweeping weedbeds along the shore. It looked good. If only there were fish in it.

I returned to my boat, pulled up on the shore of the larger lake, and carried it up the gentle rise to the smaller one. There I put up my rod and bent on a shrimp pattern to match the size and color of the ones I had dislodged under the stone.

The overcast had thickened, the sun had disappeared and the desert was gray. The wind whistled along the coulee rim and shook the bulky sage, but scarcely touched the surface of the protected pond.

I shoved off and rowed out toward the center of the lake, looking down to watch the bottom slowly slope away. It was covered thickly with weeds, good shelter for fish, good environment for their food. And then I began to fish, searching the shallows and the depths with my fly, casting in and out, keeping my eyes roving for any sign of a rise.

But there was no sign of life, and I began to fear that the lake was barren. Still, I was determined to give it a thorough trial, and I worked the fly slow and deep, bumping it along the bottom, feeling the occasional sullen resistance of a weed.

Was that a splash I heard behind me? I turned quickly, my eyes searching across the water for the sight of spreading rings. It had sounded like a slashing rise, but there was no visible interruption to the gentle rippled water. Perhaps it was only imagination; perhaps my desire to see a rise had caused me to imagine the sound of one.

Another cast, a wait for the fly to sink, and the beginning of the long, slow retrieve. And then the line was being snatched away from me, the light rod bowed toward the water and I felt the movement of a heavy fish. I felt it shake and twist and reverse itself and seek the bottom. I checked its movement and it started up and broke the surface in a flash of pure gold and flecks of red. A brown!

The trout fought with unexpected vigor, its struggle worthy of a rainbow trout, until I lifted it clear in my net. It was a thing of beauty, tawny gold with leopard's spots and great red freckles on its sides.

I opened its gullet and found snails, which was no help to a fly fisherman at all, but in among them were a few backswimmers—peculiar insects, black and brown and mottled yellow, that swim on their backs and move with incredible speed by rapid movement of their two long, oarlike limbs.

A year before, in British Columbia, I had encountered a hatch of backswimmers of several days' duration. I had been unprepared for them then, but in the interim I had worked out an imitation—a fly with black and yellow body, black wing and full brown pheasant hackle. The imitation still was untried, but I took one from my fly box and tied it on in place of the shrimp. Casting again, I switched my retrieve from the long, slow crawl of the shrimp to quick, erratic jerks, imitative, I hoped, of the rapid bursts of speed with which the natural insect moves.

Almost immediately I was into another fish, a fine, stout brown that struggled nobly. And others followed, until by the time the overcast had merged with approaching darkness, I had released eighteen plump, golden brown trout, and my new fly had won its spurs.

I went back to my little lake many times, and never saw another angler there. During the first year the fishing was as fine as I had found it on my first visit. The lake had been stocked only once, and all of the trout were of a similar size, varying only an inch or two in length and perhaps as much as half a pound in weight. There was no place where the trout could spawn, and if there were any fish of extraordinary size in the lake I never saw them. But a daily catch of a dozen and a half browns, each weighing one and a half to two pounds, is enough so that any angler should not ask for more.

But the next year the fishing declined. The trout had grown longer but had gained little weight, and there seemed to be fewer of them. Obviously, something was wrong, and it soon developed that there was a quickly growing population of sunfish in the lake, devouring most of the available food.

Still, there were some exciting times. On one hot, breathless spring afternoon I fished for hours without a sign of trout, and I had begun to think my little lake was really done. But I stayed on into the darkness, and here and there in the dwindling light the rises came. Full darkness brought a heavy hatch of midges, and in a furious half hour I brought five fish to the net and lost as many more, all on a feather-light, six-foot rod.

Since then the fishing has continued to decline, and I suspect that now only a few brown trout remain. But still I go there, and the little lake never has failed to yield a few of its treasured trout. And now that it has fallen on hard times I release each fish with extra care and hope that it will be there again when I return.

The Firehole

Far up among the mists of the Continental Divide, a small, clear lake overflows and gives birth to a river. The infant stream flows first to the north, rushing down through lodgepole ranks and wispy growths of prairie smoke and moonrose, waded in by animals, seldom seen by men, with no hint of the things that will happen to it later.

The stream grows as it accepts the water of uncounted springs and tiny tributaries, and then it starts the first of its great serpentine loops and swings to the west as if unaware of all the rocky heights that stand between it and the Pacific Slope.

It flows into lush meadows where moose browse and bison come to feed, and then it enters the first of the big geyser basins: great, roaring, whistling jets of steam, some continuous, some erratic; strange, steaming, stinking bubbles rising up from the pumice and the muck, venting part of the earth's subterranean fire with grumpy sounds like an old coffee pot; and deep, mysterious pools of hot water, rainbow-stained with turquoise, crimson and yellow algae growths, each seeking its own temperature zone. These things give the river its name: the Firehole.

Millions of gallons of boiling water pour into the river here and farther downstream, pumping in algae, salts and nutrients, acids and alkaloids, as well as heat.

Rich with warmth and throbbing life, it flows on to its destiny in a larger river, and eventually its waters are carried north again, then east and finally south to merge with other streams in the mother of rivers, the Mississippi, until at last the water that first spilled from a Yellowstone lake ebbs out through false bottoms and bayous to the Gulf of Mexico.

Of all the young rivers that grow up to become the Mississippi, there is no other like this one born in the mists and smokes of Yellowstone. It is at its best in the spring, when it flows through the water meadows with their tall grass beaten down by animal tracks and spattered with the colors of fringed gentian, goldenweed and white and yellow mule-ears, blue camas, monkshood and yellow monkey flowers. Rainbow, brown and cutthroat trout live in the river, under the cutbanks and the lava lips, feeding on the rich aquatic life and a host of terrestrial creatures swept from the meadows by the wind.

The river's beauty continues through the summer as the greens of the meadow grass turn to soft, burnished gold. Goldenrod and ladies' tresses bloom as summer turns to fall and thunderstorms crackle and roll over the valleys and drench the earth with rain and hail. Even in the dead of winter, the river still is a live thing, its steam rising above the snow as it carries down its cargo of volcanic heat while spray from the geysers freezes into frosty statues on its shores.

The Firehold is an angler's river, a difficult river that often humbles even the most expert of the experts. It is moody and enigmatic, sullen and surprising, unyielding one day and generous the next. Often the trout feed in such numbers that the rings from their rises merge and overlap, but often, too, the river's surface runs glassy and smooth as if nothing lived beneath it. Wise management has preserved its trout so that it remains something of a mecca for American anglers, a river about which it frequently is said that if you can catch fish in the Firehole, you can catch them anywhere. It has been a friendly river to me, almost from the first moment I saw it, and though other nearby streams may offer larger fish or easier fish, the Firehole is my favorite.

I first saw the river on a fine late-spring day. Alan Pratt and I had gone to West Yellowstone to watch a famous caster in action as he taught a class of novice anglers. We had been engaged to help the caster write a book, I to do the editing and Al to do the illustrations, and we wanted to observe his casting technique so that we could write about it and illustrate it as accurately as possible. But in the process, we also found time for fishing—a stop en route at Rock Creek to sample the cutthroats and the browns, an afternoon on the Madison for browns, rainbows and grayling, and some frantic hours during an incredible hatch on Henry's Fork where big rainbows splashed and rolled for fluttering sedges and mayflies.

And then we came to the Firehole, and Al parked his truck on a grassy bluff above the meadow and we looked down upon the classic river. It rippled gently through the grass, a smooth ribbon of water with clouds of steam from the geysers rolling along its upper banks. The long grass bowed before a gentle breeze that also drove great shreds and flakes of cloud across the sky. It was a day bright with light and color.

We donned our waders and jointed up our rods, then hiked down the face of the bluff and into the spongy soil of the meadow, coming out on the river where it entered a gentle bend. For a few moments we stood surveying it, watching the lush riverweeds swaying in the gentle current, looking for a rise. There was none, and it appeared the river was in one of its fickle moods.

Al started downstream and I waded out slowly and cautiously to avoid disturbing any trout that might be in the neighborhood. There were no insects on the surface and a more prudent angler might have concluded that a wet fly or nymph was necessary, but the very character of the smooth flow seemed to demand that anything but a dry fly would be sacrilegious.

And so a dry fly it was, a size 16 pattern with quill body and stiff grizzly hackle. Through my Polaroid glasses I watched the flow of the currents and subcurrents, studied the channels between the heavy weed growth and tried to gauge the float the fly would follow. In the center of the river the current broke smoothly over a lava ledge, its black shape dimly visible through the clear water. Beneath the ledge was a large expanse of dark shadow, and it seemed a perfect spot for a trout to wait under cover for food to be swept down from above.

I cast quartering upstream, and the fly dropped at the edge of the main current, floated down, slipped gracefully over the ledge and continued its jaunty ride down the river untouched. I waited until it was well below the ledge, then lifted it off the water and dried it with a couple of false casts and set it down again, this time near the center of the current. The fly cocked nicely, the hackle points dimpling the river, and rode the current down over the ledge and disappeared in a quick swirl. I lifted the rod, the line went tight and an electric weight throbbed at the other end.

The fish turned quickly from its shelter under the ledge

and started downstream. I gathered line and increased the strain to keep its head out of the moss, and the fish angled off, seeking the strongest flow. Now I was giving it line as it headed farther downstream toward faster water, but a shift of the rod turned its head and sent it swimming toward the bank. The light rod dipped into a tight arc and the white fly line seemed bent by the water's refraction of the light. Slowly the trout tired, and the line came back to the reel, a single cautious turn at a time.

And finally the fish was on its side at my feet, a thick shaft of pale cream and gold with the familiar leopard markings and blood-red spots of a brown trout. It was a male fish of about two pounds, wearing a proud hook on its lower jaw, and the drowned hackles of the little fly protruded from the bony roof of its mouth.

I grasped it gently, admired it, and slipped out the hook, then held the trout until it had the strength to swim slowly back to its refuge under the lava ledge. In just five minutes the Firehole had presented me with a fine brown trout, and if ever there was a case of love at first sight for a river, this, I decided, was it.

I changed flies and floated another pattern over the ledge without result, then moved upstream, fishing the narrow channels between the moss, bumping my fly along the splayed grass growing out of the cutbanks, but there were no other takers. Soon Al joined me and we walked upstream together, keeping back from the fragile edge of the river and watching for rises. Finally I saw one, a cautious dimple near the grass on the far side of the river.

I waded out, my feet sinking into the soft silt of the river bottom. The center of the river hid a slot too deep to cross, and so I decided to make a long cast cross-river to cover the fish I had seen rise. Working out line, I dropped the fly near the opposite bank and mended line upstream to keep drag from setting in before the fly could float over my aiming spot.

The current swept it gently down, the rise came again and I swung the rod sideways to set the hook. A small, bright rainbow broke water and I worked quickly across the current and released it.

After that, we saw no other rises, and finally we returned to Al's truck and drove upstream near the iron bridge. Here we were right among the geysers and the thermal pools, and the stench of sulfur hung heavy in the air.

We waded down the river within inches of boiling springs, but the water still was cool and fresh. We floated flies through choppy riffles and smooth glides and finally, about a quarter of a mile below the bridge, Al hooked a good fish at the foot of an orange-stained slope where a hot spring overflowed. He fought it there in the fast water and released it, a thick-shouldered rainbow of two pounds or better.

Light was fading rapidly and we had been discovered by mosquitoes, and so reluctantly we left the river to prepare dinner in Al's camper. We drove back along the river, through the geyser basin, and watched a full moon rise up through the drifting steam and the dead pines around the geysers, a scene of eerie and mysterious beauty.

It had been only a brief visit, but the charm and strangeness of the Firehole is an unforgettable memory, and I pledged to return. And I did so, one stormy September evening when dark thunderheads gathered at dusk and sent splintering bolts of blue light across the heavens as we drove into the park. Thunder rattled sullenly, a deluge of rain dashed against the windshield and the smell of ozone burned our nostrils.

The storm's violence had subsided, but a hard rain still fell when we reached the inn at Old Faithful. Nate Reed, assistant secretary of the interior, was staying in the park and had asked me to call him so we could fish together on the Firehole. But he was in Mammoth to the north and the storm had knocked out the telephone wires by the time we reached the inn.

I tried to get a message through to him, listening to the electric echo of the passing storm on the wires as the operators tried vainly to make some connection. Finally I gave up and went to a cabin, where I fell asleep with rain drumming steadily on the roof.

The next morning was cold and gray, with intermittent rain and an overcast that reached darkly down to hide the tops of the highest lodgepoles. I drove out to the Firehole and parked atop the same bluff where Alan and I had stopped before, and rigged up in the sporadic rain. The first snow of the season already had come and gone, and had drained the meadow of much of its color. The wildflowers had been put to rest for the winter and there was only the straw color of the long meadow grass, the soft green of the pine groves and the dark strand of the river running through them.

Again I hiked down the face of the bluff, through the spongy soil of the meadow to the gentle bend in the river, and again I came out where the current flowed down over the lava ledge. The river was dotted with circles from the rain, but here and there along the banks were larger swirls from rising fish. This time, I thought, the river is in one of its generous moods, and I felt the old excitement rise as I applied dressing to the fly.

But this time there was no reaction when I floated the fly down over the ledge, and I moved upstream to cover the rises along the bank.

The trout were spooky, and my first step put some of them down. Moving more cautiously, I left the water and crept cautiously upstream, well back from the riverbank, and began to cast from shore. I hooked three fish almost immediately, all of them strong, solid rainbows, and all of them fought free of the tiny hook. The sudden activity put more trout down, and, hunching over so I would not be seen, I made my way farther upstream where other fish were rising.

On the first float a large rainbow took the fly in a perfect head-and-tail rise, but plunged immediately into a bank of moss and twisted free. The other trout stopped rising and I rested the water a long time, but they did not resume.

I left the stretch, knowing now how the river had won its reputation for difficulty, and drove to the iron bridge. Here among the meadow grass there were small hoppers, and I replaced the fly I had been using with a hopper pattern. There was a rise out in the fast water; I covered it and the hopper fly was taken immediately. The fish fought well in the strong current and finally I released a fine, golden brown trout, and sat on the bank to rest under the brooding sky.

Nothing in nature is more beautiful or alive than a river. Each has its own character, no two alike, and each is worth knowing well. I have spent countless hours on mountain brooks and meadow streams, on fierce, brawling steelhead rivers and quiet sluggish sloughs.

But of all the rivers I have seen, or fished, or dreamed about, there is none quite so special as the Firehole, none with greater frustrations or rewards, and none that reaches out so well to capture the imagination or desire of anglers.

Hosmer

One of the first casualties of America's march toward industrialization was the Atlantic salmon. His native Eastern rivers were among the first to be dammed and polluted, the first to have the life choked out of them. Almost before anyone knew what was happening, the cream of the once-great American Atlantic salmon runs had been destroyed and their host rivers were dead with them.

Today, only a fragment of the salmon runs remain and biologists struggle to preserve them in the northernmost rivers of Maine. Still, after the loss of the American salmon fishery, there remained the great runs to the Canadian rivers, and to the rivers of Iceland, Norway, England, Ireland and Spain. Anglers who fished for Atlantic salmon on the rivers of these nations quickly crowned the salmon with its rightful title as the prince of fly-rod fish.

And so, indeed, it was—until less than a decade ago the feeding areas of the salmon were discovered in the North Atlantic and a disastrous high-seas commercial fishery began. Fishing fleets from Denmark, a nation which itself contributes nothing to the salmon runs, began to take immature salmon by the ton and the spawning runs returning to their native rivers dropped drastically. Organizations such as the Committee on the Atlantic Salmon Emergency and the Atlantic Salmon Foundation fought bitterly for an end to this destructive fishery, and after years of work an agreement finally was reached under which the Danes will slowly phase out the high-seas fishery.

But even with this agreement, the survival of *Salmo salar* ("the leaper") as a species is far from secure.

While man's callousness and greed were destroying the native Atlantic salmon runs of the eastern United States, his curiosity led him to try to transplant the noble salmon to distant watersheds in distant lands. Early transplants were attempted in British Columbia, New Zealand, Argentina and elsewhere. The Argentine transplant resulted in a thriving population of land-locked fish, but attempts to establish anadromous populations in the rivers of British Columbia and New Zealand met with failure.

Despite these generally discouraging results, other attempts were made over the years to transplant Atlantic salmon. In 1951, the state of Oregon received eyed Atlantic salmon eggs from sea-run fish from Gaspé Bay, Quebec. The eggs were hatched in the hatchery at Wizard Falls, Oregon, and immediately hatchery workers found the offspring were delicate and difficult to handle. Unlike trout, the salmon alevins did not swim up after absorbing their yolk sacs, and bacterial gill disease killed many of them. The survivors were slow to begin feeding, and the original stock had a survival rate of only about 10 percent—extremely poor for fish raised in a hatchery.

Though these early results were frustrating and disappointing, efforts continued to produce a healthy population of fish that could be planted in some suitable water. The work went slowly and the results were far from dramatic; still, the survival rate of eggs and fry gradually was increased to about 20 percent, and enough fish became available for planting.

The search for a place to release the salmon finally centered on a cold, clear, shallow lake high in the Oregon Cascades: Hosmer Lake.

One could search for a lifetime without finding another place with the fierce, wild beauty of Hosmer Lake. Nearly a mile above sea level, nestled in among the volcanic cones of the Oregon Cascades, it is a perfect portrait of nature, a picture of such breathtaking fragile beauty as to discourage one from entering for fear he might somehow injure it by his presence. It is really more of a marsh than a lake, with two large areas of open water connected by a channel winding through weedbeds, lava flows and pine groves. It is crowned on every side by peaks—Bachelor Butte, Broken Top and the Sisters—dark bulks of volcanic rock topped in the springtime by great mantles of blinding snow.

A stream of cold, sweet water runs into the upper end of Hosmer and eventually loses itself in the porous lava of a blind channel at the lower end. The bottom is of cream-colored pumice, crisscrossed with the tracks of clumsy sedge larvae and snails. Ospreys nest in the tallest pines, dropping in spectacular dives to crash through the surface and spear smaller fish with their razor talons, and in the deep-purple twilight of the spring evenings the nighthawks startle in their sudden, swift plunges. Under the light of a clear spring day, the forest is a deep, delicate, satisfying green, almost velvet in texture. The lake and all its surroundings are a mix of clarity and color, so vivid they defy the brightest oils of the artist's brush.

Before the Atlantic salmon came, this place of bright beauty was the home of ignominious carp and roach, and it was known then as Mud Lake. In the fall of 1957, the lake was treated to remove the carp and roach and the next year it was planted with fifteen thousand Atlantic salmon fingerlings, three to six inches long.

To almost everyone's surprise, the salmon thrived in Hosmer Lake. They grew rapidly, feeding on the huge hatches of sedges and mayflies that come on the warm spring and summer afternoons. Management officials, recognizing the great value of the fish in their new environment, made it unlawful for anglers to keep any of the salmon. Only flies with barbless hooks are allowed, and all salmon caught must be returned immediately to the water.

Word of the new fishery spread rapidly among the fly-fishing community, and in the first years after the salmon were introduced fly fishermen caught salmon weighing up to eight or nine pounds—no larger, perhaps, than the grilse of a Canadian salmon stream, but nonetheless unique in their new Western environment. Even today, some fifteen years after the first salmon were placed in Hosmer Lake, the average fish weighs three or four pounds and salmon of six or seven pounds are not unusual.

Spring was changing into summer at the lower elevations when I first saw Hosmer Lake, but high in the Cascades it still was early spring and banks of snow remained drifted up in the shady spots where the sun could not penetrate the dense pine thickets.

I had driven all afternoon through the muggy heat of

central Oregon, and as I started up the final grade out of the sagebrush and juniper country into the semi-alpine environment of the Cascades, a great parade of thunderheads marched along the row of peaks ahead. Soon they took their revenge against the hot stillness of the day, lashing out with lightning bolts and heavy detonations of thunder, spilling a cargo of rain that brought early twilight to the forest. The storm spent itself in an hour and rolled on to dump its remaining rain on some distant watershed, and the setting sun came out to illuminate the land with oblique yellow light.

The dying light struck raindrops clinging to the pines and caused them to glint like spangled tears of dew. The fresh-washed air was clean and pure and thin enough to make a little extra effort necessary to draw a full breath. The streams gossiped on the hillsides as they carried off the rain and the earth seemed to awaken after having slumbered through the day.

The twilight was deep when I drove in to the campground at Hosmer and got out to walk along the edge of the lake. The sedges were flying and far out I could see the salmon rising, throwing up silver spray as they slashed after the fluttering flies. The familiar excitement and anticipation rose up and spilled over inside, and only a practical voice in the back of my mind convinced me that it was too late to begin fishing, so I resolved that I would sleep no later than dawn and begin fishing as early as possible the next day.

And so it was. The sun had scarcely peeked around the base of Bachelor Butte the next morning when I pushed off from shore and began rowing for the entrance to the channel that led to the upper lake. The channel itself was like the estuary of a slow river, gentle and winding, with thick weedbeds growing away on every side. The water was as clear as the air so that every drowned rock and limb stood out clearly. And then, coming at me, gliding like ghosts through the clear water, I saw a school of salmon—shadowy, gray, torpedolike as they moved swiftly and effortlessly, one turning now and then to accept some small item of food, or tilting up to dimple the surface ever so slightly. I watched them pass, then bent into the oars with twice the effort. Coming out of the upper end of the channel into open water once again, I rowed around the edge of a small island, then stood up in the boat to scan the water for feeding fish.

A gentle breeze blew changing riffles across the surface with flat slicks among them, and in one of the slicks I saw a school of salmon over the bright pumice bottom in three feet of water. They were swimming in a tight circle, now and then one digging its nose into the silt in search of a nymph. Approaching cautiously to within sixty feet, I worked out line and then dropped the dry fly gently over the circling fish and waited, trying to control an involuntary tremor in my rod-holding hand.

A salmon rose leisurely and inspected the fly at length without taking, turning away finally to resume his feeding. A second fish went through the same performance, and then I wiggled the rod top slightly to impart some movement to the fly. It moved just a little, and immediately a salmon had it. It was a small fish, but I played it carefully to the boat and held the leader so that I could examine it—my first salmon. It was a handsome fish, its back showing brown through the water, lightly spotted with X-shaped markings, and a red-blue iridescence to its sides. I twisted the fly free and looked for another target.

The day that followed shall always remain bright in my memory. Before noon the sedges began to hatch, great awkward insects that fluttered with abandon far across the surface and disappeared in smashing, violent rises. After noon the mayflies came on, Dark Blue Uprights popping to the surface in unbelievable numbers, resting in rows along the gunwales of my boat and the brim of my hat, flying into my face and dancing in dark swirling cyclones across the surface. I could see the salmon approach from far off and quickly discovered that they moved far more rapidly than trout and that it was necessary to lead them by a long distance with the cast.

Time and again I would watch a salmon approach from a hundred feet away, cast far in front of him and then see every detail clearly as the fish first saw the fly, rushed toward it and took it boldly in a rising wave of water.

I learned, too, that it was necessary to delay the strike until after the salmon had turned down with the fly, and then, when the hook was set, to hold on while the salmon shot away in a long, long run far across the shallow bottom and the reel screamed in futile protest.

The day passed in a blur of motion, of casting, waiting, striking and playing salmon, of repairing smashed leaders and worn-out flies, of long, exhausting battles with great fish whose endurance was far beyond anything I had expected, of pausing occasionally to let my eyes and my soul feast on the beauty all around. When twilight came with a sudden rush, I started the long row back to camp, sunburned and weary but deeply satisfied, and spent the evening groping for superlatives in which to describe the experience.

Since that first golden day I have spent many others on Hosmer Lake and now I have seen it in all its moods—when the forest changes from green to gray under the sullen light of a mountain storm moving in, when the bitter wind from the peaks sweeps long, rolling waves across its surface, and when the mountain sunset paints it in soft, pastel shades at the end of the day. I have found that it is not always nearly so generous as it was on that first day, that sometimes the salmon are moody and cautious; but I have also had other days of wild excitement when great, silver salmon came in lunging rises,

when a sudden hole opened in the water and my fly disappeared into it, when bright fish have scattered the water in
one jump after another, and when I have stood for fully half
an hour with my slim rod bent in a futile effort to bring a big
fish to the net.

It is nearly all dry-fly fishing, and that in itself makes it
an exciting departure from the norm in Western waters. A
Dark Blue Upright or an Iron Blue Dun in size 16 imitates the
mayfly hatch, and a size 8 Salmon Candy is used almost
exclusively when the sedges are up.

The Salmon Candy is the product of Lloyd Frese, who
has spent years developing patterns for use in Hosmer Lake.
He has devised a series of four Salmon Candy patterns, but the
one I have found most useful is a sparsely tied pattern with a
thin body of dark-olive wool, a deerhair wingcase trimmed at
either end and dark-brown gamecock hackle palmered on the
forward half of the body. It is an extremely effective sedge
imitation, especially when tied sparsely, and I have even used
it with good results on the British Columbia sedge hatches far
from the Salmon Candy's point of origin.

It was Lloyd Frese who once said he feared death because
he doubted that heaven could be as good as Hosmer Lake.
And now that I know Hosmer as I do, I share his feeling that
the good Lord will have to go to some special effort to create
an angler's Valhalla surpassing this one.

It is something of a miracle that Hosmer has turned out
the way it has, and that it has managed to last as long as it has.
Efforts to establish Atlantic salmon in other nearby lakes have
proved largely unsuccessful; only in Hosmer does some
unique, indefinable combination of circumstances exist. Yet,
the success of the fishery inevitably has led to a desire to
imitate it elsewhere, and even as this is written an effort is
being made to introduce Atlantic salmon to my own state of
Washington, and discussions are underway in California to
attempt the same thing there.

One hopes that these efforts will meet with some success, and that the proper measures also will be taken to preserve the Atlantic salmon in his native habitat of ocean and stream. Truly he is a fish that deserves the respect of all anglers, of all people, for if his species should disappear the earth will never know another like it.

SUMMER

The calendar tells us the very instant when spring comes to an end and summer begins, but the transition is not so easily visible in nature. Spring often is long and cool and wet, and often it is only a gradual warming and drying of the air, a subtle disappearance of blossoms and blooms, that signals the beginning of summer. But once the transition is made, summer leaves little doubt of its presence; for days on end, the sun floats in a clear sky and sucks the moisture from the fields; the grass dries and the gentle winds carry away the thistle seeds in tumbling windrows. Life has reached the peak of the year and begun its gradual decline, and the fragile stems that pushed their way up through the spring soil live out their lush days and begin to wither in the sun.

It is a lazy time for the angler. The trout in the lowland lakes go deep and the rivers run low and clear. The cool freshness of the morning passes quickly to the heavy heat of the day. The night breezes sputter and die, and pollen hangs thickly in the air. The sun quickly saps the strength so that the angler seeks the sparse midday shade to rest and cool himself as best he can, looking forward to the coolness of the evening and hoping the trout will rise again.

The mountains, snowcapped in all the other seasons, are bare now, a distant haze of purple, green and brown. The rivers have long since carried away the runoff from the winter snows, and now they reveal their skeletons—bare, white, water-blasted rocks that are hidden at other times of year.

The trout in the rivers are quick and wary, drawn to the cover of rocky ledges and the coolness of the feeder streams and springs. They rise shyly to the summer moths and the first small hoppers from the fields.

Yet even as the rivers warm and drop and clear, the summer steelhead somehow seek out their diminished flow and enter them. These are clean, bright fish, fresh from the sea and strong, and something in their instinct draws them home in summer to lie in wait in the shadowed canyons and deeper pools of their native rivers for the higher water of fall and winter to take them to their spawning. They are among the most noble fly-rod fish and it is their presence more than any other thing that keeps the angler busy through the summer.

The early morning when the birds have just begun their song and the sky shows the first faint streaks of day is the time to fish for summer steelhead. The air still seems cool and fresh and sweet, the streams murmur softly through the alder glades and the light is soft and gentle. The fish are most active then, shifting up and down and back and forth in their waiting pools before settling down to wait out the harsh light of the day.

It is pleasant to wade under such circumstances, pleasant to be close to the water, to feel its strength and coolness through the waders, to catch a fragment of scent from wild mint growing along the river and watch the dippers at work along the shores.

A long cast drops the bright fly gently on the river and the current swallows it and draws it down to explore the hidden channels around the boulders and the ledges where the steelhead lie, sometimes momentarily visible through the shifting shadows of the stream. And there is always the familiar tenseness, the feeling of suppressed excitement as the angler awaits the heavy strike of a summer steelhead, which has been called the most vicious strike of all.

If one is not a steelhead angler, or even if he is, he may also turn to the mountains during the summer. Though the days are warm and lazy in the lowlands, the mountains are in bloom with the first full blush of life, and the mountain lakes sparkle like tiny hidden jewels, hiding the secrets in their depths. Those secrets include cutthroat, brook and rainbow trout of rare color and hue; bright golden trout and fragile grayling. Their growing season is short, and as they rise eagerly to the small insects that hatch from the cold mountain water they provide a cornucopia of angling opportunities beneath the thrusting peaks and alpine meadows of the Cascades and the Rockies.

Some anglers regard the summer as a season of diminished opportunities, but it is not so; the opportunities are at least equal to those of any other season, but they are of a different nature.

In summer, as in other seasons, the fish are where you find them, and it is those fishermen who have explored the summer rivers and the mountain lakes who have discovered that summer angling has its own pleasures and rewards, and they look forward to summer just as others look forward to their own favorite seasons.

First Encounter

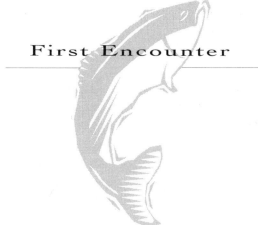

I was raised as a trout fisherman and taught by my father to fish in lakes and small streams, and for a good many years it never occurred to me that any other fishing could be worthwhile. I lived out my early years within a mile of a small stream where I fished in spring and summer for small trout, never dreaming that in the winter that same river hosted a run of steelhead, some of them nearly as large as I was the first time I had let a line down into the swirling waters of the stream. Indeed, it was many years before I became aware that steelhead existed at all, or understood what they were, or learned that they came into the rivers both in winter and summer, or knew that summer fish would take a fly almost as well as the trout I had grown used to fishing for.

Even once I had learned of the existence of steelhead, I was content to continue fishing for my familiar quarry and at first I did not angle for steelhead in any serious way. Several times in the summer I would try for them, but not with any degree of persistence, and usually after two or three hours of fruitless casting I would leave the river and go someplace where I knew I could depend upon consistent action from the trout. These early attempts resulted in a couple of quick hook-ups, one of which ended in a smashed leader and the other in a lost fish, and in neither case had the fish been on long enough to show what it could do. And so I did not have the feeling that I had really missed anything.

But gradually, my association with older, more experienced anglers convinced me that steelhead fishing held some great rewards, and so one summer finally came when I decided I would continue fishing until I had taken a steelhead on the fly.

It was this determination that led me one evening after work to the North Fork of the Stillaguamish, one of the most noted summer steelhead streams of the Northwest. It had been a hot, sticky, breathless day, but the sun was low in the sky when I arrived at the river and the air was beginning to cool. I parked the car, donned waders and vest, rigged up my rod and set out along the well-worn path through an alder thicket toward the distant sound of the river.

I came out of the woods onto the foot of a well-washed gravel bar and stopped to look around. On the far side of the river, two whitetail does were drinking in the river. Their heads came up, swiveled, and they found me with their eyes. They watched carefully, then turned quickly and bounded swiftly back into the forest, their tails waving like white flags until they vanished from sight.

The river flowed smoothly out of the east and made a

great right-angle turn at the end of the bar, dividing itself around a single large boulder, then merging below it in a run of fast water that battered itself against a high bank and then spilled into a huge, wide pool.

I waded out at the head of the bend and began to fish, letting the current swing the fly down toward the big boulder, straining to see the pockets formed by smaller rocks beneath the surface, then searching them with the fly. Slowly I worked my way down into deeper, faster water, casting short, then long, then longer still, holding the fly in the current, letting it pause, drift, tumble and sweep.

The sun had dipped below the alder fringe but the sky still was bright and small hordes of insects played over the surface of the river, their tiny sounds lost in its heavy chuckle, and small steelhead and salmon fry bobbed now and then to the surface in a frantic dash to capture one.

Now I was below the boulder in the fastest, deepest water, raising my backcast to clear the gravel ramparts piled up by the winter floods, sending the fly on long casts to the high bank on the far side where the current swept it in a long search along the ledge I imagined the water had carved into the bank. Still nothing came to the fly and I moved down, a step or two at a time, until I had fished through half the run. Another cast, and the fly dropped lightly on the water a foot from the opposite bank and the swift current carried it briefly on the surface, and then suddenly a broad silver shape was there behind it for a long instant, and then it was gone and the fly swept on, untouched.

Excited now, I cast again to the spot, and again, without result, then rested the water, tied on a new fly, and searched it further until I was satisfied that the fish would not come again. And then I fished the rest of the run and the head of the big pool where a hard double-haul was needed to send the fly across the broad water, and still there was nothing. Two other anglers passed, each answering with a shrug when I inquired about their luck, and gradually the light subsided, changing from blue-green to deep purple tinged with pink, and the first bright stars twinkled in the darker eastern sky. Still, the river whispered encouragement, and wrote strange messages in moving boils of current that spread out and dissolved themselves across the surface of the pool, only to re-emerge someplace farther on, moving ceaselessly, feeling sightlessly for the channel that would take them eventually to the sea. It was pleasant just to be there, to think and feel, to reach out with the long rod and breathe deeply the warm summer air. I felt as if I were one with the river, belonging to it as much as the fish that moved in its hidden depths or the birds that fed along its changing shores or the tiny nymphs clinging to its gravel.

It was a gentle river, and I was in a gentle mood, and I felt a rare harmony with my surroundings that one does not often feel. I had almost forgotten that my purpose in coming had been to take fish from the river; ironically I felt as if the river had captured me instead, hypnotizing with its rhythmic movements and dull reflected evening light, its deep sounds and its quiet friendliness. It sang a subtle siren's song and I had fallen victim to its wiles.

Then the reverie was gone as quickly as it had come, and my wristwatch told me that in a few more moments full darkness would be at hand and it was time to go. One more cast, I thought, and I'll call it a day.

I worked out line in false casts, then added power with a double haul and sent the line sailing far out across the pool. I had changed to a dark fly as evening came on and I watched as its small, dark shape dropped in the center of a distant boil and vanished in the shadows, then waited as the line grew taut in the pressure of the current and swung around to straighten out below me. Gradually it did so and I waited for the line to pause at the end of the swing, but it kept moving.

The pressure on it suddenly was stronger, and then the line was running off my reel and the reel was sending up a clattering stutter of protest as the line moved faster and faster.

I reared back on the rod to set the hook and the reel's stutter rose to a scream; the backing splice was gone and thin backing line was whistling out at an alarming rate. On and on the fish ran, and I looked around wildly for a way to follow it; the downstream bank was rocky and steep and, while not impassable, it would be slow and difficult to cross. But even as I contemplated my next move, the run stopped far downstream and the taut line telegraphed the movement of a heavy fish shaking its head against the hook.

Gradually the pressure eased and I regained several turns of backing on the reel, and then the fish began to move across the pool, dangerously close to its downstream lip where it spilled out into fast, shallow water. I increased the pressure so that the fish was forced to swim diagonally and gained several more turns of backing on the spool. I heard a sound off to my left and looked up to see another angler settling himself on the rocky bank to watch the struggle in progress.

The river continued its blissful conversation in the fast-fading light, but I was oblivious to it now; every effort, every spark of concentration now was on the struggle with the fish. It was a big one, of that I had no doubt. It was coming toward me now, reluctantly, shaking its head now and then, turning away in sudden, short runs, but slowly losing ground as I gathered line on the reel.

And then I felt the backing splice slide through the tip guide and reeled in slowly, slowly, until it was back on the spool and there were several turns of line on top of it.

Then the fish was off again, this time on an upstream run that started the reel whining again, and again the backing was running out and the fish broached at the foot of the fast run that glanced off the high bank and flowed down into the pool.

I looked back at the watching angler and was surprised to see he had been joined by two others who had come to watch me try to land the fish.

The run was over, but the fish still was upstream and now I had the current to my advantage. Still, the fish fought for every inch of line, straining against both me and the current, but yielding gradually until again all the backing was on the reel.

And then it was off on the most savage run of all, downstream and across, the reel whining shrilly until the run ended in a magnificent leap, the fish erupting five feet out of the water, a great, flashing silver thing, returning to the water in a fountain of spray and a crash that echoed from the rocky banks above the sounds of the river. It was a nickel-bright steelhead, ten pounds easily, maybe twelve, and I had never seen a thing I wanted so badly.

The fish was below me again, down in the deepest water of the pool, twisting and turning and shaking and sending alarming vibrations down the rod and into my wrist. It was pitch-dark now, the stars shining brightly and an owl hooting softly somewhere off in the woods. A single orange spark from a cigarette marked the spot where the other anglers still strained to watch through the gloom, and I fought the fish by feel rather than sight.

The fish was tiring, but so was I, and I transferred the rod from one hand to the other and back again to ease the strain. The backing was on the reel again and the line was coming in, a little faster now, and I began to back up toward the bank to be ready to land the fish. Now there was only twenty feet of line out, now fifteen, and now ten, and I inched my way toward the shore. And then the fish ran with fresh strength, pulling the rod tip down to the water and peeling off twenty-five yards of line as it headed out again to the center of the pool. And then we settled down to slug it out again, and I recovered line turn by turn while the fish fought stubbornly against each movement of the reel handle.

The strength of the fish was nearly gone and it was mostly his weight and the current that I was fighting now. Slowly he came in, but this time I waited before starting for the bank. The last ten feet of line came up through the rod tip and now the leader butt was showing, but it was too dark to see the fish.

And now I started back for the shore, sliding my feet carefully across the silty bottom, keeping the strain on the fish, forcing it to follow me, easing it into shallow water, now three feet deep, now two, beginning to maneuver so that I could get the steelhead between me and the beach and kick it up on the gravel. One more step, and then—with an audible "pop"—the fly came away. The leader dangled limply from the rod tip, and the fish was gone, vanished under the current boils that glinted silver in the starlight.

"Lost him," I said softly, but my audience had heard. The orange spark glowed more brightly for an instant, then disappeared, and I heard small sounds through the darkness as the watching anglers got up from their vantage point.

"Well . . . next time," a sympathetic voice said in the gloom, and then I heard footsteps as they started back along the path away from the river.

Yes, I thought. Next time. And I snipped off the sodden fly, hooked it into the lamb's-wool patch on my vest to dry, and started back for the car, with the river still chuckling softly behind me.

Once There Was a River

Once there was a river.

It gathered the waters from a quarter of the continent—the seepage from Canadian glaciers, the runoff from the Rocky Mountain snows, the cold springwater of the Cascades—and carried them all to the sea. It was called the Columbia, a name which somehow conveyed the majesty of its size and the strength of its purpose.

A thousand tributaries poured their waters into it, and their proud names are like the roll call of Northwest history—the Snake, Kootenai, Clearwater, Salmon and Deschutes; the Willamette, Wenatchee, Yakima and Spokane; the Blackfoot,

Pend Oreille, Klickitat and Wind. The river and its tributaries traversed every kind of country, from the snowswept walls of the Rockies to the pine-clustered plateaus of Montana, from the gloomy stands of Oregon fir to the desert sage of central Washington.

Even as it drained the moisture of its great watershed, the river also drew into itself the greatest runs of salmon and trout the world has ever known—giant chinook and silver coho salmon, blueback sockeye and sturdy chum, bright steelhead and golden cutthroat, drawn irresistibly from the ocean to the river's broad mouth.

In hundreds of thousands, the salmon and steelhead journeyed up against the river's heavy flow, each race turning aside to its native tributary river, some of them struggling more than a thousand miles until they sensed the familiarity of a lonely stretch of gravel in a tiny tributary high in the mountain foothills. Born of the river, their strength was that of the river, and it was enough to carry them over incredible obstacles to the very place where they first knew life.

The river basin was the dwelling place of Indians with tribal names like the Nez Percé, Spokane, Yakima, Crow, Blackfoot and Shoshoni. They hunted the deer and elk that grazed in the river bottoms and along the higher slopes, speared or trapped the salmon in their season, and knew the river as a great pulsing source of life that provided them the substance of their livelihoods.

The river also was the nesting place for the Great Basin Canada geese, a haven along the mysterious migratory route that took them from the Alberta wetlands to the rich grass of northern California, and it was a flyway for mallard, teal and scaup, goldeneye and pintail and a dozen other species of waterfowl. Herons nested along its shores, bald eagles rested in the tallest trees along its banks, and marsh hawks hunted over its sluggish sloughs.

For uncounted thousands of years, the river rose and fell

in its seasons, dug its mighty channel through the Cascades to the ocean, carried down the waters of its great basin, and nourished the life of all the creatures that lived in or around it. It changed only by the changes it wrought itself, unknown and unimagined by the white men who were working their way slowly west across the untamed continent.

It remained thus until the morning of May 11, 1792, when a small American brig under command of Captain Robert Gray, a fur trader, stumbled into its estuary. The entry in the ship's log for that date reads as follows:

"At 8 a.m., being a little to windward of the entrance of the harbor, bore away, and run in east-northeast, between the breakers, having from five to seven fathoms of water. When we were over the bar we found this to be a large river of fresh water, up which we steered. Many canoes came alongside."

Gray sailed his ship fifteen miles upriver until it grounded briefly and he turned back. For nine days he stayed in the river, trading with the Indians to obtain three hundred beaver pelts and one hundred and fifty sea-otter skins. On May 19, the day before his departure, Gray named the river in honor of his vessel, the *Columbia*.

Nowhere in the *Columbia*'s log is there any sense of historic occasion, nowhere any indication of the significance of the discovery. But after the morning of May 11, 1792, the destiny of the river and all who lived within its reach was forever altered, and the river's days of life and freedom were numbered from that moment.

The Columbia's next visitors from the outside world were the explorers Lewis and Clark, who came upon it overland from the east. Awed by the immensity of the river, the explorers studied their diaries with references to its strength and grandeur, honest in appraisal if not always accurate in spelling. "The water of the South fork Snake is a greenish blue, the north Clearwater as clear as cristial," they wrote. The Columbia Gorge they called a "Great Shute," "foaming

& boiling in a most horriable manner" with "swells & whorlpools." It was alive with salmon and with "Swan, Geese, white & gray brants, ducks of various kinds, Guls and Pleaver." And as they proceeded downstream, the explorers found the estuary teeming with sea otters and other life. One day they discovered the water had begun to taste of salt, and then came that historic morning when Clark wrote in his diary:

"Ocian in view! O! the joy."

The explorations of Lewis and Clark sealed the fate of the Columbia. Slowly at first, then more rapidly, the settlers came, both overland and by sea, and the history of the river entered the same depressing pattern that had befallen so many other rivers farther east. White men wrested the land from the Indians by force or by deceit; slaughtered the game dwelling in the river bottoms; drove the sea otters to extinction; toppled the forests along the ridges and the tributary rivers. The Indians were killed in battle or by disease, the survivors herded onto reservations. The greatest of them was Chief Joseph of the Nez Percés, whose people had lived so long in concert with the river and the land around it. It was Chief Joseph who articulated the philosophy that only today white men have begun to understand. He said:

"The earth was created by the assistance of the sun, and it should be left as it was. . . . The country was made without lines of demarcation, and it is no man's business to divide it. . . . I see the whites all over the country gaining wealth, and see their desire to give us lands which are worthless. . . . The earth and myself are of one mind. The measure of the land and the measure of our bodies are the same. . . . Do not misunderstand me, but understand me fully with reference to my affection for the land. I never said the land was mine to do with as I chose. The one who has the right to dispose of it is the one who has created it. . . ."

Guided by this philosophy, Chief Joseph and his people fought desperately for their beloved land, but they were driven from it by armed troops. Time after time the Indians defeated their pursuers in a long and bloody trek across the mountains toward refuge in Canada. But finally, half starved and frozen, they stopped to rest only a day's march from their goal. And there they were attacked and broken in a one-sided fight in the lonely Montana hills.

The survivors, including Chief Joseph, eventually were confined to a reservation, and the chief died there. On his tombstone it says he died of a broken heart.

In less than a century and a half, the river was tamed and all its native life had been destroyed or broken to the will of man. Recognizing the raw strength of the river, men built dams and drew upon it to irrigate their fields, light their cities and run their factories. One great dam followed another until now there are more than a hundred on the river and its tributaries. And the white men added a final insult to history when they named one of the dams Chief Joseph.

Slowly the Columbia ceased being a river and became a series of huge, slackwater lakes. Now, from the breaks below Bonneville Dam to the Canadian icefields, there is only one fifty-seven-mile stretch that still flows freely.

Great cities sprang up along the Columbia shores and dumped their wastes into the river and its tributaries. Fumes from the great mills fouled the air in the canyons and the valleys. The river bottom was dredged to make way for barges and ships, and its banks were buried in spoil from the dredges. Mighty steel bridges spanned the river to carry a growing cargo of rail and vehicular traffic. The rising reservoir waters drowned the nesting areas of the waterfowl and destroyed the winter range of the surviving game.

The dams blocked many of the steelhead and salmon runs from their native tributaries, and many of the surviving fish met death in commercial fishing nets. Alien species were introduced to prey upon and compete with the native runs of fish. Poison and pollution took a toll.

The virgin timber was stripped from the hillsides, so when the winter snows melted and the spring rains came, the tributaries flooded and carried the topsoil away in rushing torrents that filled the mainstem. The great surge of water spilled its way over dam upon dam in such volume that it became supersaturated with air, drawing it down into the depths of the reservoir pools. And there a strange new threat developed: The supersaturated water flowed through the gills of steelhead and salmon so that their own blood became supersaturated, and when they swam to shallow water, bubbles of air formed in their bloodstreams and they died by the thousands of bursting hearts or ruptured eyeballs.

Even the fish reared in hatcheries to replace those runs exterminated by the dams were slaughtered by the strange new environmental disease.

And still the destruction goes on. The "Great Shute" and the "swells & whorlpools" now lie deep beneath a placid reservoir. Transmission lines stretch away in barren streaks from the dams. Ancient Nez Percé pictographs, painted on the river rocks to guide Indian fishermen to a safe crossing, were shattered by a dynamite blast to clear the way for a county road. The ancient rockshelter at Marmes, site of the earliest human dwelling place yet discovered in the Western Hemisphere, disappeared under the floodwaters of a new dam, its secrets gone forever.

More than fifty other dams have been authorized, recommended or suggested for the Columbia and its tributaries. One of these, named Ben Franklin, would inundate the last free-flowing stretch of the mainstem.

On May 28, 1959, the Senate Public Works Committee approved a resolution to "determine whether any modification of the existing project on the Columbia River between

McNary Reservoir and Priest Rapids Dam is advisable at this time." Particular reference was given to "constructing a multipurpose dam and reservoir at the Ben Franklin site for navigation, hydroelectric power and allied purposes." One supposes that Ben Franklin, in his sage wisdom, would not approve of having his name applied to the last tombstone of a great river.

The dam would generate an average of 3.7 billion kilowatt hours annually. Also involved is an ambitious project that would include navigation locks and channel dredging to make the Columbia navigable all the way upstream to Wenatchee. In the laconic language of the Army Corps of Engineers, which would be in charge of the project, "the dam would complete control of the Columbia River from Bonneville Dam to the Canadian border."

The greatest native runs of salmon and steelhead the world has ever known are gone. Most of the game and waterfowl that once lived along the river are gone. The wilderness that existed along the river is gone. And all but fifty-seven miles of the river itself are forever gone. Yet men still are not satisfied, and plans have been laid to take the last fifty-seven miles as well.

What is the worth of those fifty-seven miles of free-flowing river? Government agencies, in calculating the economic worth of a project, attempt to answer such questions in monetary values. This is a most difficult thing to do. Even the angler who catches a native steelhead fresh from the sea is hard put to explain its worth. It is a thing of value to the soul, not to the pocketbook.

Perhaps the fifty-seven miles would be of little value if they had been treated the same as other sections of the river. But a peculiar combination of circumstances has made it possible for this last living stretch to escape the impact of cities and sewage, freeways and factories.

Below Priest Rapids Dam the river flows through dry,

barren hills, dotted with bitterbrush and sage, unfriendly to human life. In the early 1900s, hardy white settlers carved a small number of homesteads along the riverbanks and cultivated a few small fields with water from the river. Their orchards were rich in fruit and they built two small towns, one named Hanford and the other White Bluffs, the latter after the tall, white cliffs that line the river. But during World War II, the homesteaders were moved out and the towns were erased to make way for great, secret installations where a new substance named plutonium was manufactured, giving both hopes and fears to men.

The area was fenced and closed to public entry, and except for the ugly, gray shapes of the reactors looming starkly visible across the rolling desert, the area reverted nearly to its natural state. Inadvertently, the secrecy surrounding the arrival of the nuclear age preserved the land around the last fifty-seven miles of river.

In that fifty-seven-mile stretch, the river still runs with the energy of its days of freedom. It rips over shallow bars of gravel and boils with great force through narrow passages along the spectacular white bluffs, and splits itself around broad sand islands covered with scrub cottonwood and willow.

Here native steelhead and noble king salmon still return to spawn, evading commercial nets and anglers' wares downstream, fighting their way up the fish ladders of the lower dams, overcoming the effects of pollution and supersaturation in order to do so. The miracle of their procreation is all the more significant because of the man-made hardships they must endure.

Mule deer does still brave the current and swim to the midriver islands to give birth to their fawns, and in the late spring the mothers and fawns may be seen frolicking in the bunchgrass and scrub willow on the islands.

This, too, is still a nesting place for the Great Basin Canada geese, the dwindling remnant of the great flocks that once darkened the skies over the river. Herons still nest here and take flight on ungainly wings at any intrusion. The white bluffs are lined with the sculptured nests of cliff swallows, and doves perch in the dry limbs of the abandoned orchards. Coyotes prowl the riverbanks and swim to the islands in search of prey.

In ancient days, the Indians came to the river here and camped on its islands to fish for the returning salmon. Their campsites and house-pits still are there, together with the relics of their time, covered and uncovered by blowing sand and the shifting river.

Today the withered orchards and the shade trees of the homesteaders still line the riverbanks. The open cellars where once their houses stood are like empty sockets in a weathered skull. And except for this, the river here is much as it was when Gray sailed into the Columbia's mouth or Lewis and Clark crossed the continental divide to find its headwaters. It is alive and free and rich in life, a short stretch of living river in a stream that in every other place has died.

In some senses it is different, and in many ways it is similar to other parts of the river that have disappeared forever beneath quiet reservoir depths. There is, however, one most important difference: This is the last free-flowing stretch, the very last, and once it is gone the mighty Columbia, mother of life, will be only a memory.

The Quality Concept

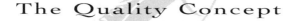

"Quality" is a favorite word of advertising agencies. In the context in which they use it, it means, roughly, getting the most for your money.

Yet there is widespread disagreement on what is "the most." To the buyer of an automobile, "the most" may mean the height of luxury; to another buyer, it may mean a vehicle that is ruggedly built and utilitarian. The different perceptions of "quality" extend to many areas. Engineers speak of "enhancing the recreational quality" of a river by building a dam on it; conservationists attack the proposal on the grounds that it will destroy the "quality" of the existing stream. Each

side believes firmly and sincerely that it is right, and
unfortunately the issue is all too often resolved in favor of the
side with the greater political muscle and not on the merits of
the issue itself.

The meaning of "quality" is nearly as elusive when
applied to angling. Some fishermen measure quality in terms
of the number of fish they are able to kill in a single day,
regardless of the size of the fish or the circumstances under
which they were taken. Other anglers regard quality as the
chance to catch large fish, even just one or two a day, and
numbers mean little to them. Still other anglers believe that
quality means the opportunity to fish in the way they choose
without interruption, or the chance to fish in wilderness
solitude. And still another definition of quality may include
something from all of these attitudes.

But these arguments are largely esthetic in nature and
often receive only passing consideration from the agencies
charged with fisheries management. These agencies measure
quality by still another yardstick—in statistical terms such as
"man-days," "catch per unit of effort" and the economic costs
of raising and planting fish.

So there is an inherent conflict between the fisherman,
who measures his success in terms of personal satisfaction, and
the fisheries management agencies, who measure success in
columns of statistics. It is unlikely that this conflict ever will
be fully resolved, but it seems incumbent upon both sides to
try a little harder to understand the other. The greater burden,
however, must be on management officials to explore the
attitudes of the public, which, after all, is footing the bill.

In many states, the opening day of the fishing season sees
huge crowds of anglers setting forth to slaughter trout literally
by the millions. This goes on for a weekend or two until nearly
all the trout have been removed, and that is the last time
many anglers will fish until the next season. The management

officials can sit back and relax for another year, satisfied that they have "given the public what it wants."

But is that really what the public wants? Could it be that the only reason the public swarms out on opening day is because it knows that two weeks later it will be too late to catch any fish? Could it be that the public really would be more satisfied to catch fewer fish on opening day in exchange for the opportunity to continue catching fish throughout the season? No one really knows, because the management agencies never have taken the trouble to find out. They have, instead, created a situation where most of the fishing public *has* to fish on opening day and the weekend thereafter in order to be assured of a reasonable chance of catching fish. If the agencies responsible for fisheries management would take the trouble to poll their constituencies, they might find the public is perfectly satisfied with the existing state of affairs—or they might discover that what the public really wants is far different from what it has received.

Of course, there are always a few fish that escape the opening-day crowds, and most states now have a few waters with special restrictions designed to ensure long-term survival and growth of the fish they contain. So, when the opening day crowds have subsided, the really dedicated anglers who fish the season long come into their own, picking up the leftovers or taking advantage of the restricted waters. Frequently, these are the fly fishermen, who have their own very definite ideas of what quality is.

While even within their own ranks there are differences of opinion, it is likely that the great majority of fly fishermen would agree that quality is the chance to fish in their own way for a few large trout, preferably wild trout, in an unspoiled environment.

There is no question that fly fishermen are in a minority, and so the waters set aside for them are relatively few. There is a definite question, however, as to whether their philosophy is a minority one, and it seems quite likely that a substantial portion of the fishing public would agree with the fly fisherman's definition of quality. Again, the problem is that no one has tried to find out.

Realistically, it seems unlikely that any such effort will soon be made. It is an old axiom that, even under our democratic system of government, the government usually is at least ten years behind the wishes of the people. So, what is to be done in the meantime, while we are waiting for the management agencies to wake up to the changing attitudes of the public?

There are a couple of very strong arguments to be made in favor of the fly fisherman's definiton of quality. What makes them especially strong is that they are arguments couched in terms that management agencies understand: numbers and costs.

The first of these arguments is economic in nature. While it is true that fly fishermen are a minority, it also is true that they fish far more often than most anglers whose choice is another method. Fly fishermen spend more on tackle; they spend more on fishing; they travel farther and stay longer to fish when they reach their destination. They spend more on guides, gasoline, licenses, food, liquor and lodging. So, even though in numbers they are a minority, they contribute a disproportionately large share to the sport-fishing economy. Thus, purely from an economic standpoint, their desires should be given special consideration. They should not be given the "leftover" waters that are not fished by the general public; they should be given the very best, most productive waters. There is no excuse for using the richest streams and lakes as receptacles for large plants of hatchery-reared fish that will be caught within a couple of weeks by the opening-day crowd. The "put-and-take" fisheries should be confined to streams and lakes whose productivity is low, because the productivity contributes nothing to the nature of the fishery anyway. The richest waters should, whenever possible, be managed as wild-trout fisheries where recreation may continue under proper regulations throughout the length of the season. To use the most productive waters for "put-and-take" fishing is simply a waste of valuable resources.

The second argument is a statistical one. It is possible to prove that, in terms of total recreational use, the *season-long* use of a fly-fishing-only water is equal to the use of a popular water that is fished out by crowds of anglers on two weekends early in the season. In other words, though a popular spot may be fished by two thousand anglers on each of the first two weekends of the season and be left virtually untouched afterward, a restricted water that draws only a hundred anglers on a weekend still will be used by more than four thousand persons in a season if a hundred anglers fish it every weekend. Combining this argument with the preceding one, it can be shown that the hundred anglers who fish every weekend through the season spend as much or more than the two thousand who fish only the first two weekends and then put away their tackle for the remainder of the year.

The problem, of course, is in gathering the data that will prove the truth of these arguments. And here, again, fly fishermen and like-minded anglers have an advantage, if they will only make use of it. Fly fishermen often are well organized in clubs and in regional or national organizations, such as the Federation of Fly Fishermen. By taking advantage of this organizational strength, they may take the creek censuses and economic surveys necessary to prove their point. The legions of other fishermen are not so organized and lack the means necessary to gather such information or express a united point of view.

The ability to present a united front is especially important. By joining together and deciding what they want, it is possible for angling organizations to go to management agencies and speak for many hundreds of fishermen. Such an approach carries far more weight and is far more effective than separate approaches, differing in nature, brought by individual clubs or spokesmen. This "united front" approach has been tried with great success by anglers' clubs in several states. However, it should be obvious that only proposals within the realm of political and scientific feasibility should be made. In other words, it is necessary first to do your homework, gather the necessary facts, and perform the necessary explorations, and then propose something that is reasonable, something that may be done without a great deal of trouble or cost. Sometimes fly fishermen are guilty of the same offense of which they accuse the management agencies: they fail to take into account the opinion of other angling groups. They must communicate and listen to ensure that their own proposals do not run against the grain of prevailing public opinion.

If the foregoing sounds like an elitist philosophy, I suppose, in truth, that it is. But it also appears to be the likeliest way of preserving something resembling good fishing in the future, to the ultimate benefit of all anglers. At the risk of being accused of snobbism, fly fishermen must take the lead in pressing for more quality angling.

Once an approach to a management agency has been made successfully and the desired goal—some sort of quality fishery—is established, the job still is not over with. Those who sought establishment of the fishery then are obligated to make maximum use of it, or they are likely to lose it later, or lose the opportunity to make further gains.

This is one of the hardest things for fly fishermen to accept. Once they have fought the political battle necessary to gain the fishing they desire, it is natural for them to be protective of it and to resent its use by increasing numbers of anglers. This, however, is an extremely shortsighted attitude. Rather than going out of their way to be secretive about such a fishery, anglers should do their best—within reason—to publicize it and ensure its use. Not only is this the surest way of keeping it for the future, but it also is the single most powerful argument in favor of the establishment of additional quality fisheries. Management officials, once they see the success and increasing use of an initial quality fishery, will be that much easier to sell on the need for more of them.

A case in point is that of Lenice Lake, in the Columbia Basin, about which I will write more later. At the request of fly-fishing clubs in Washington State, Lenice was established as a quality lake with only artificial lures permitted and a limit of three trout a day over twelve inches.

Lenice was an instant success, and its outstanding fishing led to publicity first in the local papers, then in regional magazines and finally in some of the national sporting magazines. The publicity inevitably led to greatly increased use, so that the lake was crowded every weekend throughout the season. This caused quite a bit of resentment among the anglers who had first worked on the project, but the heavy usage of the lake made it obvious that considerable numbers of people were interested in such fishing, and so the Game Department placed the same restrictions on three other lakes nearby. What had started as an effort to reserve a single lake for quality angling had grown suddenly into a chain of four lakes.

Another argument in favor of quality fisheries that seems to be gaining increasing acceptance is that some sort of special regulations are needed to protect dwindling populations of native, naturally spawning fish. The success of fly-fishing-only regulations on the Firehole and Madison rivers are outstanding examples of this. And Hosmer Lake, of which I have written elsewhere in this book, is an example of how an exotic, high-quality fishery may attract anglers from many states, thus providing a considerable economic asset to the state and community in which it is located.

Unquestionably, it has been difficult for fly fishermen

and those who share their concept of quality to gain the type of fishing they desire. Yet it now is clear that the tide is in their favor, that public concern over the future of angling is growing, that quality fishing indeed works and is economically feasible, and that, in the final analysis, it may be the only way we shall ever preserve any semblance of fishing in the future. Today there also are more fly fishermen and more anglers of kindred spirit than ever before, and whereas fly fishing once was regarded as an exclusive sport for a privileged few, it now is growing in public favor and is gaining widespread acceptance as the angling method most consistent with the conservation and wise use of fishery resources.

So the concept of quality is receiving greater understanding and the work is easier today than it was just a few years ago. Still, there is much to be done, and anglers who are concerned about the future of their sport had better be up and about doing it. The sport now stands on the threshold of achieving the kind of fishing that all men dream about, if only enough anglers are strong enough in their dedication to see it through. The choice for the future seems clear: quality fishing, or none at all.

The Brook Trout in the West

When the first colonists landed on the Eastern shores, they found the shadowed pools of the New England streams occupied by a strange, wild trout. It was colored in blue and ivory, in salmon pink and silver, with little jewels of red and yellow on its sides, and it was a willing taker of the primitive baits and flies of that ancient time.

Perhaps a little homesick for the remembered trout of the Old Country, the colonists named the new fish "brook trout," though in actuality it was a char. It was abundant in all the watersheds from the Carolinas to Quebec and inland to the Great Lakes drainage, and the first fly fishermen in this country cut their teeth on brook trout. It was the brook trout that inspired some of America's first contributions to angling literature. It was the fish of George Washington Bethune, Frank Forester, Robert Barnwell Roosevelt, Thaddeus Norris and other pioneer American angling writers.

The brook trout held its own in the East until the industrial revolution was well underway, and then quickly it was gone. Its habitat was destroyed in the short space of a few years as forests gave way to factories and cities and streams were blocked by dams and stained by pollution.

Before the sudden assault of industrialization, the brook trout melted away like snow before the summer sun, and by 1890 it had been driven into the far headwaters of the Eastern streams, where it holds forth still in the springs and tiny feeder creeks that are the beginnings of rivers. The brown trout, more hardy and adaptable, has taken over most of the brook trout's former range that has not been left totally unfit for fish to live in.

But even as the brook trout was dying in its native Eastern rivers, transplants were being made to new waters in the West—the high mountain tarns of the Rockies and the beaver ponds and marshes of the coastal plain. And today the brookie is plentiful in the streams, lakes and ponds of the Western states and Canadian provinces.

In the high mountain lakes of the West, the brook trout grows typically bright and firm with neon spots of red and yellow. It does not often reach large size in the high lakes with their short growing seasons and sparse insect life, but no other waters grow fish with flesh so firm and sweet.

In contrast, beaver-dam trout are apt to be dark from the cedar-stained waters in which they live, and the live, bright colors of the mountain trout are seldom found in the acid waters of the coastal forests. But such trout also are often apt to be large, growing deep and fat on abundant midge pupae and the populous nymphs of dragon and damsel flies.

Even so, the brook trout is not universally popular in its new Western home. He is generally conceded to be an easier fish to take than the native rainbows and cutthroats or the imported brown, and though he fights stubbornly his struggle pales in comparison with the spectacular rainbow. The brook trout breeds under a wider variety of circumstances than the native fish and consequently frequently overpopulates its range, and—perhaps because it is not native to the country— its growth rate never seems quite equal to the native species. Confronted with a choice of fishing for rainbow, cutthroat or brook trout, the typical Western angler is likely to put the brookie at the bottom of his list. The consequence of that is that good brook-trout waters seldom receive the same pressure as their counterparts occupied by other species.

These are all valid criticisms of the brook trout in the West. I have found it to be easier to catch than other species, not quite so sporting on the line, frequently too numerous, and usually slower to reach good size. But I also have found it to be a fish of unique beauty, and even if it does not fight quite so well as other species, it still is a worthy adversary on light tackle.

It was a search for this adversary that took me one late summer day down a heather-covered slope to the shore of Bagley Lake. The dark, square bulk of Table Mountain loomed up overhead, and behind us, up on the ridge, skiers left thin, twisted tracks in the snow.

The trail down to the lake still was covered in spots by aging drifts of snow, and the warm summer sun had brought the mosquitoes forth to hover around the dwarfed alpine firs and spruce that reared above the thick clumps of heather and the ripening blueberries. A bridge of frozen snow still covered the inlet to the lake, and a marmot whistled, high and clear, on the far shore.

The lake was clear as only mountain lakes can be, and the sun outlined every bit of broken shale on its bottom. It seemed impossible that trout could live in such water and not be visible at every glance, but there was no sign of life.

I made my way carefully over the snow bridge across the inlet while Joan, my wife, hiked farther up to the point where the inlet stream vanished under the snow, and began fishing there. I found a spot where the shoreline was free of snow and little buttercups grew in the meadow grass, and I jointed up the small rod and attached a little nymph to a long leader and floating line. My first cast carried into the invisible current from the inlet; the line drifted down with the gentle flow, then came to a sudden and suspicious stop. I lifted the rod tip and felt the throb of a fish and simultaneously I saw it turn, the first sign of a fish I had seen in the clear water. The brook trout tumbled out of the water in a flash of crimson spots and spray, and just as quickly it was gone. I had been too slow to strike and the hook had not been firmly set.

Then I heard a shout from Joan; her rod was bent and plunging, and moments later a fine brookie was thrashing on the wet gravel at her feet. She had let the current carry her fly down into the darkness beneath the snow bridge, and there, hidden in a little cavern in the ice, the trout had taken it. He was the best of all the trout we were to take that day, and we admired his brilliant dress against the backdrop of the snow.

I cast again, and the current carried the fly out into the lake, over a waterlogged limb on the bottom. Every detail was plainly visible through the clear water as a brook trout appeared from under the sunken limb, rose leisurely through ten feet of water and intercepted the drifting nymph in a subtle, sipping rise. To that point the whole act had appeared as if it had been filmed in slow motion, but the trout turned with a quick flash and leaped at the first feel of the hook. And then every motion of its struggle was visible as it vainly sought the sanctuary of the limb from under which it had first appeared.

And that was the way it went for an hour or more, with nearly every cast greeted by a leisurely rise followed by a dogged struggle, with every strike and turn, every twist and jump clearly visible from the first to the last. And when it was over, half a dozen brook trout lay side by side in the snow and we had released many others.

We placed the trout in a wicker creel on a bed of little sword ferns and moist meadow clover and packed handfuls of snow around them before we started back up the steep slope. The top of the ridge was crowded with skiers on their way to the slopes, and we walked to the foot of the run and watched the graceful skiers coming down with shouts of glee cut short as they plunged into a pool of ice water at the bottom. Helping hands and laughing faces greeted them as they emerged from the glacial water, and hands thrust out mugs of beer from kegs buried in the snow. And while hundreds skied and watched and laughed, we had been alone on the lake only a few hundred yards away.

Of all the places I have found brook trout, perhaps the favorite is Leech Lake, a little snowline lake at the summit of White Pass in the Cascades. It is restricted to fly fishing only, and it is ideally suited to the fly. A shallow lake with thick weedbeds growing within a few inches of the surface and sheltering deadfalls around its shore, it provides superb angling from ice-out to freeze-up. The trout never are very large, but always there are many of them, and they are as bright and brilliantly colored as any fish I have ever seen.

On our first visit we arrived late at night and drove the Jeep through the trees until we could see pale moonlight flashing on the water. We made camp on the shore and slept in the open under fragrant boughs of fir, and in the morning I came awake and stared into the startled eyes of a camp robber that was walking up my sleeping bag. The handsome bird took quick flight, and I looked beyond it to the layer of steam that was rising from the calm surface of the lake. Behind the lazy layers of floating steam came the splashing sounds of feeding trout.

Breakfast was a hurried affair, but still the rise had stopped before I was on the water. I spent the morning exploring the lake, casting off the weedbed around the outlet stream, probing the hole at the foot of the rockslide at its western end, dropping the fly around the deadfalls along the shore. Before the day was out I had released more than thirty trout, the males beautiful with the sunset colors of their early spawning dress, the females bright with spattered spots of color.

Leech Lake has given me some of the best fishing of all. On one afternoon nature forgot it was summer and a cold wind whipped a sullen drizzle of rain and wet snow across the surface, and dirty strands of dark cloud hid the ridges and drifted through the woods. But despite the cold, unfriendly weather, it was quickly apparent that this was a special day, that the trout were willing as never before, and nearly every cast over the weedbeds was met by a turning silver shape.

The trout struck hard and fought well until it seemed as if the little bamboo midge rod would be frozen into a permanent curve. The brookies were everywhere—in the weeds, along the deadfalls, in the springhole along the northern shore— and they dashed in twos and threes to strike at my imitation of a damselfly nymph. Once I hooked fish on eleven consecutive casts, something which never has happened to me before or since, and when the afternoon grew prematurely dark in the overcast and the rain, I had released more than a hundred trout.

My friend Ward McClure scoffed in disbelief at the total, and so the next weekend we went there together with a small wager as to who could catch the most trout.

At first it looked as if it would be one of those days that

are best forgotten: I had trouble with the line and trouble with the long, thin leader, and my casts never seemed to fall quite on target. Even when things went well it seemed as if the trout were determined to ignore my fly. Ward had released more than twenty fish before I had my third, and there seemed little chance that I could hope to win the wager.

But then the tide began to change. I found brook trout feeding near the springhole, and they began to come almost as willingly as they had the time before.

The same damselfly nymph that had worked so well before again stimulated their interest, and while Ward was taking an occasional fish around the deadfalls I was getting strikes on nearly every cast. When the afternoon was over and we compared notes, I had released seven more trout than Ward. The wager was settled and we joined our wives around a campfire where steaks and potatoes sputtered over the hot coals, and drank bourbon toasts to the noble brook trout. And the next morning there were brook trout for breakfast, rolled in corn meal and fried in butter, fit for a king.

Fishing in the beaver swamps and ponds is far different from fishing in the mountain lakes. Beaver-pond fishing is difficult; usually the water is dark and impenetrable, hiding a thick tangle of invisible deadfalls and snags. Where ponds have risen in the forest, groves of dead timber remain standing in them to snare the unwary backcast, and it is not unusual to see the skeletons of trees decorated with flies and strands of broken leader. There are floating islands of peat and thick beds of water lilies, and the trout hide under them and feed along their edges. Herons and occasional ospreys fish these waters every day, and the trout grow quickly wary of any quick movement, of every fragment of shadow cast by a bird in flight.

The trout are difficult to approach and difficult to fool, and because their wariness and wisdom have enabled them to survive they often grow to trophy size and weight. Fishless days occur frequently, but when the angler is lucky enough to hook a trout it is likely to be a large one, and then begins the even more difficult task of trying to land a large fish amid a jungle of dead timber and snags.

A mile beyond the end of the nearest forest road I rendezvoused with such a trout in an amber-colored pond on a dark, rainy afternoon. I had been casting along the edge of a bank of lily pads without result, working the bright fly along the silty bottom, trying to avoid the black outlines of deadfalls rearing up near the surface, hoping for a strike. Suddenly it was there: a quick pull with a sense of heavy weight behind it. Then I could feel the fish shaking its head, slowly and strongly, and immediately I knew it was a big brook trout.

It fought deep and I snubbed it hard to keep it from finding the twisted sticks and deadfalls on the bottom. Now and then a heavy boil appeared on the surface as the trout made a sudden turn beneath it, but the fish never showed itself. Gradually the strong rushes grew weaker and the leader butt was visible above the surface. I worked the fish in close and had my first look at it: short and thick, with a broad, square tail, the ivory edges of its fins showing clearly through the dark water.

And then I led it over the waiting net and gasped as the fly came away just as the mesh closed around its thrashing sides. It was a female, dark to match the water of its home, but fat and strong and in fine condition, and it brought me a gold pin from the Washington Fly Fishing Club for the largest brookie of the year and the third largest in the thirty-year history of the club.

Arguments go on over the value of the brook trout in its new Western home. Detractors claim that it is better to plant the native cutthroat or the rainbow, or more sophisticated species like the brown. But in most cases the brook trout has been introduced to waters that formerly were barren of any species, and in most cases it has adapted well enough. The West has abundant water and it seems there is enough to grant the brook trout its share without short-changing the native species or other imports. I suppose the detractors always will continue their arguments against the brook trout in the West, but as for me, I'm glad it's here.

North Fork Diary

The history of fly fishing in America had its beginnings on such rivers as the Neversink and the Willowemoc, the Beaverkill and the Brodheads. The anglers who fished these rivers developed the theories and wrote the books that still largely influence the angling tactics of the present day.

Perhaps the richest tradition of any river belongs to the Neversink. It was the home river of Theodore Gordon, the patron saint of American fly fishing, father of the dry fly in America. It also was the water of Edward Ringwood Hewitt, and in his private pools he performed the experiments and made the observations that led to so many authoritative books. It was the river of fly tiers who made lasting contributions to the art, including Roy Steenrod, Herman Christian and William Chandler. It is one of the most sacred rivers in the catalog of American waters.

Though its contribution to literature and practice perhaps was not as rich, the tradition of the Brodheads is even older than that of the Neversink. The pioneer angling writer George Washington Bethune fished there as early as the 1840s, and Thaddeus Norris, another great pioneer, came a little later. It was the river of Samuel Phillippe, who is credited with invention of modern, six-strip, split-cane fly-rod construction. George La Branche once owned a stretch of its rippling water, and its list of notables reads like a Who's Who of American fly fishing, stretching over a period of one hundred and thirty years.

The history of the Willowemoc and Beaverkill is hardly less impressive. Norris, La Branche and Hewitt also were at home on these Catskill streams, and they were followed by others such as John Taintor Foote, Ray Holland, John Alden Knight and John Atherton.

There is no stream in the West so rich in history and lore as these four little rivers in the East. Fly fishing in the West is yet relatively new and fresh, and the writers and thinkers who will shape its development are only now beginning to emerge. But if Western angling still seeks its movers and shapers, it already has a growing and impressive list of philosophers and chroniclers, including such writers as Zane Grey, Roderick Haig-Brown and Ben Hur Lampman. And if it lacks historic shrines such as the Neversink and the Brodheads, it soon will have them. And the first of them to be so recognized is likely to be the North Fork of the Stillaguamish River.

The North Fork of the Stillaguamish is not an especially large river, nor is it blessed with an abundance of good fishing water. Yet nearly every major angling writer the Northwest has yet produced has been called to its water at one time or another, and it is the source of a growing body of literature and the scene of development of several innovations and refinements in tackle and tactics.

The North Fork heads in the western foothills of the Cascade Mountains about seventy-five miles northeast of Seattle. Scarcely more than a creek at first, it gathers water from several small branches and flows south through a canyon until it makes a nearly right-angle turn near the little town of Darrington and starts its westward flow. And as it does so, it enters a narrow, verdant valley that is a place of tranquil beauty in all seasons, dominated throughout its length by the eternal, ice-covered bulk of Glacier Peak which rises more than 10,500 feet at its eastern end.

The river runs alternately through white-water, boulder-studded rapids, deep, quiet pools and smooth glides over a bed of rounded gravel. It passes through tiny settlements like Fortson, Hazel and Oso, hardly more than names on the map, and accepts the water of a dozen small tributaries, foremost among them Squire, French and Boulder creeks. And then, at the little community of Oso, it receives its major tributary, Deer Creek, a historic little river that once harbored one of the greatest runs of summer steelhead in the world.

And then it flows on past Hell Creek and Cicero, a river now grown in volume but diminished in spirit as it approaches its confluence with the equal-sized South Fork at the town of Arlington, and together the two rivers flow as one out of their peaceful valley onto the brief coastal plain until they slide into the sheltered waters of Port Susan Bay in Puget Sound.

Before white men came to the valley of the North Fork it was the home of a tribe of Indians who called themselves the Stoluck-wha-nish, a name eventually corrupted by the English tongue into the present name of the river. It was then a country vastly different than it is today. Great forests of western redcedar kept the river in eternal shade, from the salt marshes and sloughs at the river's mouth to the higher hills and valleys where they yielded their domain to fir and spruce. The river hosted noble runs of steelhead in winter and summer, of giant king salmon in the fall, of bright native cutthroat and Dolly Varden char. Great runs of humpback salmon returned to the river in odd-numbered years. The summers were warm and wet, the winters mild, and the Indians—perhaps as many as two thousand of them at their peak—found their livelihood along the river, taking from it only as much as they needed to sustain life.

The Indians were a primitive but resourceful lot, and their way of life was firmly established, ritualized by their forefathers in the misty age of prehistory. They had established a balance with the land, and it was good to them and they in turn were kind to it. But theirs was a way of life destined to fall quickly before the brutal impact of a new and alien culture that had swept across the land, and only the relative isolation of their home protected the Stillaguamish Indians from the fate that earlier came to so many other tribes.

In 1859, other Indians were fighting vainly to resist the white man's march across their land, and the white settlements around Puget Sound feared similar uprisings. In anticipation of possible conflict, military authorities built a road through the virgin forest from Fort Steilacoom, south of Tacoma, to a point beyond the Stillaguamish. It was a crude road, but it offered the first ready access to white men other than the occasional hardy traders and trappers that had ventured into the valley of the North Fork. The valley was included in a county that was recognized by the territorial legislature in 1861, even though a census showed it then had a population of only thirty-six whites, all of them men.

The existence of the military road had no immediate impact on the Indians or their valley. Until 1864 the only white settlement was in the larger valley of the Snohomish River and its tributary, the Skykomish, to the south. But then in 1864 a white man named Henry Marshall cleared a homestead and built a cabin on the lower Stillaguamish, below the confluence of the forks.

Marshall was but the first, and slowly other settlers began to trickle in. A man named James H. Perkins bought out Marshall, who seemed to be perpetually ill, and Perkins traded with the Indians and began to log the giant cedars that grew virtually in his back yard. He prospered and eventually built a hotel and saloon on the river in a community that came to be known as Florence.

Other loggers moved to the area and established small camps. The price of logs ranged from five to ten dollars a thousand board feet, and the mighty cedars were felled and sold as quickly as the loggers could cut them. Other settlers moved into the logged-off areas and began to farm. Working with shovels, plows and teams of oxen, they drained the salt marches and the sloughs near the river's mouth, built dikes and levees and planted their crops in the rich soil left by the river.

In early June, 1884, a wagon road was completed to the Stillaguamish Valley, and land hunters immediately flocked in. By 1886 the valley was considered one of the most prosperous on Puget Sound, with rich crops and heavy timber harvests that lined the pockets of many of its residents. But it was not a prosperous time for the valley's native inhabitants. They had yielded their land easily, sometimes for small sums, sometimes for nothing. They died from the white man's diseases and got drunk on his cheap whiskey, and the simple, ordered life they always had known suddenly was shattered and confused.

Logging camps sprang up along the North Fork valley, paying better wages than other nearby camps, cutting the timber, hauling it with oxen to the river, floating it down to the sawmills.

By 1889 the valley was thickly settled as far east as

Darrington, and a year later a railroad was punched into the valley from the town of Snohomish to the south. In 1890, the town of Arlington at the confluence of the North and South Forks had a population of fifty people. Fifteen years later it had grown to nearly two thousand.

In 1901, a spur railroad was built along the North Fork to Darrington, and what had been a settlement became a town. Other small communities grew up around sawmills and stores along the railroad and the river. At the point where Deer Creek flowed out of the hills a post office was built and named in honor of John B. Allen, a representative in Congress. Later, to avoid confusion with another town named Allyn, the Post Office arbitrarily changed the name of the little community to Oso, which it remains today.

By the turn of the century, the valley of the North Fork had been changed completely. The timber all had been stripped from the coastal plains, never to grow there again. Farms thrived where once the gloomy forests stood, and cornfields grew where the cutthroat had once foraged on the salt flats. The valley itself had been cleared of timber and planted with crops and orchards, the sawmill towns prospering briefly like gold-mining camps, then fading quickly into rusting, rotting obscurity. The Indians were dead or driven from their lands, less than a hundred surviving and few of those retaining the pure bloodline of their tribe.

The white men had bent the land and its people to their will, and having done that they began to turn their attention to the river. Formerly it had served first as a convenient route of transportation, then as a highway for floating logs to the mills. The railroad eliminated both uses, and as the frontier boundaries fell back, the settlers became more comfortable in their homes and occupations and began to seek their sport in the river.

There is little early record of sport fishing on the river. The Indians fished only for food, and though white fishermen captured the returning salmon in the salt water, the steelhead run had been largely ignored by everyone. Yet the North Fork hosted a great run of summer steelhead, one of the few rivers in the area to have such a run. The bright summer fish ran to the mouth of Deer Creek and held there in the pools and riffles until it was time to run up the creek itself, back into the trackless wilderness where the loggers had yet to reach. Deer Creek flowed in a succession of great, deep pools and around huge boulders, through a shaded canyon where the steelhead could rest through the long months before their spawning. No one knows the original size of that great native run, but there is little doubt that it was one of the finest summer runs in the world, perhaps the finest of them all.

Even so, it escaped all but local attention until 1918, when Zane Grey, the famous Western novelist, arrived in Seattle on his way to Campbell River to fish for tyee (chinook) salmon.

In *Tales of Fresh-Water Fishing*, Grey wrote:

"From several of the fishing tackle dealers, who kindly lent us all the assistance in their power, we got vague information about the wonderful steelhead fishing in Deer Creek. Not one of them, however, had been there. They showed us Deer Creek on the map and claimed that it was almost inaccessible. But if we could get there!

". . . At length we met the best two steelhead anglers in Seattle—Hiller and Van Tassel. They vouched for the marvelous fishing we might find in Deer Creek—if we could get there."

But it developed that neither Hiller nor Van Tassel had been there. However, one of their favorite steelhead pools was in the North Fork of the Stillaguamish at the mouth of Deer Creek. They told Grey the pool recently had been filled with fish, but they had disappeared into the creek after a rain.

Grey and his party went with Hiller and Van Tassel to Arlington, and from there they went to the North Fork.

"Before six o'clock we reached the Stillaguamish, a limpid little river, rushing and placid by turns." And the pool they elected to try was the one at the mouth of Deer Creek.

Hiller and Van Tassel were bait fishermen—the fly being almost unknown in that area at that time—but they used fly rods and "enameled silk lines, the same as those used for fly casting; a short heavy gut leader; . . . a sinker that would roll on the bottom with the current, and very small hooks."

"For bait a small ball of fresh salmon eggs that hid the hook was essential. They strapped a wire or canvas basket, large as a small dishpan, to their waists. . . .

"The use of the basket was unique. I was indeed curious about it. Van Tassel waded knee-deep into the water, put on a bait, and stripping off the reel a goodly length of line, which fell in coils into the basket, he gave his rod a long side sweep and flip and sent that bait clear across the stream. It was an admirable performance, and far from easy, as we anglers soon learned."

This, so far as I know, is the first mention in print of the "stripping basket" that later became popular on the North Fork and many other rivers. It was, at first, an invention peculiar to the North Fork, where it was used only by bait fishermen. But later it was adopted almost exclusively by fly fishermen, who used it to store loose coils of line before making the long casts so often necessary in steelhead fishing, and so difficult to perform when many coils of line are held in the hand. It was the first refinement to emerge from the North Fork, though its popularity has declined since the introduction of the shooting head as a substitute for casting the whole fly line.

Grey and his party caught no fish in the North Fork that day, and they went on to a little logging settlement on Lake McMurray to the north. There they engaged a guide who said he knew the way to Upper Deer Creek. The trip was filled with adventure, beginning on a battered logging train that carried them over rickety, wobbling trestles and once running off the track before they got to the end of the line. After an overnight hike, Grey wrote, "At last we descended to a point where, from under the giant cedars, we could look down upon Deer Creek. A beautiful, green-and-white stream, shining here, dark and gleaming there, wound through a steep-walled canyon. It was worth working for. What struck me at once was the wonderful transparency of the water and the multitude of boulders, some of them huge.

". . . Deer Creek was the most beautiful trout water I had ever seen. Clear as crystal, cold as ice, it spoke eloquently of the pure springs of the mountain fastnesses. . . ."

During his second day on the stream, Grey hooked the first steelhead of his life: "A dark gleam shot into the shallow water. How swift! Then it changed to a silver flash with glints of red. I saw a big fish swoop up and then come clear out into the air—a steelhead, savage and beautiful, fight in every line of his curved body." It was the beginning of a long acquaintance with steelhead that later would take Grey to the Rogue River, which he made famous with his writing.

After Grey's departure, Deer Creek remained inaccessible to all but foot travel, though each year the loggers pushed the forests farther back and closer to the stream. The next angler of stature to visit the area was Roderick Haig-Brown, who came as a member of a logging survey crew in 1927. Fresh from his native England, Haig-Brown knew little of the steelhead then and his first attempt at fishing for them in the Stillaguamish—like Zane Grey's—met with failure. But Haig-Brown, too, was attracted by exciting tales of big steelhead in Deer Creek, and on a June weekend he hiked through the forest to the stream, later describing the experience in his beautiful classic, A River Never Sleeps:

"The river was a lot bigger than the word 'creek' had led

me to expect," he wrote, "and it was beautiful, clear and bright and fast, tumbled on rocks and gravel bars." He caught many strange fish, disappointing both in appearance and in fight, discovering only later that they were Dolly Varden.

Then, late on his second day astream, he hooked a steelhead and lost it after the third wild jump, and knew then that the exciting tales he had heard were true. A few weeks later Haig-Brown landed his first steelhead, a seven-pounder, and he went on to write lovingly and well of these great seagoing trout.

In 1929, another angler came to the river, one who was destined to have a profound influence on it in later years. This was Enos Bradner, then on his first trip to the West Coast from his native Midwest. Liking the country he saw, Bradner decided to return and opened a bookshop in Seattle. During periods when business was slow, he studied maps of the area and spent the weekends exploring the waters he had seen listed on the maps.

In 1934 came the first suggestion that Deer Creek and the North Fork deserved something better than unlimited fishing by unlimited means. The Snohomish County Sportsmen's Association proposed that Deer Creek and one mile of the North Fork be restricted to fly fishing only, an idea that was revolutionary at the time. The proposal was quickly accepted by the State Game Commission, but led just as quickly to a public protest by bait fishermen and property owners in the Stillaguamish Valley. Faced with this opposition, the Sportsmen's Association retreated, the Game Commission rescinded its order and the river was closed to all fishing for a season.

But the idea that the North Fork of the Stillaguamish should be a fly fisherman's river would not die easily. Several members of the Steelhead Trout Club in Seattle, including Bradner, urged the club to seek a fly-fishing-only regulation on the North Fork. When the club refused to act, those in favor of the regulation decided to form a new club of their own.

During a series of meetings in the winter of 1939, the dissident members organized their new club, and in the spring of that year the Washington Fly Fishing Club was formally established in Seattle.

Bradner was elected charter president of the new club. Little known at the time, he later went on to become outdoor editor of the Seattle *Times*, a position he held for twenty-six years.

His book *Northwest Angling* was one of the first to detail steelhead angling methods and provided the most thorough description of the North Fork of the Stillaguamish published until that time. His pet steelhead fly, Brad's Brat, was developed on the North Fork and since has become popular on many Northwest steelhead rivers.

There were eight other charter members of the new club, and a distinguished lot they were. They included Charles King, Dawn Holbrook, Letcher Lambuth, Jack Litsey, Lendall Hunton, Dr. Marvin Brown, Firmin Flohr and Ken McLeod.

Lambuth performed pioneering research on rod bamboo and developed a method of spiral strip construction for bamboo rods. He also did some of the first research on Western trout stream insects, carrying on an extensive correspondence with Preston Jennings, recognized as the leading angling entomologist in the country at that time and author of the still-popular volume *A Book of Trout Flies*. Lambuth's intelligence and organizational ability were to play a major role in the future management of the North Fork.

McLeod was outdoor editor of the Seattle *Post-Intelligencer*, and a political power among the sportsmen of the state. His shrewd instincts and his influence also were destined to play a part in the North Fork story. It was McLeod who suggested the fly pattern that was to become known as the Skykomish Sunrise, perhaps the most famous of all steelhead flies.

(McLeod remembers a gorgeous dawn that prompted him to suggest to his son that he ought to tie a fly of the same colors as the vivid morning sky. His son took him at his word, tied the fly, and the Skykomish Sunrise was born.)

As its first project, the new club set out to seek fly-fishing-only regulations on a number of waters, primarily as a conservation measure to protect migratory runs of fish from overexploitation by rapidly growing numbers of anglers. Word of the effort got around and new members flocked to the fledgling group.

The club introduced a resolution calling for certain lakes and streams to be set aside for fly fishing only. The resolution was approved by the county sports council, an organization of representatives from major outdoor groups, and was transmitted to the State Game Commission in January 1941. The commission approved the new regulation for the North Fork on January 9.

Then the storm broke. When word of the new regulation got around, it was met quickly by a barrage of protest. Residents of the Stillaguamish Valley objected, as they had in 1934, and the Snohomish County Sportsmen's Association (which apparently had undergone a change of heart since it had asked for a fly-fishing-only regulation seven years earlier) led the opposition of other sportsmen. Its publication, the *Snohomish County Sportsman,* editorialized:

"Residents of Snohomish County were considerably surprised when, without warning, the State Game Commission announced that the North Fork of the Stillaguamish River had been closed to all but fly fishing. Residents of the Stillaguamish Valley were not only surprised, but shocked, for many of them were hardy pioneers who ventured into the valley years ago, carrying their possessions on their backs;

hewed out the trails, made their homes, and developed the valley into what it is today. It is no wonder, therefore, that these citizens should become indignant when they find that an elite set of Seattlelites had prevailed upon the commission to set this stream aside for the use of a favored few."

Meetings were held and petitions circulated asking the Game Commission to rescind its action. The Fly Fishing Club, in seeking the regulation, had bypassed the State Sportsmen's Council, a statewide counterpart of the county group and an organization which wielded considerable influence at the time. It quickly became apparent that an attempt would be made through the state organization to condemn the new regulation.

To head off the gathering opposition, the Fly Fishing Club decided to introduce its own resolution to the State Sportsmen's Council, asking it to commend the Game Commission rather than condemn it. With the battle lines thus drawn, the club began an intensive lobbying campaign to win support for its cause.

With Lambuth acting as organizational chief and McLeod giving political advice, club members contacted or joined dozens of other sportsmen's groups, pleading and arguing in favor of the new regulation. When the day of the state meeting finally dawned, the issue still was in doubt and it seemed the resolution had only a 50-50 chance of passage.

The debate was long and bitter, but when the vote finally was taken the resolution passed, with twenty-nine clubs voting in favor and twenty-four against. The regulation would be allowed to take effect, and the North Fork of the Stillaguamish thus became the first steelhead river ever to be restricted to fishing with the fly.

Despite the club's victory, the opposition died hard. A director of the State Sportsmen's Council charged in the press that "unfair and unethical methods" had been used by the club to obtain the favorable vote. The local Grange in the

Stillaguamish Valley took up the opponents' cause. A petition bearing 750 signatures opposed to the regulation was presented to the State Game Commission. Farmers in the valley threatened to post their lands so that fly fishermen could not gain access to the river.

But the Game Commission stuck to its ruling, and as time passed the opposition faded. Fly Fishing Club members surveyed farmers along the river in November 1941 and found twenty who said they opposed the regulation, seven who had no opinion and none at all who were in favor of it. But two years later, many of those who originally had been opposed said they had changed their minds, and the threat to forbid access never materialized. Gradually, the issue ceased to be a controversy.

To this day, the North Fork remains a fly-fishing-only river during the summer steelhead season.

Perhaps it was fitting that Bradner, the first president of the Fly Fishing Club, also was the first to take a steelhead on a fly in the North Fork after the new regulation was imposed. But it was a costly fish. So anxious was Bradner to get to the river that he was stopped for speeding on the way and had to pay a stiff fine, an incident that made humorous copy in the local outdoor columns of the time.

The club itself thrived and since has grown to more than 250 members, numbering among its ranks three national casting champions and several well-known angling writers and photographers.

In 1945, the Fly Fishing Club persuaded the State Game Commission that artificial propagation of summer-run steelhead was a project worth trying. No one ever had attempted it before, but the Game Commission dutifully built a trap in lower Deer Creek and snared seventy-five summer steelhead on their way up the creek to spawn.

The fish were transferred to a hatchery pond, where they

were kept through the long winter months while they ripened slowly. They proved difficult to handle and refused to feed, and in the end only about thirty fish survived.

But in March, 1946, thirty-five thousand fertilized eggs were obtained from those thirty fish. The eggs were hatched and the fry raised in a rearing pond until, in the spring of 1948, they were released to go to sea. Two years later the first of them returned, proving conclusively for the first time that summer steelhead reared in hatcheries would return to the rivers in which they were released.

This pioneer effort in fish propagation has since ensured the survival of the summer-run steelhead sports fishery. Rivers whose native runs were decimated by logging or other damage have been restocked with hatchery fish that now return in greater numbers than the natives ever did. Other streams that never hosted runs of their own have been given them, again with hatchery fish. And though some anglers complain that the hatchery fish are not the equal of the natives—an assertion that has strong evidence in its support—the fact remains that by far the bulk of summer steelhead now come from hatchery origin, and without them very little fishing would remain.

Unfortunately, that is true of the North Fork as well as other rivers. Deer Creek was closed to all fishing to protect the spawning run and ensure that there would always be a supply of native fish in the North Fork, but loggers finally reached the upper sheltered reaches of the stream and stripped the timber down to its banks, without regard for the priceless resource that spawned in its gravel.

Debris was pushed into the once-transparent pools and eroded topsoil washed thickly down from the ravished banks. Herbicides were sprayed along the banks to prevent the growth of alder in the wake of logging, and they also washed into the once pure, sweet water of the stream. Upper Deer

Creek became a desolate, battlefield landscape, and in the short space of a few years one of the greatest summer steelhead runs every known was gone.

Even today, years after the initial onslaught, the logging and spraying continue. A few hardy steelhead still return each year, but they are a pitiful remnant of the original run. In high water, Deer Creek runs in a brown flood with the washed-away topsoil from its upper banks, and in the late-summer months its flow is reduced to a bare trickle, ten degrees warmer than the North Fork itself. Even if the senseless destruction of the watershed is checked, it will take generations before the Deer Creek of Zane Grey and Roderick Haig-Brown returns to its former pristine glory—if ever. In the meantime, the hatchery fish compose the bulk of the run, swimming past the mouth of Deer Creek almost as far east as Darrington, and each pleasant summer day draws hordes of fly fishermen to the North Fork.

Like every river, the North Fork has its list of "regulars," many of them concentrated in the cluster of cabins on the riverbank below Oso. And an impressive lot they are.

Bradner, now in his eightieth summer, still fishes the river from his cabin below Oso. Another regular is Ralph Wahl, whose beautiful photographs—many taken on the North Fork—grace the pages of his book, *Come Wade the River*, set to the text of Haig-Brown's *A River Never Sleeps*.

Walt Johnson is a frequent visitor, and it was on the North Fork that he developed the theory that summer steelhead take a fly out of habits learned in saltwater feeding. Johnson articulated his theory in a concise treatise published in *The Flyfisher* magazine, and has developed a series of fly patterns to simulate the food steelhead find at sea (the Red and Orange Shrimp and Prawn flies). His fly-dressing theory calls for a fly with a small head for "good entry" characteristics, and suggests that the color of a fly should be chosen in relation to the reflective qualities of the stream bottom.

One of the cabins on the Hell Hole is owned by Lew Bell, Everett attorney and third president of the Federation of Fly Fishermen. Other "Stilly" regulars have included Walt (Dub) Price, angling artist, and Wes Drain, whose beautiful Drain's 20 steelhead fly pattern was so named because it took a twenty-pounder.

Rick Miller, noted both for his bold wading and his intricate fly-fishing jewelry, is another regular, as is Dr. George Keough, inventor of the "epoxy weld" for attaching fly line to backing, and of other innovations. Frank Headrick, Don Ives and Al Knudson are other anglers of note whose casts often fall upon the waters of the North Fork.

Little more than fifty years have passed since Zane Grey found his way through the cedar thickets to the productive pools of Deer Creek, but in that relatively short length of time the North Fork of the Stillaguamish has enjoyed a history every bit as rich as that of the famous Eastern streams in their first half-century of angling. And while the tragedy of Deer Creek yet remains unsolved, the valley of the North Fork is still a pleasant, tranquil place, carpeted with small farms and thriving second growths of timber. In the spring it is a rich, soft green, fresh and stimulating in the cool, clear mornings, and in the fall it changes to a rusty orange and gold, fragrant with the scent of maple leaves and woodsmoke. The train still runs over the rusty track from Arlington to Darrington and back, and local residents say it is always late because the engineer likes to stop and fish the Fortson Hole. It is not the wilderness that the Indians knew, but it remains a quiet, peaceful spot, a side valley leading away from the freeways and the cities, ending sharply at the base of an impenetrable bulwark of mountains. The steelhead return faithfully to its pools, even though few of them still are born of the river, and the fly fishermen patrol its banks through the summer mornings, searching for the shadowy gray shapes lying in the deeper pools and runs.

Its history is short, as history goes, but there is promise of a long history yet to come. And if one's imagination is vivid, he may see in the long summer evenings the ghosts of Zane Grey and his companions, wading in the mouth of Deer Creek, casting with their awkward tackle, searching the dark, rippling water for bright steelhead back from the sea.

FALL

So the year is rushing to a close, and the shorter cycle of the day alerts all the creatures of the wild to do the things that must be done. It is a time of rapid change, the days suddenly colder, the leaves turning red like the sides of the homeward salmon, the first frosts leaving the meadows silver in the morning.

The lazy days of summer are quickly gone, and suddenly there is movement everywhere. Salmon are in the rivers, leaping and struggling with reckless urgency to find their spawning grounds; the cutthroat are close behind them, more subtle in their presence, resting in the shelter of snags and waiting to begin their feast on the loose salmon spawn. Summer steelhead still rest in the canyon pools, growing restless now as the time for spawning grows closer, and fall trout in the lowland lakes are active, fat and strong.

Fall offers such an abundance of opportunities to the angler that the choice of where to fish often is a difficult one. To spend a day searching for salmon or cutthroat might be to miss a spectacular rise of trout; a journey to a favorite lake is undertaken at the risk of missing a river at its best. Yet, if one must have a problem, this is a pleasant one to have, and the agonies of choosing are lessened by the knowledge that the fishing is likely to be good, no matter what the choice.

As the days pass, the last leaves die and fall into the rivers, sucked into the current to turn and flash beneath the surface. There is a cold, hard edge to the wind, and the rain comes in stinging bursts. The pace of death and life quickens perceptibly as nature hurries to complete its work before the dawn of winter and the death of the year.

The anglers feel this, too, glancing anxiously at the calendar, fishing hard from the mist of dawn to the gloom of dusk, fearful they will miss the last opportunities of the year. The corn and beet fields are dotted with the red jackets of hunters, working over bold dogs in search of the noble peasant, and ragged formations of migrating geese are silhouetted high against the clouds. There is a sense of approaching climax in the air, and it is a time of urgency and excitement, of color and movement, a time of fresh mornings and last hopes, a sudden final quickening of energy and life.

And when it finally is over, there will be time to remember; time to remember the triumphs and disappointments of the year, to recollect the first steelhead of winter, the first trout of spring, and all the satisfactions each season has brought. But of all the seasons, fall is my favorite, when the full design of the year finally stands revealed, when the senses seem at their very height from the stimulus of change, and when there is deep fulfillment for all who love the outdoors and seek their pleasure in it.

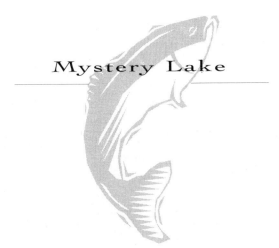

Mystery Lake

In geological terms, it was not a very spectacular event. Probably it would have caused only a minor wiggle on a modern seismograph.

Perhaps it was a great rain that caused it, or a sudden thaw after a hard winter, or even a small earthquake. But whatever the cause, it is easy to imagine how it looked: Slowly, ever so slowly, a part of the mountainside detached itself, a dull thunder shook the earth and there were sharp reports like pistol shots as smaller shards of rock split off and fell away. Moving faster now, the mass of rock began to topple into the canyon, gathering speed, throwing out a hail of great boulders and a rain of soil, splintering the timber in its path, sweeping everything before it.

With awesome force it plunged down the steep wall to the canyon floor, crushed and buried the little river running there, and rumbled on, climbing partway up the opposite slope before its speed and strength were spent. The earth slowly ceased trembling and was still, except for the occasional crash of an isolated straggling rock falling from the shattered mountainside, and the air was filled with dust and soil and spray from the murdered river.

Probably it was days before the last loose soil stopped slipping from the ravaged mountain and all the rock and splintered timber had been rolled or swept to a final resting place. And then the earth rested and set out to heal itself.

The river was damned, but still the water kept flowing down from the higher slopes and made a rising lake behind the mass of rock, soil and broken trees that shut off its passage to the sea. As the water rose, it began again to seek an outlet, probing with growing strength for chinks or weak spots in the dam.

At first there were none, but the water level crept gradually to the very top of the dam, spilled over it and dug channels through the loose soil, sweeping out the timber and the smaller rocks, eroding a path around the huge boulders that no small river could ever move, and in time the river's natural flow was restored. But still there remained a small lake behind the broken barrier, with the river flowing into its upper end, the current pressing almost imperceptibly through the lake, then passing out through what remained of the slide.

The winds carried seed to the shattered slope of the mountain, and alders and vine maples sprang up almost overnight. The alders grew in thick jungles, strangling one another until only the hardiest survived, and every autumn the soil was left richer with the fruit of their fallen leaves. A forest generation passed, and even the surviving patriarchs of

Her manner was intimidating, but I tried to sound lighthearted as I asked, "How's chances of fishing your pond?" I could see the glint of water flashing through the shade trees in back of the house.

"Wal, I dunno," she said, the canyons of her face growing deeper still. "We been havin' lots of trouble down there. Had to get the sheriff last week. Kids drinkin' beer. He run 'em off."

"I just want to fish, not drink," I said, shattering the image of fisherman everywhere.

She looked me up and down, as if deciding whether it would be necessary to call the sheriff again. But then she relented.

"Wal," she said, "I suppose it'd be OK. You kin put your boat in over there," and she gestured toward a stretch of pasture across the way.

I thanked her, returned to the Jeep and drove to the appointed spot, then unloaded the boat from its cartop rack. I lifted it awkwardly over a sagging barbed-wire fence that stood between me and the pond, then dragged it through the long grass to the shore, taking care to avoid the evidence of recent occupancy of the pasture.

The pond was small and narrow, perhaps a quarter of a mile long. Even though the sun was now high and the day was bright, it was mostly in shadow from the trees along both shores.

There were old alders, second-growth firs and cedar and even a few tall poplars on the side of the pond toward the house. A small stream entered the upper end of the pond and flowed out the other. The water was still and clear.

I assembled my rod, threaded the line through the guides and attached a fly to the leader, then pushed out from shore. In the shallows, the bottom was grown over thickly with weeds. I reached over the side of the boat, grabbed one by the stem and pulled it up to examine it. A dozen big freshwater

the canyon and it was not long before other men found it. Prohibition had ended, and two old rum-runners retired to one of the lakeshore cabins, drinking away the nights until they died there. Hunters came for the deer in their season, and a few venturesome fishermen found their way to the lake and caught the small trout they saw rising in the shallows. But of all those who came and went, only a very few discovered the thing that set the lake apart from many others like it.

Those observant few had seen what all the others had not: that in the long, dark shadows of the autumn afternoons, back among the tangled deadfalls near the shore, there came an occasional great swirl—far larger than the rises any small trout would make. To the very small fraternity of anglers who had discovered the secret of the lake, those rises had exciting meaning.

They were not the rises of small trout, but of steelhead; noble fish that had made their way back from the sea, up the swift cataracts of the lower river, over the aging remnants of the natural dam to rest in the still, sheltered waters of the lake. And there they would remain until the winter freshets rekindled their migratory urge and sent them struggling into the upper river to seek their spawning grounds.

The anglers who discovered the secret were fly fishermen, and they guarded the knowledge well. On weekday afternoons, when other visitors to the lake were few, the anglers would go there and cast their flies among the deadfalls where the steelhead lay. And there, in the silence and solitude of the mountain scene, many long and secret struggles were waged between fishermen and the fish that many anglers consider the noblest of them all.

Nearly forty years have passed, and all but a few of the old alders have died. A new stand of fir and spruce has grown up on the hillsides, the trees still young but lush and beautiful and merciful in the way they have restored the slopes. Most of the old anglers who once shared in the secret are gone, their casts falling on some uncharted water across the River Styx. But even after forty years, the lake remains unchanged, quiet and mysterious in its canyon, and the steelhead still return in the fall to rest up for the rigors of spawning.

The surviving old-timers who have fished there since the early days still guard the secret well, but they have chosen a few trusted members of a new generation of anglers to receive the knowledge on condition that they, too, keep it to themselves.

Still, for years there were rumors about the lake, fragmentary reports whispered around campfires about a Shangri-la in the mountains where steelhead were abundant and could be caught like trout. But the name of the lake never was mentioned, and when the rumors were passed back and forth in fishing camps and on river bars, it always was referred to only as the Mystery Lake.

Ralph Wahl is one of those who has fished the lake for thirty years or more, and it was Ralph who invited me to go there with him one September day. Aware that I was about to be let in on a cherished secret, I eagerly accepted the invitation.

After the long ferry ride and the rugged drive up the narrow, winding road leading to the canyon, it was dark when we arrived and we fell asleep to the sound of rain drumming steadily on the roof of Ralph's camper. When we awoke in the morning, the rain had ceased, but a dark, bulky overcast hung in the canyon and sheltered the tops of the surrounding hills. By the calendar it still was summer, but already the vine maples around the lake were bright with color, startling in the dull, gray light of the day.

A light breeze whispered along the canyon walls, shook the moisture from the forest limbs and sent gentle riffles moving on the dark, mysterious surface of the lake. Otherwise all was silent, except for the slow drip of yesterday's rain.

We carried Ralph's boat down to the water and loaded

our gear, then jointed up our rods. Ralph tied on a fly of fluorescent orange yarn, a pattern he always used in the lake because of its high visibility in the dark water. I put on a bright Skykomish Sunrise, thinking that it, too, could easily be seen.

Then, with Ralph at the oars, we set out to explore the lake. Ralph pushed the boat gently through the lightly riffled waters, giving me a tour of the lake, pointing out landmarks and the places that had produced fish for him and others in seasons past.

"Here's where Enos took a fish," he would say, "and Tommy Brayshaw got a good one there."

Water ousels hopped on the logs and a rusty-headed merganser went about its affairs with dignity. A flashy kingfisher winged overhead on its way to the hunt. Except for them, we were alone on the dark water.

Then we began to fish. Ralph maneuvered the boat expertly between a pair of deadfalls and held it there with the oars. "Put your fly next to the inside log," he advised, and I cast where he indicated. The fly sank slowly out of sight in the dark water, a tuft of bright bucktail and a splash of brilliant orange growing smaller and fainter until it passed from sight beneath the log. "Now retrieve," Ralph said.

I drew the fly back with slow, even pulls until something stopped it hard. "I've got one," I said.

Ralph quickly backed the boat away into open water. The fish followed obediently and I kept the pressure from it until we were away from the surrounding snags. Then I tightened on it and saw its sides flash silver as it turned.

It was a small steelhead and not a spectacular one. It struggled deeply, never jumping, and after a short fight I led it over Ralph's waiting net and he lifted it into the boat. It was a bright hen fish of about three pounds. "Just a baby," Ralph said. But it was tangible evidence that the lake still held its secret treasure.

We worked along the shoreline, casting in among the snags, and then moved into the outlet where the current was noticeable along the shore. We saw two steelhead in among the snags as we approached, and they moved cautiously as we drew near. We cast ahead of them, but neither would take.

Ralph guided the boat around the outlet, pointing out the likely spots and the underwater hazards that could snare a sunken fly. And then, suddenly, there was a great boil on the surface less than sixty feet away. I picked up the fly, false-cast once, and dropped it in the center of the spreading rings of water. On the first pull of the retrieve a fish struck with wild fury and the line burned my fingers as he took it away from me. Instantly the fish was away in a furious run, the line melting rapidly from the reel until suddenly it was gone and the yellow backing line was whistling out behind it.

The fish leaped twice, a magnificent bright steelhead, and then it was in among the snags along the shore and the wild throb of life at the end of the line was quickly gone.

The line went slack and I let out a long, shuddering breath. Less than ten seconds had elapsed from the first jolt of the strike to the loss of the fish, and Ralph still sat with the oars suspended above the water as they had been before the strike. There had been nothing either of us could do to check the violent run of the fish.

I started reeling in, and the line went taut again. But this time there was no life at the end of it, only the sullen, unyielding weight of a snag. And, as we found, there was more than a single snag, and we spent the next quarter-hour following the line where the fish had taken it, first around one deadfall and then another, until we came at last to one where the bright fly was stuck firmly in the rotting wood.

We fished then until it was lunchtime, taking turns rowing and casting, but saw no other fish. After lunch we worked our way down the shore toward the far end of the lake, then turned around and worked our way back again. Ralph probed every familiar spot, casting with great skill, dropping his fly within an inch of every likely resting place. But still there was nothing.

The day passed quickly, as fishing days always do, and now and then the clouds parted briefly to admit the sun, then closed up again, and the mottled light slowly faded as the afternoon died. Soon it would be time to go, but we decided to make one last swing through the area of the outlet. I took the oars and steered the boat carefully through the jumbled snags while Ralph searched the water with his fly. But there was no response.

Then Ralph took over the oars for the row back to shore, and I stood up to cast again. I had not much confidence that I would catch anything after the thorough and faultless way Ralph had covered the water without result. But on the third cast a steelhead appeared from behind a log and nailed the fly with jarring force.

Ralph saw the strike and yelled at me to keep the fish's head up. I put on all the strain I dared to keep the steelhead from diving back into the snags while Ralph rowed frantically for open water.

Luck was with us, and we kept the fish in check until the boat was drifting free in deep, unobstructed water. Then I began to play the fish, and it fought stubbornly in a series of strong, head-shaking runs, twisting and turning and struggling to free itself. But it was well hooked, and without the sanctuary of the logs it became helpless as it tired. Finally it turned slowly on its side and I steered it carefully to Ralph's waiting net.

It was a fine buck with a pale-rose shaft of color on its sides and a proud hook on its lower jaw, and it pulled Ralph's pocket scale down to the 6½-pound mark when we weighed it in the net.

I looked at the exhausted fish and thought of all the hazards it had overcome to return to this lost little lake in the mountains. It had been born in the spring floods above the lake and had spent its first summer there, evading the quick stabs of kingfishers and mergansers. It had survived the difficult journey down the white water of the lower river and its transition to the tide. Then it had gone to feed in some far unknown stretch of the Pacific, somehow surviving the deadly ocean predators that consumed hundreds of its brethren.

Finally instinct had summoned it back, calling it unerringly home across half the earth, through countless miles of strange and dangerous water, past the fatal commercial nets to the mouth of its river. And then it had thrown itself against all the weight of the falling water, struggling through the pools and fierce rapids of the lower river until at last it found a way through the debris of the ancient slide to the shelter of the lake.

And then, having met every stern test that nature could devise, it had fallen victim to my fly, and now its life was in my hands. Neither it nor its ancestors ever had known the concrete of a hatchery trough; it was wild and free, as wild as its native country before the coming of man. And it held the seeds of a future generation, strong seeds that surely would take its offspring safely on the same long, dangerous journey.

I slipped the fish gently back over the side of the boat and into the dark water, holding it carefully, moving it back and forth until its gills opened and closed again in a steady rhythm and I could feel its strength return. And then I watched it swim slowly away, its carmine-and-silver sides disappearing in the depths, on its way to join the other survivors of the journey.

And then we went home, deeply satisfied with the day.

Of course I have returned to the lake, and each time the steelhead were there, and I have waged other silent struggles, alone beneath the shadowed silence of the canyon walls. The landmarks that Ralph first showed me are familiar to me now, and I know them as well as the steelhead that seek their shelter. Still, there is always a strange excitement about this secret place, a feeling that perhaps there are other surprises yet undiscovered in its dark, mysterious waters. Other anglers still come and go without sensing there is anything more than casual observation admits, and the secret of the lake still is safe among those few who know it.

And it will remain safe with me, as Ralph knew it would when he gave it, until the day I am convinced that some brother angler will value it as much as I do. Then, and only then, will I take him there and show him what was created on that long-forgotten day when the mountainside fell and Mystery Lake was born.

The Plastic Flags Are Flying

It was one of those rare autumn days that would be more at home in May or June or in some other month when such gentle weather might be expected. I steered the Jeep over the crest of a hill and started down the rolling slope that led to the river valley on the other side.

Thick, heavy mist still hid the valley floor where the hills crowd together and the water rushes down through narrow stone walls. The sun, rising now over the massive bulwark of Mount Baker, glittered whitely off the floating layer of mist. The cornfields along the road had been freshly cut and somewhere in the rows of stubble pheasants were feeding. The apple trees still sagged under a burden of crimson fruit. There was a moist freshness to the air, and a feeling of change, and it was one of those days when the earth fairly sparkles and it seems very good to be alive.

I was on my way to test a tip about a fishing "hotspot," one of those secret places that anglers whisper about to trusted friends who have sworn oaths not to reveal them. The friend who had told me about this place had spoken of brook trout so large that I was faintly incredulous, but the earnestness of his manner had compelled me to see for myself if it was really true.

He had made a special point of advising me that I should ask the owner of the property for permission to fish in his hidden waters. The owner's careful control of the access, he explained, was what preserved the fishing in his private pond.

Following the directions he had given me, I found the place without difficulty and drove into the yard in front of a tall, rambling, old white house.

Several generations of clothing hung from a long clothesline. Five children ran into the house and three different ones came out the other side. What I had mistaken for a boulder in the yard got up and waddled away majestically, a huge sow grown fat on whatever sows eat. A fierce-looking billy goat bleated gravely at me, and I was glad to see he was tethered by a strong chain. The grass in the yard was worn thin by the traffic of children and animals, and that and the weather-beaten paint on the house gave the place a comfortable, lived-in look, like an old fishing jacket.

A very large woman came out of the house and eyed me suspiciously. She frowned, and I sensed it was a permanent condition with her: The fat had grown up around the lines in her face and made it so. Her hair was tight coils of grizzled gray, and she wore a flowered dress and an Aunt Jemima apron. She put her meaty hands upon her broad hips and took a defiant stance like a professional linebacker.

Her manner was intimidating, but I tried to sound lighthearted as I asked, "How's chances of fishing your pond?" I could see the glint of water flashing through the shade trees in back of the house.

"Wal, I dunno," she said, the canyons of her face growing deeper still. "We been havin' lots of trouble down there. Had to get the sheriff last week. Kids drinkin' beer. He run 'em off."

"I just want to fish, not drink," I said, shattering the image of fisherman everywhere.

She looked me up and down, as if deciding whether it would be necessary to call the sheriff again. But then she relented.

"Wal," she said, "I suppose it'd be OK. You kin put your boat in over there," and she gestured toward a stretch of pasture across the way.

I thanked her, returned to the Jeep and drove to the appointed spot, then unloaded the boat from its cartop rack. I lifted it awkwardly over a sagging barbed-wire fence that stood between me and the pond, then dragged it through the long grass to the shore, taking care to avoid the evidence of recent occupancy of the pasture.

The pond was small and narrow, perhaps a quarter of a mile long. Even though the sun was now high and the day was bright, it was mostly in shadow from the trees along both shores.

There were old alders, second-growth firs and cedar and even a few tall poplars on the side of the pond toward the house. A small stream entered the upper end of the pond and flowed out the other. The water was still and clear.

I assembled my rod, threaded the line through the guides and attached a fly to the leader, then pushed out from shore. In the shallows, the bottom was grown over thickly with weeds. I reached over the side of the boat, grabbed one by the stem and pulled it up to examine it. A dozen big freshwater shrimp fell wiggling into my hand. That was a surprise; I had not expected to find shrimp in this place. Perhaps my friend had not been exaggerating; an abundance of shrimp would surely grow large fish.

I let the boat drift farther out into the pond and made my first cast. The little dry fly settled gently on the surface and rode lightly on its hackles. There was a quick rise and I struck instantly.

There was hardly any resistance, and then I saw the flash of a tiny fish on the end of my line. I stripped in quickly, hoping to release the little fish without injury. Another surprise; it was not a trout, but a fingerling salmon.

I remembered then that the creek flowing through the pond entered a large river farther downstream, a river with a good run of coho salmon. Obviously some of them spawned in this tributary, and their offspring used the little pond as a nursery area, feeding and growing until they were of an age to begin their migration toward the sea. And as I looked around, I saw other tiny dimples as the fingerlings rose to feed upon small insects hatching on the surface.

But where were the trout? The water was extraordinarily clear and the bottom features stood out clearly for fifty feet around. But nowhere in among the weeds or drowned deadfalls did I see anything but salmon fry. I began to row slowly toward the other end of the pond, scanning the water as I went, hoping for a glimpse of something bigger.

Then a sudden movement caught my eye, close in. I looked down upon the back of a huge trout lying deep in the weeds. The familiar vermiculations of the Eastern brook trout were on its back and the ivory-edged fins confirmed the identification. I watched, enthralled, as the great fish balanced gently on its fins, now and then moving quickly to swallow some small thing I could not see. It was one of the biggest brook trout I had ever seen.

I eased the boat away as gently and quietly as possible,

then cast my fly over the trout's station. In the clear water, the thin leader appeared as large and heavy as a telephone cable. The trout, which had seen it all before, moved off slowly and, I thought, disdainfully.

But soon I found others, schools of them, including some even larger than the first trout I had seen. They moved together slowly, up and down the upstream end of the pond, weaving in and out among the weeds, holding now and then in the shadows of the deadfalls, seemingly unconcerned about my presence which was inescapably visible to them.

I tried for them in every way I knew. Soon concluding that they were too shy and sophisticated to rise to a dry fly, I tried them with nymph and shrimp imitations and then finally with the bright attractor patterns which brook trout have been known to take. I tried them with floating lines and sinking lines, with fast retrieve and slow, and with the smallest, lightest tippet that I had. Most often they did not respond at all, and when they did respond it was only to move away slowly, unhurriedly.

As the day wore on, insects began to hatch; chironomids first, then scattered mayflies, then even a few big, awkward sedges. And this was in October: Think what hatches must come here in the spring! With such an abundance of feed, there was little wonder that the trout were slow to take an artificial.

Finally I accepted defeat, and began to row back to the pasture without having had so much as a single strike. Too much natural feed, I thought; or perhaps it was the weather, which obviously was too good to catch fish. But no problem. The season is nearly over, but few others know about this place and next year I'll come back on a cloudy day, or when it's raining, and catch the blazes out of them.

And I did go back the next year; and all along the road there were signs advertising "Excalibur Estates," or some such, and when I reached what I had thought was my secret place there was a small A-frame cabin where I had launched my boat the year before. On it was a sign that said "Sales Office" and everywhere about there were bright plastic flags strung from the few remaining trees, flapping noisily in the wind.

The sow and the billy goat and the clothing on the line and the fat woman and the children were gone. Bulldozers had been there and had done their work around the tiny, fragile pond. Most of the trees were gone, and the stumps and slash had been raked up into smoldering piles. Survey stakes marked with plastic ribbons denoted the boundaries of postage-stamp-sized lots all around the pond. The pond itself stood naked to the sun, and the water near the shoreline was turbid with mud from the bulldozers.

Suddenly I felt very sad, and in my mind I cried for the land. The life-chain that had made the pond what it was had been irreparably broken. No longer would the earth hold the rain and release it slowly to the pond, enriched with the nutrients of the soil. No longer would the shadows of the trees keep the waters cool and protected. No longer would the water be clear and bright. The hatches still would come, but not in their former volume because now the silt would kill the eggs and larvae. Even as shy as they had been, the big trout inevitably would finally be caught, and there would be none to replace them. The salmon fry no longer would have a rich food source to prepare them for their hazardous journey. The charm that had been there in October had gone up in the smoke of burning slash in May.

All this, I thought, so that some developer can realize a small dream of short-term profit. And our children never will know what they have missed.

It was, I suppose, a small loss compared with the vastness of the country. But it was not singular; the plastic flags are flying everywhere, on countless streams and lakes, in countless forests and meadows. Each day sees fewer waters left, fewer places where trout can grow, where salmon can rest or wildlife come to feed; fewer places where man can go to restore his spirit.

October came again. The apples grew ripe and heavy on the limbs, the corn was harvested from the fields, the mist was thick again upon the meadows. But in a small way, the earth seemed a poorer place.

Duwamish Episode

Raindrops chased each other down the windowpane, and a cold wind shook drops from the old cherry tree outside the house. Even though it was October, my favorite month to fish, the day seemed so inhospitable that I felt reluctant to go out into it. Perhaps it would be a better day to light a big fire in the fireplace and set up a fly-tying vise next to it and spend the day there in hopes of better weather later.

That was my frame of mind when the phone rang. Ward McClure was at the other end, calling from his place of work at the Boeing plant on the Duwamish River.

"Are you going fishing today?" he asked.

"I'd just about made up my mind not to," I said. "It looks pretty crummy outside."

"Well, I thought I'd tell you that the river here is full of salmon. They're jumping everywhere. I'm sure you could take one on a fly."

The fireside was forgotten, and so was the tying vise. Here was a chance I had been waiting for: a chance to cast to an active school of coho, to hook one on the fly.

Of all the Pacific salmon, the coho responds to a fly more readily than any other species. But still it is a reluctant taker compared with the Atlantic salmon or the steelhead. Its feeding is done at sea, and it is hard to find there, harder still to take on a cast fly.

Nearly all the fly-caught salmon are taken by trolling flies from boats, a method I do not prefer. By the time they come to the river mouths, the salmon have ceased feeding and are even more difficult to catch. But there, at least, they are easily found, and an angler can cast to them individually and hope that perhaps one in a hundred will respond.

The boat already was on top of the truck, and it was only a short drive from my home to the river. The Duwamish is a crowded, ugly river, flowing through the heart of Seattle's industrial district. It has been abused in countless ways. From its beginning as the Green River in the Cascade foothills it flows down into a reservoir created by a dam and serves as the water supply for the city of Tacoma. The remaining water spills through the dam and runs down a spectacular gorge into the upper reaches of the broad Green River Valley. Here it is crossed by winding county roads, its banks dotted by neat dairy cattle and berry farms. In its middle reaches it flows by the valley cities, Kent and Auburn, where levees and ripraps have been built along its banks. Runoff from a thousand asphalt parking lots pours into it, and in its lower reach, where it is called the Duwamish, it carries down a weight of refuse from the mills and factories that line its shores.

Freighters and barges move upstream from its mouth at Elliott Bay, and freeways and power lines run alongside. A big shipyard stands on an artificial island at its mouth.

Still, despite all this, the river carries large runs of salmon and steelhead, most of them running back to upstream hatcheries. Perhaps they are no longer native fish, but after their years at sea they enter the river strong and bright and they bring anglers to the river in nearly every month of the year.

Finding a place where the river was not walled off by a factory was not easy, but after some searching I found one. Once a house had stood there, before the factories came, but it had long since been vacant and now half of it had burned. Behind it was a sharply sloping bank, covered with mud and scum from the river and the tide which ran up well above the spot.

I eased the truck up to the bank and slid the boat down to the water. Out in the broad river I could see the splash of salmon heading upstream. Huge trucks roared by on the freeway behind me and a passenger jet winged overhead, shaking the earth with artificial thunder. A diesel switcher moved a rattling line of freightcars somewhere near and the place reverberated with the din of the city. It seemed a very strange place to cast a fly for salmon, and I wondered idly how I would get out of the way if a big freighter came steaming down the river.

Directly across from my launching point was the Boeing plant, and Ward came out on the antenna deck and waved as I launched the boat. He could not shout above the great industrial roar all around us, but he pointed toward the far side of the river where most of the salmon seemed to be rolling and jumping.

I started rowing for the spot, and found my boat in the grasp of contending waters. The tide was flooding in fast, lapping at the base of old pilings near the shore, meeting the

strong current of the river, breaking into a changing series of
short rips and eddies. The river was too strong and deep for me
to anchor in the center of the flow, so I backtracked to the
shelter of a small point of land. From there it would be a long
cast to where the fish were showing, but I had brought a sturdy
nine-foot rod, the largest in my arsenal, and with it I was sure
I could reach the fish. Some of them were coming in close to
the boat, but most were farther out; some of them showed
color as they rolled, but most were still silver-bright. Perhaps
they would not be as strong as they were in their prime at sea,
but I was sure they would give me as much as I could handle.
There were fish of all sizes, from little jacks of less than twenty
inches to bigger brutes of fifteen pounds or better.

I had no precedent for this type of fishing, no experience
to draw from. Which would be in order, a floating line or a
sinker? Fast retrieve or slow? A small fly or a large one? I
would have to experiment to find out.

I started with a floating line, because that is what is used
by the trollers who fish at sea. I waited for a fish to roll and
saw one, then cast with a hard double-haul, dropped the fly
ahead of it and began to retrieve. There was no response. For
half an hour I cast into the ascending school with the floating
line, varying the retrieve from fast to slow with erratic stages
in between. Nothing.

Perhaps a sinking line was needed. I made the change,
and resumed casting, letting the line sink at first, varying the
retrieve again. The fish went by me in a steady march, but
none of them acknowledged the presence of my fly.

Perhaps it was the fly itself. I had tried half a dozen
patterns, and finally I turned again to my fly box, choosing a
small fly with a silver body and a polar wing with a touch of
peacock sword topping. The fly seemed too small to interest
fish of such size, and even if it did, the hook seemed too small
to hold them. But nothing else had worked, so I thought I
might as well try it.

A large fish rolled and I led it with the cast and began a fast retrieve. Suddenly the fish was there, its mouth opened and then closed around the fly. I struck hard and the fish rose out of the water, a great flash of blue and silver, ten pounds anyway. Then it gave its broad head a single, vicious shake and the eight-pound-test leader quickly parted.

My hands were shaking so that it was difficult to tie on the new tippet and another fly of the same pattern. The rhythm of casting was a calming influence, however, and soon I settled down again. Then, a few casts later, another broad silver gleam appeared behind the fly and took it suddenly. This time the small hook came away as soon as I tried to set it.

The fast retrieve seemed to be the answer, and as the afternoon wore on and the tide flooded toward its height I hooked three other salmon, but in every case the hook pulled out, too small and light to penetrate the heavy gristle of the salmon's jaw. I switched back to larger patterns and worked them with the same retrieve, but the fish seemed to have an interest only in the small fly with the polar wing, and so eventually I tied it on again.

Suddenly, as I was near the end of the retrieve of a long cast, a big salmon came out from under the boat and fell on the fly not ten feet away. Without pausing, he continued his headlong upstream rush with irresistible strength; the heavy reel squealed as line shot out; then the drag jammed, the line stretched and the leader popped and came flying back at me.

I opened the reel and doused it with a fresh coat of oil, then tested it. It seemed to be all right, so I repaired the broken leader and reached for the last of the three polar-wing patterns I had brought. The tide had nearly reached its maximum and sporadic rain still fell. The afternoon was nearly spent, and I knew that once the tide crested the salmon would stop coming.

Fish still were rolling, however, and I chose a large one and made my cast. The fish turned to follow the retrieve and took the fly midway to the boat. I struck hard and felt solid contact. The fish turned and ran far across stream toward the opposite bank, taking great, screaming gulps of line from the reel. This time the reel did not freeze, and the fish still was on at the end of its run. Then it leaped high out of the water, flashing brilliant silver through the rain. I felt its strong, heavy weight at the end of the line, and began to reel it slowly as it worked its way back toward me. Then it turned and ran again, and at the end of the run came a second jump, the big fish turning completely over in the air. And as it did so, the tiny fly came away again, and there was only the drag of the current on my line.

After that, there were no more strikes, and in a few minutes there were no more salmon to be seen rolling in the current. The tide had reached its peak and was ebbing out, leaving a wet ring around the pilings. The broad current of the river flowed smoothly past, its surface now unbroken, no evidence that fish ever had been there at all. The jets still thundered overhead, their running lights now brilliant in the wet gloom. Traffic roared by on the freeway in a confusing blaze of light and noise. I rowed back toward the burned house.

I had hooked seven big salmon, and lost them all. There had been some moments of wild excitement, for which I was grateful, but there was still the disappointment of not having landed a single fish. But now, at least, I had the experience, the precedent on which to draw on future occasions. And I was confident that with the same fly on a larger hook, I would not fail the next time.

I spent the evening tying flies, and went back the next afternoon on the rising tide. But it had rained hard all through the night and most of the day, and the runoff from the farms and parking lots of the upper valley had brought the river up and muddied it with silt. The salmon were there again, rolling out in the current, but the water was so dirty they could not see my fly.

The rain went on for several days, and by the time the river had returned to normal flow the salmon run was over. Of course I tried again the next year, in the Duwamish and in other spots. But never again have I found the salmon in such a taking mood, never again have they come so willfully for my fly with all the strength born of the sea. Perhaps there was some subtle thing I did that day that escapes me now, something that means all the difference between failure and success. If so, I can't remember what it might have been. But I will always remember that afternoon of wild excitement in the rain, hooking great salmon while the sounds of the city echoed all around me. And one day, I know, the salmon will come again as they did then.

A Lady Named Lenice

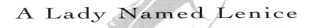

October morning.

The tires of the truck made a swishing sound on the pavement, still wet from the morning's rain. The peaks surrounding the mountain pass already were white with early snow. Winter had come early to the timberline country, but everywhere else fall still was in its glory.

The trip through the mountains to the Columbia Basin always is an interesting one, the country moving quickly past like a colored mural of changing shapes and images. In few other places can so much change be seen in so short a distance. There is the western slope with its thick fir forests drenched in rain, its old alders heavy with hanging moss; there is the mountain pass, its tangled peaks white with snow above the thick stands of alpine fir and spruce; and then there is the eastern slope, with the fir giving way quickly to the pine, and the golden aspens shaking themselves in the creek bottoms. The forest gives way to rolling hills of amber grass, and as the highway begins the last, long plunge to the Columbia River Gorge, the grass gives way to sage and dry coulees.

The Columbia is no longer a river where the highway crosses it; it is a vast, stillwater lake, its flow choked by the dam visible downstream from the windbattered bridge. From the bridge it is but a short drive south to the point where muddy Crab Creek flows out of its canyon and loses itself in the remnants of the river.

A decade ago, Crab Creek was a lonely, desolate place. The great winds that sweep up the Columbia River Gorge turn sharply into the canyon and blow along its length, whipping cyclones of sand and tumbleweeds before them. It was a dry, unfriendly place, frequented by jackrabbits, rattlesnakes and coyotes. A few isolated farms stood at its eastern end, and cattle roamed through the dead coulees, searching for sparse bunchgrass among the sage. The sluggish creek ran muddy in all seasons, with carp splashing in its shallows, and there was no reason for a trout fisherman to venture there.

But then the canyon changed. Upland farmers irrigated their lands with water from the river's reservoirs; the water flowed from the fields, seeking a way back to the river, seeping into the sandy soil. It surfaced again in the dry coulees at the bottom of the canyon, breaking through the soil in cool springs, flowing down the canyon wall in little streams. It filled a coulee and made a lake, spilled over its end and ran deeper into the canyon, forming a second lake. The second lake filled and again the water sought an outlet, flowing farther down, forming another lake and still another. And in the short space of a few years, the dead, dry canyon bottom was covered by the waters of four sparkling lakes.

The merciless rays of the summer sun reached into their depths and brought life out of them. Aquatic insects found a haven in the drowned sage, and enormous numbers of damselflies, dragonflies, chironomids and mayflies hatched in the lakes. Shrimp found their way into them and snails found the waters rich and hospitable. Rainbow trout were stocked and grew quickly to enormous size and weight on the great abundance of food.

The oldest lake, and the first to contain fish, was named Lenice, and it was Lenice where Enos Bradner and I were headed on this October day. We drove down the last stretch of gravel road to the cleared spot which was as far as vehicles could go. From there it was a quarter-mile trail through the desert rock and sand to the lakeshore.

Lenice is a large lake, and though it is possible to fish successfully from shore, it is easier to fish from a boat. The quarter-mile hike keeps many anglers from trying this, but others have rigged ingenious sets of wheels to carry their boats into the lake. Brad's boat already was there, his friends having carried it in earlier and left it padlocked to a fence post. I mounted my own boat on the set of wheels I had brought with me and we set out across the desert for the lake, invisible from the road.

Lenice is more than just an exciting place to fish. It also is the scene of a research program which, it is hoped, will lead to better fishing there and in many other waters.

When the lake was opened to fishing, the rich productivity of its waters was recognized by the Washington Game Department and it was restricted to "quality" fishing. Only artificial lures with barbless hooks were allowed; bait was outlawed and the limit was reduced to three fish a day over twelve inches. In the first two years, the rainbow trout in the lake grew quickly, some of them reaching weights of five pounds or more. With the great source of feed in the lake, they should have grown much larger, but few, if any, did. Instead, they reached sexual maturity at the age of two years or a little more, and most of them died.

To the anglers who fished the lake, this was no real surprise; they had come to expect it from their experiences in other lakes. The reason is that the rainbow trout now stocked by nearly all the Western states is far removed from the wild rainbow that was found by the first settlers. Population growth and the advent of "put-and-take" fishing that accompanied it led management officials to try to develop fast-breeding strains of rainbow trout so that new crops for stocking could be raised in as little time as possible. Those trout which matured at the earliest age were selected for brood stock in the hatcheries. The final, inevitable result was a strain of rainbow trout that spawned at the age of two years or even less.

This was a desirable goal from the standpoint of "put-and-take" management, where it makes good economic sense to have such fish. But these same fish were stocked in the "quality" lakes, where the intent of management was to produce fewer, larger fish. The trout grew rapidly in these lakes, but because of their genetic history they became sexually mature before they had lived long enough to grow to real trophy size. Few of them survived the effects of sexual maturation to grow larger.

Cognizant of this trend, the members of the Washington Fly Fishing Club proposed the Lenice Lake experiment. Financing the program themselves, and with the cooperation of the University of Washington Cooperative Fisheries Research Unit and the Department of Game, they proposed the following: Lenice Lake should be stocked each year with trout from the short-lived hatchery strain and an equal number of wild trout with a genetic history of longevity. Then, for a five-year period, the population would be monitored by creel censuses and netting and tagging operations to see which strain of fish lived longer and grew larger.

A search was made for a strain of wild trout, and finally eggs from the Kamloops trout in Pennask Lake, British Columbia, were obtained. These Kamloops trout spawn at an average age of four years, and this, according to the theory behind the experiment, would give them at least two years more growth than the hatchery fish.

The experiment now is in its third year, and the first plant of Kamloops trout is beginning to reach large size. Two years of work remain before any conclusions can be drawn, but in the meantime Lenice Lake has provided some of the most memorable fishing ever seen in the Northwest.

I rolled my boat down the last sandy grade to the lakeshore and Brad and I began to rig up for the fishing day ahead. I had been there only two weeks previously and had enjoyed one of the finest days in my memory. Anchored in the shallow west end of the lake, I had landed seven fish consecutively, each of them over four pounds, each of them desperately strong. All of them had run far into the backing, and each alone would have made my day on some other lake. An eighth fish of a size at least equal to all the rest had run my line around a submerged sagebrush plant and broken the leader. And so I had expectations of another wonderful day as we pushed our boats away from the shore and started rowing for the same place at the western end.

It was a typical fall day in the Columbia Basin. A solid, high overcast hid the sun and a changing breeze chased riffles across the water. The great hatches of spring were long gone, but a second generation of damselfly and dragonfly nymphs was active in the water. Coots clucked and bobbed in the shallows and the cattails were alive with the raucous calls of yellow-headed blackbirds. A marsh hawk glided on motionless wings over the swampy ground at the end of the lake.

We anchored our boats in the shallows and began to probe among the weeds and sunken brush with sinking flies. There was little surface activity, but occasionally we would be startled by the sound of a fierce, heavy rise from a large fish feeding. It became quickly obvious that there would be no fast fishing as there had been two weeks before; the trout were more cautious now, having been fished heavily since the opening of the fall season, and the algae bloom that had been on the lake earlier was gone, the water was clear, and no doubt the trout were more wary because of this.

Still, it was not long before I felt a hard, vicious strike, and a trout ran well with my fly, leaping high and tumbling at the end of its long run. It was a strong fish, and I coaxed the tackle to its limit to keep it from the thick weeds that grew within inches of the surface in many spots around. There was a satisfying feel to the plunging rod that signaled a heavy fish, and it fought stubbornly, showing itself in silver glimpses as it twisted and drove vainly to reach the bottom. Eventually it tired, and I led it to the net. I weighed it quickly in the net and it pulled the spring balance down nearly to the five-pound mark; a good start for the day, I thought. And as I twisted the fly free from its jaw, I saw where it had been hooked at least three times before. A good example of the quality concept: at least three anglers had enjoyed sport with this prime fish before I had; with luck, others would do so after I released it.

But after that the fishing was very slow for me. I caught and released a couple of scrappy smaller fish, but as the afternoon wore on nothing more moved to my fly.

Brad, meanwhile, had maneuvered his boat into a shallow pocket inshore of a small island, and there he found a school of large fish lying in among the weeds. He took three or four in rapid-fire order, setting quickly against the solid strikes, steering them masterfully through the weeds, bringing them to the net and releasing them. The old man was in his element, as excited as a boy, and I admired the enthusiasm that he could still feel after so many fish on so many waters in his long, illustrious life.

After that there was no action for either of us for a long while. The overcast grew darker with approaching twilight; soon it would be time to go, and I had taken only the one good fish.

The boat was drifting on a soft breeze that was pushing it gently toward the line of cattails that grew along the shore, where the coots still played noisily. I cast in front of the drifting craft, searching the water in a semicircle, hoping for one more good fish to end the day. And suddenly it was there, a hard strike followed by the sight of a big rainbow coming out in an arching leap, returning to the water with a heavy splash.

"Sounds like a big one," Brad's voice said across the water.

"It is," I said, and held on as the trout ran far along the edge of the cattails and jumped again. The wind quickened a little and began to push the boat faster toward the shore. There would be no chance to land the fish before the wind carried the boat into the cattails; somehow I had to stop its progress. Trying to keep the line taut with the rod in one hand, I worked an oar with the other, backing water, praying that the fish would not find a handy sagebrush plant and foul the leader. I gained a few feet and used both hands to play the fish, now slugging it out with shakes of its heavy head. Then the wind gained the upper hand again, and it was back to one hand on the rod and one hand on the oar until once again I had room to play the fish.

In that awkward way I fought the fish until its rushes grew shorter and it came obediently as I reeled in the last line until the leader knot was up to the tip-top of the rod. Then the wind was pushing on the boat again, carrying it toward the threatening line of cattails; quickly, I stabbed at the fish with the net. The mesh closed around it and I lifted it, dripping and squirming, from the lake. It was no longer than the big fish I had caught earlier, but it was immensely broad and thick. On the pocket scale it weighed more than five pounds, the largest trout I ever had taken in Lenice, and somehow it made the trip out easier as I wrestled the heavy boat up the sandy grade.

The fierce winds still blow up Crab Creek Canyon, and when they blow no trout fisherman goes there. It is still good country for jackrabbits, rattlesnakes and coyotes, and the cattle still graze on the dry hillsides. But now the chain of lakes at the bottom of the canyon is something of a mecca for Northwest anglers, and they come on the calm days to fish for the big rainbows that lurk among the sunken sage. The Kamloops trout are growing large and strong and hold the promise that in future years a five-pounder may no longer be unusual. Outwardly, the canyon still appears a foreboding place, but those anglers who are willing to challenge the heat and the barren, broken country will find Lenice a lake with rich rewards, and exciting promise for the future.

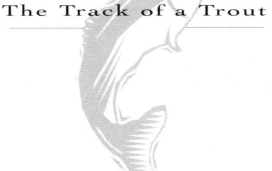

The Track of a Trout

The boat seemed suspended over a black abyss populated with the ghosts of fishes moving quickly in thrusts of pale, milky light. The landmarks of the estuary had long since been lost in the approach of night, and now there was no other light at all except the far twinkle of lamps in a small town miles distant across the dark water. There was no sound except for the persistent, eerie echo that came to me through a pair of earphones from a sonic tag planted in the belly of a sea-run cutthroat trout.

It seems there ought to be a simple key to the behavior of the sea-run cutthroat, some single explanation that would lead to understanding of its habits and movements. But perhaps that is a forelorn hope. Anglers, being human, think more or less in logical patterns, and they seem to expect the same of fish. But there is no reason to believe that fish are capable of any sort of logic, and so the search to find some rational explanation for their movements probably is doomed in advance to failure. Yet fishermen still search, and perhaps it is the fun of searching that keeps them going.

It was as a part of this search that I found myself at Dewatto estuary on this dark, overcast night, listening to the pulse from a trout hidden from sight but not from sound.

Dewatto is a bay in Hood Canal, a deep cut carved by the Dewatto River which flows into it. The name is a corruption of the Indian word *Du-a-ta*, which meant "the place where sprites come out of the ground." On this evening it seemed an appropriate name as we watched the silent, phosphorescent wakes left by countless fish moving through the plankton of the estuary. It was easy to believe how these strange, glowing shapes in the sea had led the Indians to imagine ghosts emerging from the dark waters to stalk through the forests that grow down to the water's edge.

The chain of events that had taken us to Dewatto had begun months before in a conversation among cutthroat-fishing enthusiasts in the Washington Fly Fishing Club. Cutthroat traditionally are caught on the rising tide, and few anglers can recall having seen them at low water. The question, debated for years, was where do the cutthroat go during low water, and why?

The members decided to pool their money to buy some sonic tags and track the movements of cutthroat. The money was quickly raised and more than thirty members volunteered to take part in the experiment. Battery-powered tags were purchased, one emitting a fast-pulsed sound signal and the other a slower pulse. Tracking gear was borrowed from a government agency, and on the appointed weekend the club members flocked to Dewatto with campers, trailers and boats to begin the experiment.

Dewatto had been chosen because it is well sheltered from the southwesters which regularly sweep the open waters of the canal, and because it was a place where anglers had taken cutthroat regularly on the fly. The plan was to use a beach seine to capture fish on Friday evening, then plant the sonic tags in the two largest fish and track them around the clock through Monday. But at first the beach seines yielded nothing, and it was Saturday morning before a club member succeeded in taking a cutthroat on the fly. The fish was partly anesthetized and the capsule-shaped tag worked down its gullet and into its stomach before it was returned to the estuary.

Later in the day, the seine finally turned up a second fish, a husky nineteen-incher, and the second tag was planted. And then the club members began following the movements of the fish, using boats to trail the telltale echoes and plotting the positions of the trout on charts of the estuary.

It was nearly dark on Sunday when I arrived for my "shift." Most of the members had gone home by then and the few of us remaining gathered in a camper to draw up a schedule for the night. At ten o'clock I climbed into a boat with Curt Jacobs and he took the oars to steer us gingerly out into the dark estuary. Each stroke of the oars set the water afire with pale, shifting waves of phosphorescent light, with bright, gleaming sparks here and there among them.

As we moved past a row of old pilings to the deeper water of the estuary, we began to see the tracks of countless small fish, glowing with ghostly flame as they darted away. Occasionally, a larger fish—perhaps a salmon—would swim by, and we could measure its length in light. Curt struck his foot against the side of the aluminum boat and the water exploded with light as a thousand fish fled the sound like Roman candles in the fog.

I donned the earphones and checked the listening gear, which consisted of a cone-shaped hydrophone mounted on a metal shaft, with wires leading to an amplifier and then to the earphones. By dipping the hydrophone in the water and turning it until the sound signal reached its peak it was possible to take a bearing on the direction of the sound. Then the boat would be moved to another location to take another bearing so that a fix on the fish could be obtained by triangulation and noted on the chart.

I thrust the hydrophone over the side and soon picked up the faint, chirping signal from one of the fish. We followed the sound, using flashlights to spot landmarks on the shore to plot our position, and got a fix on the trout in shallow water near the mouth of the river. Then Curt started the motor on the stern and we moved to the mouth of the estuary where the other fish had last been pinpointed, leaving a trail of phosphorescent fire in our wake.

A faint breeze stirred the water at the estuary's mouth and tiny wavelets slapped against the sides of the boat. Occasionally, out in the darkness, we could hear the heavy splash of a leaping salmon. We quickly picked up the signal from the second fish and plotted its position, which had changed little from the last plot.

I looked at my wristwatch and was surprised to find that an hour had passed. Curt started the motor again and we headed back toward the camp, with Curt steering and I in the bow with a flashlight to search for pilings and deadheads in our path. Back at camp, Curt headed for a sleeping bag in the back of his truck and I roused Harry Ludwig from his. For the next hour Harry and I tracked the fish, which had moved little, and then I turned in for a few hours' sleep while Harry woke Dick Thompson to continue tracking.

At five o'clock I got up to join Harry for another tracking session. The tide had run far out, and with our flashlights and lanterns we could see that most of the estuary was bare mudflat with little more than the river running through it. As we shined our lights across the river to the far bank, two pairs of glowing eyes stared back at us—perhaps raccoons, or even bears, that had come down from the woods.

The lower water made it difficult to maneuver the boat, and the last watch had lost track of both fish. This was the crucial test: to find where the cutthroat had gone at extreme low water. So far we had no idea where they were.

Harry and I made our way out through the sticky mud to the small, water-filled channel where the last tracking crew had left the boat. We pushed off into the shallow water, less than three feet deep and clogged with heavy mats of eelgrass. There was nowhere to go but downstream; upstream it was too shallow for the boat.

"I've got a hunch," I told Harry. "Before we go anywhere, let's take a sounding right here." We dipped the hydrophone into the shallow water and the grass, and immediately there came a strong signal. With a little maneuvering we determined that one of the cutthroat was almost directly beneath the boat, holding in the protection of the thick grass.

Having noted the fish's position on the chart, we slowly worked our way downstream, shining lights over the side to keep from running aground on the mudbanks. As we got closer to the mouth of the estuary, the water deepened and the flashlights caught patches of gravel showing through the mud, and soon we were in the open water of the canal. Using the motor, we cruised back and forth until we picked up a signal from the second fish and found it holding close to shore off the north headland at the estuary's mouth.

We plotted the position of the fish and then drifted, talking and drinking coffee from our vacuum bottles, watching the phosphorescent display. After a while we took a second sounding and found that the fish now was on the move. The tide was changing, imperceptibly to us but not to the trout, and we followed the fish as it began to move rapidly into the estuary toward the mouth of the stream. For perhaps a quarter of a mile we followed and then took a final fix of its position as it became time for us to wake up the next watch.

I crawled back in my sleeping bag and slept until after it was light, then fixed a breakfast and rejoined the tracking effort. The tide was high now, but the relative positions of the two fish had not changed much. One was resting under a log close to shore, well up in the estuary and not far from the channel where we had found it at low water. The other trout still was at the mouth of the estuary, moving occasionally, but not far.

We combined fishing with tracking through the day, casting in the likely spots and breaking every half hour or so to plot the positions of the tagged fish. Through the morning and afternoon they hardly moved. I took two trout on the fly, one with a stomach full of sticklebacks and the other filled with fir needles, maple seeds and bits of leaf, indicating it had spent some time in fresh water upstream.

Both fish were bright-silver, typical of cutthroat in salt water, and both were covered with sea lice, copepods that attach themselves to the backs and bellies of trout.

At four o'clock I quit fishing to make a final plot on the two fish. The first still was content under its log, but the second had moved, and at first I could not pick up its signal. Steering the boat back and forth across the mouth of the estuary, I finally picked up a faint signal and followed it until I found the fish, a mile out in deep water and still moving. After that, we packed our gear and set out for home.

And so the experiment was at an end, and it was time to evaluate what we had learned. Somewhat to our disappointment, but not necessarily to our surprise, the plots revealed little discernible pattern to the movements of the trout other than a general tendency to swim in with the flood tide and out with the ebb. And so our search for some common denominator to the behavior of the nomadic cutthroat was, in this case at least, largely unsuccessful.

Still, it is difficult to draw hard conclusions from such an experiment. Three days, perhaps, was too short a time to track the fish. A longer time might have revealed a more meaningful pattern to their movements. Perhaps at a different time of year or in a different place the trout would have behaved differently. And who is to say that their behavior at Dewatto was natural with the strange burden of the sonic tags in their bellies?

So we know little more than we knew before, and what little we have learned offers no encouragement to anglers who seek the cutthroat in salt water. Yet it seems safe to say that as long as cutthroat continue to prowl the beaches, anglers will continue to search for them there, relying on luck and persistence if not knowledge.

The End of the Year

And so the cycle now is nearly at its end. The earth once more has completed its whirling course, and its life has followed the well-ordered sequence of the seasons, the rise and fall of the tide, the rising and setting of the sun.

Always there is a little sorrow at the passing of the year, perhaps because each of us realizes another year is gone and our time on earth is measured less. But the feeling passes quickly, supplanted by the return of the old fever, the familiar excitement of the chase. Always, it seems, there is time for at least one more trip before the snow flies, before the rivers run with the first winter floods.

Sometimes the last fish of a year is as memorable as the first, memorable in size or strength or circumstance. One year on the trout season's last day the termites hatched in the forest and the wind swept them out on the lake in countless numbers where they fell and struggled on the surface, and the trout fed on them wildly. I had nothing to imitate them, but in the bottom of a fly box I found a large Green Drake tied with hackle-point wings. I spread the wings flat and coated the body with mucilin paste to hide its color, then cast the unlikely fly to the feeding trout. In their unwary anxiety to feed, three of them took it, and one was a strong, fat rainbow, one of the best of the year.

Another year there was ice around the edge of Morgan Lake on the day before Thanksgiving, but the rainbows still were active and feeding. They came willingly to the fly, fighting well, each of them a near twin to all the others, all of them weighing within ounces of two pounds. The next strike was no different in feel from all the others, but by the time I raised the rod the backing splice already had run out through the guides and an enormous trout was jumping far across the lake. It jumped free and escaped before I had a clear look at it, but there was little doubt it had been the largest trout of the season.

Disappointed, I fished on into the cold gloom of the evening, and then another great trout took my fly. In the gathering darkness I played it to the net, a great old buck, and I decided it was a good fish to end the year.

Even in December when the Basin lakes freeze over and the rivers flood, the sea-run cutthroat still move in and out on the tide and there is no lack of fishing. Braving the winter gusts and the stinging sleet, hardy anglers fish on through the short, dark days that signal the dying of the year. In every month, in every season, there are men who fish as long as there are trout or salmon in the rivers and the bays.

Why do men fish? What is it that makes angling not just

a sport, but a philosophy and a way of life? Many good men have addressed themselves to that question throughout the long literature of angling. Their answers vary; some contend it is instinct inherited from man's early days as a hunter and gatherer, and some say it is because fish are found in such pleasant places; some say they fish because fishing is a contemplative sport, and some because it is a gentle art that relieves them from the pressures of their daily lives.

I suspect it is a little of all of these things, and something more. I suspect each individual angler has his individual reason, whether or not it is within his power to express it, even to himself. Indeed, it is difficult for me to know my own reasons; but I think I fish because there is a challenge in it, and because fishing forces the angler to observe nature and become a part of it. I fish because I love rivers and the life in them, because I love their sound and color and quick movement and the scent of forests on their shores. I fish because trout and salmon are honest and uncompromising creatures and one can meet them only on their terms.

I fish because fishing takes me to places where the land is still as it always has been, and as long as such places still exist there is hope for mankind. I fish because fishing humbles a man, and humility is a rare virtue. But most of all, I fish because it makes me feel closer to myself.

For whatever reason men fish, they are rewarded simply by the things they see. All the mechanisms of life are visible to those who look for them, from the nature of the very smallest creatures to the natures of men. A man's behavior on the stream is likely to tell much about the kind of man he is, and the deepest friendships are those made along rivers. And perhaps this is another good reason why men fish.

In his searching, the angler sees many things. Often he is the first to notice change, because change always has meaning for an angler. It may be nothing more than the subtle shifting of the current in a river, a day's delay in a faithful hatch, or some small thing a casual observer would not see or under-stand. But often the change is sweeping and drastic; a forest cut away to change forever a river's flow; a dam; a bridge; a new road where there was none before.

In this book, I have written often of change. And the changes that have come to the watersheds, the forests, the rivers and the wilderness seldom are for the good. Always they are justifiable in terms of profit, economics or convenience, but rarely are they good for the land, the creatures that live on it or the waters that flow through it.

The technology of man has given him almost infinite power to destroy life, but little knowledge to restore it. Early in our history the land was so vast and so wild it seemed there never would be an end to it, nor to the fish and game that it sustained. Now the end clearly is in sight, but the human juggernaut rolls on, unchecked. Though now it is possible for man to enjoy a life of plenty without the total, wasteful destruction of resources, the momentum of the past still carries forward the bulldozers and the dams.

There must be a better way, and all who love nature share a responsibility to help in finding it. There is more at stake than the future of angling; the future of man also rests in the balance, and time is running out. The Year of the Angler is coming to a close, and it is time to think hard about the future.

The year ebbs. It is raining now, and soon the rain will become snow. In the high country the snow already is falling. The maples and alders, once bright, are starkly barren now, their dark, decaying leaves tumbling in the currents of the rivers flowing down from the hills. The rivers are running slow and dark, but the salmon still are there. Like the leaves, they have lost their brightness, and the once great silver shapes are ugly now, black and yellow with fungus, fins worn ragged by their spawning ordeal. Their last life ebbs along with the last moments of the year. Another cycle nears its end, another ring is added to the tree.

Some who were with us when the year began are not with us now; for them there are memories of shared campfires, of laughter and disappointment, of days both difficult and fruitful. Their cycle, too, is ended, but we will keep their memories with us as we continue on our own.

The earth is hushed, waiting the ordeal of winter. The farms and the fields are barren and bleak, and there is ice on the rims of the marshes. The ducks and geese are long departed for the warmer south, and the bright songs of the summer birds are still.

A cold, wet mist floats thickly in the forests, and the old cedars and the firs loom through it like gray ghosts from another time. There is only the slow, even drip of rain and the silence of decay as rotting limbs and dead leaves return forever to the soil.

As the year came softly in the January dawn, so it softly goes in the late December dusk. The sky is dark and low, and the first snowflakes begin to fall in aimless, twisting patterns, growing ever thicker until they form a solid moving wall of white. The snow collects in the crevices between the rocks on the river bars, fills them and grows deeper. It clings like fragile lace to the fir limbs and gathers in the crotches of the naked alders. It hides the wounds of clear-cuts on the foothill slopes and masks the filth of the city streets. It swirls through the distant valleys and mingles with the woodsmoke from the cabin chimneys, falls gently on the meadows and holds the fresh, bold track of a foraging deer.

It has been a good year, and it dies peacefully and well. But there is no end to time or life; life sleeps, and awaits the beginning of another year.

PART TWO

The Year of the
TROUT

CREDITS

Some portions of this book were published previously in various magazines or periodicals or are based on works by the author published in such form.

"The Next Best Thing" is based partly on "An Angling Library for the '80's," originally published in *The Flyfisher*, Vol. XVI, No. 4, 1983.

"Cutthroat Slough" originally appeared in slightly condensed form in *Fly Fisherman Magazine*, Vol. 14, No. 3, May 1983.

"Like Father, Like Son" first appeared as "The Legacy" in the July 1982 issue of *PSA Magazine*, carried aboard Pacific Southwest Airlines.

"Fishing the Misty Fjords" originally was published in slightly different form in *The Flyfisher*, Vol. XII, No. 3, 1979.

The account of the eruption of Mount St. Helens in "Pages from a Trout Fisherman's Diary" is adapted from "A Day of Fishing Became a Night of Fear," first published in *Sports Illustrated*, July 14, 1980.

"The Once and Future River" is adapted from "It Was A Sad Day for A Fisherman When the Green River Lost Its Glitter," first published in *Sports Illustrated*, October 20, 1980.

"Hello, Dolly!" is expanded from an article first published as "Hello, Dolly, It's So Nice to Have You Back," in *Sports Illustrated*, March 26, 1979.

"Blackberry Run" was first published in *Fly Fisherman Magazine*, Vol. 14, No. 5, July 1983.

Portions of "Fall Favorite" are adapted from "The Dry Fly in Salt Water," first published in *Fly Fisherman Magazine*, Vol. 10, No. 3, March 1979.

"A Fish to Remember" was first published in slightly different form as "A Steelheader's Autumn" in *Fly Fisherman Magazine*, Vol. 11, No. 1, October–December 1979.

ACKNOWLEDGMENTS

Many persons made generous contributions of time and information to this book. I am especially indebted to Professor Charles J. (Jack) Smiley of the University of Idaho for sharing his findings from the fossil site at Miocene Clarkia Lake and for showing me the site and the surrounding countryside. A special word of thanks also is due Professor Smiley and his family for their warm and generous hospitality.

I am deeply grateful to Dr. Robert J. Behnke of the Department of Fishery and Wildlife Biology at Colorado State University for his advice and for permission to quote from his published research. His monograph on Western trouts was of invaluable assistance in preparing the chapter of the evolutionary history of trout, and his careful study of the history of the

Lahontan cutthroat trout provided much of the information reported in the chapter on that fish. Without Dr. Behnke's generous help, this book would have been two chapters shorter.

Dr. Gerald R. Smith of the University of Michigan Museum of Paleontology also was most helpful in answering my questions about the evolutionary relationships of trout and provided a great deal of valuable information on recent fossil trout discoveries. It also was Dr. Smith who examined and identified the fossil fish from Miocene Clarkia Lake and suggested its possible history.

A word of extra thanks is due to all three men for reading, criticizing and suggesting changes to the chapters on the Clarkia fish and the trout family tree. They share no accountability for any conclusions or opinions expressed in those chapters, however; I am solely responsible for those.

Others who provided generous assistance were Bill Rember of the University of Idaho and Dr. Fred Utter of the National Marine Fisheries Service in Seattle, plus the efficient staffs of the Libraries of Fisheries and Natural Sciences at the University of Washington.

I shall always be grateful to Dale Pihlman and Tom Ramiskey for arranging the trip that led to the chapter "Fishing the Misty Fjords." I wish only that I could have found more vivid words to describe that wonderful country.

James G. Swan's account of the Chehalis River treaty council, quoted in "Steelhead Blues," is a brief excerpt from his long and colorful diary of life on the Northwest frontier. Swan's diary, now in the public domain, has been published in book form by the University of Washington Press under the title of *The Northwest Coast, or Three Years' Residence in Washington Territory*. Anyone with an interest in the history of the region will find it worth reading.

Finally, to my wife, Joan, and my children, Stephanie and Randy, some very special words of thanks for being so patient and understanding.

—*Steve Raymond*

INTRODUCTION

to the 1995 Edition

The trout are still there. There are fewer now than a decade ago, and now there are many more anglers seeking them and many new things threatening them—yet somehow they endure, and in some places even thrive. But there have been many changes in the world of trout, and trout fishing, since this book was first published.

Even the names of some trout are different than they were then. The rainbow and cutthroat retain the popular names by which they have always been known, but taxonomists have changed their scientific name from *Salmo* to *Oncorhynchus*, acknowledging new research findings that link them more closely to Pacific salmon. The rainbow and its seagoing version, the steelhead, have gone from *Salmo gairdneri* to *Oncorhynchus mykiss*, and the cutthroat in all its varied forms is no longer *Salmo clarki* but *Oncorhynchus clarki*. The change means little to anglers—the fish are thankfully the same—but the rainbow and cutthroat now occupy slightly different places in the trout's family tree as described in these pages.

Perhaps in part because of this change, there is now more widespread interest in the study of the complex evolutionary history of trout. The best work on this subject is Dr. Robert J. Behnke's landmark treatise, *The Native Trout of Western North America*. Dr. Behnke's work existed only in draft form when this book was first published and I was fortunate to obtain one of the few copies then available; now it has been updated and published by the American Fisheries Society and is available to everyone.

The passage of time has healed much of the bitterness over the 1974 Boldt decision on Indian fishing rights. All but a few diehard steelhead anglers have since learned that cooperation is a better tactic than confrontation, and today many steelhead sport-fishing groups and Indian tribes are working together on enhancement projects that ultimately will serve the interests of both.

Unhappily, that has not meant an improvement in the overall fortunes of steelhead. For a host of reasons, many wild steelhead runs have been reduced nearly to the point of extinction. In particular, the once-great run of wild summer steelhead in the North Fork of the Stillaguamish has continued its decline over the past ten years.

I have written about the fate of the North Fork steelhead in this book and others. For the most part it has been a sad story, one I would rather not have had to tell. But the conclusion has yet to be written, and there are a few small, hopeful signs that the river and its steelhead may have begun the long, uncertain process of recovery. One of my fondest hopes is that I might live long enough to record a happy ending to the North Fork story.

Elsewhere, the landlocked salmon that were planted with such high hopes in Oregon's Hosmer Lake have turned out much different from their sea-run predecessors, and the differences have been almost uniformly disappointing. The landlocks neither grow as large, rise as willingly, nor fight as well, and Hosmer Lake sadly is no longer the angling showcase it once was.

My son, Randy, whom you will meet as a small boy in these pages, has grown to manhood and now complains he cannot go fishing as often as he would like—a feeling I know well. But I am grateful he still feels the tug of that first trout that took his fly in a little side channel of the North Fork when he was only eight years old. I hope he always will.

As for me, I have also grown older, and the trails do seem a little longer, the river's current a little stronger, and a No. 16 dry fly at the end of a long cast is much definitely a harder thing to see. Yet I perceive no decline in my enthusiasm for fishing, and the approach of each new season still brings forth the familiar feelings of anticipation and excitement. Trout still display the same noble fighting spirit that has always placed them foremost in the affections of anglers, and there are still enough of them—and they still inhabit the same wild and beautiful places—to make trout angling the worthwhile avocation of a lifetime.

I have been lucky to have it as my avocation, and I treasure the store of memories it has given me—but I still look forward to adding more of them. I envy only those who are coming now to the sport for the first time, who still have ahead all the joys of discovery, all the pleasures of trying new things and new places, all the many levels and textures of reward that come with each new season in the Year of the Trout.

I hope they will enjoy these things as much as I have.

—*Steve Raymond*

PREFACE

to the First Edition

A new book by Steve Raymond is always an angling-literary event. For Steve is that rare blend of angler *and* writer, a man who knows and loves his fishing intimately and who writes of it with deft skill. And since he writes too little, any new book—and especially one this fine—is all the more to be cherished.

In *The Year of the Trout* he follows the seasons, as he did in *The Year of the Angler*, but here the focus is more persistently outside, less on the man than on his quarry and on the world of his pursuit. Steelhead, brook trout, Dolly Varden, Atlantic salmon transplanted to a western lake, rainbows, cutthroats, and browns—we find these, in their seasons (especially the steelhead, which Steve chiefly loves), and we find also the special places in which they live. Like all of us who fish, Steve has a deep affection for those "lonely, wild, and beautiful" places, and through the year he finds us a full measure of these in which to fish.

Steve Raymond is a writer on whom little in the natural world, or in the experience of fishing, is lost: the cryptic codes on the surface of a river, the history of a particular fallen tree on which he's chanced to sit, the dramatic early life of the steelhead he's tenaciously pursued and finally caught. He is always interested in the "now"—in what's before him—but also, always, in what has gone before and what someday will be. So you get a special density in a Steve Raymond book, quite unlike that in any other angling writing I know—a movement into the natural world in which its author stands, a movement back into the history of a place or thing, and, always, a solicitude for the future.

Often, as in his writing on New Zealand and the Misty Fjords area of Alaska, you feel a past that will never truly be past pushing up against a present that is more than it seems merely to the senses. So the angler's New Zealand that everyone writes about these days is only a part of what Steve offers; we also get a textured history of several years, only some of which is even associated with trout. And we hear, in other instances, of lesser-known little rivers and their historical origins, of matters paleontological, and, of course—because he has long been one of our finest book reviewers—of books, which are crucially part of the history, the substance, the world of angling, and where the past also presses up into the current moment.

But the most vivid parts of this wonderful book, like those parts in any fine book about fly fishing, are the worlds of the angler and his quarry, in the present. We get winter steelhead on a day so cold the author's fingers, as he tied on a new leader and fly, were so numb he lit a pipe for warmth; then he cupped his "frozen hands around its bowl to feel the heat come slowly through the brier." We get winter cutthroat in an Indian slough, too—and some unexpected new friends. We get that special bond between father and son, built uniquely by fishing. "Call it an attitude or feeling," Steve writes, "a sort of inner excitement that returns each spring when the green buds burst open on the trees, the mayflies hatch, and trout begin to rise. It's that and more—a kind of understanding and appreciation that fishing is one of the very best things that ever a man can do, and trout fishing is the very best of all. It is one of my father's most precious gifts to me, and now I hope somehow to impart the same feelings to my son."

That's fine, memorable prose, isn't it?

But we also get a special "birthday trout," a gift to make us smile, and we get an inutterably sad and moving description of a trout river devastated by the eruption of Mount St. Helens. "It was a dead river," Steve says, "flowing through a dead land."

One of my favorite sections treats his diaries—with pages in one that still have trout scales stuck to them, and a motto that such a book, an angling diary, is not to be measured "by how much information it can hold, but how well it preserves the memories of a fishing lifetime." And I am especially moved by the section on his fishing camp, bought from friends with whom he has shared wonderful days astream, blessed finally by a visit with the ashes of one of those old, dear friends.

What a wonderful trip, then, this book offers. We travel from the icy days of one winter until the final changes of another fall are registered in the chill air and the colors of the cottonwoods. Along the way we see lots of new water, feel the powerful fight of a sea-fresh steelhead, slip back into the past, laugh and cry a little, and catch some memorable fish.

How I'd like to have spent that year fishing for these trout with Steve!

But maybe, through this splendid book, I have. And so will you.

—Nick Lyons

WINTER

The days of winter seem so short yet the season seems so long. The mornings are calm and cold, with frost forming beneath a floating layer of mist. The woods are still, the streams dark and low with a grudging flow of water from the snowfields on the foothill slopes. But the trout are there.

Perhaps nothing is as deceiving as the appearance of a winter stream. Though the trees along its banks are barren, though the snow reaches down to the water's edge, though the river itself seems slow and dark and sullen, beneath the surface there is abundant life. True, there is less of it and it moves at a slower pace than in summer rivers; yet still it moves. Though the earth seems to hold its breath in winter, the cycle of predator and prey, of life and death and procreation still goes on in the rivers. And the trout are always there.

The steelhead returns in winter. It has done so since long before calendars were kept, for with its instincts it has no need to number days. But now men know the timing of its ways and wait with rod and reel and feathered fly to greet the first returning fish, still sea-fresh and shining bright.

They also know the ways of all the other kinds of trout and seek each one in its proper season. They know the landlocked rainbow usually is a bold and reckless fish, at its best in the spring when the mayflies and sedges are hatching; and yet they know too that sometimes the rainbow may be as elusive as its name, a momentary bend of color in the sky, then vanished.

They know the cutthroat as a clan of many cousins, each a little different from all the rest, yet each a practical, pragmatic fish that makes the most of things in almost any season, in saltwater or in fresh. They know the brown trout as a street-wise fish, cunning, tough, and smart. A wary brown is a challenge for any fisherman and rare is the angler who does not respect it.

They know the golden trout is as spectacular as its name suggests and as rare as a gleaming nugget in the gravel of a mountain stream—and just as much worth finding. They know the Atlantic salmon is a grand fish that does things on a grand scale, that it is the largest of all the trouts and a great prize for any angler. They know the brook trout really is a char, but one that has earned a trout's name, a fish of unsurpassed beauty and grace.

All these they know as members of the bright firmament of fish called trout. And from the very first cold dawn of winter to the very last gray twilight of the fall, men seek them through the changing seasons of The Year of the Trout.

Upstream Journey

Snow had fallen overnight, a soft wet snow that pressed heavily on fir and cedar limbs and broke off and fell in cold little clots as I passed through the woods on the way to the river. The highway was a long way off, the river was quiet within its channel somewhere up ahead and there was not a sound to disturb the tranquility of the cold, empty morning.

A pair of anglers had preceded me along the snowy trail, leaving a double set of footprints, but where the trail forked near the river I was relieved to see that both had turned downstream. I was headed for an upstream drift, hoping for a steelhead to start the year.

I found the familiar path bordering the river and picked my way over slippery, snow-covered rocks and fallen logs, grasping the trunk of a friendly alder and using it as a lever to swing across a place where some past flood had washed away the trail. Other anglers who had passed this way had done the same for so many seasons that their hands had worn a groove in the alder's trunk.

I walked a mile or more before I came upon the run. It looked as I remembered it from times before, 200 yards of good steelhead water, shallow on my side but dropping steeply to a deep slot against the far bank. But one thing was new: Halfway down the run a tree had dug itself top-first into the river bottom and now its drowned trunk angled up through the water and its roots tilted crazily out of the current. It would be a difficult place to fish without hanging up a fly, but the tree would offer shelter where a steelhead might hold; it would be a place worth fishing.

I walked up to the head of the drift and waded in slowly, gauging the strength of the current and feeling its chill come quickly through my waders. Then I stripped out the fast-sinking line and began casting a big bright fly, quartering downstream and lengthening line until the fly was dropping within a foot or two of the high bank on the far side. The current was swift and acted quickly on the line. Each cast required two or three quick upstream mends to hold the fly where I wanted it, to give it a chance to sink to the depth where a steelhead might be waiting.

But if any were waiting, they ignored the fly as I fished through the upper part of the run. Near the middle of the drift the current quickened even more, so I switched to upstream casts to give the fly more time to sink. After the first two or three of these the line drew slowly tight against a weight that wouldn't yield; somewhere, down below, the fly had found a snag. I worked hard to free it, but in the end there was nothing left to do but break it off and go ashore to replace the leader tippet and the fly.

As I waded out I noticed a large log lying near the water's edge. It was just the right size for sitting, so I sat down and fumbled in the bulging pockets of my fishing vest for a spool of the right-sized leader material. I found it and cut off a measured length, but my fingers were so nearly numb it took three tries to tie the knot to join it to the remnant of leader the river had left me. It was a similar chore to tie on a duplicate of the fly I'd lost, so after that I reached again inside my vest and found the old tobacco pouch and battered pipe. I filled the pipe and lit it, then cupped my frozen hands around its bowl to feel the heat come slowly through the brier.

I watched the river as I waited for my hands to warm; its surface spelled out hurried messages in a cryptic code, erased them, then quickly wrote others in their place. Beyond the stream, a line of cottonwoods stretched naked limbs against a leaden sky and the ground still was bleak and white with snow.

I chanced to look down at the log upon which I sat. It was a stout log, splintered at each end, but the river's abrasive silt had long ago worn away the splintered ends to harmless rounded stubs. Still, it was obvious this was a broken section of what once had been a large and substantial tree.

I brushed away some snow to see if I could tell what sort of tree it might have been, but the wood beneath was old and gray, weathered and bleached by countless days of sun and wind and current. It had been tossed against a hundred gravel bars and beaches, and particles of sand and silt had worn its surface smooth—so smooth it was hard to see the grain of wood, hard to tell what kind of wood it was. But whatever sort of tree it once had been, the splintered ends were proof that it had not been cut by saw or ax; some natural force had brought it down.

I wondered what that force was and when and where it had happened. For how many scores of years had the tree lived? Had it stood proudly near the river, watching salmon and steelhead passing upstream and their offspring coming down, season after season, until suddenly a great spring flood had reached out and claimed it? Had it once grown straight and tall on a windward hillside, stretching its limbs among eagles? Had lightning brought it down, or fire, or a great wind? Or had it merely died a quiet, natural death and gone on standing until weather, birds and insects turned it to a gaunt old snag, a tombstone to itself, before it finally fell?

All questions without answers. And yet for some reason I wanted to know the answers, wanted to know where this tree had lived and how it had died and what convoluted route it had followed to this place.

Perhaps the strange handwriting on the river held the answers, but if so I could not read them.

The last tobacco had burned out of my pipe and the river beckoned, so I stood, stiff from cold, moved around a bit to loosen up, then waded once more into the current and resumed casting. At first nothing happened, and after a while my mind began to wander as I settled into the mechanical routine of casting so that I failed to notice when the line came to a slow and subtle stop at the end of a long cast. The line began to move upstream, slowly at first, then with increasing speed, and in the instant I took to ponder this development the line came tight and suddenly the reel was spinning wildly.

I raised the rod then and felt furious resistance. The line already was off the reel and the backing followed swiftly as I started for the beach. Then the long run finally ended and the fish broached in the current, far upstream, and I caught a glimpse of its silver shape.

A hooked steelhead that runs upstream places itself at a disadvantage, for it must contend with both angler and current. This one quickly realized its error and changed directions, heading downstream so rapidly that a dangerous belly formed in the trailing line. I cranked the reel as quickly as I could until finally the line came tight again, though it slanted downstream at a dangerous angle.

I followed the fish down, putting on all the strain I dared to keep it from the hazard of the drowned tree in the center of the run. The fish came reluctantly away from the snag, then turned and ran once more, and again I was forced to follow. It was a stubborn fish, strong and determined to keep its freedom, but the unyielding spring of the long rod finally proved stronger; the steelhead turned on its side and I led it carefully into quiet water and eased it up onto the snow-covered river rocks along the beach.

It was a classic sea-fresh winter fish, slim and bright steel-gray on its back and gleaming nickel on its sides. I judged it was easily eight pounds. Carefully I twisted the fly free from its jaw, then held the fish gently in the shallow water. The decision to release it had long ago been made, but I found myself holding it for a long time, admiring its beauty and graceful shape as I eased it back and forth to restore rhythm to the movement of its gills. Slowly its movements grew stronger and at last I let it go; it swam slowly outward and down along the sloping cobble bottom.

I watched it go and thought of the path it had followed to reach this place. Like the log behind me on the beach, the stream had borne it down from the hills, yet unlike the log the fish had come willingly and with purpose. It had reached the sea and gone about its life's clear and uncomplicated mission: to forage in the rich ocean pastures, to survive and grow, and finally to return to its native river and spawn. I had briefly interrupted its progress toward this goal, but now it was free to resume its upstream journey and complete its purpose. And if it did, it could then die peacefully with whatever dim sense of accomplishment a trout may have.

I thought of my own life in comparison with the

steelhead's and of the course that had brought me to this cold and quiet beach on a winter morning. It was a course infinitely more complicated than the trout's, filled with unexpected twists and sudden turns, false starts and fitful purposes, satisfying advances and sorry retreats. It also was a course without a clear and certain purpose, for unlike the steelhead a man has no familiar river to which one day he knows he will return. A steelhead always knows where it is going, but a man seldom does.

I rested for a while and smoked another pipe, then waded in and fished out the remainder of the run, but no more fish touched my fly. The morning was well spent, the overcast showed signs of breaking and the snow had begun melting from the sagging limbs along the river. The stream continued to scrawl its mysterious moving messages, but their meaning was no clearer now than it had been before. I decided it was time to move on, to head upstream and try another pool and see what surprises it might hold in store.

I walked up from the tail of the long run, past the submerged tree with its roots waving in the current, past the spot where I had hooked the fish, on up to the point where the trail disappeared among the trees. For some reason I paused there and took a last look back and my eye fell upon the log still resting on the beach.

The snow had melted from it and it looked different with its dull bleached wood gleaming darkly through the wet. It lay there, an unknown soldier of the woods, waiting for the river to bear it to some final resting place far from its home. I wondered how long its wait would be, and how many more seasons it would spend on lonely beaches before it finally reached the end of its halting, uncertain journey.

Then I turned away and continued upstream on an uncertain journey of my own. But I was pleased; I had taken the first fish of a new year, a good and satisfying fish, and upstream, through the woods, I could see the sky was bright.

The Land of the Long
White Cloud

Back home the winter winds were blowing and the rivers were in flood, but it was early summer in New Zealand and the morning air was fresh and sweet as I stepped for the first time into the Major Jones Pool of the Tongariro River. After only a few casts I hooked a strong fish that fought with all the vigor of a fresh-run steelhead, as indeed its ancestors once had been.

In all, five bright rainbows took my fly on that first pass

through the Major Jones, one of the most famous trout pools on earth, and I marveled at the fact that it was possible for an angler to trade seasons and travel to the Southern Hemisphere to find trout fishing such as this.

New Zealand now is justly famous as a Mecca for trout fishermen, though its rich waters have held trout only a little more than a hundred years and the country itself was not discovered by European explorers until the 17th century. But its history reaches back much further and it is a history worth knowing—a fascinating story that begins in misty legends a thousand years old, passed down from generation to generation in tales told over campfires in the long antipodean twilights.

By most accounts, it began with a voyage from a legendary island known as Hawaiki, somewhere in eastern Polynesia. There, it is said, a warrior named Kupe murdered a carver named Hoturapa, took Hoturapa's wife and escaped in the slain man's canoe. Learning of this, Hoturapa's relatives gave pursuit, chasing the fugitive pair far across the ocean until they finally were lost from sight.

For day after day and week after week, Kupe and his consort traveled across the long rolling swells of the South Pacific with only flying fish and porpoises for company. Each morning the sun rose at their backs and each evening it beckoned them onward as it sank, blood-red, back into the restless sea. Ever southwestward they sailed, across the lonely heaving landscape of the ocean, until at last came a morning when the far horizon was hidden by a long layer of white cloud—perhaps a sign of land!

With gathering hope and excitement, Kupe and his woman sailed on until they were close enough to see there *was* land ahead—a great land that stretched beyond sight both to the north and south, a land of high forested hills that rose to the dim and distant shapes of enormous mountains far inland. And when Hoturapa's canoe finally grated safely on the sand

and Kupe stepped ashore, he was ready with a name for the new-found land: Aotearoa, the Land of the Long White Cloud.

Kupe's tale is apocryphal, one of many legends about the settlement of Aotearoa. Another version suggests that Kupe returned to Hawaiki and told others about Aotearoa so they were later able to find it for themselves. The exact truth probably never will be known, but there is little doubt that sometime within the past 600 to 1,000 years at least one canoe, and perhaps many, traveled from somewhere in east Polynesia to the mysterious country far to the southwest.

The newcomers found a magnificent land of two great islands and many smaller ones, covered with thick forests and stands of giant ferns and riven by cold, rushing rivers that hurried down from the hills. One of the big islands had a volcanic spine, a chain of fiery mountains, geysers, steaming lakes, and strange pools of boiling mud, and right in the middle of it was a great blue inland sea. The other island had a range of even higher mountains, glacier-crested peaks that disappeared into perpetual cloud, and a ragged coastline punctured by deep saltwater fjords with lush rain forests growing down to their shores. In the forests lived parrots, parakeets, and a whole galaxy of other birds.

But the new arrivals also found they were not the first people to reach this land. Some earlier migration, now forgotten even in legend, had brought primitive tribes that lived by hunting enormous emu-like flightless birds called moas, some standing as much as ten feet tall—the largest birds ever to live on earth. The primitive culture of these tribes was no match for the more advanced Polynesian way of life, and as the newcomers spread out to occupy the islands, the moa hunters slowly melted away until both they and the moas were extinct.

The Polynesians brought with them food-bearing plants and a tradition of agriculture, but they also were skilled fishermen and found bountiful harvests of fish in the seas around the new land. They also found rich, oily eels that migrated into the rivers; a small fish they called Inanga that entered the estuaries in great numbers every spring, and a handsome, grayling-like fish called the Upokororo that followed the Inanga and fed upon its schools. They also learned to spear or snare the abundant waterfowl and birds, and occasionally they augmented their largely meatless diet by eating one another. They called themselves the Maori.

For several hundred years the Maori had Aotearoa to themselves. But in 1642 the Dutch East India Company sent out two ships under command of Abel Tasman to search for new lands in the South Pacific, and on December 13 of that year Tasman sighted the west coast of the southern great island of Aotearoa, which he recorded as "a large land uplifted high." His first contact with the Maoris ended in a violent clash in which four of Tasman's men were killed, and the explorer sailed away without ever setting foot on his discovery.

Over the next 150 years Aotearoa was visited by other explorers flying British, French, and Spanish flags. By 1790 New Zealand—as it was then called in Europe—was considered fair game for exploitation by the outside world. Hundreds of vessels arrived to begin hunting the fur seals that clustered on the South Island beaches and these were quickly followed by whaling ships and timber traders.

Close on the heels of the exploiters came Anglican, Wesleyan, and Catholic missionaries bent on bringing God's word to the Maoris. They sent back tales of tragedy and atrocity, and these stories, combined with concerns over French territorial ambitions in the South Pacific, prompted a reluctant British government to annex New Zealand. Capt. William Hobson of the Royal Navy was sent to negotiate a treaty with the Maori chiefs for transfer of sovereignty to

Britain; the result was the 1840 Treaty of Waitangi, which opened the way for full British settlement of New Zealand.

In the years following, as more and more British colonists arrived, they began yearning for two of the favorite things the British already had carried to so many other far-flung lands: tea and trout.

New Zealand's climate and waters seemed ideally suited for trout. In fact, the colonists found one trout-like fish already living there, the fish the Maoris had called the Upokororo and which the settlers soon named the New Zealand grayling. Formally classified *Prototroctes oxyrhynchus*, it was a curious fish, growing as large as 18 inches and appearing in lowland streams during the summer and fall, then disappearing during the winter only to turn up again in the spring to feed on schools of young Inanga in the estuaries. The Inanga itself, *Galaxiias attenuatus*, was called "whitebait" by the settlers. It was one of a number of galaxiids—slim, scaleless pike-like fish—common to New Zealand's streams and lakes.

But the New Zealand grayling had little opportunity to prove any sporting qualities it may have had. Along with the whitebait it was considered an excellent food fish, and both species were netted in great numbers when the whitebait were running. Catches were so plentiful that surplus fish sometimes were used as fertilizer in colonists' gardens. This kind of heavy pressure, combined with changes to the environment and other factors, was too much for the New Zealand grayling; its numbers dwindled rapidly and it soon became rare.

But even if the New Zealand grayling had fared better it almost certainly would not have made the colonists forget their favorite fish. The task of obtaining trout from overseas sources was taken on by local "acclimatisation societies," groups of sportsmen organized expressly for the purpose of bringing in exotic species of game and fish to improve sporting opportunities in New Zealand.

In 1867, the Canterbury Acclimatisation Society obtained brown trout eggs from Tasmania, where trout had been introduced three years earlier. The eggs were hatched at the society's pond in Hagley Park in Christchurch on the South Island, but only three fish survived and all three managed to escape into a nearby swamp. Two were later recaptured, and by great good fortune one was male and the other female. They were returned to the hatchery, presumably under better security, and over the next few years they provided many offspring for stocking in Canterbury waters.

In 1870, the Auckland Acclimatisation Society introduced brown trout to the North Island. These fish also were hatched from eggs received from Tasmania, the source of all the brown trout stocked in New Zealand until 1883. In that year the Dunedin and Wellington Acclimatisation Societies imported a shipment of eggs directly from Loch Leven in Scotland. Later shipments came from Rhine River stock and from Italian waters.

But brown trout alone were not enough to satisfy the members of the acclimatisation societies. They were eager to import other species as well.

The Auckland society's minute book for August 1878 records the arrival of a shipment of eggs from Lake Tahoe, California, a gift from a Mr. T. Russell. After hatching, 2,000 fry survived and it was left to the society's chairman to decide where they should be released; unfortunately the minute book contains no record of his decision.

There also remains some question about just what kind of trout these were. At the time, and for many years afterward, it was generally assumed they were rainbows, but that assumption has been challenged by recent research. In findings published in 1978, D. Scott, J. Hewitson and J.C. Fraser pointed out that it now appears doubtful rainbow trout ever were indigenous to Lake Tahoe, but the Lahontan cutthroat, *Salmo clarki henshawi*, was native; therefore, the trout imported by the Auckland society may very well have been Lahontan cutthroat. If indeed that was the case, there is no record of what finally became of these fish; presumably they either died out or were absorbed through hybridization into rainbow trout populations introduced later.

For its next shipment the Auckland Society decided that it wanted Eastern brook trout (char) from the United States. The minute book for April 3, 1883, reports "the Secretary announced the arrival of 10,000 brook trout ova from San Francisco by the *City of New York*, from which 500 healthy young fish had been hatched, and also of 12,000 ova of the same fish by the *Zealandia*, about 5,000 or 6,000 of which appeared in good condition."

At first these fish did well in the Auckland's Society's ponds, but the following spring brought unusually warm weather and soon dead trout fingerlings were found floating in the ponds. Society members quickly transferred the survivors to cooler ponds along the Waihou River near Okoroire, 120 miles south. There they survived and flourished and many subsequently were released into North Island rivers.

Some fish were kept for breeding stock, however, and by 1886, when they were starting to reach sexual maturity, their appearance was beginning to puzzle members of the society. The minute book for September 7, 1886, describes them as "black-spotted Brook trout," although the true Eastern brook trout has no black spots. Later it became clear these fish were actually rainbow trout and the 1883 shipments represented the first successful introduction of rainbows in New Zealand.

For many years it was accepted as gospel that the eggs in these shipments had come from steelhead in California's Russian River. But the research of Scott, Hewitson, and Fraser turned up convincing evidence that they actually came from a run of winter steelhead returning to Sonoma Creek, a tributary of San Francisco Bay. Confirmation is found in a report published in the *Sonoma County Weekly Index* on July 21, 1883:

"Mr. A.V. La Motte, superintendent of the Lenni Fish Propagating Company, informs us that the company sometime since shipped 30,000 trout eggs to the Auckland, New Zealand, Acclimatisation Society, and have received the report from them that they arrived in better order than any prior lot they had received from other parties. This we consider another feather in Sonoma's cap, and a big, bright one, too." La Motte's hatchery was on Sonoma Creek, although much later he operated a hatchery on the Russian River—a fact which probably explains the long confusion over the source of New Zealand's first rainbows.

But no matter where they came from, brown and rainbow trout adapted quickly to New Zealand's cold, fertile rivers and lakes, finding abundant food in the native smelt, galaxiid, crayfish, and insect populations. Some grew to phenomenal size in a remarkably short time; in 1891 anglers reported catching rainbows weighing up to 9 pounds in Lake Takapuna on the North Island, and in 1892 a 28-pound brown trout was taken from Butel's Creek, a tributary of Lake Hayes near Queenstown on the South Island.

Perhaps the most spectacular fishing developed in and around Lake Taupo, the great blue 400-square-mile inland sea of the North Island. Taupo is fed by scores of rivers and streams, most notably the charming little Waitahanui, the gentle Hatepe, the tranqil Tauranga Taupo, and the big, swift Tongariro. The first brown trout were released in Lake Taupo by the Auckland Acclimatisation Society in 1886, and 11 years later the Wellington Society liberated rainbow trout in the lake. The rainbow, descended from the original 1883 Sonoma Creek shipments, quickly reverted to the migratory habits of their ancestral stock, feeding on the rich store of natural food in the lake, then migrating up its tributary streams to spawn.

O.S. "Budge" Hintz, New Zealand's best-known angling author, relates an early record of the fishing at Taupo from the diary of a British angler named King-Webster. On his first visit in 1908 King-Webster traveled 56 miles by horse-drawn coach from Rotorua to the town of Taupo on the northeastern shore of the lake, then by steamer the length of the lake to the settlement of Tokaanu near the mouth of the Tongariro at the lake's south end. "King-Webster fished triumphantly, at times almost incredulously, on the Tongariro," Hintz wrote. "Fish running into double-figure weight were common, and his best was one of 19 pounds."

King-Webster also spent three days fishing the Waitahanui, which drains the volcanic slopes on the eastern shore of Lake Taupo. During those three days he took 17 fish with a combined weight of 166 pounds. His best was a 14-pound rainbow taken from the little Mangamutu Stream which enters the Waitahanui just before the latter flows into the lake.

Another early visitor to the Waitahanui was Major Percy Stewart, who recorded his adventures in a 1924 book, *Round the World with Rod and Rifle*. Stewart made four trips to the Waitahanui during the years 1909-1914. On his first visit he caught trout averaging slightly more than 10 pounds, but on subsequent trips he noted a gradual decline in the size of the trout until by 1914 the average weight was only five pounds.

There is a famous, oft-published photograph taken in 1911 of a pair of Taupo anglers displaying a single day's catch of 78 trout taken at the mouth of Waihaha Stream, another Taupo tributary. Seventeen of these fish weighed 16 pounds or more; none was less than 12 pounds.

But the native Maoris who lived around the lake accounted for the largest catches. There are stories of a 37½-pound rainbow taken by Maoris from Mangamutu Stream and of a huge, 51½-pound brown trout captured near the south end of Lake Taupo. Like Kupe's tale, however, these stories are largely apocryphal.

Whatever the truth, by all accounts the early-century fishing in Lake Taupo was nothing short of incredible. But as Major Stewart's records indicate, a rapid decline in the average size of trout was becoming evident as early as 1914. Soon it became apparent the trout had succeeded only too well in taking advantage of the hundreds of miles of spawning water in Taupo's tributaries and had reproduced at an explosive rate. Their rapidly increasing numbers had seriously depleted the lake's great store of natural food, something no one had ever thought possible. By 1918 the average weight of Taupo trout had fallen to a little over three pounds.

Commercial netting for trout was allowed in the lake starting in 1913, but at first there was little market for the fish and few were taken. But as more shipments made their way to the cities, demand increased and the numbers of trout taken went up rapidly. By 1921, when commercial fishing was halted, the trout population had been thinned to the point that equilibrium with the food supply had been restored; the average weight of Taupo trout in that year was between five and seven pounds and by 1924 it topped 10 pounds. In 1926, three anglers took 450 pounds of trout from the Tongariro in a single day.

But it took only a decade for the trout population to build itself back to the point where the balance of the lake again was disturbed. By 1939 the average weight of Taupo trout had declined to about four pounds, and in an effort to reverse the trend the government began transplanting native smelt from the Rotorua lakes into Lake Taupo. Gradually the smelt took hold in their new home and began to multiply and the trout turned to them as a new source of food. The average weight of trout slowly increased until it leveled off at around five pounds. It has remained close to that figure ever since.

The advent of jet travel in recent years has made New

Zealand a favorite refuge for anglers seeking escape from the Northern Hemisphere winter. The South Island fishery, still primarily for brown trout, usually is best in January and February, when the northern winter is at its worst. The best fishing on the North Island comes a bit later when the Lake Taupo rainbows begin running to the tributaries, and the runs peak in the early southern winter months of May and June. Lately, however, Taupo fishermen have noted increasing numbers of bright fish entering the Tongariro as late as spring or even early summer.

It was one of these late runs of rainbow that greeted me that first memorable morning on the Major Jones Pool. The smallest fish was a little over three pounds, the largest a little over five, and all behaved with the explosive violence I have learned to expect from sea-run rainbows in the brawling rivers of the Pacific Northwest.

I landed the last fish just above the tail-out of the pool, then found a place to rest in the shade and watch other anglers work their way through the long curving reach of the Major Jones. They were the latest in a long line of Taupo anglers dating back to the days of Major Stewart, King-Webster and before, and I was glad to be among them—glad to find my own small place in the century-old tradition of fishing for transplanted trout in the Land of the Long White Cloud.

The Next Best Thing

A good fishing book is a joy in itself, but a good book is even better when it is read in front of a warm fire on a long winter evening while the wind is strong and rain is rattling like buckshot on the windowpanes. A book read under such circumstances can very easily become a magic thing, lifting the reader's mind and carrying him forward to the pleasures that await on spring ponds and summer rivers, or transporting him back to memories of past rewarding days. Books speak to us of all the mysteries that make trout fishing such a captivating sport; next to fishing itself, there is nothing better than a good fishing book.

There are many to choose from. In terms of importance, fishing can scarcely be said to rank with such matters as war or statecraft, but the literature of angling is hardly less extensive than the literature for either of those subjects. Fishing for trout has prompted as much study and debate as any of the arts or sciences; it has evolved its own philosophy and ethics, its own customs and codes, its own language and technology, and all of these are described in books.

It's often said that a trout fisherman passes through a predictable evolution, starting with a desire to catch as many fish as possible and working up to a point where he ignores all but the most difficult or demanding fish. I believe a student of angling literature must pass through a similar metamorphosis. It begins with an indiscriminate desire to read as many fishing books as possible, then progresses through stages of increasing selectivity until it finally culminates in a preference for the most challenging or thoughtful works. At least that has been true in my case.

The first fishing book I ever read was Zane Grey's *Tales of Fresh-Water Fishing*. I was no more than 10 years old when I found the tall green volume in my father's library and took it down from the shelf. Grey's prose style was flamboyant, sometimes given to exaggeration or extreme, but I didn't realize it then; to me his book was a collection of thrilling angling tales in which I could easily imagine myself as the central character. Thanks to my father's interest in fishing I already had gained a fair amount of experience with trout, but Grey's book provided an inkling that there was more to the business of fishing than I had supposed.

The next angling book I read was Roderick Haig-Brown's classic *A River Never Sleeps*, which broadened my horizons much further. Haig-Brown articulated many things about fishing that I was beginning to sense or feel but had yet to translate into thoughts or concepts of my own. His book was full of rich feeling and warm expression; it was an ideal book for an angler to read in his formative years, and though I have since reread it many times, I always have been glad that I first came upon it when I did.

After my early acquaintance with Grey and Haig-Brown, I began haunting the aisles of the public library, checking out all the fishing books I could find on the shelves. It was a mixed bag if ever there was one; I found myself reading not only about trout, but also about salmon, tarpon, bonefish, bass and other species. Some of the books were just awful—there is no other honest way to describe them—and some were about fish or fishing I would never likely see or do. But they were all about fishing, and so I read all of them faithfully.

It did not take very long to read most of the fishing books the library had to offer (there were others listed in the card catalogue that I wanted very much to read, but the fishermen who borrowed them never brought them back. That suggested a lesson: Never loan a book to a fisherman). And the more I read, the more I began to understand which authors and which books had most to offer, or which ones were held in highest regard by other writers. With this knowledge I was able to begin reading more selectively, and since the only way I could obtain some of the books I wanted was to buy them, I finally took the ultimate step and started an angling library of my own.

It was a small thing at first, just a few volumes tucked between a flimsy pair of bookends on a single shelf, but over the years it has grown massively until it now occupies a full wall of shelves in my office. During the time it took to reach such size its contents changed character many times, always reflecting my current interests—and that, I think, is what a good library should do.

But every library also should contain at least a few of the truly seminal works on angling. By these I mean books that were first to express important new ideas—Halford's works on the dry fly, Skues on the nymph, Jock Scott on the greased-line method, La Branche on the dry fly in American waters, Jennings and his successors on trout-fly entomology, Marinaro on minutae—to mention just a few.

Studying the works of these masters also is likely to stimulate a reader's interest in history and the cultivation of such an interest is the next logical step in becoming a literate angler. The scholarly works of John Waller Hills, John McDonald, William Radcliffe, and Alfred Joshua Butler together will provide an angler with a solid background in the origins and development of the sport. Arnold Gingrich's *The Fishing in Print* also qualifies here because Gingrich, in summarizing the work of nearly every important fishing writer, managed to span most of the known history of angling—and angling literature and history often are synonymous.

Many fishing books are of the instructional variety, and any student of the sport should begin by reading some of these. It is not necessary to read very many in order to become thoroughly grounded in the principles and techniques of trout fishing, and one would not really wish to read too many or he would soon begin to notice a depressing similarity among them. Most cover essentially the same ground, often in the same way, sometimes even in the same words. Such books are necessary, but they do not represent angling literature at its best. I keep some in my library, not because I enjoy reading them but because they are valuable for reference; if I need to know how to dress a certain fly or tie a certain knot, I know that somewhere in these books I will find the answer.

The highest level of expression in angling literature is found in books about the philosophy and appreciation of the sport. These subjects have inspired more eloquence than any others, and in dealing with them some writers have found ways to touch a reader's heart and soul.

A River Never Sleeps would have to rank near the top of any list of such books. It is generally considered Haig-Brown's greatest work, but he produced many other classics of nearly equal stature. They include *Return to the River*, a novel about the great race of spring Chinook salmon that once populated the Columbia River, and his famous "season" series—*Fisherman's Winter, Fisherman's Spring, Fisherman's Summer,* and *Fisherman's Fall*, four of the most beautiful fishing books ever written.

Another writer who has given me almost as much satisfaction is Robert Traver, whose books *Trout Madness* and *Trout Magic* are among the most touching and amusing I have read. Traver writes exclusively of his passionate, whiskey-fueled pursuit of brook trout in the backwater ponds and creeks of Michigan's Upper Peninsula, and his books contain some of the funniest and most heartwarming tales in fishing literature. Traver is the pseudonym for John D. Voelker, a former justice of the Michigan Supreme Court who is better known as author of the best-selling novel *Anatomy of a Murder.*

Nick Lyons is another favorite. His books, *The Seasonable Angler, Fishing Widows,* and *Bright Rivers*, are written in a gentle, self-deprecating style with the sort of good-natured despair of an angler whose work has trapped him in the city and limited most of his fishing to daydreams; even on those rare occasions when he is able to get away, nothing ever seems to go quite right. Every angler who has experienced the frustration of being unable to go fishing, or of having something go wrong while he is fishing, will recognize something of himself in Lyons' tales.

Lyons also is a skilled editor who compiled one of the finest all-around collections of fishing stories ever published, an anthology titled *Fisherman's Bounty.* It would be hard to find another book capable of giving so much pleasure, but three other anthologies come very close—*In Trout Country,* compiled by Peter Corodimas; *Silent Seasons*, edited by Russell Chatham, and *The Ultimate Fishing Book*, with Lee Eisenberg and DeCourcy Taylor.

Chatham also is the author of *The Angler's Coast*, another well-crafted, entertaining book that never has received the attention it deserved. Other titles of equal merit are Ben Hur Lampman's *A Leaf from French Eddy*; Gingrich's *The Well-Tempered Angler* and *The Joys of Trout*; Edward Weeks' *Fresh Waters*; William Humphrey's *My Moby Dick* and *The Spawning Run*, and any book by Dana Lamb.

Where the Bright Waters Meet, by Harry Plunket-Greene; *A Summer on the Test*, by John Waller Hills, and *Thy Rod and Thy Creel*, by Odell Shepard, are three older classics that contain some of the finest lyric writing ever lavished on the sport. All three have recently been reissued and are available to the angling public for the first time in nearly two generations. Any one of them would be a solid cornerstone on which to build an angling library.

Bryan Curtis' *The Life Story of the Fish* is a book that deals more with appreciation for fish than for fishing, but it is so filled with sparkling insights and wry wisdom that any reader, even one not the least bit interested in fish, could scarcely fail to find it entertaining. Curtis was a respected scientist with well-honed literary instincts and this book displays both talents at their best; unfortunately, it is the only one he ever wrote. It too has recently been reissued.

Another unusual book is *Come Wade the River*, by Ralph Wahl, my friend and fishing mentor. For nearly half a century, Ralph has roamed the rivers of the Northwest with a camera in his vest, capturing the moods and scenes of angling more vividly than any writer ever could. Some of his best work is featured in this book, matched to some well-chosen words from *A River Never Sleeps*. The result is a stunning display of imagery and prose.

So far I have mentioned only titles which are still in print, recently reissued, or at least not so old they have grown difficult to find. There are others, dating all the way back to the 19th century or before, which are equally worth reading but are now nearly impossible to obtain.

One exception is a book that is more commonplace now than at any time during its 330-year history—Izaak Walton's *The Compleat Angler*, perhaps the most popular and enduring work ever penned in the English language. But it took a while for Walton's masterpiece to achieve such stature; shortly after it was published a London review damned it with the faint praise that it was "Not unworthy the perusall." Even today, revisionists attack some of Walton's prose as awkward and his literary devices as contrived, and we also know now that he copied shamelessly from the works of other writers—though such practice was rather more common and accepted in his time than it is in ours.

But whatever the revisionists may say, there is no denying that *The Compleat Angler* forever established angling as "the contemplative man's recreation" and made it a socially acceptable pastime for people of all stations. Any book capable of doing that had to be very special, and Walton's was—and is. It's also clear that whatever Walton may have borrowed from others he improved greatly by himself, and his prose evokes a spirit of serenity that has rarely been matched in all the centuries since. *The Compleat Angler* is a book every fisherman should read at least once in his life in order to fully comprehend the nature and meaning of his sport.

I have tried in this brief list to single out those books which have given me the greatest pleasure and fulfillment, those I believe would grace the shelves of any library and enlighten the mind of any fisherman. But regardless of which books an angler chooses to read, he will find the time it takes to read them is time not idly spent. In books he will share the excitement of the early discoveries of those who fished with horsehair lines and wrote by candlelight; he will fish alongside the masters, test their theories and take sides in the righteous fury of their great debates. Their rivers will become his rivers, their successes his to share, their traditions his to carry on.

All this and more is waiting, always waiting, just as often as one is willing to open the pages of a book.

Steelhead Blues

If you go up to the headwaters in winter, you will see them: the survivors of the long return. They are steelhead, paired together in lonely pools or huddled on the redds, their bodies lean and dark and scarred from the stress of their upstream passage. They are a stirring sight, these great fish so far from the sea, so intent on fulfilling the purpose of their lives.

How far they have come! Perhaps from this very pool they began their long journey years before, following the river's flow blindly to the sea, riding the crest of the spring runoff down through the rapids and the pools until they felt the first lift of the rising tide. Then, following some ancient imprint of their race, they left the river to steer a secret course far across the sea, feeding and growing as they went, shedding the parr's bright paint for the silver gloss of ocean fish.

For two years or more they foraged in the trackless depths, growing fat and rich and strong. And then, one by one, each sensed a signal to return, a message from the past written in a genetic code a thousand generations old, and each responded to retract its path homeward through the twilight of the sea, back to the river of its birth.

They found Indian nets and anglers' lures waiting in cruel welcome for their return and many fish were taken. Those which escaped faced an even greater test: A hard dash against the river's cold, full winter flow, with each fish spending its stored-up strength in a ceaseless struggle against the falling weight of December's rain and January's oozing snow.

Finally the survivors reached this place, this pool, somehow sensing it was right, and waited for nature to unfold the next step in the ancient drama of their race. And now at last they spawn, spilling their precious eggs into the gravel, committing them to the care of the river, trusting instinctively that in the fullness of time the river will bring forth life.

Days and weeks will pass and the raw winds of March will give way to the gentle rains of April. The snow on the higher slopes will begin its long retreat to the summits and the rivers will swell with its melt. The woods will brighten with the first fresh blush of spring and the tight red willow buds along the riverbanks will break; only then will the steelhead's progeny thrust themselves one by one from the gravel and into the light.

The adult fish never will see what they have bred. By the time the timorous alevins push out to begin their lives as fish, the surviving parents will be far again at sea, feeding on its riches, healing the wounds of their spawning and restoring the strength they spent against the river. And of those that do not survive the ordeal of spawning there will be no sign. The

ragged remnants of their flesh long since will have been
reclaimed by the ever-strict economy of the river, devoured by
bird and beast and all tiny teeming life of the stream, life
which in its own turn will bring nourishment to the young
steelhead emerging from the gravel.

For as long as man has walked the shores of the New
World's rivers, the miracle of the steelhead has been played
out before his eyes. At least some steelhead return in every
month, but the greatest runs always have been in winter; yet
even when the runs were still untouched by man, the
steelhead always were much less numerous than the Pacific
salmon with which they share so many rivers.

The salmon and steelhead were two of the most important reasons why Indians first settled in the Northwest and
made their homes along its rivers. To the Indians, the
primitive country must have seemed like a kind of rain-
washed Garden of Eden—there were rivers full of fish, rich
wild berry crops in summer, prairies filled with edible camas
root, and forests of cedar from which to make longhouses and
canoes. It was a place where Indians could live easily, and in
time the river basins of western Washington became more
densely populated with Indians than any other area north of
Mexico.

Salmon were the mainstay of the Indians' life. They
returned to the rivers at predictable times each year and the
Indians knew this and waited to catch them. Five of the six
Pacific salmon species are found in Northwest waters—the
chinook, coho, sockeye, chum, and pink—and it seemed as if
at least one of them was always running, from spring clear
through to the early days of winter.

To most tribes, steelhead were less important simply
because they were less numerous and because the largest runs
came in winter when water and fishing conditions were often
at their worst. But in some rivers, steelhead and salmon runs
peaked together and the Indians caught them both, and the

steelhead became nearly equal to the salmon in importance. And nearly every Indian fisherman knew that even when the rivers were empty of salmon, at least a few steelhead could probably be found.

The Indians fished with dip nets, crude gill nets, reef nets, spears, and cleverly constructed traps; they caught fish in weirs and impoundments, and they used trolling and jigging methods. They fished mostly in the estuaries and the rivers, but some ventured far out onto Puget Sound or onto the wild north Pacific Ocean. They learned not only the seasons but the locales in which the fish would run, and year after year they returned to the same fishing stations to await the returning salmon and steelhead.

Since salmon and steelhead play such vital roles in tribal life, it is hardly surprising that over time they took on a mystical, even religious significance to the tribes. Nearly every Indian group had its own version of the "first salmon" ceremony, a rite of celebration at the capture of the first salmon of the season. It included ceremonies whose purpose was to assure that the first fish would be the harbinger of a healthy run, and to remind tribal members they should do nothing to offend or waste this great natural gift that was so essential to their existence.

The Indians even saw salmon in the stars. Those who lived along the Nisqually River, south of the modern city of Tacoma, would watch by night as the constellation Orion ascended slowly in the autumn sky, knowing that when it reached a certain point the chum salmon, which they called Tl'hwai, would return to their river, and with it would come Skwowl, the steelhead. To them, the three stars in Orion's belt symbolized Indian fishermen drawing in schools of fish; the bright stars of the Pleiades cluster resembled a school of fish, and on clear nights, when the northern lights flickered on the far horizon, the Nisquallys thought it looked like a giant school of herring turning up their white bellies.

It was important to the Indians' philosophy never to take more fish than they needed in order not to offend the beneficent spirits who sent them. As long as that was their belief the runs remained healthy, for even at their peak the Indians never were numerous enough to have a significant impact on their size. For countless centuries the tribes lived in harmony with the salmon and steelhead, timing their travels to the migrations of the fish, carrying on the rituals they believed would assure their return, and tracing the shapes of salmon and steelhead among the stars. But late in the 18th century they began to feel the first touch of the outside world.

That touch seemed light enough at first, a series of brief encounters with strange white men who appeared off the coast on great sailing ships such as the Indians never before had seen. Sometimes these meetings led to bloody clashes, but more often they were peaceful and the sailors traded with the Indians for fish and pelts.

The white men always sailed away as mysteriously as they had come, but they left behind an invisible legacy of disease that spread rapidly among the tribes; lacking immunity, the Indians died in great numbers. Perhaps as many as half of all the Indians living in the Puget Sound area died in the period of early contact with the whites.

And then the white men began to come and stay—a few fur traders and trappers at first, then prospectors and speculators, finally settlers lured by a promise of unclaimed land and a dream of cities rising on the shores of Puget Sound. In the beginning there were not enough of them to have much effect on the Indians' way of life, for the land and its resources were large enough for both. The Indians continued fishing for themselves and increasingly were hired to fish also for the whites, and a mutually beneficial commerce grew up between them.

The settlers had little interest in the fishery, except for their own use. Their techniques for preserving fish were primitive, and since the Northwest was so far from the rest of the civilized world, shipments of steelhead and salmon spoiled long before they could arrive at market. In fact, Puget Sound salmon soon gained a bad reputation among the fish dealers of distant cities because it always was in such poor condition when it arrived, and this effectively discouraged any thoughts of a commercial fishing industry among the early settlers.

But the increasing settlement of the Northwest drew the government's attention to the potential value of the region and the United States negotiated a series of treaties to extinguish the conflicting claims of Spain, Russia, and Great Britain. Then, on August 14, 1848, Congress approved an act establishing the Oregon Territory, which included the present bounds of Washington state.

Five years later Washington was split off as a separate territory and Isaac Stevens was appointed governor. Stevens' instructions were to unite "the numerous bands and fragments of tribes," negotiate treaties with them, and furnish the government with a map showing the areas occupied by each tribe and the territories it claimed.

The notions of political structure and land ownership were foreign to the tribes, but Stevens set out to educate them on the rudiments of both. He appointed Col. Michael T. Simmons to visit the Puget Sound tribes, determine their numbers and the boundaries of the territories they claimed and try to organize them into political entities with which Stevens could negotiate. Stevens also enlisted the help of George Gibbs, a lawyer, surveyor, and ethnologist, and Col. B.F. Shaw, an interpreter, to help with the forthcoming negotiations.

After much preliminary work, Stevens and Gibbs compiled a census that showed 7,559 Indians were living in western Washington in 1854, although their count almost certainly was inaccurate and incomplete. The white population of the territory at the time has been estimated at about 2,000.

Stevens and his assistants also succeeded in dividing the Indians into discrete tribes and bands, simultaneously appointing many chiefs and subchiefs to represent their fellow tribesmen in negotiations. In one case, the Skopamish, Stkamish and Smulkamish Indians, who lived along the White and Green rivers a little east of Puget Sound, were combined into a group Stevens called the Dwamish, under a chief whose name the white men had difficulty both pronouncing and spelling. The name they finally settled on was Seattle.

Having made everything ready, Stevens scheduled a series of parlays with the tribes for the purpose of concluding the treaties. Among those invited to attend one of these meetings was the diarist James G. Swan.

"During the winter I received from Governor Stevens a letter inviting me to be present at a meeting to be held early in the spring on the Chehalis River, for the purpose of making a treaty with some of the Coast tribes relative to a purpose of their lands," Swan wrote. "This meeting was to take place at the clearing of a settler about ten miles from the mouth of the river, and the day designated was the 25th of February, 1855."

In the company of William B. Tappan, Indian subagent for the southwestern section of the territory, a certain "Dr. Cooper," and a contingent of local Indians, Swan left his home on Willapa Bay and traveled by canoe to the rendezvous site. "As we approached the camp we all stopped at a bend in the river, about three quarters of a mile distant, when all began to wash their faces, comb their hair, and put on their best clothes," Swan wrote. "The [Indian] women got out their bright shawls and dresses, and painted their faces with vermillion, or red ochre, and grease, and decked themselves out with their beads and trinkets, and in about ten minutes we were a gay-looking set; and certainly the appearance of the canoes filled with Indians dressed in their brightest colors was very picturesque, but I should have enjoyed it better had the weather been a little warmer. . . .

"Governor Stevens gave us a cordial welcome, and, after expressing the gratification he felt at the sight of so many canoes filled with well-dressed Indians, told us to go to the campfire, where he had ordered a breakfast to be ready for us, and we soon had a hearty meal of beefsteak, hot biscuits, and coffee, and were then shown in the tent which had been assigned to us, where we proceeded to put ourselves to rights, and then took a look around to see the lay of the land.

"The campground was situated on a bluff bank of the river, on its south side, about ten miles from Gray's Harbor, on the claim of Mr. James Pilkington. A space of two or three acres had been cleared from logs and brushwood, which had been piled up so as to form an oblong square . . . In the centre of the square, and next to the river, was the governor's tent, and between it and the south side of the ground were the commissary's and other tents, all ranged in proper order. Rude tables, laid in open air, and a huge framework of poles, from which hung carcasses of beef, mutton, deer, elk, and salmon, with a cloud of wild geese, ducks, and other small game, gave evidence that the austerities of Lent were not to form any part of our services.

"Around the sides of the square were ranged the tents and wigwams of the Indians, each tribe having a space allotted to it. The Coast Indians were placed at the lower part of the camp; first the Chenooks, then the Chehalis, Queniult and Quaitso, Satsop or Satchap, Upper Chehalis and Cowlitz. These different tribes had sent representatives to the council, and there were present about three hundred and fifty of them, and the best feelings prevailed among all." Only 14 white persons were present, including Stevens, Gibbs, Shaw, and Simmons.

"The next morning the council was commenced. The

Indians were all drawn up in a large circle in front of the governor's tent and around a table on which were placed the articles of treaty and other papers . . . His excellency the governor was dressed in a red flannel shirt, dark frock-coat and pants, and these last tucked in his boots California fashion; a black felt hat, with, I think, a pipe stuck through the band, and a paper of fine-cut tobacco in his coat pocket. . . .

"After Col. Mike Simmons, the agent, and, as he has been termed, the Daniel Boone of the Territory, had marshaled the savages into order, an Indian interpreter was selected from each tribe to interpret the Jargon of Shaw into such language as their tribes could understand. The governor then made a speech, which was translated by Colonel Shaw into Jargon, and spoken to the Indians, in the same manner as good old elders of ancient times were accustomed to deacon out the hymns to the congregation. First the governor spoke a few words, then the colonel interpreted, then the Indians; so that this threefold repetition made it rather a lengthy operation. After this speech the Indians were dismissed till the following day, when the treaty was to be read.

"We were then requested by the governor to explain to those Indians we were acquainted with what he had said, and they seemed very well satisfied. The governor had purchased of Mr. Pilkington a large pile of potatoes, about a hundred bushels, and he told the Indians to help themselves. They made the heap grow small in a short time. . . .

"The second morning after our arrival the terms of the treaty were made known. This was read line by line by General Gibbs, and then interpreted by Colonel Shaw to the Indians." The treaty called for the tribes to cede their lands and agree to be placed on a reservation between Gray's Harbor and Cape Flattery. For this they were to be paid $40,000 in installments, plus $4,000 to enable them to "clear and fence in land and cultivate."

"No spiritous liquors were to be allowed on the reservation; and any Indians who should be guilty of drinking liquor would have his or her annuity withheld," Swan recorded. "Schools, carpenters' and blacksmiths' shops were to be furnished by the United States; also a saw-mill, agricultural implements, teachers, and a doctor. All their slaves were to be free, and none afterward to be bought or sold. The Indians, however, were not to be restricted to the reservation, but were to be allowed to procure their food as they had always done, and were at liberty at any time to leave the reservation to trade with or work for the whites.

"After this had all been interpreted to them, they were dismissed till the next day, in order that they might talk the matter over together, and have any part explained to them which they did not understand. The following morning the treaty was again read to them after a speech from the governor, but, although they seemed satisfied, they did not perfectly comprehend. The difficulty was in having so many different tribes to talk to at the same time, and being obliged to use the Jargon, which at best is but a poor medium of conveying intelligence. . . .

"Several of the chiefs spoke, some in Jargon and some in their own tribal language, which would be interpreted into Jargon by one of their people who was conversant with it; so that, what with this diversity of tongues, it was difficult to have the subject properly understood by all. But their speeches finally resulted in one and the same thing, which was that they felt proud to have the governor talk with them; they liked his proposition to buy their land, but they did not want to go on to the reservation.

"The speech of Narkarty, one of the Chenook chiefs, will convey the idea they all had. 'When you first began to speak,' he said to the governor, 'we did not understand you; it was all dark to us as the night; but now our hearts are enlightened, and what you say is clear to us as the sun. We are proud that our great father in Washington thinks of us. We are poor, and

Indians were all drawn up in a large circle in front of the governor's tent and around a table on which were placed the articles of treaty and other papers . . . His excellency the governor was dressed in a red flannel shirt, dark frock-coat and pants, and these last tucked in his boots California fashion; a black felt hat, with, I think, a pipe stuck through the band, and a paper of fine-cut tobacco in his coat pocket. . . .

"After Col. Mike Simmons, the agent, and, as he has been termed, the Daniel Boone of the Territory, had marshaled the savages into order, an Indian interpreter was selected from each tribe to interpret the Jargon of Shaw into such language as their tribes could understand. The governor then made a speech, which was translated by Colonel Shaw into Jargon, and spoken to the Indians, in the same manner as good old elders of ancient times were accustomed to deacon out the hymns to the congregation. First the governor spoke a few words, then the colonel interpreted, then the Indians; so that this threefold repetition made it rather a lengthy operation. After this speech the Indians were dismissed till the following day, when the treaty was to be read.

"We were then requested by the governor to explain to those Indians we were acquainted with what he had said, and they seemed very well satisfied. The governor had purchased of Mr. Pilkington a large pile of potatoes, about a hundred bushels, and he told the Indians to help themselves. They made the heap grow small in a short time. . . .

"The second morning after our arrival the terms of the treaty were made known. This was read line by line by General Gibbs, and then interpreted by Colonel Shaw to the Indians." The treaty called for the tribes to cede their lands and agree to be placed on a reservation between Gray's Harbor and Cape Flattery. For this they were to be paid $40,000 in installments, plus $4,000 to enable them to "clear and fence in land and cultivate."

"No spiritous liquors were to be allowed on the reserva-

smuggled some whisky into the camp, and made his appearance before the governor quite intoxicated. He was handed over to Provost-marshal Cushman, with orders to keep him quite till he got sober. The governor was very much incensed at this breach of orders, for he had expressly forbidden either whites or Indians bringing one drop of liquor into camp.

"The following day Tleyuk stated that he had no faith in anything the governor said, for he had been told that it was the intention of the United States government to put them all on board steamers, and send them away out of the country, and that the Americans were not their friends . . . That evening the governor called the chiefs into his tent, but to no purpose, for Tleyuk made some insolent remarks, and peremptorily refused to sign the treaty, and, with his people, refused to have anything to do with it. That night, in his camp, they behaved in a very disorderly manner, firing off guns, shouting, and making a great uproar."

The next morning, Governor Stevens called Tleyuk before the camp and gave him a severe reprimand, "and taking from him his paper which had been given to show that the government recognized him as chief, he tore it to pieces before the assemblage. Tleyuk felt this disgrace very keenly, but said nothing. The paper was to him of great importance, for they all look on a printed or written document as possessing some wonderful charm. The governor then informed that, as all would not sign the treaty, it was of no effect, and the camp was then broke up."

Tleyuk was not the only chief to defy Stevens, but the governor succeeded in getting most tribes and bands to sign treaties covering all of western Washington north of the Chehalis River. In each case the treaties were explained to the Indians in the crude Chinook Jargon, a trade language which had only a few hundred words—and no word at all for steelhead.

It seems doubtful the Indians ever had more than a

general concept of the details of the treaties, but there is little doubt that each side in the negotiations knew what was foremost in the minds of the other. The white men wanted title to the Indians' land, and the Indians understood this; for their part, the Indians were determined to have continued access to the salmon and steelhead runs that had always sustained them, and the white men knew this. The whites also knew that if the treaties denied such access, there was no hope the Indians ever would agree to sign them.

Even so, Stevens and his associates might have made a bid to obtain some of the Indians' fishing rights if they had thought them worth very much; as it was, the Puget Sound salmon already had a poor reputation in the marketplace and seemed of little commercial value. In any case, the steelhead and salmon runs seemed limitless, and no one could foresee a day when there might not be enough for everyone. Allowing the Indians to keep their right of access to traditional fisheries therefore seemed a minor price for the whites to pay in return for the signatures they sought on the treaties, which would give them title to the Indian lands.

So a clause was written into the treaties to assure the tribes they would be able to continue fishing, and Governor Stevens was able to say to the Indians, as he did at the Point No Point Treaty council, "This paper secures your fish." The clause said that "the right of taking fish at usual and accustomed grounds and stations" was secured to the Indians "in common with all citizens of the Territory."

The treaties gave the whites what they wanted—title to the land—but they were not enough to avert bloodshed. Before the year 1855 was out, violence between Indians and whites had flared on both sides of the Cascades and an ugly little war was under way. It was a conflict that has all but escaped mention in history books, with the notable exception of the so-called "Battle of Seattle," but it continued well into the spring of 1856 in a series of nasty little skirmishes and ambushes in the woods and along the river bottoms south and east of Seattle.

Suffering and loss was heavy on both sides, but in the end triumph went to the whites with their superior weapons and firepower. Most survivors of the vanquished Indian bands were forced onto reservations, joining other tribes which had gone there peacefully after the treaties were signed.

Indians still outnumbered whites in the territory and at first, after things had settled down, most were able to leave the reservations and continue fishing at their traditional sites. The settlers offered encouragement by serving as a willing market for the Indian catch. The steelhead and salmon runs themselves apparently were as abundant as ever. The Northwest still seemed far from the heart and nerve center of the nation, and in any case the country soon found itself totally preoccupied with the bloody conflict of the Civil War. Even Governor Stevens was caught up in the war's violent vortex, becoming a brigadier general in the Union Army. On September 1, 1862, near the country estate of Chantilly in northern Virginia, he snatched up a battle flag, led his men in a charge on Stonewall Jackson's lines and was shot dead. His sacrifice won him a small place in the history books, but for the next hundred years his role as the chief architect of the treaties was all but forgotten.

When the Civil War ended, a new wave of settlers came pushing westward and the white population of Washington Territory began to increase dramatically. The new arrivals claimed lands, cleared farms and built sawmills and towns, usurping some of the Indians' traditional fishing sites in the process. That was bad enough for the tribes, but a much more significant and subtle change also was taking place: Logging in the lowland valleys was beginning to strip the rivers and their tributaries of the shade that had kept them cool and comfortable for fish. Also, once the trees were gone, there was little to hold back runoff from the fall and winter rains; the rapid runoff eroded the soil and carried silt into streams where steelhead and salmon spawned. Enterprising farmers caused other problems, draining saltwater marshes and freshwater sloughs where young trout and salmon had sheltered and fed, converting them instead to croplands.

All these things were done without much thought for the fisheries, for the runs still seemed limitless; in any case, few people realized what consequences their actions ultimately might have upon fish or the rivers that sustained them.

Then a canning process was perfected that made it possible for the first time to ship salmon and steelhead to distant markets with assurance they would arrive in palatable shape. With this discovery, the fish runs suddenly took on enormous potential economic worth, and white fishermen moved swiftly to take advantage of it.

The first cannery on Puget Sound was built in 1877 at Mukilteo—ironically, the site where Chief Seattle and other Indians had signed one of Governor Stevens' treaties 22 years earlier. By 1894 the number of canneries had grown to three; by 1905 there were 24. The cannery fishermen borrowed a traditional Indian fishing method, the fish trap, and elbowed the Indians aside to stake their traps at sites where tribesmen had fished for countless generations. Once in place, the traps functioned with deadly efficiency on the returning runs.

At first there were no restrictions on the commercial fishery—no one ever had foreseen a day when restrictions would be needed—and whole runs were decimated or wiped out. After a few years of this, the decline in numbers of returning fish became so obvious that it was apparent something had to be done. Washington had become a state in 1889, and the next year the Legislature passed a measure that outlawed salmon fishing for three months of the year. Soon thereafter, the state began to require commercial fishermen to have licenses and started regulating the types of fish traps that could be used and their hours of operation. The Legislature also prohibited spearing, snagging, or snaring of fish.

Conservation was the motive for all these regulations, but they also had the practical effect of denying Indians access to the fishery and outlawing many of their traditional fishing methods. The tribes' original fear that they would lose the opportunity to fish was being realized.

Meanwhile, logging had grown into a major industry and many watersheds were stripped of their timber. After it was gone, tributaries used by salmon and steelhead for spawning began to flood in the spring and subside to low, warm flows in summer. Spawning beds were choked with silt, and logging slash formed barriers that kept fish from ascending streams. These drastic changes, coupled with the relentless pressure of the commercial fishery, reduced the runs from massive abundance to a shockingly low ebb in a few short years.

State authorities responded by authorizing construction of the first state salmon hatchery in 1895, beginning a long series of efforts to use hatcheries to overcome problems of damaged habitat and too much fishing pressure. In 1897 and again in 1899 the Legislature also approved additional conservation measures, ordering the closure of fishing in all tributaries and many estuaries of Puget Sound—once again denying the tribes access to some of their most valued salmon and steelhead fishing stations.

Despite the declining runs, the non-Indian commercial fishery continued to increase. Development of gasoline-powered engines allowed purse-seine vessels to venture into the outer waters of Puget Sound where they were able to intercept returning salmon in deep water long before other fishermen had a chance. Use of the highly efficient purse seines "stole upon us like a thief in the night," a state fish commissioner observed.

Engines also increased the mobility of gillnet boats, but

the new technology actually reduced the overall efficiency of the fishery. Always before, mature salmon which had finished feeding and reached their peak weight and condition had been taken in river-mouth fisheries; now, seiners and gillnetters ranged far and took fish which had not yet reached their maximum size.

The Indians, mostly crowded onto reservations and living in poverty, lacked means to purchase boats and motors and join in this fishery, so they were left with a chance to fish only for those salmon which had been able to evade the outlying seines and gillnets.

By 1904, things were so bad that State Fisheries Commissioner T.R. Kershaw reported that "on Puget Sound the salmon have been steadily decreasing in numbers each year until even now the most optimistic concede that this industry will soon become one of comparatively little importance unless active steps . . . are taken." Steps were taken: more and more hatcheries were built, and more controls were imposed on fishing. But there were still no laws to protect against logging-caused erosion or pollution from the growing number of towns and mills on Puget Sound and its tributary rivers.

The steelhead runs, whose fate always has been inextricably intertwined with the salmon, suffered from the same problems. But although their numbers already had declined to a fraction of historical size, steelhead were beginning to win a small but dedicated following among sport fishermen. These were men who had discovered that the steelhead provided a rare quality of sport, enough to justify the effort of hiking or riding horseback to untrammeled upstream sites where it was still possible to fish the surviving runs.

For their part, the Indians seemed powerless to resist the changes that had taken away their right to fish as they always had. They were not even citizens of the country that had imposed itself on them, and thus had no representation on the councils that set fishing rules and regulations. They were also still widely regarded by the whites as little more than ignorant savages. As one early decision of the Washington State Supreme Court put it, "The Indian was a child, and a dangerous child, of nature, to be both protected and restrained. In his nomadic life he was to be left, so long as civilization did not demand his region. When it did demand that region, he was to be allotted a more confined area with permanent subsistence. These arrangements were but the announcement of our benevolence which, notwithstanding our frequent frailties, has been continuously displayed. Neither Rome nor sagacious Britain ever dealt more liberally with their subject races than we with these savage tribes, whom it was generally tempting and always easy to destroy and whom we have so often permitted to squander vast areas of fertile land before our eyes."

Considering a mind set like that, the Indians had little hope of obtaining relief in the state's courts. But federal courts were more friendly to their cause, and in one of the earliest fishing-rights cases, *United States versus Winans*, a white settler was ordered to remove four fish-wheel traps he had placed in the Columbia River at one of the Yakima Nation's traditional fishing places. In that 1905 case, the beginning of more than half a century of litigation, the U.S. Supreme Court observed that the Yakimas' right to fish at their accustomed places was "not much less necessary to the existence of the Indians than the atmosphere they breathed."

But even such words from the nation's highest tribunal were not enough to stem the tide running against the Indians. By the end of World War I, the non-Indian fishery had expanded to include a growing offshore troll fleet, which reached out beyond the seiners' territory to intercept returning fish at an even earlier stage in their migration. The salmon now had to run a triple gauntlet—the offshore trollers, the purse seiners and the inside gillnet fishery—before they reached the Indians' traditional estuarine and river fishing sites. By then their numbers had been so reduced that often there were barely enough remaining to meet spawning-escapement needs; Indians who tried to catch them were accused of trying to destroy the runs.

During the 1920s, the number of commercial fishermen increased faster than the catch and the average fisherman's income declined. The various fishing groups—trollers, seiners and gillnetters—squared off in bitter political contests to try to wrest a greater share of the rapidly declining resource for themselves.

Several other significant events occurred during that turbulent decade. On June 2, 1924, Congress passed an act that made every Indian a citizen of the United States. A year later, the Washington Legislature, responding to the rapidly growing popularity of the steelhead as a sport fish, declared that steelhead returning to fresh waters were to be classified as game fish and could not be taken in nets. At first this provision did not apply to steelhead in streams flowing across or next to Indian reservations, but two years later the Legislature eliminated that exception. Finally, in 1929, the Legislature also prohibited the commercial sale of steelhead.

The result of all these actions was to reserve the steelhead as a sport fish, protected from any kind of commercial fishery or exploitation. Aside from complying with the desires of sport fishermen, there were some very good economic and biological reasons for doing this, but as a practical matter it shut off still another traditional tribal fishery. The steelhead never had been as important as the salmon to most tribes, but the Legislature's move to close the steelhead fishery, coming as it did after the non-Indian commercial fishery had effectively usurped the salmon, was a bitter blow to the Indians.

But that wasn't the end. In 1935, state voters adopted an initiative prohibiting all "fixed-gear" fisheries. By this time, the Indians had few fishing sites left, and few were the salmon that returned to them, but the initiative made it illegal to use traditional trapping methods at these few remaining sites. It also closed inner Puget Sound to fishing by any means other than trolling or gillnetting, and the trollers and gillnetters quickly stepped in to take the fish Indians no longer were permitted to catch in traps.

Meanwhile, dams were beginning to add to the habitat problems already caused by logging, pollution, irrigation, and increasing industrial development in the Northwest. The Columbia River and its tributaries were hit hardest, beginning with completion of Rock Island Dam in 1933. That same year, making good on campaign promises, President Franklin D. Roosevelt commissioned a massive federal hydroelectric and irrigation development program on the Columbia, beginning with construction of Grand Coulee and Bonneville dams.

The Army Corps of Engineers' original design for Bonneville Dam contained no provision for fish passageways, which would have meant complete extermination of the Columbia's vast upriver salmon and steelhead runs, largest in the world. This was simply too much, and public protest finally forced the corps to reconsider and hire a team of biologists and engineers to design ladders to enable fish to ascend the 65-foot dam.

But Grand Coulee Dam would be 550 feet high, and there was no possible way fish ladders could be designed for a dam of that height; construction of Grand Coulee shut off the entire upper Columbia River Basin to migratory fish, blocking access to hundreds of miles of spawning water.

Over the years, dams proliferated on the Columbia and Snake rivers until they became a series of slackwater lakes behind stairstep barriers. Other dams were built on many of their tributaries, and west of the mountains many key rivers flowing into Puget Sound suffered a similar fate.

Both the state and federal governments continued to try to deal with these problems by building more hatcheries.

Beginning in the early 1940s the Washington Department of Game, which was responsible for steelhead management, began propagating winter steelhead. But as often had been the case with salmon, little attention was paid to the origin of the stock used in these hatcheries. Steelhead from one river were trapped and spawned and their offspring were released in other rivers where they were expected to behave as if they were the progeny of natural runs that had returned to those rivers for thousands of years. Not surprisingly, they did not behave as expected, and those which managed to survive usually returned much earlier in winter than the native runs.

In a way this was good, for it spread the winter sport fishery over a longer time. Encouraged by these results, the Game Department began in the late 1940s to experiment with hatchery-reared summer steelhead. The first limited plants of these fish were made in lower Columbia River tributaries early in the 1950s and in 1956 a hatchery was completed to provide fish for a large-scale stocking program. By the early 1960s this program was under way.

Logging had been particularly harmful to the state's summer steelhead populations, destroying the cold, clear summer flows the fish needed to survive. The Game Department's stocking program succeeded in rebuilding some depleted runs and even created new ones in rivers which lacked them, most notably the Toutle River and its tributaries. Restoration of the steelhead runs provided great encouragement to anglers and the ranks of the state's license-holding steelhead fishermen swelled to several hundred thousand.

Meanwhile, intensive commercial net fisheries had developed in Alaskan and Canadian waters, intercepting Washington-bound salmon many hundreds of miles from their rivers of origin. Despite this increased competition, the number of commercial fishermen continued to grow and more hatcheries were built to pump out salmon in ever greater numbers.

All these things helped crowd the Indians into an even

smaller corner. Many Indians gave up fishing and left the reservations that always had been their homes, but a small cadre continued to eke out a bare subsistence on the tiny share of the resource that was left to them. Time and again they had appealed to friendly federal courts, and time and again the courts upheld their treaty rights with noble words that were largely ignored by state authorities, and nothing changed.

But in the 1960s Indians began to take notice of the growing success of the black civil-rights movement and decided to borrow some of its tactics. They began staging "protest" net fisheries for steelhead on the Puyallup River, challenging the state to intervene. A series of confrontations followed, some of them violent, and a number of Indians and their sympathizers went to jail. But these incidents drew widespread public attention to the fishing-rights issue, which was exactly what the Indians wanted.

Public attitudes had changed since the days when the state Supreme Court had called the Indian "a dangerous child" and the tribes found they had a great deal of sympathy from the majority of the white population not directly involved in fishing. Playing on these sympathies and the publicity generated by their protest fisheries, the tribes and their activist supporters began to bring pressure on the federal government to do something.

In September 1970, 115 years after the last treaty was signed, those efforts finally paid off when the United States, acting as trustee for seven western Washington Indian tribes, filed suit to enjoin the state from interfering with the fishing rights Governor Stevens had promised to the Indians. The case was assigned to U.S. District Judge George H. Boldt of Tacoma.

In many respects it was an unequal contest. After years as underdogs, the tribes suddenly had the full weight and resources of the federal government on their side. As additional tribes were allowed to intervene, their lawyers, together with those representing the federal government, grew to outnumber the state's attorneys by more than 10 to 1.

The state Department of Fisheries and Game intervened as separate defendants in the case, but non-Indian sport and commercial fishermen had no direct voice in the proceedings. One reason may have been that they underestimated the importance of the case; after more than a half century of Indian fishing-rights litigation which had changed nothing, there was no apparent reason for them to believe this case might end differently.

The trial finally began on August 27, 1973, and continued for three weeks. Nearly 50 witnesses testified, including anthropologists, Indians, biologists, and fishermen, and the transcript ran to more than 4,600 pages. But when all was said and done, the issue boiled down to what Governor Stevens had meant when he told the Indians they had the right to fish "in common with all the citizens of the Territory."

On February 12, 1974, Judge Boldt ruled that "in common with" meant to share equally. In an historic opinion, the judge wrote: "It is the responsibility of all citizens to see that the terms of the Stevens treaties are carried out, so far as possible, in accordance with the meaning they were understood to have by the tribal representatives at the councils, and in a spirit which generously recognizes the full obligation of this nation to protect the interests of a dependent people . . . the mere passage of time has not eroded, and cannot erode, the rights guaranteed by solemn treaties that both sides pledged on their honor to uphold."

The essence of his ruling was that the treaties had reserved the Indians' right to fish, which meant that for non-Indians fishing was not a right but only a privilege. And Boldt departed from all earlier court decisions by quantifying the Indians' right; it meant, he said, that treaty fishermen were entitled to fish at their traditional off-reservation stations and catch half of all the returning salmon and steelhead not needed for spawning escapement. Non-Indians would have the opportunity to catch only those fish not needed to provide the Indians with their share, less whatever fish were necessary for spawning escapement. The tribes also were to become equal partners with the state in managing the fisheries.

The decision was a total victory for the tribes. Never before had their fishing rights been more than a vague legal concept; now they had firm meaning. And Boldt, a feisty and dedicated jurist, was determined to see that the meaning was enforced.

It took a while for the full impact of the decision to register on non-Indian fishermen. But then Boldt took control of the state's fisheries management, ordered early closures of the non-Indian commercial salmon fishery and sent state and federal agents to enforce his rulings, and suddenly the full meaning of his decision was clear to all.

It also was soon reflected in the catch statistics. In the years before the decision, the tribes had averaged only five percent of the area's salmon harvest; in 1974, after Boldt imposed restrictions on the non-Indian fishery, the tribal share increased to nearly 12 percent. Each following year saw more and more restrictions on the non-Indian fishery and a larger tribal catch.

The impact on steelhead was even more dramatic. In the three years before Boldt's ruling, the tribes' reservation net fisheries had taken about 23 percent of all the steelhead caught in the case area. In 1974 that figure jumped to 38 percent, in 1975 it surpassed 50 percent, and by 1976 it was nearly 66 percent. In some rivers, Indians caught nearly 100 percent of the harvestable steelhead run, leaving sport fishermen with nothing.

As these impacts became visible they stirred conflicts nearly as violent as the Indian war that had followed the signing of the treaties: Shots were exchanged, people were hurt, fishing boats were rammed, and angry sport and commercial fishermen marched in the streets and hung Judge Boldt in effigy.

Fate had played a cruel trick on the non-Indian fishermen. Most had fished all their lives, just as the Indians once had; for many, fishing had become a way of life, just as it once was for the Indians. Nearly all considered that fishing was their natural right, just as the tribes had once believed. Suddenly, through circumstances beyond their control, that right had been wrenched away from them, just as it had been taken from the Indians a hundred years before. And now they felt the same bitter hurt and blind frustration the Indians had felt in their darkest days.

Steelhead anglers were hit hardest by the ruling. Always before the Indian fishermen had been at the wrong end of a long funnel; now, with Indian nets strung across the mouths of nearly every steelhead river, it was the steelhead sport fisherman who suddenly found himself at the wrong end. The tribes concentrated on the winter runs, and soon the upstream reaches of the coastal rivers were lined with anglers waiting for fish that never came.

Angry though they were, the non-Indian commercial and sport fishermen seemed incapable of doing anything about their plight. Just as the Indians had been at the time of the treaties, non-Indian fishing groups were fragmented, disorganized, and at odds with one another, each group apparently unable to see beyond the limited horizon of its own selfish interests. They staged protests and wrote angry letters to editors and congressmen and cursed the Indians, Judge Boldt and one another, and some of them went to jail. But nothing happened.

Meanwhile, subsequent court decisions made matters even worse. Boldt's ruling was determined to apply not only to wild salmon and steelhead, but also to fish raised in state hatcheries; these were seen as replacements for wild stocks which had been depleted by the white man's careless treat-

ment of their habitat. This meant that hatchery-reared
steelhead, paid for by sportsmen's license fees, could be caught
in Indian nets, a fact which further incensed steelhead
anglers. A federal judge in Oregon also applied Boldt's 50-50
formula to the steelhead and salmon fisheries of the Columbia
and Snake rivers.

In an ironic reversal of earlier history, many steelhead
sport fishermen gave up fishing in disgust and many non-
Indian commercial fishermen were forced out of business by
the increasingly severe restrictions placed upon them; others
fished in defiance of the regulations and went to jail for
poaching.

In 1979 the U.S. Supreme Court upheld Boldt's ruling in
nearly every important respect. After that the protests slowly
sputtered out, the picket signs disappeared and in their place
"For Sale" signs appeared on many fishing boats. Various
legislative proposals or public initiatives to decommercialize
steelhead were trotted out but most were beaten back, and
these failures finally led some non-Indian fishing groups to
belatedly conclude that compromise was their only hope—
though they had little left with which to bargain. Meanwhile,
federal promises of funds for fisheries enhancement went
unfulfilled, and some fish runs, already endangered, declined
even further.

For the Indians, the Boldt decision has meant greater
self-esteem, a return of tribal members to the reservations,
and a large increase in the number of Indian fishermen. Yet
only a few members of the largest tribes have been able to
make enough money from fishing to join the ranks of the
middle class; most reservation families still have incomes far
below their white counterparts.

The decision also revived many old prejudices that would
have been better left forgotten. And by their actions in its
aftermath, both sides have proved that prejudice and greed are
not the exclusive traits of any race.

Despite the controversy, any careful reading of the Boldt decision or the long preceding record can hardly fail to lead a reasonable man to conclude that the decision was both morally and legally correct. But that is not to say it is without flaws; indeed, it has at least one very serious flaw, perhaps a fatal one: It requires biologists to predict run sizes and measure catches with a degree of precision that is impossible to meet—yet such precision is necessary in order to divide catches equally and assure enough fish are left for spawning. Judge Boldt failed to recognize that the chances for error in this approach are much greater than the chances for success, and any error that cuts into spawning escapement can very quickly bring a run of fish to the edge of extinction.

To be sure, Boldt's ruling has stimulated significant improvements in management techniques and knowledge, and this is all to the good; but it is unlikely that fisheries science ever will advance far enough to achieve the kind of absolute management precision that Boldt assumed was possible. That shortcoming, coupled with the fragmentation of management between federal, state, and tribal governments, could pose a grave danger to the future of the runs.

Beyond that, there is the larger question of whether it is wise social policy to divide the fish equally between a small number of Indians and the much larger community of non-Indian sport and commercial fishermen. As long as either side feels it is getting less than a fair shake, there is bound to be conflict, and this is a problem that ultimately must be resolved by the people rather than the courts. Unfortunately there is little sign that a solution is taking shape.

And so, from the early days of plenty, when the rivers ran full of fish and the Indians lived easily on their shores, we have come down to this: A divided society scrapping over the pitiful remnants of the once-mighty runs, arguing in court over who should be allowed to catch what little is left. It is, altogether, a sad story, a tale of greed, injustice, irony, and weakness on all sides, a tragedy for men and for fish—but especially for the fish.

If you really wish to understand it, then you must go up to the headwaters in winter and search for those scarred survivors of the long return. If you look long enough you will find them, paired together in the lonely pools or huddled on the redds. They are a stirring sight, these great fish so far from the sea, the last wild survivors of their kind. How far they have come!

If you see them, then you will know why men have followed them, worshipped them and fought so long and so hard for the right to fish for them.

And then, perhaps, you will truly understand.

Cutthroat Slough

Winter was hanging on like an old overcoat. It was the eve of April, but there was still no hint or sign of spring. Day after day the skies and the rivers were cold and gray. No flies hatched; no trout rose.

Faced with a restless urge to fish, I surveyed the limited prospects and decided to go in search of cutthroat. The cutthroat is a good fallback fish; no matter what the season or the weather, it seems there always are a few of them around. If you can find them, you can nearly always catch them.

A friend had told me about a slough where cutthroat sometimes were plentiful late in winter or early in the spring.

Following a map, I drove to the spot, crossing a bridge over the outlet of the slough, then turning off on a pair of ruts that led across a farmer's frozen field. Beyond the field I could see the glint of water.

The road ended at the edge of the slough, near a ring of fire-blackened rocks that marked the remains of an old camp. Old maples grew along the water's edge, their winter-barren limbs leaning out over the slough like skeletal fingers. It was quiet there, and cold. The field behind the maples was deserted; there was not even a house in sight. But others had used the spot to camp, so I supposed it would be all right if I did so, too.

I was chilled by the time I had finished setting up my camp, manhandled my little aluminum pram down to the water and set up my rods. An icy wind scrawled changing patterns on the surface of the slough and the sky overhead was the color of slate, threatening snow.

The slough was wide near my camp, narrowing farther upstream until it disappeared among the trees. From the map I knew it was several miles long and I was near the lower end of it. It was actually the side channel of a great river, forming a giant arc from its upstream source until it emptied back into the main flow through the outlet I had crossed. Within the arc was a large island; my camp was on the island's edge.

The water was cold and dark with a slow current running through. The bottom, carpeted with the rotting remains of last year's leaves, sloped away quickly toward the far shore. It looked deep there, with a steep, moss-covered cliff dropping down to the water's edge.

I eased the little boat quietly into the channel and rowed within casting distance of the face of the cliff. There I began probing the deep water with a sinking line and a bright fly that was the only spot of color in the darkening day. Everything remained quiet. No birds sang, no insects hatched, no trout moved.

After a while thin tubes of ice began to form around my line, and I realized the air was growing even colder. The ice broke off and jammed in the rod guides so that after each few casts it was necessary to thrust the rod down into the water, which was only slightly warmer than the air, and leave it there long enough for the ice to melt away. Then I noticed a few flakes of snow were falling.

I had dressed warmly, but the cold had long since cut through my clothes and was toying with my bones. What was intended as enjoyment was rapidly becoming misery, and I was giving thought to quitting when a trout suddenly took hold. There was no warning; one moment the sinking line was slack, the next it was taut and throbbing with the feel of life on the other end. My numb fingers struggled for a grip upon the line as the graphite rod bent and bowed in cadence with the fish. The trout came to the surface and thrashed around, the first sign of life I had seen, and when it finally surrendered I led it to the side of the boat and saw with satisfaction that it was a bright cutthroat of a pound or better. I twisted the fly free and the fish quickly turned away and vanished in the dark water.

By then it was snowing harder, but the trout had revived my interest and I went on fishing. Soon I took another trout, a twin of the first, and then a third, smaller than the others. That was all for a while, but then I noticed a quiet dimple on the surface a little way upstream. Others followed, and it was obvious that several fish were feeding on the surface there. They were making quick, delicate rises, perhaps to the snowflakes that were striking the water in growing numbers.

I rowed within range of the rising fish and took up a rod equipped with a floating line and a small dry fly and began casting. The rises continued, but none came near my fly, so I replaced it with a small nymph and resumed fishing. Almost immediately the floating line gave a twitch and I raised the rod and set the hook in what turned out to be a feisty, plump whitefish—an unexpected bonus for what had started out as such an unpromising day. Moments later I hooked another, just as fat and feisty as the first.

I had grown so intent on fishing that I didn't see the canoe approach. It was less than a hundred feet away when I first noticed it, looming like a ghost through the gathering snow. It held two stern-looking Indians, their solemn eyes fixed steadily on me. Then I remembered from the map that the island where I'd camped was part of an Indian reservation—and I had not seen anyone to ask for permission to camp there, or to fish. The Indians did not look friendly; I wondered if there was going to be trouble.

The Indian in the bow of the canoe was short and stocky with a round face. His companion was tall and powerfully built, with long hair. Neither spoke nor changed expression as they drove the canoe closer with powerful paddle strokes. They came alongside, close enough to touch my boat, and then the short Indian suddenly grinned broadly.

"You shouldn't be out fishing on a day like this," he said. "It's too damn cold. Come ashore and we'll get you warm." Without waiting for an answer, he and his companion turned the canoe toward shore and quickly beached it. Within moments they had gathered wood and had a fire blazing.

I rowed ashore and beached my boat alongside the canoe and joined them at the fire. The smaller Indian reached inside his jacket and produced a bottle. "Here," he said, "this'll warm you up on the inside."

The fire was good and we passed the bottle back and forth while the smoke spiraled up into the thickening snow. The tall Indian sat and said nothing, and I never learned if he could speak. Perhaps he was one who followed the Old Ways and chose to speak only in a tongue I could not understand. But the other Indian—his name was Joey—more than made up for the silence of his friend. He was voluble and friendly and talked freely of fish and fishermen, of salmon and trout and their mysterious ways. He had seen few fly fishermen and knew little of the sport, but seemed fascinated when I opened up a box of flies and took some out and placed them in his hand. He was vastly pleased when I told him to choose a couple and stick them in his hat where they would always be handy for his use.

But he also was puzzled that I had come so far on such a cold day to fish only for cutthroat. "The cutthroat is such a small fish, he is not worth your time," Joey said. "You should come here later, in November, when the coho salmon are in and try to take them with your flies. I bet you could. I'd like to see you try." He made me promise that I would.

We talked on while the fire burned lower, the surrounding fields grew white and the nearby mountains disappeared behind a moving mist of snow. Soon there would be enough snow to make the roads difficult, possibly for days to come. I began to think better of my plan to spend the night.

Finally I said goodbye to Joey and his silent friend and left them by the fire. I rowed back to my short-lived camp, packed up, and drove away across the snowy field. Outside was an arctic scene, but inside my truck was warm and I felt good. I had caught some fish, and that was fine; but better yet, I felt I'd made a friend.

And I'd forgotten all about the long-delinquent spring. I was already looking forward to November.

SPRING

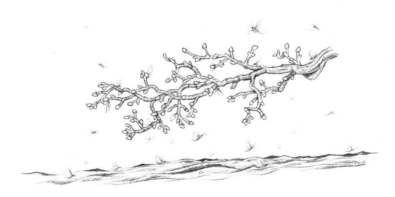

Spring begins in March, a month named after Mars, the Roman god of war. And March is truly a month of conflict, a clash of seasons. Spring advances tentatively, then retreats before the last-ditch assaults of winter. Winter uses every weapon at its command, sneaking through the nights to leave killing layers of frost, or attacking boldly by day with knife-edged winds, lightning bolts, and bursts of rain or stinging hail.

Through the whole long month the battle rages, some-times lasting well into April, which is supposed to be a peaceful month for planting. But despite the fury of the struggle, the outcome always is the same; the storms slowly lose their strength and ebb away, and spring presses forward to reclaim the barren battlefields of winter.

At first the signs are fitful, but then they come together all at once: Buds break open and leaves unfurl to catch the warming rain; mayflies come out to join the midges hatching on the lakes, and suddenly swallows and nighthawks are there among them. Trout and steelhead fry emerge from the river gravel, and soon the streams are filled with their quick, darting movements, masking the more cautious maneuvers of the older, wiser trout. At last the season has arrived; at last it is the time for which the trout fisherman awaits.

I remember going out on a spring morning after a long winter's wait to renew acquaintance with a river that February's floods had changed. The changes were many, but I was pleased to find one spot along the bank was still the same—a pleasant open patch of grass amid a growth of ferns. I stopped there to rest in the gentle warmth of the early afternoon and stretched out to watch the current flowing idly by.

Six weeks earlier the river had been gray and ugly and near flood, its surface swift and barren of any sign of life, its banks overhung with gaunt limbs that long ago had lost their last trace of foliage. Now the stream was clear and bright, with mayflies and midges dancing on the surface and trout rising eagerly to catch them; the trees were all in full green leaf, and everywhere there was color, sound, and movement. And I thought what a miracle it is that seasons can so swiftly pass and life so quickly reappear, and how spring is like a promise kept—especially for a trout fisherman.

A verse began to take shape in my mind and I reached inside my fishing vest and found a scrap of paper and an old blunt pencil and wrote it down. When I was finished I stuffed the paper back inside my vest, then returned to my fishing and soon forgot about it. Many seasons later I found the scrap of paper at the bottom of a pocket in my vest and wondered what it was. I took it out and unfolded it carefully; the paper was wrinkled, faded and yellowed by the years, but the words remained clear:

> *Spring brings*
> *fulfillment*
> *of an angler's winter dream;*
>
> *A chance again*
> *to solve*
> *the silent silver secrets of the stream.*

And now, each time winter sounds retreat and spring returns, I think again of those words—and give thanks once more for fulfillment of the dream.

Like Father, Like Son

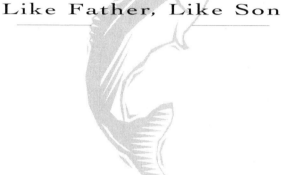

Something magical happens the first time a father puts a fishing rod in his son's hand and leads him to trout water. It happened to me when I was five years old, going on six, and now I have seen it happen to my own son at the same age.

I hope he remembers it as well as I remember that first trip with my own father. It was a spring morning and the air had never been so clear. We followed a dirt road toward far mountains that stood out so vividly it seemed as if the horizon had been ripped along its edge. The road wound through pastures where white-faced Herefords grazed behind split-rail fences, then climbed into aspen groves and pine thickets where the ground still was wet with dew.

We came to a bridge over a small stream and my father stopped the car. The bridge was just a pair of heavy planks and the stream was hardly a stream; I could jump across it easily on my short, five-year-old legs. But it was filled with trout, which was the reason why my father stopped.

The trout had run up from a nearby lake and now they were spawning. Some of them were longer than the stream was wide and it was difficult for them to maneuver in the close quarters between the banks. But they went about their business purposefully, the females probing the gravel with their tails to prepare their nests while the males slashed and fought for the privilege of pairing with them. It was a fascinating sight, unlike anything I'd ever seen, and it prompted a feeling of awe and respect for trout that is with me still.

Later we drove on to Big Bar Lake, our destination, and spent the night in a log cabin on the shore. The next morning there was bright frost on the meadows and a thin layer of ice around the margins of the lake. Fire crackled in an old wood stove in the cabin and the sweet smell of alder smoke soon mingled with the odor of frying bacon. Breakfast was a hurried affair and then we rushed down to a leaning dock where a rowboat was waiting. My father took the oars and pushed off onto the still surface of the lake. When we were out far enough he took a fly rod, worked out the line, then placed the rod in my hand. "Hold tight, son, or the fish will take it from you," he warned.

We rowed slowly across the lake, and I held tightly to the handle of the long bamboo rod, trailing the sinking line behind the boat. The line slanted gently away into the depths and I wondered what was going on down there, and whether any trout could see the bright fly at the tip of the leader.

Soon enough one did, and the rod suddenly came alive in my little hand, throbbing with a strong, electric pull. Instinctively I thrust it back at my father, who took it and played the fish to the side of the boat. It was a foot-long trout, all bright and gleaming silver and quite unlike the dark and ruddy fish I had seen spawning in the stream. And it was a small matter that my father had landed it; I had hooked it, so it was "my" fish, and I proudly proclaimed it so while Dad grinned from ear to ear.

My father and I fished together many times thereafter, but never quite as often as we would have liked. He was an Army officer, a career that left few opportunities for fishing, so the opportunities took on added importance when they came. Always there were elaborate preparations—food to be bought, sleeping bags and bedding to be aired and packed, fresh flies and leaders to be purchased, maps to be studied, plans to be made. But my favorite time was when we took the tackle out to see what things needed to be repaired or replaced.

Each item had its own special feel and scent. The reels were cold and solid to the touch and held braided silk lines with a strong aroma of linseed oil and silicon dressing. The bamboo rods had a musty scent mixed with a lingering odor of varnish, and the long brown shafts felt smooth and strong. We would join the sections together to test the fit, then flex the rods in the air and imagine them bending under the weight of a heavy fish. The fly boxes held a kaleidoscope of colors and textures and the names of the patterns were nearly as exciting and colorful as the flies themselves—Colonel Carey, Black O'Lindsay, Alexander, Nation's Special, Cummings Fancy, Rhodes' Favorite, Lioness, and others whose names escape me now.

Finally, when all was ready, we would pack the car the night before departure, and I would toss and turn in bed and be up well before the dawn, waiting impatiently until it was time to go. Usually my mother or one of my uncles or a fishing companion of Dad's would come along.

But on the last trip it was just the two of us alone. We didn't know, of course, that it would be our last trip together. We set out with the usual bright hopes, and Dad wore the happy look he always had when going fishing. It was not the best fishing we ever had, but neither was it bad, and on the last day we fished into the twilight in a driving rain until both of us were soaked. My father was shivering when we started back to camp, and by the time we reached it he was trembling uncontrollably. I built a fire, wrapped him in a blanket and made some soup and gave him some. After a while he seemed all right again, but it was the first time I had ever really worried about him.

I was 17 then and just about to start college, and back in Washington, D.C., they were cutting orders that would take my father to Germany. We saw each other only a few times after that, and there was never enough time for fishing. And then he suffered the heart attack that killed him.

Now his old reel sits atop my bookcase, the pungent smell of oil and dressing having long since faded. His old bamboo rod stands in its case in the corner, the luster long gone from its varnish. His old flies are carefully put away, but their colors, too, have faded over time.

But the memories remain—recollections of sunlit days and days of rain, of full creels and empty ones, of misty mornings full of promise and evenings spent cleaning a catch by lantern light. Remembered too are his lessons about what knots to tie, how to gauge the wind and light, and where to place the fly. But the brightest memory and the best lesson was one he taught subtly, a little at a time. Call it an attitude or feeling, a sort of inner excitement that returns each spring when the green buds burst open on the trees, the mayflies hatch, and trout begin to rise. It's that and more—a kind of understanding and appreciation that fishing is one of the very best things that ever a man can do, and trout fishing is the very best of all. It is one of my father's most precious gifts to me, and now I hope somehow to impart the same feelings to my son.

His name is Randy, the same as his grandfather whom he never had a chance to know. He is a strong and sturdy boy with a quick mind and many interests, of which fishing is one. It is not something that he has ever been compelled to do, nor has he ever been told that he should want to do it. It has been offered to him as an opportunity that is available whenever he wishes to take advantage of it. And often enough, he has.

The first time was at Dry Falls Lake. It was a spring morning, but a very different one from the long-ago day when I "caught" my own first trout. The sky was dark and streaked with lightning, the wind was cold and strong, and rain came in hard bursts. Randy was bundled up in heavy clothing that made it difficult for him to move, but he was at my side when I hooked a husky little trout and passed the rod to him. He squealed with delight when the fish jumped, then cranked the reel so furiously he nearly wound the fish up to the top guide of the rod before I could stop him. It was a proud moment for him, but an even prouder one for me.

Not long after that he asked if he could have his own rod, and I gave him one my father had given me, along with an old reel and a line. Soon he asked to learn to cast, and I have tried to show him how—sometimes to our mutual consternation, but sometimes, when all goes well, to our mutual delight.

Watching me tie flies one night, he asked to be shown the secrets of that art. Now, with a little instruction, a hand-me-down vise and hand-me-down materials, he is tying his own, which get a little better all the time. He has yet to take a trout on a fly he tied himself, but surely that day is not far off.

Some years ago we bought an old cabin on the North

Fork of the Stillaguamish River, and when Randy watched me wade the stream he asked to follow suit. Not yet, I said; you're not quite old enough for that, and besides you have no boots or waders. But then a friend gave him a pair of children's-sized hip boots, and I no longer had a good excuse.

So on a summer day I helped him into the boots and strapped them to his belt. Even though they were children's size, the boots were too long for his short legs and they hung loosely in accordian pleats. Undaunted, he walked with me down to the river, and I showed him how to slide his feet over the slippery rocks, how to plant one foot firmly before moving the other, and how always to keep his body turned sideways to the flow. Then he put his warm little hand in mine and held tightly as we started out across a side channel to a small island. We reached it safely, waded back, then crossed again. In all, we waded the channel six times before Randy decided he had finally had enough. "Dad, I think that was the funnest thing I ever did," he said.

I thought it was one of the funnest things I'd ever done, too.

Each of these things has pleased me, as my own childhood fishing exploits must have pleased my father. But what a boy does is not always an indication of what he will do when he becomes a man, and there have been times when I have wondered if Randy's interest in fishing is a permanent thing or merely a passing fancy.

And then, last year, I think I got my answer.

Randy was eight then, and decided for the first time to go fishing by himself. He donned the hip boots—they fit a little better now—put his rod together, attached the reel, and threaded the fly line through the guides. He chose a fly without asking my advice, knotted it to the end of his leader, walked down to the river and waded alone into the same side channel we had crossed together a couple of years before. He found a spot to his liking, worked out line and began to cast, while his mother and I settled down to watch from among the trees on the high bank above the river.

Soon we heard his shout and saw the rod bend in a pulsing bow.

I saw the look of joy upon his face, and understood.

"He's hooked one," his mother said.

"No," I told her. "I think maybe it's the other way around."

The Dawn Trout

The St. Maries River is a placid little stream that follows a meandering course through a peaceful valley in the hills of northern Idaho. In most respects it seems an unremarkable little river, but there is much more to the St. Maries than meets the casual eye.

It is, for one thing, a very old river. The weathered ridges that define the limits of its valley once were shoals in a Precambrian sea, and they have shaped the flow of water through the valley since the world was young. For millions of years the river has carried the runoff from these hills, twisting and turning in its channel but always bearing northwestward in the direction dictated by its confining ridges. The Pacific Northwest has hundreds of rivers of greater volume or personality or consequence, but few as old as this one.

You would not think it so old to look upon it now. In the early spring its valley still seems fresh and new, with creeks running full and grass growing tall and clots of winter snow lingering in the shaded hollows. Fat cattle and handsome Appaloosa ponies graze in meadows along the river, and columns of woodsmoke rise into the morning air from the little settlement of Clarkia, a cluster of neat houses built on potholed streets with logging rigs parked out in back. The rigs are there because of the white pine, fir, cedar and hemlock that grow in the hills.

Below Clarkia, where Emerald Creek comes down from the hills to meet the St. Maries, dredges churn the creek sediments to recover garnet sand, but the dredge spoils are dumped in holding ponds so that both the creek and the river still run clear. Above the dredging on Emerald Creek, you can find caddis larvae with cases made of garnets, looking like little living jewels as they crawl slowly and awkwardly among the rocks and debris on the streambottom.

The logging and dredging provide most of the local jobs, but there are not very many of either, and the valley remains sparsely settled. It is far from any major highway or any city of consequence, and far from all the problems that highways and cities bring. Its life is measured and orderly, its rituals defined by the seasons, and its people are accustomed to hard work and hard play. Their recreation reflects their attitude and spirit: They like to race snowmobiles in the winter and trailbikes in the spring and summer. And strangely enough, it was this interest in racing that led to the discovery of some of the secrets hidden in the St. Maries' ancient past.

It began with a man named Francis Kienbaum, who owned property near Clarkia and was well aware of the local interest in racing. Kienbaum had an idea that a commercial racetrack might be a profitable enterprise, and his own land seemed an ideal site; it lay in a hollow between a pair of wooded knolls and was just the right size and shape for a track. All that was needed was a little fill dirt to build up the turns of the track, and there was plenty of dirt for the taking in the knolls at either end of his property. A bulldozer could move it quickly and easily where it was needed.

Having made these plans, Kienbaum decided one day in 1971 to carry them out. He climbed into the cab of a bulldozer and began slicing into the base of one of the knolls, cutting away the topsoil and pushing it toward what would be the north turn of the track. On the first day he worked through the afternoon and into the evening and finally ran the bulldozer far into the night, digging ever deeper into the face of the slope.

But Kienbaum was scarcely prepared for what he found when he returned to the site next morning. What had not been visible in the darkness of the night before was revealed clearly in the morning light: His bulldozer had cut through the topsoil into a layer of soft clay, and the clay had broken up to reveal thousands of fossil leaves. And these were not ordinary fossils; to Kienbaum's astonishment, the leaves appeared to be intact and perfectly preserved. As he watched, some began to dry out, curl up and lift off the clay. One by one, they peeled off and were carried away by the morning breeze.

Kienbaum tried cutting into the clay with a knife and found that it split easily into thin layers like a pastry, with each layer containing more fossils. He found leaves that still wore green, red and golden colors from the springs and autumns of ages past, and again as he watched they dried out quickly, their colors faded, and the leaves curled up and blew away. He opened another layer of clay and this time found what appeared to be the fossil remains of a small fish.

Certain by now he had found something important, Kienbaum decided to report it to someone who could evaluate it properly. He made a telephone call to the University of Idaho in Moscow, 55 miles away, and ended up talking to a secretary at the College of Mines and Earth Resources. She jotted down the details of his story and gave the message to Charles J. (Jack) Smiley, a geology professor and a specialist in the arcane science of paleoecology, the study of prehistoric ecosystems.

Smiley is a wiry, energetic man with a powerful intellect and the kind of strong, innate curiosity that leads a man into science. He also is a man of omnivorous interests, and such a broad range is practically essential in the study of paleoecology. A paleoecologist is like a detective following a very cold trail—a trail that may be 20 million, 50 million, even 100 million years old or more. Even the very smallest clues—fossil flecks of pollen or tiny spores—may have meaning to such a scientist, and his work requires the utmost patience and perseverence in evaluating every detail.

So when Smiley received the message, he was anxious to see what Kienbaum had found. Early the next morning, he drove to the racetrack and quickly confirmed that Kienbaum had made a major discovery—a treasure trove of unusually well-preserved fossil leaves and fish. Subsequent analysis would show them to be from the Miocene Epoch; in other words, the leaves turned up by Kienbaum's bulldozer and carried off by the morning breeze had last known the light of morning nearly 20 million years before.

Kienbaum's find would provide Smiley and others with much work in years to come—the work of taking, preserving, and classifying samples, of analyzing and interpreting them, then finally of translating all the results into a written record to become a permanent part of the published knowledge of earth's past. In the process of this work, a picture of the prehistoric St. Maries valley began to emerge:

Sometime during the Miocene Epoch, a tongue of

molten magma had forced its way up through a fissure in the ancient rock that bounded the St. Maries and spilled out onto the surface as a lava flow. The lava had hardened into a dam that blocked the river, causing the valley to fill with water and form a lake nearly 25 miles long. Smiley and Bill Rember, a graduate student who assisted in the research, named it Miocene Clarkia Lake.

The Cascade Mountains had yet to rise when the lake was formed, and northern Idaho was near the eastern edge of a plain that extended almost unbroken to the Pacific Coast. The climate was much warmer and more humid than it is now, and the fossil evidence showed that swamp cypress, water lilies, and cattails had grown up around the shoreline of the lake. On the lower slopes of the surrounding hills were stands of oak, maple, sycamore, sweetgum, tulip trees, magnolia, and other plants now commonly found in forests of the southeastern United States, but long gone from the Idaho hills. Coniferous trees grew on the higher, cooler slopes above the lake, and all the plants shed their leaves and seeds and pollen to the wind, which carried them out over the open water. There they had fallen to the surface and sunk slowly to the soft muck of the bottom, where they were joined by the remains of beetles, bugs, caddisflies, ants, and other insects that also had fallen into the water, and by the remains of sunfish, minnows, and other aquatic organisms from the lake itself.

The fish had lived near the wind-stirred surface of the lake, above a thermocline that protected a layer of cold, stagnant water near the bottom. It was in this bottom layer where all the plant and animal remains came finally to rest, where each in turn had been covered by a slow rain of silt washed in from tributary streams, or by great falls of ash carried on the wind from distant volcanoes. The lake bottom was a static, sterile environment, so lacking in oxygen that there was no decay. And that is why leaf tissues still wore their colors when Kienbaum's bulldozer sliced into the knoll so many millions of years later; few other sites in the world have yielded fossils preserved so perfectly as those from Miocene Clarkia Lake.

The site of Kienbaum's racetrack, which he promptly named the "Fossil Bowl," once had been a small bay near the upper end of the lake. Surveys disclosed other fossil deposits in the valley, but none as rich as the racetrack site; a layer-by-layer analysis of a thin column of lake-bottom clay from the racetrack yielded a count of more than 10,500 fossils.

Despite the richness of its fossil deposits, the lifespan of Miocene Clarkia Lake was hardly more than a mere flickering instant on the grand scale of geologic time. Ash and silt accumulating on the bottom filled the lake so that its outlet cut an ever-deeper channel through the lava dam. Without the dam to hold it back, the lake quickly disappeared, and once again there was only a placid little river flowing through the long valley. The lake had been born and had lived and died in less than a thousand years, and when it was gone there was hardly any evidence that it had ever existed—except for the fossils that would remain hidden for so long.

In the years immediately following Kienbaum's discovery, the ancient lake gave up its secrets generously, including some that were new to science. Among its fossil fish was a new species, *Archoplites clarki*, a sunfish that may have been a predator with habits similar to those of the modern bass. Among its fossil leaves and fruit were specimens that Smiley classified as a previously unknown genus, *Pseudofagus*, an extinct relative of today's beech trees. And there were many other matters of scientific interest.

But Miocene Clarkia Lake still had one more surprise in store, and nine years would pass before it came to light.

The morning of June 12, 1980, was warm and still with a

threat of thunder in the air. Mount St. Helens had erupted less than a month before, and a fresh layer of powdery volcanic ash lay upon the earth exposed by nine years of digging when Smiley, Rember, and two other students arrived at the racetrack site to begin searching for more plant fossils. They had been at their work only a short time when Rember thrust his knife into a piece of clay, split it open and found himself staring at what appeared to be the bones of a fish— one much larger than any ever found before. Rember thought it might be the remains of a gar, a primitive freshwater fish whose descendants still live in the eastern and southern United States. He shouted and the others came running.

Excited by the size of the find, they began working carefully to lift up other pieces of the clay that concealed the rest of the fossil. It was ticklish work; the fossil was embedded in a layer of clay only half an inch thick, already fractured in places, and below it was a layer of ancient volcanic ash from which the clay could easily separate and fall. Slowly they exposed more and more of the fossil, but by lunchtime the task still was not finished. The foursome covered the fossil with a plastic sheet and drove to a cafe in nearby Clarkia.

The thunderstorm struck while they were at lunch, and by the time they returned to the fossil site the diggings had turned to sticky mud and water was rushing down the slope. Despite the downpour and the uncomfortable conditions, they resumed work until finally the full outline of the fossil was revealed—not that of a gar, but of a large, distinctly trout-like fish. The fish was complete except for a few parts of the skull; even its lateral line was still evident.

The fossil was removed in several pieces; wrapped in newspaper and placed in a box for transportation back to the geology laboratory at the University of Idaho. When the pieces were reassembled at the laboratory, the fish was measured at a length of 72 centimeters, or slightly more than

28 inches. Then the still-wet pieces of thin clay, reassembled in their original shape, were placed in a press and left there to dry out and to harden and compress the clay.

After five weeks the fossil finally was dry and work began to try to identify what kind of fish it was. All the other fish fossils unearthed from Miocene Clarkia Lake had belonged to the sunfish or minnow families, and none had measured more than eight inches long; this one was clearly something quite different.

Smiley and Rember photographed the fossil and sent slides and prints to Dr. Gerald R. Smith of the University of Michigan Museum of Paleontology, an expert on the taxonomy of early fish. Smith sent a graduate student to retrieve the fossil and carry it from Moscow back to Michigan where he could study it in person.

Smith's verdict was that the fossil was that of a "large trout" with characteristics "unlike any other genus of North American salmonid." Its jaws and teeth were too large for it to have been a grayling; it had too few vertebrae, scales and anal-fin rays to have been a Pacific salmon; its scales and vertebrae were larger than those of any existing North American trout, and its dorsal fin had more rays than any char. But if it was not any of those things, then what was it?

Smith concluded that there *was* one fish which shared all the characteristics of the fossil trout: The *Hucho*, a Eurasian salmonid commonly known as the Huchen. The Huchen, which bears a superficial resemblance to the Atlantic salmon, today is found in the Danube Basin of southern Europe, Siberia, and waters of the Far East, and in some of those areas it is prized as a sport fish.

But the identification raised a major question: The Huchen has not been known on the North American continent within the history of man's occupation; if the Clarkia Lake fish really was a Huchen, then where could it have come from?

Smith proposed an answer for that, too. He theorized that millions of years ago, when the Bering Land Bridge was in place between Siberia and Alaska and the Bering Strait was closed, there was a free interchange of fish between North America and Asia. Sometime during that period, the Huchen may have migrated from Asia and found a hospitable home in the prehistoric lakes of the Northwest, where the climate was moist and mild. Or, conceivably, it might have been the other way around—the Huchen could have evolved here first and emigrated to Asian waters.

Wherever it came from, there was other circumstantial evidence to support the identification of the Miocene Clarkia fish as *Hucho*. Earlier fossil finds in sediments of prehistoric Lake Idaho on the Snake River Plain also closely resembled Huchen, although these fish were perhaps 10 million to 15 million years younger than the Clarkia Lake fish.

Still, Smith labeled his identification of the Clarkia fish "preliminary." He has suggested the fish may have been an intermediate, ancestral evolutionary line that led to the modern Huchen and the modern chars, and although he believes his identification of the fish as *Hucho* is "pretty solid," there is always the chance that future discoveries might show it was part of a line that led to the chars. If that happened, the Clarkia Lake fish might have to be reclassified.

At approximately 20 million years, the Miocene Clarkia fish is the second oldest salmonid fossil ever found. The oldest, at 40 million years, is *Eosalmo driftwoodensis*, described in 1977 from the Middle Eocene Driftwood Creek fossil beds near Smithers, British Columbia. Bone fragments and scales of even older fish have been found, but the type specimen of *Eosalmo* was nearly intact.

Compared with the Clarkia fish, *Eosalmo* was small, about 11½ inches long, with features intermediate between those of the grayling family and the Salmoninae—the Huchen, chars and trouts. But Smith reported no indication of a lineage from *Eosalmo* to the Clarkia fish, or to the still younger fossils from the Snake River Plain. Nor was the Clarkia fish apparently the ancestor of any living North American salmonids. "Its relationships seem to be with Eurasian forms," Smith wrote.

So the Huchen apparently ran its course in North America for several million years, then vanished. Why did it disappear? Again, there are only theories: Perhaps it lost out in competition with separately evolving chars and trout, or perhaps it was a victim of a change in the climate that began about 2 million years ago when the first of successive waves of glaciers swept down over the roof of the continent. No fossil remains of *Hucho* have been found from after that time.

Whatever the reason, when the first men arrived to begin exploring the rivers and lakes of North America, they found Pacific salmon, trout and char in abundance, but no trace of Huchen. Its former presence here was never guessed or imagined until its fossilized remains were unearthed so many years later. And even now, after those remains have been studied and identified, the idea that Huchen once lived in our lakes and traveled our rivers is so remote that it almost seems an abstraction.

But there is nothing abstract about the fossil fish of Miocene Clarkia Lake. Once it was a living creature, with instincts and purpose; it sought food and fled danger and perhaps rolled in the evening twilight even as large trout do in the twilights of our time.

Perhaps it was the offspring of a race of fish that had ranged far across a prehistoric sea and found their way into the rivers of a new continent, with each generation working farther inland along a network of rivers and lakes far too old for any human to remember. Perhaps it had traveled far itself, spending its life in a compulsive urge to press forward and see what lay beyond the next bend of the river—until one day, after rounding hundreds of bends in scores of rivers, it came finally to the foot of a heavy flow spilling from a lava dam that held back a lake high in the hills. The falls would have been a formidable obstacle, and it may have taken the fish many tries to clear them, but eventually it did, and its reward was a chance to rest in the quiet waters of the lake.

But its rest would have been brief, for a new compulsion would have hurried the fish along through the lake to the mouth of a small tributary rushing down the slopes of a ridge that once was a shoal in a Precambrian sea—perhaps a tributary where caddis larvae crawled on the bottom and made their cases of tiny garnets plucked from the sand. And in that little tributary, the fish might have found another of its kind, a veteran of the same long journey; and there, in a quiet pool under the protective shade of sweetgum and magnolia trees, the two of them would have made a redd and filled it with their spawn.

After that the end would have come swiftly for the fish. Having spent its last energy in spawning, it could not long resist the tributary's flow; the current would have swept it downstream, tumbling and drifting until it was back in the quiet waters of the lake. Even those restful waters would not have been enough to restore its strength, and finally, in a little bay near the lake's upper end, it would have settled slowly down into the cold, dark water and the silt, joining the day's harvest of fallen leaves and insects. And there it would remain until a warm spring morning with a threat of thunder in the air, 20 million years later.

A fanciful tale? Perhaps. But if we could ever learn the full story of the fossil fish of Miocene Clarkia Lake, it might not be so very different. Possibly one day we shall know more: Chemical analysis of the fossil may yet reveal more of its life's history.

Meanwhile, the valley of the St. Maries remains a sleepy,

peaceful place, little changed by its scientific notoriety. Except for the "Fossil Bowl" sign on Kienbaum's racetrack, there is not much to suggest the area's ancient heritage.

But if you should go there in the spring, when the camas lily is blooming in the meadows near the river, you might see a reminder of the past: Stand on a high hillside and look down at the fields of waving blue blossoms and it will seem very much as if you are looking out upon a sparkling lake—like one that filled the valley 20 million springs ago.

Family Tree

Man's unending search for the origins of life has impelled him to look from the deepest seas to the most distant corners of the universe, and far back to the very beginning moments of time. He is understandably most curious about his own origins, but he has not neglected the other forms of life with which he shares his world—including trout.

Yet in many ways, searching for the trout's lineage is even more difficult and demanding than searching for our own. One reason is that the quest for early man is a more glamorous undertaking and therefore commands more attention, time and money; another is that the trout's span of history is much greater than our own, and so it is necessary to search much farther back in time for its origins. Early man also left more for us to find; besides his own remains, he left primitive tools and spearpoints, the campfire middens of his dwellings, and galleries of enigmatic artwork painted on the walls of ancient caves. The trout left us only its bones.

Even when we are lucky enough to find some of those bones, it sometimes only makes matters more complicated. The story of the fossil fish of Miocene Clarkia Lake is a case in point: Here were the remains of a fish long extinct in North America, found where no one really expected them to be. Finding them did not simplify the effort to trace the evolutionary lineage of trout; instead, it merely forced scientists to come up with an explanation for how a fish previously thought native only to Europe and Asia could have been living in northern Idaho 20 million years ago.

But even if they present new problems, such fossil finds always are valuable because they offer a snapshot of how matters stood on the evolutionary scale at a particular time and place. They also are the best evidence we have of things gone before, key parts in a giant jigsaw puzzle from which most of the pieces are still missing.

Other evidence may be obtained by examining the distribution and genetic relationships of living trout, but here again there are complications. The problem is that trout and their kindred species still are dividing themselves up into separate forms, so that it becomes necessary for scientists to try to determine the point of their last division, plus the one before that, and all the other ones before that, in order to figure out where they came from and how they got to be the way they are.

Scientists have employed a formidable arsenal of weapons in an effort to solve these problems and trace the trout's lineage back to a common ancestor, or at least a group of ancestors. These include such sophisticated modern tech-

niques as electrophoresis, an electrochemical means of measuring genetic similarities among living fish; complex studies
of comparative anatomy, and computer methods for discerning relationships among fish. But they also still include the
sweaty, unsophisticated work of swinging a pick against a hard
surface of sun-baked clay or rock to get at the fossils presumed
to lie underneath.

These methods, and the hard work of the men and
women who wield them, have led to a theory of how trout
evolved. It does not attempt to say precisely when or exactly
where the first trout-like fish appeared, nor does it seem likely
that any theory ever shall be able to say so with very much
certainty. Neither is it a finished theory; like the trout itself, it
continues to evolve. And not all of its elements are unani-
mously accepted; some remain in hot dispute. Yet for all that,
it is the best explanation we now have.

It supposes that the lineage of trout extends back at least
as far as the late Cretaceous period, about 100 million years
ago. The seas of that time held fish belonging to an order that
men much later would call the Salmoniformes, a diverse group
whose modern members include the freshwater pikes and
mudminnows and marine forms such as the strange deepsea
bristlemouth, the spookfish, viperfish, and deepsea dragon-
fish.

Sometime within the late Cretaceous period there
occurred a "polyploid event," a doubling of chromosome
numbers and DNA in an ancestral species that caused it to
diverge from the evolutionary path of the other Salmoniformes. This divergent line apparently developed mostly or
entirely in the cold, fresh waters of the northern latitudes of
Eurasia and North America, and gradually, over millions of
years of geological upheaval and climatic change, it began
sending out branches of its own. Some quickly withered and
died, others survived for a time and then vanished, but others
flowered and eventually sent out cautious tendrils of their

own. And through this slow process of evolutionary winnow-ing, there eventually began to appear a glittering array of graceful, brightly colored fish that men one day would call the Salmonidae.

The common ancestor of the Salmonidae is long since extinct, but one of its earliest divergent lines led eventually to the subfamily Coregoninae, a nearly toothless group of fish whose modern living members include *Prosopium*, the Rocky Mountain whitefish; *Stenodus*, the huge, Arctic sheefish; *Coregonus*, the lake whitefish, and *Leucichthys*, the ciscoes.

A split in the line that gave rise to the whitefish led independently to evolution of another subfamily, Thymal-linae, whose surviving members are the delicate and beautiful grayling of Europe and North America.

From the same common ancestor that gave rise to all the Salmonidae, another separate line developed eventually into the most complex subfamily of all, the Salmoninae, a many-splendored group of fish whose modern members include *Brachymystax*, the Siberian lenok; *Hucho*, the Huchen; *Sal-velinus*, the chars; *Salmo*, the trout, and *Oncorhynchus*, the Pacific salmon.

The earliest species of *Salmo*, the trout, remains un-known and long extinct, and there is even uncertainty over which is the most primitive living species. Some believe it is the trout of Lake Ohrid, Yugoslavia, which sometimes is classified *Salmo ohridanus*. Others disagree, and consider the Lake Ohrid trout a wholly separate genus, either *Salmothymus* or *Acantholingua*. If one discounts the Lake Ohrid trout, then some of the Mediterranean-Adriatic varieties of the brown trout, *Salmo trutta*, probably rank as the most primitive surviving members of the genus *Salmo*, followed by *S. salar*, the Atlantic salmon, a trout despite its name.

A separate line from the same extinct common ancestor of *Salmo* led eventually to development of more advanced, specialized forms of trout now generally classified in the subgenus *Parasalmo*. These include the well-known trout of western North America, the cutthroat, *S. clarki*, and the rainbow, *S. gairdneri*. The same line also gave rise to the Pacific salmon, *Oncorhynchus*, which split off at some point either before or after the cutthroat and rainbow trout appeared.

Among the qualities of modern salmon and trout that man has found most endearing is their instinct to range far at sea and then return almost unerringly to their home rivers. This powerful drive reaches its peak in the steelhead and Pacific salmon, making them especially romantic and enduring symbols of stamina and strength. But migratory behavior is present to some degree in almost all salmonids and is a habit acquired very early in their evolutionary history—most likely even before the division into separate lines leading to the modern subfamilies. It happened at a time when there were waters of intermediate salinity in thousands of estuaries throughout the Northern Hemisphere, making it possible for the ancestors of trout and salmon to travel easily from the rivers to the oceans, with their vast stores of food. The ancestral fish took advantage of this rich food resource, which quickly proved to be a successful evolutionary strategy, and over time the migratory habit became deeply rooted in their instincts. Thus we see it now in their modern living relatives.

But that is about the extent of what is known or assumed of the evolutionary history of trout. Much of the theory rests on guesswork, without very much supporting evidence from the scant fossil record of ancient fish. But as one gets closer to the present, the fossil record improves, particularly in western North America, where many salmonid fossils of more recent vintage than *Eosalmo* or the Miocene Clarkia fish have been found.

Those fossils reveal glimpses of some highly unusual fish.

But the strangest by far was one called *Smilodonichthys Rastrosus*, a giant "saber-toothed salmon" whose remains have been found in Oregon and California. It was named for the enormous curved breeding teeth on its upper jaw, and with these teeth and a maximum length that may have exceeded six feet, *Smilodonichthys* surely must have been a threatening specimen. Ironically, its one or two pairs of huge front teeth were virtually the only ones it had, and apparently it fed entirely on plankton.

Salmo Australis was another unusual specimen, both because it represents the southernmost occurrence of Salmonidae in North America and because it also had very odd teeth. It was found by workmen digging a cellar out of sandy soil in the village of Ajijic near the northwestern end of Lake Chapala in Mexico—at only 20 degrees north latitude, nearly 250 miles farther south than any salmonid had been found previously. *S. Australis* was a large fish, reaching nearly 40 inches in length at adulthood, with big, powerful jaws and a mouthful of formidable sharp teeth set in large round bases marked with vertical striations.

S. Australis is believed to have lived during an ice age that caused a cool, moist climate to extend southward into Mexico. Although classified within the genus *Salmo*, it was different from any other fossil or living member of the genus.

The most dominant salmonid in the recent fossil record of western North America is a trout called *Rhabdofario*, found in southern Idaho near the Oregon border. Except for a rod-like maxillary (upper jaw) bone it probably was not unlike modern trout in appearance and habit, living in lakes and perhaps growing to a maximum length of 40 inches. At first scientists believed its maxillary bone was simply too different for it to have been part of the line leading to modern cutthroat and rainbow trout, but some now say it is not unlike the maxillary which develops in modern rainbow trout as they reach old age. This has led some taxonomists to suggest that

Rhabdofario should be abolished as a separate genus and reclassified as *Salmo*, possibly ancestral to *Parasalmo*, the modern rainbow and cutthroat trouts. Others regard the question as still open.

Dr. Robert J. Behnke of Colorado State University, one of the most eminent authorities on trout taxonomy, attempted to unravel some of the complex evolutionary relationships of western trout in an extensive monograph, "The Native Trouts of the Genus *Salmo* of Western North America," written in 1979 for the federal government. Unfortunately, it never was formally published because funds were lacking—a sad thing for scientists and anglers alike, because it is certainly the most definitive paper ever written on western trout, even though subsequent research already has altered some of its conclusions.

In it, Behnke presented a case for North America as the "center of origin" of *Parasalmo*. But he also remarked on a strange fish known as *Salmo formosanus*, "a most interesting and significant species, now perhaps extinct and known only from one river in the mountains of Formosa." Only two specimens are known to exist, both collected in 1917 "near wild country controlled by fierce headhunters."

Studies of these fish by himself and others led Behnke to conclude that *S. formosanus* is—or was—a distinct species that "may represent an early separation of the *Parasalmo* line or its direct ancestor which dispersed in Asia but became extinct except for a single river in Formosa." Unfortunately, the watershed in which *S. formosanus* was discovered was logged off many years ago and converted to agricultural use, and it seems very unlikely that any more specimens of this fish ever will be found. That is another sad thing for both anglers and scientists, for *S. formosanus* might have told us much about the recent branches of the trout's family tree.

Other than the possible *S. formosanus*, the only representative of the subgenus *Parasalmo* now living in Asia is

S. mykiss, found in the lower Amur River of the eastern Soviet Union and along the coast of the Sea of Okhotsk to Kamchatka and the neighboring Commander Islands. But *S. mykiss* is identical to the coastal rainbow trout of North America, and Behnke suggests its foothold in Asia was gained recently, probably "no more than 11,000-12,000 years ago, or since the disappearance of the Bering Land Bridge at the end of the last glacial epoch."

Behnke's studies indicate the cutthroat "was first on the scene" in western North America and was able to colonize the waters of the upper Columbia River Basin before they were isolated by barrier falls downstream. Geographic barriers also apparently divided coastal and inland cutthroat populations, leading to divergence of the two. Glacial upheavals further split the interior group into two major subgroups, and later changes in climate and drainage patterns subdivided these into many smaller groups, each evolving and adapting to the conditions in which it found itself.

Today the range of the coastal cutthroat extends from Prince William Sound in Alaska to the Eel River in California, while the numerous interior populations are scattered all the way from southern British Columbia, Alberta, and Saskatchewan to New Mexico, Nevada, and northeast California.

The rainbow trout arose from the more primitive cutthroat, and Behnke speculates there also was a major split into coastal and inland groups early in the rainbow's history. These two populations eventually became genetically distinct, but unlike the cutthroat, the interior rainbow—which Behnke calls the "redband" trout—may again have come in contact with the coastal rainbow after the last glacial epoch, leading to some genetic mixing of the two. Another theory is offered by Dr. Gerald R. Smith of the University of Michigan, who suggests the interior "redband" trout actually may be the closest living descendant of *Rhabdofario*.

The natural range of the modern coastal rainbow extends from the Kuskokwim River of northwest Alaska to the Rio del Presidio in Mexico. The interior form inhabits the Columbia Basin east of the Cascades, except for the isolated headwaters originally colonized by the cutthroat, and is native to the desert basins of Southern Oregon, the upper Klamath Lake Basin, and the Sacramento Basin. The "redband" complex includes the famous Kamloops trout of British Columbia and the California golden trout, *S. aguabonita* and *S. gilberti*. Steelhead are found within both the coastal and interior rainbow groups, with the latter ascending the Fraser River above Hells Gate in British Columbia and the Columbia River east of the Cascade Range.

There are still other trout, native to Gulf of California drainages, at least some of which apparently are not part of either the cutthroat or rainbow line, but may have arisen separately from some early common ancestor. These include *S. chrysogaster*, the Mexican golden trout, generally considered the most primitive of the western trouts; *S. gilae*, the Gila trout of New Mexico, and *S. apache*, the Apache trout of the White Mountains of Arizona. All are distinctive in their vivid yellow or gold coloration, and *S. apache* is notable for having the largest dorsal fin of any western trout.

Dr. Robert Rush Miller, who was first to describe both *S. gilae* and *S. apache*, postulates that during the ice age the ancestral stock of *S. gilae* crossed the Baja California peninsula by way of a marine corridor near 28 degrees north latitude, or at the Isthmus of La Paz, or possibly migrated around the tip of Cape San Lucas and into the Gulf of California. From there it penetrated the Gila River drainage where it subsequently evolved in isolation to its modern form.

Miller suggested several possible origins for *S. apache*, but favors the theory that it derived from an ancestral cutthroat trout that made its way from the north into what is now the

Little Colorado River basin, became isolated there and evolved into its present form.

Behnke, however, suggests all these trout are more closely related to one another than to either the rainbow or cutthroat lines, and may have evolved from "an early branching from the main line leading to cutthroat and rainbow-redband trouts."

There are still other trout, not yet formally assigned to any species, that dwell in the Rio Yaqui, Rio Casa Grandes, and Rio Mayo drainages of Mexico. Perhaps one day, when more is known about these fish, they will add to our knowledge of the evolution of western trout.

In the process of dividing and scattering themselves across the western portion of the continent, modern cutthroat and rainbow trout have split into many small but distinct local populations, and some of these have evolved in unique or unusual ways. Behnke, for example, lists 15 different sub-species of cutthroat, from the widespread coastal type to tiny isolated inland groups found only in one or two small streams.

This great diversity of forms has prompted a continuing taxonomic debate. On one side are the "lumpers," who hold that many of the differences among modern western trout populations are too small to warrant classifying them as separate subspecies. On the other side are the "splitters," who argue that populations with unique or unusual characteristics should be granted status as separate species or subspecies in order to preserve their uniqueness.

To anglers, this may seem an esoteric subject for debate, the kind of thing that could only arouse a musty scientist surrounded by mouldering books and dusty manuscripts, and to some degree it is exactly that—a long-winded technical argument. But it has implications that extend far beyond the realm of science. What it boils down to is that some people think there is special value in a name; if an animal has one all its own, it is more likely to be given respect and protection than an animal which hasn't. It is sort of like saying "birds" on the one hand and "bald eagle" on the other.

The importance of all this to sport fishermen is that the outcome of the debate could decide the future of many kinds of trout with characteristics that could be of great value in fisheries management.

For example, there are some populations of rainbow trout—such as the Gerrard strain of Kamloops trout in Kootenay Lake, British Columbia—that do not spawn until they are at least four or five years old, by which time they may have attained weights of 15 to 20 pounds. Such a long-lived stock could be invaluable to managers attempting to establish trophy fisheries.

Behnke writes of another example, a remarkable strain of rainbow trout he found in a tributary of the Owyhee River (coincidentally, just 12 miles from the fossil beds where *Rhabdofario* first came to light). The tributary's watershed had been devastated by grazing and the stream had been reduced to slow, intermittent pools, with a water temperature of 83 degrees, but despite these extreme conditions, the trout fed normally, came willingly to a fly and fought well. The potential management implications of a stock adapted to such temperatures, which would be lethal to most trout, can scarcely be imagined.

On the surface, there appears no reason why fish with such potentially valuable adaptations cannot be protected regardless of classification. Again, the answer is that classification—that is, the formal assignment of a name—has value in some bureaucratic quarters. Conversely, a fish without a name conferred by science may be in danger of being treated as if it were no different from any other trout.

Treating all trout as if they were alike is an approach with powerful appeal for bureaucrats, particularly on the federal level, because it promises to make their jobs much easier. After all, if a trout is just a trout, then there is no extraordinary need to protect its wild populations or the habitat which sustains them—and besides, such protection requires a lot of money and effort.

The all-alike idea also appeals to some hatchery managers; it would relieve them of the bother of separating different strains of fish in the hatchery, or of considering which ones should be planted in a particular stream or lake. The danger of this is that indiscriminate hatchery breeding soon culls out unique wild adaptations and produces homogenous populations of assembly-line fish—something which already has happened to an alarming degree. Many unique and useful adaptations, the final fruits of 100 million years of evolution, probably already have been lost in hatcheries; we cannot afford the loss of any more.

It is unfortunate that the debate between the "lumpers" and "splitters" has carried over into the bureaucratic arena. Both sides should set aside their differences long enough to join forces and insist on protection for all trout populations with unique characteristics that have value for future management, or which are valuable simply because they *are* unique— regardless of how they may be classified now or in the future.

As a practical matter, the debate over classification probably will never end. As Behnke has written, the native trouts of western North America "can never be reduced to a system of classification into species and subspecies that accurately reflects all of the degrees and nuances of evolutionary relationships." A more realistic goal, he suggests, would be to try to establish the approximate major and minor branching sequences on the basis of the evidence and "create a classification best reflecting evolutionary history."

So the arguments will go on, along with the work of trying to pinpoint the origins of trout and sorting out the many modern forms into which they have evolved. It will go on in lakes and streams, under microscopes in laboratories, and out in the countryside where the fossil bones of ancient fish lie frozen into stone.

Even if we are not able to learn everything we would like to know about the origins of trout—and very probably we shall not—at least we can learn something about the past history of these noble fish which have ascended the rivers of time to become those most favored by man.

Fishing the Misty Fjords

It did not look much like a morning in May. A low overcast made the day seem dark and spurts of rain dashed hard against the wheelhouse windows on the *Phaedra Mae*. Choppy seas battered the hull until Tom Ramiskey, the boat's skipper, guided her out of the wind and into the calmer waters of Port Stewart, north of Ketchikan.

Port Stewart is where Capt. George Vancouver anchored his ships in August 1793 and sent out boats to search for the fabled Northwest Passage, which he never found. The *Phaedra Mae* was bound on a mission of a different sort—to search for cutthroat trout and steelhead in the streams flowing into Port

Stewart and the countless other fjords and bays nearby. Errol Champion and I were the "explorers" and Ramiskey's boat would be our traveling home and headquarters for the week-long voyage.

We hoped for better luck than Vancouver had found.

The trip had been arranged by Dale Pihlman, president of a fledgling company called Outdoor Alaska. His idea was to set up a business to take fishermen and sightseers into the Misty Fjords wilderness northeast of Ketchikan and he had teamed up with Ramiskey, who ran the *Phaedra Mae* as a charter service out of Ketchikan.

The saltwater passages leading into the Misty Fjords are famous for their salmon fishing, but the freshwater fishing potential of the area has scarcely been explored. That was where Errol and I came in; Dale had asked us to try to find some likely spots where he and Tom could take their future customers.

It was no coincidence that our visit came at a time when the Misty Fjords were part of a raging congressional debate over which of Alaska's unspoiled lands should be preserved as wilderness. Dale, as much an environmentalist as a businessman, was hoping to prove that wilderness has economic worth as well as aesthetic value, thereby providing another good reason for Congress to preserve the Misty Fjords.

Errol and Tom and I had rendezvoused in Ketchikan and Port Stewart was our first stop. It's a narrow harbor on the eastern edge of the Cleveland Peninsula which dangles awkwardly from the Alaska mainland, and except for a few floating log rafts it probably looks much the same as it did when Vancouver chose it for an anchorage.

After the *Phaedra Mae* was safely anchored in quiet water, we launched her little Boston Whaler skiff, started the outboard and set out for the beach to explore an unnamed stream. Errol and I wore waders and fishing vests while Tom had donned a pair of boots and stuck a hefty revolver—he called it his "cannon"—into his waistband, just in case we had a surprise meeting with an angry bear.

It was a long run to the shore where the wide opening in the woods marked the location of the river, but at last we beached the boat at the edge of a tidal marsh near the river's mouth. Once ashore, we hiked upstream a little way, following the creek's meandering course through soft muskeg and back into the rainy gloom of the spruce forest. Then we began to fish our way back down, using bright flies and roll casting to avoid the brambles at our backs.

But we soon had the feeling we were searching barren water. The stream flowed evenly over a flat bed of gravel with very few sheltered spots where a fish might hold—and those few spots were empty. We had thought the stream might host a run of cutthroat and that some might still be there in early May, but if there were any they had all gone farther upstream than we had time to go. So we headed back to the *Phaedra Mae*, hoisted anchor and got under way again. Vancouver's luck was holding.

Our next stop was Spacious Bay, another anchorage a little farther north, which we reached late in the afternoon. The rain had stopped, but the day remained threatening and the wind blew dark shreds of cloud across the sky. Despite the uncertain weather, Errol and I again ran the skiff ashore, this time near the mouth of a stream called Wasta Creek. It was a noisy little stream flowing downhill over a rocky bed, filled with very dark water—almost the color of poor claret. We found nothing in its lower reaches, but a faint trail led upstream and we followed it.

About a half mile inland we came to a boggy lake that fed the creek through a pair of slow-moving outlet channels. At the far end of the lake the sun was shining brightly through a hole in the overcast, but where we stood it had begun to rain again—scattered drops that left tiny spreading rings on the surface of the twin outlet channels. But there were also much larger rings among them, the unmistakable marks of rising trout.

Errol took one channel and I waded into the other and began casting with a small Skykomish Sunrise on the end of my leader. The very first cast was met by a strong answering pull and a handsome fish came tumbling end-over-end across the surface, then began a frantic search for refuge in the brush along the channel's edge. Stopped short by the pressure of the rod, it soon came writhing to my hand—a fine cutthroat, about 15 inches long, dark silver in color with big, black leopard spots on its sides and bright crimson slashes on its lower jaw.

Twenty more fish followed in the next half hour, none larger than 16 inches but all firm and fat and brightly marked. It was preposterously easy fishing—nearly a fish on every cast—but memorable because such fishing has grown so very hard to find.

It also was very hard to leave, but the day was well spent and we still had at least an hour's run to our night anchorage. So reluctantly we reeled in and started the hike downstream, leaving fish still rising in the outlet channels.

Two sea lions popped up to inspect us and hundreds of ducks wheeled overhead as we motored back to the anchored *Phaedra Mae*. It was a wild, exciting place—Alaska as I had imagined it would be.

Tom was waiting aboard the boat with potatoes baking in the galley oven and a big bowl of tossed salad. After we had secured the skiff, raised the anchor and gotten under way, he threw steaks on the fire and we soon sat down to an enormous meal. Then, in the very last light of the long northern day, we slipped into a sheltered cove behind a point and dropped anchor in Yes Bay, a deep narrow fjord that received the flow from Wolverine Creek, which was the reason we had come.

Next morning we motored in the skiff to the float at Yes Bay Lodge, a famous salmon-fishing resort built on the site of an abandoned cannery at the creekmouth. From the lodge a crude trail follows Wolverine Creek to its source in McDonald Lake; the creek was known to host a good run of spring steelhead.

The scale on the map showed the trail to the lake was only nine-tenths of a mile, but on foot, through muskeg and up and down granite outcrops, it seemed more like four miles. The trail was blocked frequently by deadfalls, forcing us to detour through thickets of devil's club or swamps filled with skunk-cabbage blooms and clinging black mud. In places there was no defined trail at all, only an occasional strip of surveyor's tape tied around a limb to mark the way. It was tough, hard, sweaty going, made more uncomfortable by the weather—mild and humid, with occasional spurts of rain.

Wolverine Creek is more of a full-fledged river than a creek. In its lower reaches it thunders through a narrow bedrock canyon in its eagerness to reach the sea, but farther upstream it holds a succession of fine pools, some as large as a small lake. In the first of these we saw half a dozen large steelhead lying in the tail-out, easily visible through the clear water. The pool was too deep to wade except at the very edge, and the brushy shoreline left no room for backcasts, so we began roll casting to drop our flies where the current could carry them over the fish.

The fish were nervous in the low, clear water, and they shifted and turned as our sunken flies swung past them, but made no effort to follow. A dry fly brought the only real show of interest; a single fish followed the float and surveyed the fly closely, but still refused to take.

At length we decided to rest the pool and resumed the difficult hike upstream. After half an hour we came to a rotting lean-to on the bank of a vast pool above a split in the river, and there we were met by a breathtaking sight: At least 50 steelhead were scattered up and down the length of the pool. Water and the imagination of fishermen both magnify the size of fish, but even after taking both factors into account Errol and I agreed that at least a dozen of those steelhead had to exceed 20 pounds in weight.

Forgetting the weariness of the trail, we started in after them—then spent hours changing flies and lines and techniques as the fish greeted every presentation with indifference. Once again a dry fly seemed to evoke the greatest interest, and several times a fish came up closely to inspect a floating fly and follow its downstream float, sometimes even bumping it with its nose—but not one fish would actually open its mouth to take the fly.

Then Errol finally had a take on a wet pattern fished deep. The fish hit hard, but was on only a moment before the line went slack. Errol retrieved the fly to find the fish had straightened out his stout-wire hook.

My bag from the pool was a single Dolly Varden that emerged from behind a rock to intercept a sinking fly the steelhead had greeted by parting ranks to let it pass. The Dolly was a handsome two-pound fish, but it seemed a dwarf compared to the huge steelhead in the pool.

Finally we yielded to frustration and left the pool as full of fish as we had found it—even my Dolly Varden had been returned. On the downstream hike we stopped again at the first pool and found the same steelhead still lying in the tail-out, but these fish were no more willing to take than they had been before.

Then it was back to the trail, with sticky mud clinging to our boots, brambles stinging our faces and rubbery roots tripping us at each unwary step. Weary, drenched with sweat and thirsty, we finally reached the lodge—and as fate would have it, the lodge was out of beer. That prompted a dash in the skiff back to the *Phaedra Mae*, where we began depleting the ranks of cold cans in her refrigerators before we got under way for Bell Island, where we planned to spend the night.

There is another famous salmon-fishing camp at Bell

Island, and when we arrived we found a skeleton crew on hand preparing for the season opening in another week. The owner invited us to use the pool, fed by hot geothermal springs, and we eagerly accepted the invitation. The steaming, buoyant water was a welcome antidote to those long hours on the trail, and we relaxed in front of the thermal jets and watched as the clouds parted to reveal a gathering host of stars. When we finally trooped back to the *Phaedra Mae* at dockside, the sky was alight with the silent shifting curtains of the northern lights.

Next morning we left Bell Island and entered the heart of the Misty Fjords wilderness, a land where deep wounds left by mighty glaciers have been flooded by the sea. The evidence of this violent geological past is preserved in shadowed, somber fjords surrounded by great folds of granite—one of the most spectacular and beautiful landscapes on earth.

As we turned southeast into Behm Canal, a long line of snowy peaks unfolded before us, row upon row of whitecapped ridges extending as far as the eye could see. From our vantage point they appeared impenetrable, but the map showed these walls of rock were pierced by fjords whose entrances were invisible until the traveler was almost upon them. We passed several such entrances, narrow chasms opening suddenly to reveal long veins of water thrusting back into the mountain fastnesses, then disappearing quickly behind us—almost as if a secret door had been briefly opened, then quickly closed.

Then we came to the fjord that was our destination and turned into it, entering a narrow passage with great walls of gray rock rising 3,000 feet on either side. Here and there the walls were stained with silver waterfalls plunging down from snow on the clifftops, or hanging in frozen drifts in shadowed fissures in the rock. A few wind-twisted spruce had gained a fragile purchase on the walls, and these stood out like solitary climbers halfway up the rock, with great wispy chains of moss hanging from their limbs.

The sea in the narrow passageway ahead was as smooth as a ribbon of glass, and it seemed a long way up to the sky. The chart showed nearly 1,800 feet of water beneath our keel, so there was nearly a mile of distance from clifftop to seafloor.

We cruised for several miles through this awesome scenery until suddenly one wall of the fjord opened to disclose a bay at the foot of a narrow valley with great peaks and snowfields looming on every side. Out of the valley flowed a river, entering the bay between grass-covered headlands in a perfect, park-like setting. We dropped anchor in the bay and Errol and I climbed into the skiff for the run to the mouth of the river.

Reaching shore, we pulled the skiff up into the deep grass near the river's mouth and began the hike upstream. A little way up the valley opened into a great natural amphitheater, with tiered rows of stone rising to the snowline on either side and waterfalls streaking down to the valley floor. The river whispered softly as it carried the snow-cold water in graceful curves toward the sea, and the water was as clear as the mountain air so that every detail of the fine golden gravel on the river bottom was exposed in sharp relief.

The river ran alternately in smooth, deep glides and burst into noisy, rock-strewn rapids, sparkling in the shafts of sunlight that poured down from beyond the peaks. There were tracks of deer and bear on the sandbars, and high on the slopes we could see a group of mountain goats cavorting near the snowline. It was a scene too perfect for pictures or for words; of all the other rivers I have ever seen or heard about, there is none that could compare.

But where were the fish? The river was so clear that if it held trout of any kind we surely should have seen them. Bleached bones from last autumn's salmon run lay half-buried in the sand, but there was no sign of any living fish.

And then at last we found them: In the pool above the first rapid, well back, lying in deep water behind a lichen-stained rock, were five steelhead, clean and bright and fresh from the sea. It had to be; the river was too perfect in every other way not to host such a noble race of fish.

We tried for them cautiously with small flies fished just under the surface on fine leaders, and then with dry flies and a riffle hitch, but the fish were spooky and nervous in the clear water and moved away as the flies passed overhead. At first I was frustrated, but after a while I found myself past caring; it was exhilarating just to be there, where so few other men had ever been, and to see these magnificent sights that so few other men had ever seen. The river suddenly seemed a hallowed place, a place where the steelhead were better left undisturbed, where it seemed wrong even to leave a footprint in the sand along its shores.

I quit fishing then and concentrated on trying to remember every detail of this enchanted place, knowing that very likely I would never have another chance to see it. And when it finally was time for us to leave, I left sadly, though I knew my memories would be greater reward than any trophy fish could be.

In the days to come we explored other rivers and saw more magnificent country. We watched eagles spiral overhead and traveled with a school of porpoises that rode the bow wave of the *Phaedra Mae* so closely we could nearly reach out and touch them. We hiked along streambanks where the only human footprints were our own, and cruised along great empty waterways where no ships ever came in sight. We were alone, just we three, in a country still untouched by man, and it felt very good to be there. I am not sure I have felt as good anywhere else.

Looking back on it now, I suppose in one sense our trip was a failure because we had largely failed to find the object of our search. Going in, we had known little about the timing of the runs in the rivers of the Misty Fjords, and we found fish in only a few of them. Even when we found them, we were not always able to catch them. But we saw enough to know that the wilderness has a wealth of good water, and surely its rivers and lakes must hold cutthroat and steelhead in abundance at times. I envy those who will carry on the exploration and finally establish the timing of those runs.

But even if there were no runs, the scenery is so spectacular that everything else is secondary. If there is one place in the world where an angler can go fishless and not be unhappy about it, it is in the Misty Fjords.

Both the fishing and the scenery still are there. The congressional battle finally was resolved and most of the Misty Fjords have been formally classified as wilderness, off-limits to any permanent habitation or alteration by man.

The wilderness area includes a certain unnamed river that flows through an enchanted valley and whispers softly as it carries snow-cold water in graceful curves toward the sea. In the spring it welcomes home bright steelhead that hold nervously in its deepest pools, and in the fall the salmon return to it and leave their bones to bleach in its golden sand.

It is a river I may never see again, but it will always flow through my memory, through my dreams—perhaps even through my soul.

A Well-Traveled Fish

The story of the diplomat and the salmon is one of the most charming chapters in Northwest angling lore. T.W. Lambert was among the first to tell it in his book, *Fishing in British Columbia*. His version, published in 1907, goes like this:

"There is another story very popular in the West, relating what happened at the time when the great fur companies held the country and were disputing and even fighting for its possession. The (British) Imperial Government sent out some illustrious diplomat to report on the situation, and he described the country as of no value and so hopeless that 'even the salmon would not take the fly.' It is a tradition in British

Columbia that on this ground the now flourishing states of Idaho, Montana, Washington and Oregon were handed over to the Americans."

It would be ironic if there were any truth to the story, for we now know that Pacific salmon will take flies, at least under some circumstances. But it's easy to understand how the diplomat—if there ever really was such a person—could easily have grown disgusted at the dour behavior of the Pacific fish when he was used to the magnificent Atlantic salmon of the British Isles. In fact, such an attitude would have been typical of most men, who never seem quite satisfied with the hand that nature deals them.

That was certainly true of the men who settled the Northwest; even though their adopted country was favored by great natural runs of salmon, steelhead, cutthroat and char, the settlers weren't content: They wanted Atlantic salmon, too. So did the men who settled many another far-flung land, and so they do today; wherever there are rivers and men to fish them, those men will wish for Atlantic salmon.

There is hardly any mystery in this. The Atlantic salmon reaches a greater size than any other trout (as a member of the genus *Salmo*, it is a trout despite its common name). It also has a character and reputation all its own, a mystique that has caused many anglers to regard it as the ultimate fly-rod challenge in fresh water.

The Atlantic salmon also is by far the most prestigious of all fish, a consequence of many years of private ownership of the best salmon rivers. Only the very wealthy can afford access to these rivers, and this has made salmon fishing an aristocratic sport, with the best reserved for kings and dukes and famous statesmen (or diplomats). That's another reason why men of all nations want salmon in their rivers; they envy the status of those who fish for salmon, and the opportunity to catch one is a way for even the most humble commoner to feel—if only for a moment—that he is on equal footing with a king.

All this has made the Atlantic salmon the world's most well-traveled, oft-transplanted fish. But the salmon also is a most particular fish, both in its habits and its choice of habitat, and only recently has man learned very much about either one of these. His earlier lack of knowledge led to the failure of many attempts to introduce salmon to foreign waters, and when he succeeded it was largely a matter of luck.

The eager settlers of New Zealand were among the first to attempt long-distance transplants of Atlantic salmon; they also have been among the most persistent. They began way back in 1868 when the provincial government of Otago on the South Island received some salmon eggs from the Tay and Severn rivers in Britain. These were hatched and reared to an average length of about six inches and 500 were released in the Waiwera River—the beginning of what turned out to be 40 years of effort to establish salmon in New Zealand waters.

During those four decades, eggs were imported from many sources and salmon were planted in many waters on both the North and South Islands. Many fish were released into river systems that drained to salt water in hopes the salmon would migrate to sea and return as large adults, just like their European ancestors. But despite all the hope and effort, to this day there never has been a single authenticated report of a seagoing Atlantic salmon returning to any New Zealand river (although transplanted Pacific salmon have done so for many years). In fact, most of the Atlantic salmon planted in New Zealand waters seem simply to have vanished.

But not all of them. A 1908 shipment of eggs from Canada hatched into fry that were liberated in a tributary of the Upukerora River, which flows into Lake Te Anau, a huge natural lake near Fjordland National Park in the southwest corner of the South Island. The next year another shipment was obtained from the British Isles, and fry from these eggs also were placed in the Upukerora. Eggs from other stocks, including the English Test, the Dee, the Wye, and even the German Rhine, were hatched and released at various times into the same stream or into Lake Te Anau itself. It is impossible now to say which of these plants succeeded, but at least one of them did. However, contrary to the hopes of their liberators, the fish did not migrate out of the lake to the sea; instead, they stayed where they were, feeding on the rich aquatic life in Lake Te Anau and running up its tributaries to spawn.

Rich as it was, Lake Te Anau could not provide growth comparable to the sea. G. Stokell, in his book *Fresh Water Fishes of New Zealand*, says the average weight of 114 salmon taken from Lake Te Anau in 1932 was 4.2 pounds—a nice-sized fish, to be sure, but no larger than a precocious sea-run grilse. Stokell also mentioned a mounted specimen of 29½ inches which he found hanging on the wall at the Te Anau Hotel, a fish which might have weighed as much as nine pounds. While that was certainly exceptional for Lake Te Anau, it would be a small fish by the standards of most seagoing salmon.

Today, rainbow and brown trout greatly outnumber salmon in Lake Te Anau, but in Lakes Gunn and Fergus—part of the watershed of the Eglinton River which flows into Lake Te Anau—Atlantic salmon are still abundant. Salmon up to eight pounds have been reported from Lake Gunn, although I saw none of that size during a visit to the lake in 1980.

Atlantic salmon also are taken occasionally from Lake Manopouri, downstream from Lake Te Anau, and sometimes from the Waiau River between those lakes, and they may exist in a few other New Zealand waters. That seems little to show for the decades of work New Zealanders have invested in these temperamental fish, but it is perhaps a measure of the difficulty of transplanting Atlantic salmon that New Zealand's experience ranks as one of the more successful.

One of the earliest attempts to transplant Atlantic salmon in North America was in the Delaware River, where the New Jersey state Fish Commission planted salmon fry for several years in the early 1870s. Some of these fish apparently survived, went to sea and returned, for in 1877 a few salmon weighing as much as nine pounds were taken from the Delaware and a fish of 24 pounds was reported the following year. But despite this promising start, no effort was made to nurture the fledgling run and it soon disappeared.

Atlantic salmon also were planted in Yellowstone Lake shortly before the turn of the century, but these fish also failed to become established, possibly because they were unable to compete with the large population of native cutthroat.

Perhaps mindful of the legendary diplomat's harsh judgment of their land, British Columbia fisheries authorities tried during the early years of this century to establish runs of Atlantic salmon in some of their waters. "Atlantic salmon have been introduced into the waters about Vancouver Island, and quite a number of specimens have been reported as having been taken in some years by anglers," the pioneer biologist J.R. Dymond reported. However, Dymond was able to collect only two specimens for his own studies, and both were small: "One had been taken in Cowichan Lake, September 3, 1913; it was less than six inches long. The other, eleven inches in length and nine ounces in weight, was taken in the Lower Cowichan River on May 31, 1926."

Noting the diminutive size of these fish, Dymond went on to report that "in the opinion of A.A. Easton, fisheries inspector at Duncan (Vancouver Island), the Atlantic salmon introduced into that district may have stayed in the lakes and rivers, as they have done in New Zealand, where they act like landlocked fish." Dymond concluded his report by writing:

"The planting of this species in British Columbia waters has now been discontinued, on account of the lack of success attending its introduction."

So another experiment ended in failure. But it would have taken much more than a dubious record of earlier results to deter the indefatigable Edward Ringwood Hewitt, the famous angler, innovator, and author. Hewitt began experimenting with Atlantic salmon in his private water on New York's little Neversink shortly after World War I. Over the years, he imported salmon eggs from Norway and Scotland, hatched them and planted the fry in his beloved Neversink. Yet despite his determination and enterprise, his efforts also went for naught; although two anglers later reported catching and releasing Atlantic salmon in the Neversink, there is no documented record of any of these fish ever having been seen again.

One of the few successful experiments in transplanting Atlantic salmon, and surely the most widely publicized, was that carried out by the state of Oregon in Hosmer Lake. The lake itself covers an old creek channel meandering across an alpine meadow that once was a pumice plain, ringed by spectacular snowcapped volcanic cones and a labyrinth of twisted lava flows surrounded by thick forests of lodgepole pine. Fed by Quinn Creek, which flows at a nearly constant temperature of 42 degrees, Hosmer measures only 11 feet at its deepest point and most of it is much shallower. It is an exceptionally rich lake, with enormous spring hatches of mayflies, caddisflies and damselflies, and few better trout environments could be imagined.

Until 1957 the lake was occupied only by a few brook trout and large numbers of carp and roach which had been introduced sometime before 1940. It was known then as Mud Lake, probably because the carp kept the pumice bottom stirred up constantly so that the water was never clear. The lake was chemically treated in the fall of 1957 and the carp and roach were removed, although some brook trout survived—probably by taking refuge in Quinn Creek.

In 1951, the state of Oregon obtained 10,000 eggs from Gaspe Bay sea-run Atlantic salmon stock, provided by the Quebec Department of Game and Fisheries. The eggs were hatched at the Wizard Falls Hatchery on the Metolius River, but the fry proved extremely hard to handle; at first they would not feed, and many lingered on the bottom of the hatchery raceway and eventually died of bacterial gill disease. About 90 percent of the first lot died in the fry stage, but there were still enough fish left alive after five years to breed a second generation, which proved somewhat more adaptable to the hatchery environment.

A second shipment of Gaspe Bay eggs arrived at Wizard Falls in 1958, adding to the stock already on hand. In the spring of that same year, the first liberations of Atlantic salmon from the original lot were made into Hosmer Lake—6,015 yearling fish averaging six inches and 9,014 fry averaging three inches. The lake remained closed to fishing until 1961 when it was opened under regulations that allowed anglers to keep a single salmon. State officials estimated that 2,956 were caught that first year, the largest measuring 27½ inches and weighing 6¼ pounds. The average of all fish caught was 20 inches.

Removal of the carp had allowed the suspended particles of silt to settle out of the water and the combination of the clear, shallow water and pumice bottom made it possible for anglers to see fish cruising at great distance. The salmon also proved enthusiastic risers to the heavy hatches of mayflies and caddisflies, and these factors soon made Hosmer a favorite spot for dry-fly fishermen. The lake's spectacular alpine beauty and exotic fishing also made the name "Mud" seem singularly inappropriate, so in 1962 it was officially changed to Hosmer Lake, in honor of Paul Hosmer, a naturalist of local renown.

That same year the fishing regulations were changed to

catch-and-release and fly-fishing-only with barbless hooks, and they have remained so ever since.

Oregon fisheries authorities had great hopes that the Hosmer Lake salmon would reproduce by spawning in Quinn Creek. The fish did indeed spawn, but winter anchor ice destroyed their eggs. That made it necessary for the state to take on the costly business of maintaining a large hatchery stock of salmon in order to replant the lake periodically. The investment paid off, however, for Hosmer's reputation quickly spread far beyond the borders of Oregon, with unexpected benefits for the state. A 1971 study estimated that 90 percent of the anglers visiting the lake had come from out of state—a rich source of income for the Oregon license fund and a significant source of business for the local economy.

From 1962 to 1970, Hosmer Lake provided wonderful fishing. Most of the fish measured 20 inches or more, with quite a few in the four- to five-pound class and some larger. Although this was still only grilse-sized by sea-run standards, the opportunity to fish for salmon provided a marvelous new experience for Western anglers.

But the fishery began a slow decline in the early 1970s. One problem was that the salmon had a bad habit of escaping from the lake. Harkening back to their sea-run ancestry, many yearling fish tried to migrate by swimming out over the top of a crude outlet dam during periods of high water. Water spilling over the dam flows about 100 yards and disappears into a sump in the porous lava; fish washed down this sump are never seen again, and many were lost this way.

The disappearance of yearling fish was accompanied by a natural die-off of older fish in the lake, and together these factors established a downward trend that reached a low point in September 1975, when all 4,317 yearling salmon remaining at the Wizard Falls Hatchery were stocked in an effort to restore the Hosmer Lake fishery.

In the years since, the fishing has been up and down, but mostly down, defying the best efforts of biologists to restore it to its early days of glory. In 1982 it hit bottom; in the spring of that year, biologists estimated the total population of salmon in the lake was only 75 fish. A fall plant brought the population up to several thousand fish by the following spring, but by summer's end most of them were gone.

Fish escapement during high water has remained a serious problem, but not the only one: The shallow, clear water of Hosmer Lake makes the salmon especially vulnerable to attack from a burgeoning population of ospreys and it is not uncommon for these magnificent birds to take at least 50 fish a day. A thriving group of otters also takes its share. Another problem is growing evidence of genetic stagnation among the breeding stock, which has not had an infusion of new blood since the last shipment of eggs in 1958. The offspring of these fish have shown an increasing lack of vigor and an ever-higher incidence of albinoism and other symptoms of inbreeding within a small, closed population.

In the fall of 1983, two significant steps were taken to try to solve some of these problems: Local fly fishermen joined state workers to repair the outlet dam and make it more difficult for fish to escape from the lake, and 20,000 landlocked salmon eggs from Maine were received at the Wizard Falls Hatchery. The Maine fish, from the so-called "Grand Lake Stream" stock of landlocked salmon, presumably lack the smolting instinct that has caused so many of the Gaspe Bay fish to leave the lake; they also should add fresh vigor to the hatchery stock. But it will take several years for the Maine fish to prove themselves, and at this point the future of the Hosmer Lake salmon fishery is highly uncertain.

The early success of Atlantic salmon in Hosmer Lake is all the more remarkable when one considers that efforts to introduce these fish into nearby waters ended in total failure.

Fish from the Gaspe Bay stock also were planted in several
other lakes in the Oregon Cascades, including Sparks and
Davis, two well-known fly-fishing waters, but only a few
survived long enough to be caught by anglers. The rest died
out.

The good early fishing at Hosmer also inspired Washington state anglers to lobby for an Atlantic salmon experiment
within their own state, and the Washington Game Department finally acquiesced and obtained some of Oregon's Wizard
Falls stock. The fish were held in a hatchery while a search
was made for a suitable lake to put them in. That proved to be
a difficult task, for even though the state had more than 8,000
lakes to choose from, not a single one could be found with
characteristics as favorable as those of Hosmer Lake.

Chopaka Lake, a popular, scenic, fly-fishing-only lake in
the Okanogan country of north central Washington, finally
was chosen as the best candidate, even though it had only a
few similarities to Hosmer. In the spring of 1973, Chopaka
received a plant of 7,920 Atlantic salmon averaging 10
inches.

Ken Williams, the state biologist assigned to monitor the
experiment, later reported that the Atlantic salmon began to
lose weight as soon as they were planted in the lake, and by
fall they had become "emaciated . . . with significant numbers on the verge of starvation." Williams also put his finger
on the reason why: For years the Washington Game Department had planted enormous numbers of rainbow trout in
Chopaka Lake; more than 50,000 had gone into the lake in
1972 alone. In retrospect, it was hardly surprising that a small
number of Atlantic salmon were unable to compete with a
large, well-established population of rainbow trout.

"The salmon appeared to have a difficult time adjusting,"
Williams reported. "Salmon would meander slowly but constantly back and forth over a large but definable area. If they

got too close to the trout, they were immediately subjected to strong acts of aggression, including nipping. In every case observed, salmon were submissive to trout aggression. Aggression was never noted among the salmon."

The Chopaka experiment ended in failure, but the next year the state tried again in another lake—this one with an environment about as different from the natural habitat of sea-run Atlantic salmon as it would be possible to find. It was called Quail Lake, actually little more than a pond formed by irrigation seepage in the hot desert near the little town of Othello in central Washington. Surrounded by barren basalt outcrops and clumps of sage and bitterbrush and swept by howling winds and sandstorms, the scenery around Quail Lake probably bears a closer resemblance to the surface of Mars than it does a salmon river.

But Quail Lake had produced large trout in the past, and its trout population was small enough that biologists felt it would not pose a competitive threat to the salmon. So, in October, 1974, 580 Atlantic salmon averaging 10 to 12 inches were planted in the lake.

When the lake was sampled eight months later, the fish averaged 18½ inches—a nearly unheard-of rate of growth approaching an inch a month in some cases. It looked as if Washington state finally had found a lake where Atlantic salmon could survive and thrive.

But the jubilation over Quail Lake was short-lived. The salmon were so efficient in feeding on the lake's aquatic insect population that they soon destroyed it, leaving themselves with nothing to eat. A second plant of yearling fish in 1975 scarcely grew at all, and the older fish—those which had grown so rapidly during their first year in the lake—grew thin and sluggish and began to die. Quail Lake turned out to be a flash in the pan; no more salmon were planted there.

However, some Atlantic salmon were planted in a third

lake, a small, high-altitude tarn in the mountains of the Olympic Peninsula. At first they did well, feeding on a natural population of scuds, and anglers who hiked into the lake two years after it was stocked caught salmon weighing more than three pounds. But the state has since ended its Atlantic salmon program, mainly for lack of success, so there will be no further stocking of this lake.

There is more than a little irony in the fact that Washington state finally gave up trying to establish Atlantic salmon in its own waters, because it is playing a vital role in the effort to restore salmon to the New England rivers where they were once native. Several different stocks of Atlantic salmon, including some descendants of the original Gaspe Bay-Hosmer Lake fish, are being held in saltwater pens in Puget Sound to provide eggs and fry for planting in New England streams. Puget Sound was chosen as the holding site because, unlike most New England harbors, it remains free of ice in winter.

In a way it is sad to visit the floating pens and see these great fish in such small enclosures, with walls of mesh that keep them from fulfilling their age-old instinct to head for the open sea. But there is consolation in knowing that they may hold the seeds of restoration for the faraway rivers of New England, whose original salmon stocks were wiped out by dams and pollution a century ago.

It also seems entirely in keeping with the salmon's reputation as a well-traveled fish that some are being held in Pacific waters for the benefit of restoring vanished runs in the Atlantic. And surely that is not the end of the story; ambitious Atlantic salmon stocking programs are now under way in the Great Lakes and in other waters, and more will certainly follow. As man continues to learn about the salmon, it also is reasonable to expect that more transplants will be successful than in the past.

So the salmon's travels are bound to continue, and

perhaps one day fisheries biologists will even find a way to make it more than just a token resident of the Pacific Northwest. Though that might cause some temporary restlessness in the immortal sleep of a certain legendary British diplomat, I think anglers would welcome it.

I know I would.

Price's Lake

It had been a long time since my last visit to Price's Lake. Each year I'd plan to go there, just as I had gone so often in the past, but something always seemed to interfere. I'd postpone the trip, thinking that I'd get another chance, but somehow those second chances never came. Before I knew it, five years had passed.

Finally I set a date to return and vowed this time I'd let nothing interfere. At last the day came and Randy and I set out on a fresh spring morning over roads still wet with rain.

I went with some misgivings, remembering that often I'd returned to a favorite water after a long absence and found many changes, seldom any for the better. Price's Lake was well off the beaten track, but not so far that it was invulnerable to change.

I wondered if it would still be anything like it was on the very first day I fished it, nearly 20 years before. I caught nothing that day, but I watched another fisherman take a four-pound rainbow on a fast-stripped Muddler Minnow back in the weeds. It was a fine bright trout, one that would have been a trophy from any lake, and I remember wishing keenly that it had been my fish instead of his. Just the sight of it—plus the knowledge that here was a lake capable of producing such fish—inspired me to return. And for the next few years I did so often.

It never was an easy place to reach. The dirt road was always rutted and always wet and ended a quarter of a mile from the lake. Near its end was a ramshackle cabin surrounded by second-growth firs and rusting hulks of cars, machinery, and other detritus from someone's lifetime in the woods. An old couple lived there and rented boats on the lake and sometimes when I stopped to pay they would invite me into their cluttered kitchen for a mug of steaming coffee.

The kitchen was a period piece, with pots and pans hanging from nails driven in the walls and a linoleum floor that had been buckled by the damp until it undulated like the surface of the lake when the wind was up. While I sipped coffee the old man would always say the fishing had been good and if I tried a Yellow Professor I would surely catch my share. He would say that even if the fishing had been poor.

The road beyond the cabin was little more than a muddy trail. It led down through an old apple orchard that was under attack from the woods, which had sent fir seedlings as scouts to grow among the apple trees. It was a battle the orchard was bound to lose, but each fall its defiant trees still bent under a heavy weight of fruit, and every spring their blossoms lit the trail.

The road finally petered out at the edge of a swamp and from there it was a 10-minute walk over a boardwalk to the lake. The boardwalk, fashioned of split cedar sections laid across a pair of wooden rails, followed a zig-zag course through dense thickets of fern and skunk cabbage and scattered pools of dark water with great old cedars growing out of them. The cedars trailed long strands of moss and snake-like vines and their thick foliage held the rain and dripped it slowly. It was a dark and eerie place, filled with the moist scent of slowly rotting leaves and wood.

Often enough the odor of rotting wood came from the boardwalk. Although sections of it had been replaced from time to time, decay had begun the very moment the new planks were set in place and some always were broken or missing at vital points along the way. The gaps revealed stagnant pools of black water and sticky ooze below, and the only way to get across was to walk tight-rope fashion on the narrow wooden rails. It was not an easy thing to do, especially if one was carrying a heavy pack, or if mosquitoes decided to attack—as they often did just at the instant when one's balance seemed in greatest peril.

Even on a dark day, stepping out of the shadowy swamp and into the open would leave a fisherman blinded and blinking while his eyes adjusted to the sudden light. When he could see again, he would find himself looking out on a leaning dock attached to unsteady posts driven into the muddy bottom of the lake. An assortment of battered wooden rowboats was kept tied to the dock, and these were the source of the old couple's income. It was a monopoly business; no one in his right mind would have tried to carry a boat over the boardwalk, and float tubes had yet to come in fashion.

But the rowboats always lacked something—sometimes something vital, like an intact hull, but more often something a little less essential, like an oarlock, a seat or a matched pair of oars. Ingenuity usually could provide at least a temporary substitute for whatever was missing, but when the substitutes had been devised and a boat was as seaworthy as a fisherman could make it . . . well, usually that was just the beginning of his problems.

Price's Lake is one of the wettest places in a state famous for its rain. Annual rainfall at the lake exceeds 100 inches, and rarely a day goes by without at least a little rain; more often there's a lot. I've spent days there when I had the feeling that the rain and the lake were in a race to see which could be first to sink my boat—the lake seeping or spurting in through cracks in an old, poorly caulked hull, while the rain hemorrhaged from clouds that had gathered an oceanful of it in their long journey across the Pacific. Sometimes I'd bail until I could barely lift my arms, but then I'd drift over the watery grave of a sunken rowboat, dimly visible on the bottom. There were many sunken boats on the bottom of Price's Lake, and the sight of one always was an inspiration to keep on bailing.

The reward for all this risk and effort was a chance to catch large rainbow, Eastern brook, or cutthroat trout, and Price's Lake is the only place I've ever fished where it was possible to catch all three. It also was a lake ideally suited to the fly, shallow and weedy and filled with massive stumps and snags. On spring days it produced good hatches of large mayflies, and at dusk blizzards of smaller mayflies and caddisflies would rise from its surface. Later it would come alive with squirming damselfly nymphs searching for stumps or stems to crawl out upon and hatch. Sporadic hatches continued even in the fall, and sometimes late in October there would be a great flight of termites from the woods and the awkward insects would fall on the water and set off a frenzied rise of fish.

It also was a lake with a firmly established place in local angling lore. It had given up many large fish—brook trout to five pounds and rainbow to seven, if you could believe the tales—and any lake which produces trout or trout stories of that size is bound to attract a large following of anglers. Among the Price's Lake "regulars" were some of the Northwest's most famous fishermen, including Enos Bradner, outdoor editor of *The Seattle Times* and one of the founders of the Washington Fly Fishing Club. Bradner caught two brook trout in Price's Lake which still are the largest ever entered in the records of the club, and it was on Price's Lake where Bradner and Frank Headrick perfected a fly pattern they dubbed the "Dandy Green Nymph" which has since become a Northwest standard.

Price's Lake also has an unusual natural history. Geologists say it was created by an enormous earthquake that pushed up a scarp to block a stream flowing through a gentle valley. Water backed up behind the scarp, forming the lake and flooding a stand of huge firs and cedars; the trees died and gradually rotted away at the waterline, but their stumps were preserved under water. Based on the age of the stumps, geologists believe the earthquake occurred between 1,100 and 1,300 years ago.

I'd heard the stories about Price's Lake and went there to see if they were true. That first visit 20 years ago convinced me that they were, and after that I fished it many times—in spring and fall, in the usual rain or during rare spells of sunshine, on calm mornings or windy afternoons. I found it an intriguing and strangely enigmatic water, slow to share its secrets. Often it was sullen and unyielding, devoid of any apparent sign of life, and occasionally it was grudgingly friendly and granted me a fish now and then. But every once in a very great while it could be unbelievably generous, both in numbers and size of trout.

Once I went there with Bradner. He was an old man by then but age had not impaired his skill. By the day's end I had caught more fish, but the ones he caught were much larger. Another time I went with Ward McClure and we found the way blocked by a fir tree that had fallen across the road. Somehow we had forgotten to bring along an ax and a dull machete was the only cutting tool we had. It took nearly an hour to cut through the tree and there were blisters on our hands when we finished, but we went on to the lake anyway. We found it in a stingy mood and fished painfully through an afternoon of blinding rain with only three small trout to show for our efforts.

Ed Foss and Vince Sellen joined me there one day when the wind blew so hard we swore there were whitecaps in our coffee cups, but we caught fish anyway. And once when I went alone the old couple in the cabin said I was the first person they had seen in more than a week. Nevertheless, the old man still said the fishing had been good and if I used a Yellow Professor I would surely catch my share.

There were days when I did catch my share. Once I caught a brook trout of nearly 2½ pounds, the largest I have taken. I landed many rainbow over two pounds and some over three, mostly on dry flies during mayfly hatches in the spring, and one day after taking several brook trout and rainbows, I caught the first cutthroat I had ever taken there—the first time I had ever caught all three species in a day.

I learned to know the lake in all its moods. I grew to love it in the spring, when the apple blossoms burst open in the old orchard, the skunk cabbage flashed its yellow blooms like lanterns in the darkness of the swamp and everywhere around the lake the cottonwoods and alders and maples were in fresh green leaf. But I loved it just as much in the fall when those once-fresh leaves would change to rusty red and gold and the slightest breeze would shake them loose and send them gliding in gentle spirals down to the water. I even loved it on days when the woods dripped rain and the sky was heavy with the dark promise of more, or when a chilling fog settled down on the water and blotted out the hills so that it seemed as if I had floated off the earth into a mysterious gray void.

More often than not I fished with only ducks or muskrats or a solitary heron for company, and sometimes at dusk I'd hear the quavering howl of a coyote close at hand or the sound of something large crashing through the nearby brush. All these things were a part of the peculiar charm of Price's Lake; it had taken hold of me, and I found it a strangely wild and beautiful place.

But some things did change in the years that I fished it. The old couple's cabin, which stood on land leased from a logging company, was swept by fire one winter and the old man suffered burns. They took him away to a rest home and when he was unable to return the logging company canceled the lease and closed the road. A new road was opened to the opposite side of the lake with a trail down a steep hillside to the shore.

About the same time, responding to lobbying by fly fishing clubs, the state declared Price's Lake a "wild trout" water. No more trout would be stocked, and those already in the lake would be allowed to spawn naturally in its two small inlet streams. Fishermen would have to use artificial flies or lures and release all the trout they caught.

I fished it a few times after that, using the new road and the new trail and carrying in my own boat. The lake itself had seemed the same and I enjoyed it just as much as always.

But five years had passed since my last visit there. And now, as I drove up the eastern flank of the Olympic Peninsula, I could see that ugly real-estate "developments" had metastasized far up into the foothills. The sight of them kept me in suspense until we drew closer to our destination and I saw with relief that the spreading blight had yet to reach into the secluded valley of Price's Lake.

The dirt road leading to the lake was just the same as it had been the last time I had driven it and I found the trailhead easily, though the trail itself showed little evidence of use. It also seemed a little longer and steeper than I'd remembered it, but then all trails are beginning to seem that way to me.

Randy helped me with the boat and we got it down to the lake and set up our rods and pushed away from shore. There was no one else in sight, but it would be wrong to say we had the lake entirely to ourselves; three ospreys circled overhead and two of them were busy building up a nest—a knobby-looking affair in the top of an old fir near the shoreline of the lake. We watched them carry limbs and branches to add to the considerable bundle they already had assembled.

The day was mixed with changing patterns of sun and cloud and drizzle and a variable breeze. The water was cold and clear and the weeds were barely beginning to sprout from the bottom, though the annual crop of water lilies already was appearing near the shore. During periods when the sun was out and the lake was flat, big dark *Callibaetis* mayfly duns popped to the surface and hoisted their wings like tiny sails. Occasionally a trout would follow one up and take it, but most of the fish were feeding on the nymphs, leaving only little wrinkles on the surface to show what they were doing. We put up a size 12 *Callibaetis* nymph on a floating line and quickly found action.

The first fish was a rainbow, strong and fat and firm. The second was a cutthroat, dressed in a beautiful shade of olive with bright red slashes under its lower jaw. The third was a brook trout, also handsomely marked with bright pink and lemon-yellow spots floating in the sunset colors on its sides. All were wild, naturally spawned trout, their fins perfectly shaped, their colors those nature gave them. It would be hard to find three prettier trout anywhere. Once before I had caught all three species in a single day on Price's Lake, but this was the first time I'd ever done it back-to-back.

All the fish were fat and in good condition, but each was only about 11 inches long and I remembered that Price's Lake was capable of better. The next fish proved the point; it was a bright rainbow that jumped high and took out line and weighed a little over two pounds when I finally brought it in. It was followed by another rainbow only a little smaller, then by two smaller brook trout.

We fished leisurely with time out for lunch and a couple of newt-hunting expeditions. Price's Lake abounds with rough-skinned newts and they seem to have a special fascination for kids. Randy caught a couple and kept them as temporary "pets" until we were through fishing; then, like the trout, they were returned to the lake.

At last we steered the boat back through the ancient stumps to the muddy launch at the foot of the trail, then loaded our gear and started up the hill. Behind us the lake sparkled in the afternoon sun, still the same lonely, wild and beautiful place that it had always been. And I was glad.

Some places are perfect just the way they are. Price's Lake is one of them.

SUMMER

If you go out on a summer morning when the day is just breaking you will find the river in its loveliest mood. The air is cool and fresh and full of promise and the river seems hushed and quiet as it flows through meadows still sparkling wet with morning dew. Deer slip down from the woods to drink in the cool eddies, and you may see a great blue heron standing stock-still in the shallows; it has begun its fishing day even before you have begun yours.

Winter's violence and river-changing floods are a fading memory now, for by summer the river has assumed the shape it will hold for the remainder of the year. With the slow passage of the long warm summer days it will shrink ever deeper in its channel until by August it will begin to show its bones—the bleached white water-blasted rocks that shaped its currents during the high water of seasons past. If you look at them closely you may see the vacant shucks of stonefly nymphs that crawled up on them to hatch and enjoy a brief caper in the air during the latter days of May or early June. Perhaps you also will see some tiny empty tubes of gravel, calling cards left by caddis pupae that have long since passed through their miraculous metamorphosis into flies.

Yet even during August's low water the river still bustles with life. Steelhead and cutthroat fry that hatched in April are busy feeding in the shallows and the long pale ghosts of Dolly Varden stalk them there. Spring Chinook salmon have returned to the river for their long rest before spawning and they hold in the deeper quiet pools, rolling noisily in the twilight and sending ripples all the way to the shore. And even when the current subsides to its weakest flow the summer steelhead somehow are still able to find where it mingles with the sea and follow it upstream.

During the hot, still, lazy days of August the steelhead pause to rest in shaded runs and there they may be tempted by a floating fly or a gleaming bit of fur and feathers offered at the end of a long floating line. Then, if an angler is lucky, he may witness the heart-stopping sight of a fresh-run summer fish rising to a high-floating fly, or the great swirl of a strong subsurface take.

Even the excitement that follows cannot compare with that first electric moment of the take. It is the ultimate reward of summer, surely one of the best moments of the year.

Birthday Fish

On the morning of my birthday I awoke with a raging sinus
headache. I lay in bed a while, hoping the headache would go
away, but all it did was move around a little until it found a
spot it seemed to like, just to the left of my nose. There it
settled down and felt as if it meant to stay.

I had been planning to spend the day on the river. A few
days earlier it had been too high to fish, but there had been
dry weather since—dry enough to bring the river down to
fishing shape. It would be the first chance of the year to try for
a summer steelhead.

The thought of a steelhead contended with the headache

and the steelhead won. I crawled out of bed, swallowed two cups of coffee and some aspirin, loaded my waders and tackle in the truck and started out for the river.

It was a warm day but not too bright, some fluffy clouds were scattered around the sky and there was a gentle breeze. That much was good, but the headache was persistent; it grew worse as I drove north on the freeway in heavy summer traffic.

The trip took an hour and by the time I reached the river I was feeling sorry I had come. The river looked in shape, as I thought it would, but a bad sinus headache can destroy your enthusiasm for just about anything—even the chance for a steelhead on the fly.

I sat in the shade, thinking what a lousy way this was to spend a birthday, and waited to see if the pain would go away. After a while it did subside a little, and though I didn't feel quite up to fishing I decided I felt well enough to tie a fly or two. The stock in my steelhead fly boxes was low; it had not been replenished since the last summer season.

I don't know whether any medical authority has ever investigated the therapeutic value of fly tying, but if not then someone should. After a dozen flies had emerged from my vise the headache had vanished and I felt some of my usual vigor starting to return. By then it was late afternoon, the day was cooling and long shadows were beginning to reach out across the stream, but from where I sat I could see my favorite run was empty—I hadn't seen anyone there all day—and that was the last bit of encouragement I needed.

Returning to the truck, I removed the graphite rod from its long tube and joined the sections together, mounted the reel and strung the sinking line through the guides, then took one of the flies I had just tied and knotted it to the end of the leader. I slipped on a pair of stocking-foot waders and laced up the wading shoes, then wriggled into the overloaded vest with its bulging pockets and headed for the river.

I scrambled down the bank, started upstream toward my favorite run and stopped. Another fisherman was just wading in at the head of the run. He moved around a little until he found a spot he seemed to like, just to the left of the tongue of current flowing through the pool. There he settled down and looked as if he meant to stay.

I stood there, muttering single-syllable words, and wondered what to do next. Then I remembered another promising run a little way downstream and decided that it might be worth a look.

The run was empty when I arrived so I waded in and began casting. The water was cool and so was the air above it and both felt good, and soon I found myself caught up in the gentle rhythm of the river. It was satisfying to be there, to reach out with a long line and drop the fly close to the far shore, then feel the line come alive in the current as it started its downstream swing. But I was hoping for something more than just the feel of the current on the line.

I fished patiently and thoroughly through the run, stopping after each pair of downstream steps to search the water with several casts before I took another pair of steps and stopped to search again. In such methodical fashion I fished almost to the end of the pool—and there, just as a long cast straightened out below, I felt the heavy pull of a steelhead.

Perhaps it was because I was out of practice, or perhaps just because the fish took me by surprise, but for whatever reason I struck too hard. The leader tippet parted like a cobweb.

That brought quite a few more single-syllable words to mind. I was angry and disgusted—not at the fish, but at myself for having missed the chance. There are not so many opportunities to hook a steelhead on the fly that an angler can afford to waste many of them—especially one that falls upon his birthday.

There were no more steelhead waiting in the remainder of the pool and finally I left it and started back, still feeling most unhappy with myself. Wading across the river, I glanced upstream, and saw the same angler still planted in my favorite run. That did not make me any less unhappy. Soon it would be too dark to fish, and I faced the specter of a fishless birthday.

Then the other fisherman abruptly reeled in, waded out of the river and vanished into the woods, leaving the empty pool to beckon. Quickly I considered the possibilities: The other fisherman had spent a lot of time in the pool and probably had covered it thoroughly; if he hadn't taken a fish that likely meant there were no fish there to be taken.

Still, there was no harm in trying.

There was not enough light left to fish the full length of the run, so I started in near the tail where I'd always had the best results. Immediately everything went wrong; the fly line came up tangled from the stripping basket, and no sooner had I got it straightened out than it tangled once again. With little patience I plucked at the loops and coils until the line was free and I could cast, but then the leader snarled. Finally exhausting my vocabulary of one-syllable words, I picked through the monofilament maze in the fading light until once again the leader was free of knots, or nearly so.

At last I made a decent cast, then another and a third. The third cast had barely settled to the water when a fish seized the fly. This time I set the hook more gently and the fish reacted slowly, moving out into the center of the run and taking a few turns of line from the reel. It didn't feel especially large, but it was a fish and that was all I wanted.

Then the fish ran strongly, taking the line down into the backing. It jumped at the head of the pool and I could see that it was big and bright. I was well below it, just where I wanted to be, and I recovered line as the fish fought the pressure of both the current and the rod. It ran again and jumped a second time, far out of the water in a graceful parabola. After that we traded line, the fish jumped again, and then I got the upper hand and led it into shallow water. It turned on its side and I thought it was done, but suddenly it turned upright and ran again, the strongest run yet, and took all the line and much of the backing as it headed far upstream.

When the run finally ended I began reeling in as quickly as I could, but it seemed the fly line would never come in view. At last the backing splice came through the guides and several turns of fly line came in on top of it, but then the fish ran again, stopped and thrashed heavily on the surface.

The line went slack. I reeled frantically but there was no answering pull. With growing despair, I kept reeling until all the line was on the reel and the leader butt was showing.

Then I felt the fish again. It had gone around me and was holding just below, almost within my reach. The current had formed a slack belly in the line when the fish made its sudden move, and in the dim evening light I couldn't tell where it had gone.

But now I knew. I went ashore, got below the fish again and steered it close enough so that finally I was able to reach down and give it a gentle shove onto the wet stones along the river's edge.

It was the most beautiful fish I had ever seen—snow white on its belly, bright silver on its sides and gleaming steel-gray on its back, without a single flaw or blemish. Its form was just as flawless—a small head, thick body and powerful tail, every fin shaped perfectly. This was no hatchery fish; only nature could have made a fish as beautiful as this.

I measured it against my rod—29 inches—and guessed its weight at somewhere between eight and nine pounds. Then I carefully removed the fly and lifted the fish gently back into the river, holding it there until it exploded from my grasp and went on about its interrupted way.

I stood again and looked around. The sun had set, bats were feeding on the evening hatch and the day was nearly done.

But I felt good. It was my birthday, and the river had remembered.

Pages from a
Trout Fisherman's Diary

Trout fishermen are known for the diaries they keep. Their journals, dating back almost to the misty origins of the sport, have given us a rich and colorful record of trout fishing through the ages. Few other activities of man have inspired such proliferacy and devotion for so long.

That devotion remains true to this day. In fact, it shows signs of growing—in recent years angling diaries have become more commonplace than ever. But there are signs their purpose may be changing: Many anglers seem to have dismissed the notion of the diary as a personal angling journal and have begun using it instead as a repository for technical

information that might have future use. If there is a hatch of
pale sulfur duns on a particular river at 2 p.m. on July 11, they
record that information faithfully; then, if they should happen
to be fishing the same water a year hence, they can look in
their diaries and learn what to expect.

Sensing this trend, various entrepreneurs have begun
selling printed page forms with neatly arranged columns and
spaces in which a trout fisherman can record just about any
kind of technical information he could possibly want—water
temperature and clarity, hatches observed and the times they
began and ended, fly patterns used and results obtained,
weather data, trout species caught and the length and weight
of each, and so on and on. I suppose such forms have a proper
place, but it always has seemed to me they are better suited for
accountants than for anglers. Certainly they do nothing to
encourage free expression.

It's not that I don't keep detailed records in my own
journal, but I do so in my own fashion—and once having
recorded the information, I seldom refer to it again. "You can
look it up," as Casey Stengel used to say, and I can; but I
hardly ever do. For I learned long ago that the best reason for
keeping a fishing journal is to preserve the treasured experiences of a fishing lifetime—experiences that might suffer from
distortion or disappear if left to the mercies of a frail human
memory.

Now I read my journal to relive those moments from the
past. Its faded pages bring to mind old names and familiar
places and revive the vivid excitement of times gone by. In it I
can find the triumphant words I wrote after the capture of my
first steelhead, or the joyful account of my first salmon on a
fly—along with records of all the unsuccessful trips that led up
to those happy days. It holds the description of my first
rainbow from Lake Taupo, the story of my first Alaska cutthroat, and the records of countless fish caught in waters close
to home. For me, it is the best of all fishing books.

Some of its pages still have trout scales stuck to them, preserved for study under a miscroscope but serving also as reminders of struggles with memorable fish. Between other pages are copies of old licenses, souvenirs of trips to exotic places; still others bear scribbled maps of routes to obscure waters or notes on the fly patterns that succeeded in them. There are details of a thousand trips, some delightful and others disappointing, but each one worth recording at the time, and worth remembering now.

My diary reminds me that I was fishing in a mountain lake on that historic day in 1969 when men first landed on the moon, and that I caught and released more than 50 lively brook trout before racing home to watch on television as that first giant step was taken for all mankind.

It also brings back to mind my first impression of the mighty Deschutes River in Oregon. "The Deschutes is aptly named," I wrote on that July day in 1973, "a swift-flowing river with many rapids breaking over lava ledges and great boulders. It is different from any river I have fished before—a wide, mostly shallow stream that carries a good amount of glacial silt . . . The walls of its canyon are spectacular basalt terraces and turrets, and the river is lined with trees of sparse foliage, all flat-topped from the wind. It is a strange country, both friendly and forbidding, and I am glad for a chance to see it. . . ."

Reading that now, I can see it all again—as well as everything that followed: "We went up about 12 miles and began fishing at 6:15 a.m. By 7 the sun was over the rim of the canyon, but it never did become too warm—though the sky was clear—because the river itself was cool and a strong wind came up with the sun . . . I went without a fish until about 2 p.m. At that time I was fishing a drift right below an abandoned railroad water tower, using a No. 6 Skunk, which is about all I used all day. Suddenly the fly was taken by a strong fish that took me about 200 yards downstream in a series of short rushes before I beached it—a fine bright buck steelhead of about 25 or 26 inches and around seven pounds—a very solid, block-shaped fish."

Two months later I was in British Columbia fishing for Kamloops trout, and my diary holds the record of a remarkable sight on a wilderness lake: "Two large bears standing upright, grappling and wrestling in the water. They began to roll around and kick spray at each other and appeared to be having as much fun as a couple of kids in a water fight." I watched them for a long time, and I remember wondering if man's traditional view of bears as dangerous animals might be wrong; perhaps I was witnessing a display of their true nature.

Those preprinted diary forms offer no space for observations such as that.

A year later I returned to British Columbia to make a fishing film for a network television program. The network had chosen Peter Duchin, the famous band leader, to be the "featured fisherman" and I was to be his guide. Each of us was "wired" for sound and kept under the unwavering eye of a camera while we tried to coax trout to floating flies.

My journal tells the story: On the first day "a few sedges were on the water, but no fish were rising. We fished seriously for an hour or an hour and a half without result . . . I could not help but feel badly that we caught nothing, but apparently the film crew is used to this sort of thing. I hope the lake is cooperative tomorrow; I feel the pressure to produce results."

Next day was a little better: "Shortly before noon, the traveling sedges started coming off in good numbers and the fish started rising. I rose one and broke it and Peter rose two and broke both of them. Then I rose and hooked a fish of about 2½ pounds and landed it—our first fish on camera." But the effort was for naught: "The noise of cattle and the appearance of many other boats soured the camera crew."

It was a busy week. We were up early each morning for breakfast and the long drive to the lake that we had chosen for the filming. Then we would fish and film all day—work which turned out to be much more difficult than I'd ever imagined it would be—and drive back for a late dinner at the lodge where we were staying. After dinner I would usually stay up until the early hours of the next morning, tying flies for use in the day's fishing or talking with members of the film crew.

The fishing never was very good, but the trout cooperated just often enough for the camera crew to get what it had come for—and our six days of fishing eventually were condensed to 12 minutes of film shown on the network.

When the work finally was done and the director pronounced himself satisfied, there was still one day left to fish for fun. And on that day my journal says we found "the finest hatch of traveling sedges I have ever seen . . . I rose and hooked a fine trout that jumped several times, took line and gave an excellent account of itself before I finally landed it. It was the best fish of the week—and, of course, better than any we filmed on the show."

Later that summer I visited the little upper Gibbon in Yellowstone Park. "The river is hardly more than a brook at this point, meandering through a lush meadow," I wrote. It was full of small brook trout—"and, much to my surprise, a 14-inch, 1¼-pound rainbow."

My journal rekindles the memory of that fish: I had fished upstream through the meadow to the point where a highway bridge spans the creek, and by then I had nearly given up hope of finding any sizable fish in that tiny stream. I was ready to leave when I heard a heavy splash under the bridge.

The meadow was bright with sunshine, but under the bridge it was pitch dark in the shade. I listened for a while and the splash came again. There was no way to see what was causing it but I guessed it might be a trout, feeding somewhere back in the shadows. So I stripped line from the reel, stood well back from the bridge and pitched my little dry fly far up into the darkness underneath. The current brought slack line back to me and I gathered it in and waited until I heard the splash again. Then I struck.

A large rainbow came tumbling out of the darkness into the sunshine, and it was hard to tell which of us was more surprised. The fish's size and strength was far out of proportion to the stream, but it fought as hard as the close quarters would allow. When it finally came trembling to my grasp I released it quickly and carefully, then watched as it headed swiftly back for its dark lair beneath the bridge. I wonder now if its descendants still sip flies in the shadows of that little bridge.

There are many entries from Hosmer Lake in my diary, simply because I have fished for the transplanted Atlantic salmon there so often and so long. There is one about a salmon that jumped into the boat and just as promptly jumped out again, another that recalls the time an osprey plunged from the sky and tried to catch a fish I was playing and another about the time an otter seized a fish right beneath my fly.

It also was at Hosmer where my backcast once hooked a nighthawk on the wing. My diary reports what happened next: "After what can only be described as a very interesting fight—or flight—with the line wound twice around my spare rod and once under the outboard motor shaft, I got the bird to the side of the boat, where I could see it was hooked near the base of one wing. By then it was angry—no doubt about that—and it opened its mouth and said 'Scrawwk!' With a healthy respect for its talons and beak, I broke off about 30 inches of tippet and the bird flew off with my No. 16 Blue Upright still stuck in its wing.

"Well, after all, this is supposed to be a catch-and-release lake."

A few days later my friend Dave Draheim also accidentally hooked a nighthawk. This one flew in circles, trussing up

Dave in four turns of his own fly line—one of the funniest sights I have seen in all my years of fishing.

Of all the Hosmer Lake entries in my diary, my favorite is one written on the last day of a long stay:

"The morning dawned cold with a solid overcast and a threat of rain. More or less as a pilgrimage, I went to the upper lake, not really expecting to find anything there. The wind was cold and cruel and Mount Bachelor and the stately South Sister lay hidden in the lowering mists. But all the other familiar sights were there—the moss-covered snag on the point beyond the lava reef, the tules bending and bowing gracefully in the wind, the withered pines in the encroaching meadow around the lake. Ospreys and eagles floated overhead against the dark backdrop of the sky and when the wind died momentarily I could hear birdsongs from the meadow, mixed with an occasional whistling flight of ducks. Even in the cold, gray light of this somber day, Hosmer is a magical place, a place of wild and magnificent beauty.

"And while taking it all in, I searched also for the elusive dark shadows of salmon moving beneath the waves. The usual haunts seemed empty of fish, so I drifted on the wind, past the point with the old snag, past the mouth of the little lagoon where last year I went swimming on a hot, still day, and on to the next point with its short skirt of dark lava rocks where, every once in a great while, I have found the salmon gathered and feeding.

"And they were there again today, rising and boiling in the rough, wind-whipped water. Quickly I was fast to one, an angry salmon flashing away on its first fierce run, then jumping high and throwing a burst of spray into the wind. Then came a long struggle of give and take, the salmon taking line in shrill bursts from the little Hardy reel, then yielding sullenly to the pressure as I regained the line. After several shorter runs and two or three more tumbling jumps, we approached the end game—two determined players, each making careful moves, each trying to avoid a fatal error that would result in loss of the game. For the salmon, the stakes were his life, for he could not know that I would let him keep it. And when his last energy ebbed and he came alongside in obedience to the spring of the rod, I twisted the fly free and the salmon knew that he had won as well as lost.

"Throughout the long, cold, windy afternoon the salmon came, sometimes in quick succession. I raised many more than I could hook because the wind was unrelenting, blowing wide bellies in the line so that I couldn't set the hook before the quick salmon was gone. And late in the day the wind blew hard pellets of rain onto my glasses as I fought a last strong fish that ran twice into the backing and gave me a long, stirring fight before I twisted the fly free and restored him to the lake.

"And when it was finally over, I had felt the weight of 26 salmon on my line, 15 of which I landed. In addition, there was a single plump brook trout.

"So another fine year at Hosmer Lake is over. It has become so much a highlight of my year that I think of it often during the long days of winter work. I hope it will be here, waiting, for as long as I am able to come, and for my children after me."

It is still there, waiting, although the fishing has declined sadly in recent years. I hope it will soon be restored and that Hosmer Lake will yet account for many more pages in my diary.

Over the years my diary has grown to fill 28 notebooks and I am just now starting number 29. Many hours and much work has gone into those pages, but "it was an employment for his idle time, which was then not idly spent," as Izaak Walton once succinctly said. It also has been time spent in the most pleasant way, transcribing adventures as they happened, then reading and re-reading about them later.

I do not know or really care if anyone else will ever read what is written in these notebooks, but I do know they have always pleased their intended audience of one. If someone else should read them, I suppose they would seem less interesting to him than they have always seemed to me. But if he had the patience to keep reading, he would find the account of one fishing trip that was extraordinary by any standards—a trip that literally became a voyage into the twilight zone. It is the entry dated May 18, 1980.

On that bright spring Sunday morning I had taken my family to Dry Falls Lake in eastern Washington. We arrived early, just as a trendmendous dragonfly hatch was getting under way. Dozens of big, stubby nymphs had crawled out of the lake and up onto dry land, leaving awkward trails as they crossed the dusty road to the grass on the far side. There they climbed the stalks and began the slow process of extracting themselves from their nymphal shucks. The children went to watch this curious pilgrimage while Joan, my wife, set up a camp stove to heat the morning coffee and I made preparations to go fishing.

The coffee perked and added its pleasant scent to the fresh morning air and we were just about to take the first sip when the sounds came. At first there was only a gentle ripple in the air, so soft and subtle I was uncertain I had heard anything at all. Then it came again, much louder this time, a deep, ominous rumble that grew in volume until it became a mighty swell of sound that washed against the coulee walls, echoing and re-echoing around the great amphitheater of the Dry Falls.

The children were frightened and came running to ask what was happening, but I had no explanation to offer. The sound was not thunder or a sonic boom, nor did it seem possible it could have carried from the Army's Yakima Firing Range; it was too far away. Then I had a joking thought:

"Maybe Mount St. Helens blew her top," I said. The children laughed, reassured that I could jest, and soon returned to their play.

The sound faded as abruptly as it had come and we soon forgot it. I started fishing about 9:30 a.m.; the dragonfly hatch had ended, but within an hour the damselfly nymphs began to move and fish started rising. Four good rainbows came to my fly and fought well, giving me a difficult time in the weedy shallows. It was a good morning, passing quickly as all good mornings do.

It was nearly noon when I glanced over my shoulder and noticed for the first time an ominous dark cloud spreading over the coulee rim from south and east. It looked like a big thunderstorm headed our way, and remembering the violence of some other storms I'd experienced at Dry Falls, I knew it would be a good idea to seek cover before it hit. Perhaps I could go ashore and have lunch, then wait for the storm to pass and resume fishing in the afternoon.

I made a few more casts, then started for shore, keeping a wary eye on the approaching cloud. It seemed to be moving in quickly, though the lake was still strangely calm and trout were still rising.

Other fishermen also were heading for shelter. Most loaded up their gear and left, and we sat and ate our lunch and watched them go until only one or two remained. The dark cloud now covered half the sky.

I walked up the road to the top of the first rise where I could look south along the coulee. The cloud extended for as far as I could see; it was a big storm, one that looked as if it would last at least throughout the afternoon. Reluctantly, I decided we should pack up and follow the others who had left.

I told Joan and the children to gather up their things while I put away my rods and hoisted my little pram atop the truck. We worked quickly, expecting the storm to strike at any moment, but though it grew ever darker there was still no wind, nor yet a hint of rain.

It was completely dark by the time we were ready to leave—not just storm-dark or twilight-dark, but as dark as the deepest, blackest night. The cloud had filled the sky, stretching from one rim of the coulee to the other, and it had completely swallowed up the day. All the familiar landmarks of the Dry Falls had disappeared and we were surrounded instead by vague shapes and masses that we felt rather than saw. Even the noisy yellow-headed and redwing blackbirds in the tules around the lakeshore had suddenly grown still.

It was 1 o'clock in the afternoon, but it was night.

I started the truck, switched on the headlights and shifted into low gear for the first hill on the tortuous, rocky road out of the Dry Falls. By this time only one other fisherman remained and he also was working hurriedly to load his boat and leave. He looked anxiously at the sky as we drove slowly past. "I've never seen anything like this," he said.

Neither had we.

By the time we had driven a quarter of a mile the darkness had become so murky and impenetrable that even the high beams of the truck's headlights could scarcely drill a thin tunnel of light ahead of us. Then I noticed a thick, heavy mist floating in the headlights and beginning to collect on the windshield. The storm was at last beginning.

"Here comes the rain," I said.

"That isn't rain," Joan said quietly. She was right. Whatever it was, it was dry.

The bright morning, so full of promise, had dissolved into total, impenetrable darkness. And now something was falling from the sky and it wasn't rain. We could see nothing, except for the pair of ruts that appeared dimly in the headlights, and hear nothing, except for the truck's engine straining to overcome the grade. It was as if we had made a wrong turn to another planet, or had suddenly crossed the threshold of a forbidden dimension.

There had to be some rational explanation and I could think of only one: That Mount St. Helens *had* exploded, with more cataclysmic force than anyone could ever possibly have imagined.

"Turn on the radio," Joan said. "There must be something on the radio." I hadn't turned it on before because reception is difficult down in the rocky pocket of the Dry Falls. But I did so now.

There was lightning in the air. It crashed and crackled across the radio band as I dialed, searching for a station. There were snatches of faint, far-off music, blurred by static. And then the frightened voice of a disc jockey at a station in nearby Moses Lake: "Mount St. Helens has erupted and ash is falling everywhere in the Columbia Basin. All roads in the area are closed. If you're in a car, pull over and stop!"

The voice was near panic; the disc jockey obviously was having as much trouble coping with the situation as we were. And yet his voice was somehow comforting, a link to the familiar world that had disappeared so suddenly an hour before. And it confirmed the explanation for the explosions we had heard and for our present plight.

But I was not about to take the disc jockey's advice. Pulling over and stopping was the last thing I wanted to do. Ash from the exploded volcano was falling thickly outside the truck; already I could smell and taste the stuff and it made my throat dry. It might be toxic. If we stopped, it seemed possible we might not be able to go on breathing in the gritty atmosphere. I decided to try to get away from this phantom rain and ugly darkness as quickly as I could, back to someplace where the air was clear and it was light.

It was a strange ride out of the Dry Falls, with the windshield wipers working to keep the ash from piling up and the headlights illuminating a dim path through the darkness that had come up out of the earth. But finally the rocky ruts gave way to a narrow band of asphalt that led southwest toward the nearest highway, and eventually we found our-selves in a line of other cars fleeing from the cloud. Each car stirred up an enormous roostertail of blinding dust that forced those behind to slow or stop until it settled.

In such halting fashion we made it to the highway and turned north, crawling through the dusty darkness until the headlights dimly picked out the sign for the junction with U.S. Highway 2, the route westward to the Cascades. If we went that way, I hoped, perhaps we could escape the cloud; we might even be able to make it over the mountains to our home in Seattle.

For 10 or 20 minutes we drove slowly westward in darkness. Then, far ahead, a dull gleam of light appeared, low on the horizon as if it were shining under the hem of a curtain. It grew larger and brighter as we continued toward it. The announcer at a radio on in Wenatchee assured us that Highway 2 was closed, but we kept on going.

Soon it was bright enough to see beyond the cone of light from the truck headlights. Everything was gray; ash swirled on the highway like new-fallen powder snow and filled the furrows of the plowed fields along the road. I thought about the ash being sucked into the truck's air intake and worried that it would choke the carburetor and kill the engine, but the truck plowed ahead steadily into the storm of ash.

It was sometime after 3 when we reached Wenatchee. The sun was a sullen glow in a dusty sky and thick ash and dust were blowing in the streets, but still it was a scene that seemed infinitely hospitable compared to the one we had left at Dry Falls. We had come from darkness into light, traversing a dusty moonscape which only that morning had been lush with green grass, freshly plowed dark rows of earth and trees filled with ripening fruit.

From Wenatchee we drove into the mountains toward

Stevens Pass, soon leaving the last of the ash behind us. The sky again brightened to a faultless blue and afternoon sunlight glinted from the silvery caps of late spring snow still clinging to the Cascade peaks. We breathed cool, clean air and gave silent thanks.

In another two hours we were home.

We were lucky. Thousands of others were not so fortunate. They were stranded for days in tiny, ash-choked towns or roadside rest areas, forced to a halt by blinding, blowing ash or by car engines that choked to death on the noxious stuff.

We also were lucky in another way: We had witnessed the awesome power of nature in a way that few people ever have. Those in other parts of the world who read of the explosion of Mount St. Helens in newspapers or watched it on television will never comprehend the full magnitude of the event; even the most powerful descriptive phrases or the most startling photographs cannot convey it properly. In order to understand how big—how incredible—it really was, you had to see it for yourself.

Now my vision of it is preserved in the pages of my fishing diary, along with the accounts of many less eventful days. It is there among the yellowing licenses, scribbled maps and fly patterns and the pages with trout scales still stuck to them—each one a separate record of some adventure from the past.

And that, I think, is the true test of what a trout fisherman's diary ought to be—not how much information it can hold, but how well it preserves the memories of a fishing lifetime and reminds a man of all the fun he's had.

The Once and Future River

The Green was only a little river, a mere capillary in the giant circulatory system that feeds the great Columbia. It emerged quietly from between high timbered ridges in the south Cascades, and all through the long summers it carried away the snowmelt in a gently diminishing flow.

Winter was a different story. In winter the river often shed its quiet personality and sometimes flooded violently, and the torrents would change it so that when anglers returned in the spring they could never be certain what they would find. The Green was a river one had to learn again and again.

But it was a river well worth learning. Despite its diminutive size and distance from the sea, it drew into itself large runs of bright steelhead in the summer and handsome sea-run cutthroat in the fall. It had salmon, too, a big early-autumn run that returned to a hatchery near the river's mouth. From the eve of summer to the twilight of the fall, an angler could always find fish in the Green.

There are dozens of rivers named Green, perhaps scores. Some are large; some, like this one, small. Only a few are actually green. This one was not—at least I never saw it so. Maybe it was once, back before loggers cut the giant firs that grew along its banks; back then it might have reflected the soft, deep green of fir boughs that stretched across its narrow width. But all trees of that stature were long gone by the time I got to know the Green, replaced by a host of maples, cottonwoods and alders and a new generation of firs not yet tall enough to be reflected in the stream. Perhaps if one looked into the depths of the river's largest, deepest pools he could have seen a hint of green, but I will always remember the Green as a silver-colored river, sparkling and lively and full of highlights in the bright summer sunshine.

It also was a generous river, easily waded and easily fished. In most places it took only a gentle roll cast to cover the most promising water with a fly, and often in the low water of late summer the steelhead would be plainly visible—sleek, silver-gray shapes lying in the hollows between boulders in the tailwaters of the pools. It was necessary to be cautious in order to see them without them seeing you first, and I remember spending a long time crawling through the brush to the edge of a pool, then cautiously raising my head to see if a fish was there.

If one was, the next problem was to find a way to put a fly over it without causing it to take alarm. Sometimes the solution was to go back through the woods and well upstream, then wade out cautiously, hunched over, and make a sidearm cast with a long sinking line and let the river carry the fly down to the fish. Or sometimes the answer was to go downstream and approach the fish from below, casting up with a long line and a big high-floating dry fly. Sometimes, no matter what you did, the fish would sense your presence and vanish so quickly it would leave you wondering if you had ever really seen it at all. But every now and then things would go just right, the cast would fall on target and the fish would take the fly.

It's hard for a steelhead to show all its strength in a small river, but the Green River fish always did the best they could—and often that was enough to leave you breathless and trembling, with a broken leader, a lost fly and shattered hopes. But again there were times when all would go well, when the tackle would hold despite the best efforts of the fish, and a long fight would end with a bright steelhead on the beach. Those were the times that made the Green a steelheader's favorite—my favorite.

The first time I went there was with Joe Pierce and Enos Bradner, two river-wise old veterans who had spent more years chasing steelhead than I had been alive. It was good to have such men as teachers, and I watched and listened to them carefully as we explored the river from the salmon hatchery downstream to the enormous pool where it joined the larger North Fork of the Toutle. It was late July and the water was low and we soon found three fish shifting nervously in the shallow tail-out of a riffle. We took turns casting to them but only Bradner could solicit one to strike. The fish followed his fly and took it hard, but the connection was only momentary before the fly came free. After that the fish ignored our offerings.

We finished the day without catching any fish, but the chance to see the river was reward enough for me. It was an intriguing little river, large enough to hold big fish but small enough to share its secrets, and I found myself wanting to return. Soon enough I did so, and that was the beginning of a long friendship with the Green.

It was not until my third trip that I hooked my first steelhead. It happened in a long pool on the lower river, a fine stretch of wrinkled water with good depth and plenty of places for fish to hold. I found nothing in the upper half of the pool, but midway through a fish took my fly solidly, ran hard and jumped twice, revealing itself as a bright summer steelhead of perhaps 10 pounds. I was afraid the fish would run out of the pool into the rapids down below, but it suddenly changed direction, dashed upstream the full length of the pool and jumped again, far out of the water in a somersaulting leap. It fell back with a crash, then darted into the remains of an old log jam and broke the leader somewhere in the jackstraw tangle of waterlogged limbs. It happened so quickly that I scarcely had time to draw a breath, but I still remember the sight of that great silver fish hovering over the water at the apex of its final leap.

Early that evening I returned to the same pool and hooked another fish, a smaller one. This time the contest went my way and when it was over I had captured my first Green River steelhead—a handsome fish that glowed softly silver in the mother-of-pearl light of a rising full moon.

I grew to love that pool. My private name for it was the Long Pool, simply because it was the longest of all the pools I fished on the river. It began where the river made a narrow right-angle turn, skirting the edge of the log jam where the first fish had broken me, and then it widened out and flowed along a gravel bar that offered ample backcast room. On the far bank was a big alder whose shadow would fall across the pool on summer afternoons; usually it wasn't long before a fish moved into the shadow, and I discovered I could go there each day with the almost certain knowledge that a steelhead would be waiting. It was the closest thing to clockwork fishing that I've ever seen.

Once I hooked a fish on my first cast into the shadow. The steelhead jumped once, then ran out of the pool into the rapids down below and took my line around a rock. I followed it down and waded out cautiously in the fast water until I found the rock and freed the line. The fish ran again, this time across the river to a spot where the current had eaten into the bank and left a tree leaning dangerously with one limb trailing in the current. There the fish jumped again and carried my leader over the limb.

There was nothing to do but try to wade across and free the leader. The current was strong and the rocks were slippery, so I took my time and chose each foothold carefully until at last I reached the trailing limb. I stripped away the leaves and removed the leader. Once it was free the fish ran again.

So far the fight had gone all the fish's way, but now it made its first mistake. Its run carried it downstream, out of the rapids into a quiet pool, and for the first time I began to think I might have a chance to land it. But first I had to wade all the way back across the river, through the same fast water and over the same slippery rocks, trying to remember where I'd put my feet on the first crossing. It was a near thing, but I made it without falling, scrambled up onto the bank and dashed downstream to the next pool, where the fish was rushing around busily. Finally it was too tired to resist any longer and I steered it safely to a patch of sandy beach. It was a bright-eight-pounder, far from the largest steelhead I'd ever caught, but it had put up one of the longest, toughest fights I'd ever had from any fish.

The Long Pool was more than generous all that first summer, but the next winter a flood gnawed away its lower end and filled in part of its head and after that it wasn't such a long pool any more. But the big alder survived the flood and still gave its shade on summer afternoons, and for another year the steelhead still sought shelter there. Then came another

winter and another flood that took the alder and all that
remained of the pool.

It was a loss the river never quite replaced, though there
were other good pools and it was seldom one could not find a
fish in at least one of them. Once I found one holding in the
tail-out of the very last pool in the river, just above the
Toutle. The fish stood out in bold relief in the low, clear
water, and it must have been able to see me as clearly as I
could see it. But after I stood and watched it for a while it
seemed to accept me as a normal part of things and showed no
alarm when I began to cast.

After a few casts I was able to gauge the current and
distance well enough to swing my fly within inches of the
fish's snout, but the steelhead eyed each offering stoically and
made no move. I began changing flies after each half-dozen
casts, alternating size and color, and went on casting until the
fish finally began to display some little signs of interest. At
first these were no more than subtle movements of the fins,
repeated each time the fly transcribed its arc past the fish's
nose. Then the steelhead suddenly shifted to its left and half-
turned toward the fly. But its pursuit was brief and ended
without a take, and the fish settled back in its familiar lie.

I sensed the fish had grown excited, but so had I and my
fingers trembled as I changed the fly one more time.

Once more I made the familiar cast. Two pairs of anxious
eyes—mine and the fish's—followed the fly as it settled just
under the surface and began its semicircular swing. I thought I
was ready for what would happen next, but the steelhead
attacked the fly so savagely it nearly pulled the rod from my
grasp. In the split second it took me to recover, the fish let go
of the fly.

It was hard to believe a fish could hit so hard and escape
without being hooked, but that is what had happened. I
couldn't see where it had gone, but after a while I found it
again, lying between two boulders a little way downstream. I

resumed casting, but this time there was no sign of interest; it was clear the fish could not be tempted a second time.

By then it was nearly dark and time to go. I reeled in and started up the trail, heading into evening gloom that was no deeper than my own.

But such disappointments were more the exception than the rule, and over the years I built up a store of many happy memories of the Green. There were pleasant trips with Ralph Wahl, Ted Rogowski, Ray Kotrla, Alan Pratt, Errol Champion, and Ward McClure; there was the time we found wild blackberries ripe on the Fourth of July and ended up eating baked steelhead and wild blackberry pie, and there were many morning walks along the dusty road that paralleled the river, always cool in the shade of the leafy woods.

Now those memories are all that remain, for the Green River as I knew it is no more. It vanished forever on that tragic May morning when Mount St. Helens unleashed her devastating wrath.

In those first few flaming moments the volcano's blast reached out over the ridgetops and down into the headwaters of the Green, searing trees with its heat and flattening them with its incredible force. A great streaming mudflow raced down the Toutle's North Fork and carried away everything in its path. The mud filled in the junction pool and pushed up the lower Green, burying half a mile of river and the hatchery that had kept it filled with salmon in the fall. Whatever was spared by blast and mud was covered by a steady rain of ash.

A month after the eruption I went looking for the Green. The area was closed to entry because of continuing danger from the simmering volcano so my search was from a plane. It was a sad, strange flight over an alien landscape. Nothing was familiar; all the old landmarks were gone or changed beyond recognition.

Finally I found the remains of the river. Its headwaters were choked with downed timber and cloaked in ash. A narrow band of dirty gray-white water oozed between its banks, flowing past the corpses of a thousand fallen trees to vanish somewhere in the sea of muck that filled the river's lower end. It was a dead river, flowing through a dead land. I flew home sadly, feeling as if I had just come from the funeral of an old friend.

Nature works slowly, but in time it will cleanse and heal the river. Many years from now a new generation of firs will grow up to stretch their limbs across the Green and shade the mountain slopes so that the snow again will slowly melt and fuel the river with a steady cold clear flow. Perhaps wary summer steelhead will pause again to rest in sheltered pools and anglers once more will cast their flies in the bright riffles of the Green. My son may be among them, but the Green will never heal in time for me.

Yet I feel no envy for those anglers of the future, for I remember the Green River as it was.

Hello Dolly!

Most trout have names that are at least suggestive of their nature. The rainbow, cutthroat, and brown trout all were named for their appearance, the steelhead's name tells something about both its color and its disposition, and the common name for the Eastern brook trout gives a pretty good idea of where it might be found. But there's one fish whose name doesn't fit the pattern: The Dolly Varden.

Of course the Dolly Varden is not a true trout, but it looks enough like one that most anglers call it a trout, and it shares waters occupied by both trout and salmon. Unlike those fish, however, the Dolly Varden isn't one that wealthy industrialists or beer barons would travel a thousand miles to catch before retiring for cocktails on the veranda of a private lodge. The Dolly Varden is a fish with few followers or friends.

Yet there are some anglers who fish for Dolly Varden; they've found it a useful fall-back fish when trout are scarce or unwilling. But they generally keep quiet about it, because being a Dolly Varden fisherman is not something you'd want to admit in polite company. That's because most high-minded trout fishermen think of the Dolly Varden as a fish with a five o'clock shadow and a blackjack in its pocket, the kind of fish you wouldn't want to meet after dark. In their view, Dolly Varden might make a good name for a motorcycle gang.

The object of all this contempt is actually a char, a member of the genus *Salvelinus*, a close kin of the Arctic char, a cousin of the Eastern brook trout and lake trout and a distant cousin of the true trouts. It dwells in rivers and lakes of the Pacific Coast from the Aleutian Islands through Alaska and as far south as northern California, and reaches inland through parts of Nevada, Idaho, and Montana into British Columbia and Alberta. There are numerous sea-going populations throughout the northern part of its range, but they do not migrate long distances like steelhead or salmon. Instead, they mostly hang around estuaries, waiting to mug any small fish or other unsuspecting prey that may happen along.

Dolly Varden are similar in color to other chars. Their backs are dark green, sometimes with faint worm-track vermiculations, and their flanks are pale yellow or olive with distinctive scattered red and yellow spots. The leading edges of their pectoral and ventral fins are white, though less so than the ivory etchings on a brook trout's fins. Sea-run fish invariably are bright silver with only faint red and yellow spots.

The Dolly Varden is not wary or graceful like a trout; it's a voracious feeder, a vacuum cleaner of riverbottoms. It gobbles up the eggs of salmon and steelhead and their hatching fry as well. It even has been known to eat shrews, mice, moles, frogs, and small birds. It is extremely vulnerable to all angling methods, especially bait and spoons. It is often caught by steelhead fishermen, but despite its fearsome predatory habits its fight pales in comparison with the steelhead or any other trout. The Dolly Varden rarely jumps, preferring instead to fight in a series of short rushes. Dolly Varden of two to five pounds are common and fish of more than 10 pounds are not exceptional in Alaskan waters, and though fish of such size will put a healthy bend in any rod, they seldom fight as long or as hard as their size would indicate they should.

During past episodes of taxonomic confusion the Dolly Varden was known variously as *Salvelinus spectabilis*, *S. confluentus*, *S. bairdii*, *S. parkei* and *S. campbelli* until general agreement finally was reached on thee name *Salvelinus malma*. But in 1978, Ted M. Cavender of the Museum of Zoology at Ohio State University proposed that *S. malma* actually was two different species with overlapping distribution. He re-vived the name *S. confluentus* for the second species and suggested the common name "bull trout," which somehow seemed more fitting.

Cavender's findings were based on analysis of character-istics of fish taken at many different locations. Those characteristics which distinguish the bull trout from the Dolly Varden include "a long, broad head which is flat above and sharply tapered through the snout," large jaws and teeth and heavy jaw muscles. Cavender concluded the bigger jaws, teeth and muscles were all the better to eat other fish with; in other words, they were the result of piscivorous dietary habits. The bull trout was even more of a fish-eater than the Dolly Varden.

The bull trout is present in some coastal drainages, but the heart of its natural range is inland along the Cascade Range and the Rocky Mountains. It also extends east of the

Continental Divide in Canada to the headwaters of the South
and North Saskatchewan rivers and the Athabaska, Peace and
Liard rivers. Cavender suggests the species may have origi-
nated in the Columbia Basin because it is widely distributed
there and because that basin borders on the other river basins
where it is found.

Cavender's findings have been widely accepted by taxonomists, but few anglers have yet to hear of the new species.
When they do, many will discover they have been fishing for
bull trout all these years when they thought they were fishing
for Dolly Varden.

Not that names or taxonomic differences matter much to
casual fishermen. The early white settlers called the Dolly
Varden a "red-spotted salmon trout," which would have been
an eminently sensible and dscriptive name were it not for the
fact that the Dolly is neither a salmon nor a trout. The
Nisqually Indians got along fine calling it the Pus-sutch; so did
the Klallams, who named it Com-mah-mah.

And where did the name Dolly Varden come from? Dolly
Varden was a leading character in Charles Dickens' novel,
Barnaby Rudge, a sort of Victorian *femme fatale* who left a trail
of broken hearts through 72 chapters. To quote Dickens:

"When and where was there ever such a plump, roguish,
comely, bright-eyed, enticing, bewitching, captivating, mad-
dening little puss in all this world, as Dolly! . . . How many
coachmakers, saddlers, cabinetmakers, and professors of other
useful arts, had deserted their fathers, mothers, sisters,
brothers, and, most of all, their cousins, for the love of
her! . . . How many young men, in all previous times of
unprecedented steadiness, had turned suddenly wild and
wicked for the same reason, and, in an ecstacy of unrequited
love, taken to wrench off door-knockers and invert the boxes
of rheumatic watchmen! How had she recruited the king's
service, both by sea and land, through rendering desperate his
loving subjects between the ages of eighteen and twenty-five!

How many young ladies had publicly professed, with tears in their eyes, that for their tastes she was much too short, too tall, too bold, too cold, too stout, too thin, too fair, too dark—too everything but handsome! How many old ladies, taking counsel together, had thanked Heaven their daughters were not like her, and had hoped she might come to no harm, and had thought she would come to no good. . . ." But you get the idea.

What has all this got to do with a fish? That's a complicated story. To quote Dickens again:

"As to Dolly, there she was again, the very pink and pattern of good looks, in a smart little cheery-coloured mantle, with a hood of the same drawn over her head, and upon the top of that hood, a little straw hat trimmed with cherry-coloured ribbons, and worn the merest trifle on one side—just enough in short to make it the wickedest and most provoking head-dress that ever malicious milliner devised." When Dickens toured the United States sometime after publication of *Barnaby Rudge*, Dolly Varden hats became all the rage, and one of the most popular was a calico pattern with pink spots. According to legend, some fashion-conscious young lady was shown a freshly caught char with prominent pink spots and promptly exclaimed that it was a regular "Dolly Varden trout." The name stuck, and the Dolly Varden became the only fish ever named after a hat.

It also would be hard to find a more misleading name for a fish. It's not that the Dolly Varden isn't a handsome fish; it's just that it has such a reputation for nasty habits. At one time there was even a widespread notion that the Dolly Varden's habit of eating fish eggs and small fish posed a threat to the survival of salmon and steelhead runs. Overlooking the fact that salmon and steelhead somehow had managed to survive thousands of years despite the predatory habits of the Dolly Varden, anglers began a sort of informal campaign to eradicate the species. Since it was an easy fish to catch, it was caught and killed in wholesale quantities, and logging-camp inhabitants frequently joined in the fun by dynamiting pools where Dolly Varden were known to congregate. It wasn't long before the Dolly Varden became relatively scarce in coastal rivers south of the Canadian border.

But these days, when even the snail darter is grudgingly conceded a right to life, there is a somewhat more benevolent attitude toward the Dolly Varden. Its numbers are gradually increasing and some anglers even have begun to consign to it a sporting value, especially when there aren't any steelhead around—as increasingly there aren't.

My first encounter with a Dolly Varden came while I was dry-fly fishing for steelhead in the North Fork of the Stillaguamish River. The fly had just touched down after a long cast across a pool when a six-inch steelhead smolt rose and took it. Immediately I gave slack in hopes the little fish would not hook itself, but a gentle tugging on the line signaled that it had. I started stripping line rapidly, hoping to bring in the fish and release it as quickly as possible but not paying very much attention to it. Suddenly there was a much stronger pull on the line.

Looking down through the clear water, I was amazed to see that I was fast to a fish at least four times longer than the one that had taken my fly, a fish that was twisting and turning powerfully in the current through the pool. Slowly I played it until I could see its jaws were clamped around the six-inch smolt that had risen to the fly. I fought the fish until it was within arm's length, and only then did it grudgingly release its grip and swim past me, almost brushing against my waders. I could see then that it was a big, mean-looking Dolly Varden, obviously disappointed at having had to give up what it had thought would be an easy meal. For me, the incident confirmed all the unpleasant things I'd heard about this fish.

The first Dolly Varden I actually caught also was while I was fishing for steelhead in the Stillaguamish. My fly was taken at the tail of a riffle by a strong fish that ran well and I thought surely it was a good steelhead. But the fish turned and came to the surface at the end of its run and I caught a glimpse of green and gold and knew immediately it was not a steelhead. It proved to be a fat Dolly Varden whose uncharacteristically vigorous fight was due to the fact that my hook had found a place in its dorsal fin rather than its mouth.

At first I was disgusted, but as I eased the fish up onto the stones of the riverbank the sunlight struck full upon its side and I realized what a handsome fish it was. I understood then how it could have been named after a calico hat with a cluster of pink spots. I gently removed the fly from its dorsal fin and returned the fish carefully to the stream.

Since then I have caught Dolly Varden all the way to Alaska, where they are extremely numerous and still sometimes regarded as something of a nuisance. I've even coaxed a few fresh sea-run Dollys to rise to a dry fly, although such a delicate and esoteric act seems against their general principles.

The Dolly Varden never will be my favorite fish, but it has its own place in the river and its presence has saved me from some blank days. It never will match the speed and power of a steelhead or the stamina of a cutthroat, but nowadays it is something of a bonus to find the Dolly Varden in rivers where once it was so scarce. And in these days of ever more fishermen and fewer fish, it is slowly becoming a target species in its own right. Perhaps someday someone will even write a book about Dolly Varden the fish instead of Dolly Varden the flirt.

Which brings us back to the *other* Dolly Varden, in case you were wondering whatever happened to her. She had a few bad moments, but came through them all unscathed and ended up marrying a poor fellow named Joe, who long before had given up all hope of winning her. They lived happily ever after, and as Dickens wrote: "Go to Chigwell when you would, there would surely be seen, either in the village street, or on the green, or frolicking in the farm-yard . . . more small Joes and small Dollys than could easily be counted."

Truth sometimes imitates fiction, and now in the rivers of the Northwest you will again find more small Dollys—and some bigger ones—than could easily be counted. And some people think it's nice to see the Dolly back where it belongs.

Bucktail Camp

A dozen years ago, in *The Year of the Angler*, I wrote at some length about the history of the North Fork of the Stillaguamish, most celebrated of all Northwest steelhead rivers. Much of the lore and many of the techniques of steelhead fly fishing were developed on the North Fork, and virtually every famous angler or angling writer the Northwest has produced first cut his teeth on the North Fork's summer steelhead run.

The North Fork was where Zane Grey and Roderick Haig-Brown first fished for steelhead, and it was in Deer Creek, the North Fork's principal tributary, where each succeeded in landing his first steelhead. The North Fork was the river of Enos Bradner, Walt Johnson, Ken McLeod, Wes Drain, Lew Bell, Frank Headrick, and many other famous fishermen. Thanks mainly to the efforts of Bradner and other early members of the Washington Fly Fishing Club, the North Fork became the first steelhead river anywhere to be placed under fly-fishing-only management, a status it has enjoyed since 1941.

What made the North Fork especially unique was the great run of summer steelhead that ascended it to spawn in Deer Creek, and although that run has been all but destroyed by logging abuses, a hatchery program has kept the river populated with at least some summer fish. Now it is not uncommon to drive along the North Fork on a summer afternoon and see license plates from half a dozen states or Canadian provinces at the fishermen's access areas. If the Northwest has a single river that qualifies as an angling shrine, the North Fork of the Stillaguamish is it.

But there have been many changes to the North Fork since I first wrote of it. Its valley remains unrivaled for its pastoral beauty, but there are more homes and fewer farms along the river now. Summer weekends bring swarms of people to float the river in rubber rafts, inner tubes, kayaks, and canoes, and of course there are more fishermen every day of the week, so that it is much harder now to find a place to fish in solitude. The Boldt decision on Indian fishing rights has revived the spirits of the little Stillaguamish Tribe and its members now fish the river with their nets, and although they fish mainly for salmon, many steelhead inevitably fall victim to their monofilament mesh. Logging continues in the Deer Creek watershed, with its disastrous impacts becoming ever more evident, and together all these things have increased pressure on the river and its precious fishery.

Simultaneously some threats have eased. A plan by the Army Corps of Engineers to build a dam at the little community of Oso appears finally to have died a quiet death, as it should have long ago, and the big timber on upper Boulder Creek—another main tributary of the North Fork—now is safely preserved inside a wilderness area established by Congress. Efforts to gain a small measure of additional protection for the river under the National Wild and Scenic Rivers Act have been stymied by lack of support from the local congressman, but such ideas have a long life and congressmen do not remain in office forever, so there is still hope.

But the biggest change has been in the people of the river. The anglers who first cared and fought for it and secured its reputation have grown old and their ranks are thinning. Lew Bell and Al Knudson both are gone, and although Ralph Wahl and Frank Headrick still visit the river from time to time, they rarely fish it any more. The row of cabins along the river below Deer Creek, once owned exclusively by these and other Stilly "regulars," has changed hands or been handed down to members of a younger generation, most of whom do not have the same deep feeling for the river or its fish.

It is this transition from old hands to new which has most affected me, for I have been a part of it.

At first the North Fork was just one river on a list of many that I fished, and although I had proper respect for its colorful history, it held no more affection for me than any of the others. True, it was the river where I had nearly landed my first steelhead, but that long battle finally had been won by the fish, and along with the fish I had lost any chance for the special sentiment a victory would have given me. To me the North Fork was merely a pleasant place to fish and a handy place to go, near enough so I could reach it after work and fish several hours on a long summer evening.

But that was before my first visit to Bucktail Camp.

Bucktail Camp was the name of one of the cabins in the row below Deer Creek, probably the smallest cabin in the lot. It was owned by Enos Bradner and Sanford (Sandy) Bacon.

It was Bradner who first took me there. We had spent most of the day prospecting for steelhead on the upper river, but late in the afternoon we drove downstream and turned off the main road onto a pair of muddy ruts that led a short distance through the woods to a little cabin perched on the edge of a small clearing. It was a plain and simple cabin, hardly more than a hut, 15 feet square and raised up on blocks in a hopeless effort to keep the winter floods from entering. It had a peaked roof, the shingles overgrown with moss, and a rusty stovepipe that belied the fact there was no stove inside. Over the single door was a large sign with the words "Bucktail Camp" inscribed in the wood. Stuck in its side was its namesake—a faded bucktail fly.

Bradner was an old man even then and fished the river less often than before, and Sandy Bacon had moved away to Oregon to retire. As a consequence the place had suffered from neglect: There were cobwebs in the windows, paint was peeling from the outside walls and a large family of mice had taken up residence inside. Cottonwoods, cedars, maples, hemlocks, and some huge old firs grew around the clearing, and these had sent seedlings that were rapidly reclaiming it for the woods. The woods made the place seem distant from everything, though it was barely half a mile from the old general store at Oso. There was no telephone and no water, except what could be dipped from the river, but a fisherman's wants are simple—and this place had everything a fisherman could want.

The clearing was in a hollow, separated from the river by a dike that was overgrown with swordfern and salal, huckleberry and wild rose, osoberry and Oregon grape. On the other side of the dike the river had built a large sand bar, and it had been there long enough for horsetail, thistle, and cottonwood seedlings to take root in it and begin to grow.

Beyond the sandbar was some of the best water the North Fork had to offer. Just downstream was a place called the

Elbow, once one of the most famous pools on the river; here the river made a nearly right-angle turn, tumbling down over a series of gravel terraces, then merging into a fine tongue of current split by Volkswagen-sized boulders. For many years it had been Bradner's favorite pool, and although the river had since filled in some of its best holding water, it still yielded an occasional fish. Below it was the Upper Rip-Rap Pool, also sometimes called the Stump Pool, one of the longest reaches of good fly water on the North Fork, deep and fast and with room enough to hold at least a dozen steelhead at a time. Upstream was another good stretch called the Pocket, where a long run of broken water dissolved into a gleaming slick that was made to order for a riffle-hitched dry fly. And above that it was only a short hike to the famous pool where Deer Creek plunges into the North Fork.

These were the places we explored in the dying light of that long afternoon, and I listened closely as Bradner recited tales of memorable contests between men and fish in these waters. We caught no fish ourselves, but I came away with a deeper understanding and appreciation for the river and its history. And I envied Brad for owning such a place as Bucktail Camp.

So a few years later, when Brad offered to sell Bucktail Camp to me, I was absolutely delighted. He was in his 84th year then, and though he still fished often from a boat, the river had become too much for him to wade. He had written Sandy Bacon, who had agreed the place would be of little further use to them, and they had decided it was time for someone else to use and care for it. I was their choice if I wanted it.

I took my family to see the place and they fell in love with it at once and on Labor Day weekend 1976, we met Bradner at Bucktail Camp for a picnic and to hammer out the details of the transaction. We quickly agreed on the terms and shook hands on the deal, and once our business was concluded

Bradner settled back to tell us something about the history of the place.

At some point in its history the land had been used as a gravel quarry, which explained its conformation. After that it had been a dump, which explained the faded bits of old glass and rusting metal that turned up in every shovelful of earth. Then it had been part of a family farm, which was subdivided by its owners shortly after World War II. Nearly all the subdivided lots eventually were acquired by the fly fisherman who by then already had made the North Fork a famous place.

Bradner had been away at the time the Bucktail Camp property was offered for sale, covering the atomic-bomb tests at Bikini Atoll for *The Seattle Times*, so Bacon handled the purchase. When Bradner returned from the Pacific, the two built a wooden floor in the clearing to serve as a platform for a tent. A trap door in the platform concealed a barrel hidden underneath which was used as a cache for equipment and supplies. A hole was dug in the moist earth of the nearby dike to serve as a cooler, and that was the extent of the original camp. Some years later the existing cabin had been built atop the original floor and since then many visiting fishermen had contributed to its upkeep and improvement.

When he had finished his discourse on the history of the cabin, Bradner turned to his pet theory about steelhead fishing in the North Fork, one I had heard him express often. He claimed that if, as you drove past the dairy farms along the North Fork, the cows were standing up and swinging their tails, then you had better hurry to the river for the fishing was bound to be good. But if the cows were lying down there was no need to hurry, for lazy cows meant the steelhead would be lazy, too. He espoused this theory with great conviction and claimed to have proven its validity through many years of observation, though on this occasion, as before, it was not quite possible to tell whether he was really being serious.

When he had finished defending his theory and the last

cold fried chicken was consumed, we went our separate ways. But later that week we met again to sign the papers and Bucktail Camp was ours.

There was much to do around the place. We cut away the brush that had grown up around the margins of the clearing, discovering in the process an old stone fireplace that had been completely concealed by ferns and moss. The cabin got a badly needed coat of paint, though there was a startling moment when a sleeping bat fell out as we moved the "Bucktail Camp" sign to paint behind it. The rusty old stovepipe gave way to a new and larger one, and this one was connected to a new fireplace in the cabin. Rock and sand were hauled up from the riverbank to patch holes in the road, and an old wooden bench at the base of a big fir overlooking the river was braced to hold the weight of resting anglers. Trails were cleared and leaning trees were cut and a modest treehouse was built for the children. With trepidation, we plugged in the old refrigerator in the cabin—Bradner had bought it used for ten dollars years before and its motor had been submerged in the waters of several winter floods—but it started up and soon chilled the beer.

But it wasn't all work. Our labors were interspersed with long walks along the river, where we often saw deer and nearly always saw at least one heron fishing motionlessly in the shallows. We found bits of soapstone and river jade among the gravel, and in the spring there were sweet wild strawberries to be picked and eaten and a winter's supply of new driftwood to be gathered for summer campfires. Sometimes when we paused in our work we could hear grouse drumming in the woods or an osprey calling as it searched the river for its prey, and we soon found that Bucktail Camp was a community all itself, with shrews and squirrels and lizards and robins' nests and hollow trees where woodpeckers made their homes. And every weekend, when we left the cabin, the mice would move back in.

And then there was the fishing.

The best of it was gone by the time we became the owners of Bucktail Camp, but there were still moments when it was good, sometimes even great, and only rarely did I wade the river without faith that I would find at least one fish if I looked long and hard enough—even on days when the cows were lying down. Two kinds of steelhead returned to the river, the slender, gleaming, streamlined fish of the native Deer Creek run, and the stockier, heavier fish from the state rearing ponds upstream. A fish of either kind was always welcome.

But I got off to a slow start in my first full season on the river. In fact, I was in a terrible fishing slump, having gone for months without hooking a single steelhead. I was still looking for my first fish from the waters around Bucktail Camp when I came upon Walt Johnson fishing the foot of the Rip-Rap Pool near darkness on a July evening.

Walt is among the last of the old corps of Stillaguamish veterans who still fish the river faithfully and in recent years he has become something of a legend, both for his prowess with a fly rod and for the stealth with which he comes and goes. Like the deer along the river, he is most often seen at twilight or at dawn, moving softly through the woods to emerge and take up a stance in one of his favorite pools. When I found him he was casting a long line and a dry fly, and I settled down to watch—a rare chance to glimpse a master at his craft.

He soon noticed me there and we began to chat while he continued fishing. Then a big steelhead rolled far down in the corner of the pool, and Walt's fly was over him like a shot, floating down over the spot before the current had swept away the ripples from the rise. The fly passed over unscathed and Walt plucked it smartly from the water and cast again, but the result was the same. Several more times he cast, and although the fish rolled a second time, it was not in pursuit of the fly.

Walt reeled in. "What kind of line do you have on?" he asked.

"A sink-tip," I said I had been fishing earlier, but as usual without success.

"Well, you'd better get out here then. This fish isn't going to take a dry, but I'll bet you could take him on that line."

"Oh no," I said. "That's your fish."

But Walt already was wading toward the beach. "Wade out there, just above that break in the current, and cast down to him," he said.

I followed instructions and waded to the spot, then stripped line from the reel and tried to gauge the distance to the last place where the fish had risen. Then I began to cast.

Now our roles were reversed and Walt was watching from the beach. "You're going to get yourself a fish, Steve," he said in such a way that I believed it.

But after half a dozen casts my confidence began to wane. The fish had not shown itself again, and I resolved that if something didn't happen after the tenth cast I'd leave the pool and let Walt try again.

The steelhead took on the ninth cast. The fly came to a sudden hard stop as if it had found a snag where none had been before, and I reared back and felt the weight of a heavy fish. It jumped only once but put up a long and sullen fight and I handled it carefully in consideration of the light leader I was using, but finally beached it in the quiet water below the Rip-Rap Pool. It was a bright silver buck of about ten pounds.

The darkness was nearly total by then, but Walt was still watching and I carried the fish up to him and thanked him as best I could for his generosity in yielding the pool and giving me the chance to catch it. We stood and talked until the darkness was full and a soft rain had begun to fall. As we parted, I thanked him again and told him that I'd been in a terrible slump and this was my first fish in a long while.

"This fish will break the slump," he said. "You'll see." Then he vanished into the woods while I began the walk back to Bucktail Camp, the fish hanging heavily from my hand.

Next morning the rain was still falling and fat clouds filled the valley clear down to the firtops. I stayed in the cabin during the morning to tie flies, but when the overcast showed no sign of lifting I finally put on a rain jacket over my fishing vest and hiked up to Deer Creek. No one was fishing at the creekmouth, so I waded out carefully over the big, slippery boulders in order to cast down to the point where the current from the creek merged with the North Fork's main flow.

After just three casts I was into a steelhead that raced downstream out of the pool and into the long Deer Creek Riffle down below. I waded ashore and stumbled over the toaster-sized boulders that littered the beach in an effort to follow. Looking downstream, I saw an older fisherman I knew was hard of hearing and for an instant I was afraid he wouldn't hear me coming, but at the last moment he turned and saw me. His eyes widened and he reeled in quickly and backed out of the way.

The steelhead finally ran itself out and I beached it midway down the riffle. It was a Deer Creek fish, slim and bright and probably no more than five pounds, but it was full of spite and spunk as Deer Creek steelhead usually are.

I released the fish and went back up to the head of the riffle to resume fishing. The current at the head was swift and it was hard to hold a fly in it for any length of time, but there was one place where the current curled around a boulder, leaving a quiet patch of water just below. I dropped my fly in that little pocket and a steelhead seized it instantly.

The fish ran downstream and once again I found myself on the beach, stumbling over rain-slickened boulders in breathless pursuit. Then the fish began to jump, giving me a chance to catch up with it, but after its third leap it fell back squarely on the leader tippet and broke it.

So I lost that fish, but I didn't really mind. Counting the fish from the night before, I had hooked three steelhead in five casts—something I'd never done before and have never equalled since. And after that day, I've always considered Walt Johnson a pretty fair prophet in addition to his other talents.

There have been many other exciting moments during the year since that first summer at Bucktail Camp. The 1980 season was the best of all; that year the river swarmed with steelhead all through the summer, and old-timers said it was the best they had seen since the war. Why it was so good is a question that confounded even the biologists responsible for managing the river, but whatever the reason it lasted only that single year; next season steelhead were few and far between.

Over the years I've grown to know the moods of the North Fork in both good times and lean. Early in the season, when the water is high and cold and fast, the river is hard and uncomfortable to fish, but often it is most generous then. The fishing is easier in August when the water is low and clear, the current slow and big rocks are showing like the bones of some prehistoric beast, but that also is when the river is most difficult and unyielding. Still, there are times in August when steelhead will rise to a riffle-hitched dry fly, and if there is a more exciting sight in fishing I have yet to see it.

The North Fork also is a different river in the morning and the evening and at midday. In morning, when the sky is just beginning to lighten in the east, the river seems new and full of promise, as if it had been reborn overnight; but later, in the heat of the day, it grows languid and lazy and the summer sun glares fiercely from the surface of its pools. Finally, in the evening, as darkness spills down the valley like a rising flood, the river becomes mysterious and alive, with trout rising in the shallows, bats plunging to feed on the twilight hatch and the slap of a heavy salmon leaping in the quiet water of a distant pool.

No matter what time of day I visit the river I rarely fish alone, for the North Fork's fishermen are many and not all fish with rod and reel. They include the herons, most patient of all fishermen; the kingfishers, perhaps the most impatient, and the ospreys, surely the most spectacular fishermen of all. I enjoy fishing in their company and do not begrudge them their success, for I admire them and I know they are entitled to their share of the river's yield as much as I am.

But unhappily both for them and for me, the fishing trend in the North Fork has been inexorably downward in recent years—with the marvelous exception of the 1980 season. It is now obvious that the steelhead run is in serious decline and that its decline is but one symptom of a multitude of problems, most related to the continuing mismanagement of the Deer Creek watershed. Each winter the creek sheds massive loads of silt into the North Fork and great drifts of it have piled up behind every rock for many miles downstream. Silt has filled the crevices of the river-bottom gravel, rendering it unsuitable for spawning, and has covered gravel bars, hardening into lunar landscapes in the summer sun. So much silt has been washed down that it has filled the riverbed to the point that the North Fork no longer can carry all the water that seeks to use it for a channel, and when Deer Creek floods—as it does now several times each winter—the river often overflows and spills out into the adjoining fields and farms.

This has happened at least three times in the past few years, a little worse each time. All three floods have filled the hollow of Bucktail Camp and reached inside the cabin, but fortunately the damage has been small and miraculously the aging refrigerator still runs.

Even in summer a brief shower is enough to turn Deer Creek an ugly ruddy brown—some anglers say a hard sweat would be enough to knock Deer Creek out of shape—and a heavy rain destroys all fishing in the lower river for days on end. The silt drifts that fill the river also make for dangerous wading, and altogether the North Fork has become less hospitable both for fishermen and fish.

Anglers have watched all this happen and have known the reasons for it, but in a state long dominated politically and economically by logging interests, the casual destruction of watersheds has almost become a way of life; little was said about Deer Creek and nothing was done. Of all the state or federal agencies that might have intervened, only the state Game Department—a poor stepchild of state government—showed any interest, and that interest was confined mostly to periodically cataloguing the decline of the native steelhead run. That decline finally reached such alarming proportions that in 1983 the department imposed a 30-inch minimum size limit on steelhead caught in the North Fork below Deer Creek in hopes of assuring the return of a few more of the smaller Deer Creek fish. It was largely a token gesture, however, since many North Fork "regulars" already had long been in the habit of releasing most or all the fish they caught.

But then a young Forest Service biologist named Jim Doyle began to take an interest in the problems of Deer Creek. He made a survey of the condition of the watershed and a public meeting was called to hear his report.

The meeting was held on a spring evening in the Fire Station at Oso. Early arrivals found seats on folding chairs, but as more and more people came they began lining up against the walls; some even stood outside in the rain and listened through an open door. Walt Johnson was there, and Ken McLeod, and many of the river's other less famous personalities. Of the three major landowners in the watershed, the Forest Service and state Department of Natural Resources both were represented, but the Georgia-Pacific Co., the major private landowner, did not bother to send a representative. Biologists from the Game Department and the Stillaguamish and Tulalip Indian Tribes were there and so were many local landowners and fishermen. Rain drummed steadily on the roof and a few hundred feet away Deer Creek was high and roaring.

Doyle began by showing color slides he had taken in the watershed, numbing images of landslides, washouts, ravaged slopes and gutted streams, a realm of destruction that in some cases resembled that left by the eruption of Mount St. Helens.

Doyle explained that Deer Creek and its tributaries originally had cut their channels through unstable glacial silt and clay. So much of the watershed consisted of this unstable soil that natural landslides undoubtedly had occurred long before man first set foot in the area, and these slides probably had kept the silt load in Deer Creek at a near-critical level even in its natural state. Still, the amount of silt entering the stream under natural circumstances had not been so great that the stream was unable to carry it away, and the pristine Deer Creek managed to remain healthy and clear.

When logging began, most of it was in the lower watershed where slopes were not so steep and the impacts not so great. But as those areas were turned into graveyards of rotting stumps and slash, the loggers were forced to begin cutting timber on higher ground. They built more roads, which added to natural erosion, and began logging steep hillsides, which accelerated it even more. The faster runoff and erosion began filling Deer Creek and its tributaries with more silt than they could handle.

The streams probably would have suffered even if proper forest management practices had been followed, but they suffered much more because they were not. Doyle's survey turned up a sad litany of abuses. Among them:

—Insufficient buffer strips had been left along streams. Instead of providing cover and protection, as they were meant to do, trees in the strips had blown down into the streams, gouging out soil from the soft banks and adding to the erosion problem.

—Logging roads were built without proper drainage, or with culverts that were too small, resulting in washouts. Even when culverts of proper size were installed, they had been damaged and left unrepaired, or had become plugged up and were never cleaned. Result: More washouts.

—So much forest cover had been removed that during warm weather the water temperature in portions of Deer Creek was reaching levels dangerous to trout.

—Logging slash had been left in natural runoff channels, causing more washouts and erosion.

—Slash burns had been allowed to get out of control and become so hot they literally "cooked" the soil in portions of the watershed so that nothing could grow in it.

—Protective measures written into timber-sale contracts or specified by state guidelines had been neither observed nor enforced.

The cumulative effect of all these abuses was greatly increased and more rapid runoff and erosion, leading to sporadic flooding of Deer Creek and increasing the width-to-depth ratio of the stream. In other words, the farther Deer Creek flowed, the wider and shallower it became, until at low water it was very nearly dry, devoid of pools or enough water for fish to live in. Steelhead spawning and rearing habitat on the creek and most of its tributaries was rated at zero.

The most pressing problem was a huge slide emanating from an area that had been logged off years before. The slide, fed by springs, was pumping a kind of silt slurry into Deer Creek which promised to keep the lower North Fork unfishable all year long, perhaps for years to come.

The Forest Service, meanwhile, was planning to build another 16 miles of logging roads and clear-cut another 1,000 acres of the upper watershed.

As a result of his findings, Doyle proposed a monitoring program to try to document the decline of water quality and fish runs in Deer Creek. Then, if the results so indicated, perhaps the agencies responsible for managing the watershed could be persuaded to leave what was left of it alone. It was a rather feeble proposal, but with senior Forest Service bureaucrats listening in the room it took no small amount of courage to make it.

The audience listened with a mixture of sadness, frustration, and fury, and the meeting finally broke up with no clear sense of accomplishment or purpose. But it caused enough of a stir to get others interested in the plight of Deer Creek: *The Seattle Post-Intelligencer* and *The Seattle Times* both published extensive articles. The state Game Commission approved an emergency resolution extending the 30-inch minimum size limit downstream from the confluence of the North and South Forks all the way to salt water. And the state Department of Natural Resources, while hastening to disclaim all responsibility for the latest slide, sent in work crews and heavy equipment to divert it at least temporarily and assure one more summer of fishing on the North Fork.

But the future remains as murky as the waters of Deer Creek after rain. There is yet no long-term commitment on the part of any agency to improve current management in the watershed, let alone to stop cutting timber or begin a restoration program; on the contrary, there seems to be much more interest in escaping blame or liability for everything that has happened. The official bureaucratic line is that there is no proof logging has had anything to do with the flooding, erosion, or siltation of Deer Creek or the disappearance of the steelhead—although logging is the only activity that ever has taken place in the watershed and it's hard to see how any reasonable person could possibly conclude that the damage was caused by something else.

It is especially sad when one considers that the value of the timber removed from the Deer Creek watershed almost certainly has been worth far less than the value of the fishery destroyed in the process. At best, timber can be harvested only once every 50 to 60 years; the fishery, if left to itself, would have produced a handsome annual yield to the local economy, easily surpassing the one-time value of the timber harvest in the long run. To be sure, Deer Creek is not an isolated example of such false economy, but the destruction of its unique summer steelhead run makes it an especially outrageous one.

It would be less than fair to say that Deer Creek is responsible for all the North Fork's ills. Poaching also is a serious and growing threat, and on any given weekday the number of legitimate fishermen on the river probably is a minority compared to those using weighted hooks, spears, guns, or other illegal methods. Most, but not all, are local fishermen, and most of them know better, but the authorities seem unwilling or unable to do anything to stop them. The situation is now out of control.

As this is written, the state Game Department is preparing for yet another count of the number of adult summer steelhead returning to Deer Creek. This time, however, the purpose of the count is to determine if the run is on the verge of extinction. When the results are in, a decision will be made whether it is worthwhile to trap the few remaining fish and spawn them artificially in hopes of keeping the genetic stock alive until Deer Creek may again be fit for spawning or rearing summer steelhead. The alternative may be that the run will have to be written off as a resource too far gone for saving. It is not a pleasant choice, made less so by the fact that either alternative would give the timber companies and their subservient management agencies free rein to do as they please in what remains of the watershed.

Even if the native fish somehow should manage to survive, either on their own or with help, it will take many years to heal the damage that already has been done. Even then it is unrealistic to expect that Deer Creek or the North Fork ever again will be anything like the cold, clear, steelhead-filled rivers that Zane Grey, Roderick Haig-Brown or Enos Bradner fished. Those of us born too late to enjoy those happy times must take our satisfaction from what remains.

Bradner himself made his last visit to Bucktail Camp in his 90th year. There was no fishing that day—the occasion was a picnic with family and friends—and there are photographs commemorating the event. They show a group of happy faces, with nowhere a hint of realization that the day might signal the end of an era of the Stillaguamish.

After the photos were taken and the table was cleared, Bradner climbed the dike one last time and stood under a big fir and looked at the river for a long time. His legs were stiff and unsteady, his frame was bent and frail, but there was still the look of eagles in his eyes as he gazed at the Elbow Hole and remembered what it had been like when both he and the river were young.

In January 1984, Bradner passed away quietly in a nursing home where he had spent most of the last year of his life.

That spring, on a dark rainy afternoon in May, there was another gathering at Bucktail Camp. A few members of Bradner's family and two old friends met at the cabin, greeted one another, then walked together down the path to the edge of the Elbow Hole. And there they scattered the old fisherman's ashes over the water he had fished so long and loved so well.

When they had finished, they returned once more to Bucktail Camp and stood before the fire to drink a final toast to their relative and friend.

And now he belongs to the river.

Blackberry Run

I discovered Blackberry Run early on an August morning when the air was fresh and cool. At the time I didn't know its name, but I could see at once that it was a classic stretch of steelhead water, made to order for the fly.

At its upper end the current hustled down through a narrow chute, then fanned out in a long even flow against the base of a high rock bank covered with berry vines—the namesake of the pool, as I would later learn. Breaks and swirls on the surface gave hints of big boulders and hidden pockets down below; surely this was a place where summer steelhead would stop to rest and seek shelter on their journey home.

Downstream a thick layer of morning mist floated in the valley, but overhead the sky was blue and brightening with the onrushing light of day. I chose a fly from the collection in my box, then waded out and took position in the flow.

At first I searched the water close at hand, watching carefully as the large dry fly bounced along on the current, hoping a fish would rise to meet it. But I had fished only a little while before the sun's disk topped the serrated ridges to the east and lit up the layer of mist a mile downstream. Then the light advanced upstream as the sun rose higher, and I began hurrying my casts to cover as much water as I could before sunlight stained the pool.

I made a long cast across current and dropped the fly near the high bank on the far side. The fly floated only for a foot or two before a steelhead came in a sudden rising wave and took it down. I set the hook and the fish jumped immediately, out of the shadow and into the advancing sunshine.

It was not a large fish but it was strong and active and quickly took the old Hardy St. John twice into the backing. Four more times it jumped, then made half a dozen lesser runs before I led it slowly to the beach. It was a fine native fish, a buck of five pounds or a little better, and the big hair-wing fly was stuck firmly in the corner of its jaw.

I worked the fly free and slipped the fish gently back into the river and waited until it was gone. Then I fished down the remainder of the run, raising nothing more, and by the time I had finished the sun had warmed the air and the day had turned lazy. But it was a fine start for an unfamiliar pool, and I knew I would return.

Naturally it was with great expectations that I did so, but the circumstances were far different from before. It was still August, but this time it was near the end of a misty day, already growing dark as I found the path leading down to the river. The path led through a gallery of ancient firs, standing as tall and straight as the masts of a sailing ship, with a few old cottonwoods scattered among them, bent by years of wind. Together they groaned and creaked in the evening breeze and dripped the day's accumulated rain, so that my fishing vest was soaked by the time I left them.

The rain also had fueled the river so that it was much higher and faster than before. It seemed dark and unfriendly in the fading light, and I guessed that a dry fly held no prospect in its current mood. So I chose a sinking line instead, and knotted on a small dark fly.

I waded in near the foot of the chute, stripped line and rolled out a short initial cast, then added length with each succeeding throw. I had fished down just a little way below the chute when something grabbed the fly and pulled the line rudely from my grasp. Then the fish was in the air—once, twice, three times—and back in the current, running hard. At first it took my breath away, and then it took my line. I held the rod high and headed for the beach.

But it was a long way back to shore and I struggled to keep my balance while the river teased me with slippery gravel and a strong, uneven flow. Meanwhile the fish was gaining line and when I finally made it to the beach I could not tell where it had gone.

I reeled in and the backing came easily, followed by a long length of line. But then the line came tight against unyielding weight and I thought surely I'd lost the fish around a snag. I waded out, sliding my fingers down the line, following it under the surface until I felt where it was caught firmly on a rock. With arm immersed, I groped until I found the leader butt. Suddenly there was a great throbbing movement at the other end, the leader came free and the fish, still hooked, surged out into the center of the run.

This time it chose to run upstream and for the first time I thought I had a chance to gain control. It jumped again, and through the misty rain I caught a silver glimpse of it. It was a very large fish, perhaps the largest steelhead I had ever hooked, and the sight of it destroyed the confidence I'd briefly felt.

It turned then and headed downstream at a furious rate, so that again I had to follow. Then came another jump and once more I was awestruck by the fish's size. After that we traded line, back and forth, for what seemed a very long time, but gradually the fish began to tire and yield. Carefully I led it from the main current into quiet water and began to look around for a place where it might be safely beached.

But then it ran again, as strongly as before, and the run ended with a high and tumbling leap. I had expected this and dipped the rod to give it slack, but the fly still came away. When I got back I saw the reason why: The hook had been forced open so that the point was at right angles to the shank.

I felt the icy pang of disappointment as keenly as a knife, and for a long time I stood there, with the river curling round my knees, and stared at the wrinkled gray surface of the Blackberry Run. Perhaps I thought I could somehow will the river to deliver up my fish, but it merely mocked me with the whisper of its flow. Finally I waded out of the pool and started back along the path through the dark woods, where the limbs still dripped their saved-up rain.

Now the seasons have gone their way and August and its fellow months are buried under autumn leaves and snow. But I tell myself it won't really be so very long before August comes again.

And when it does, I plan to go back to Blackberry Run.

FALL

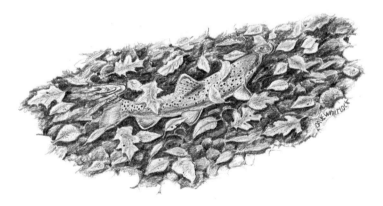

The cottonwood leaves are the first to fall. They turn pale yellow in the August sunshine and spiral down in the easy breezes of the afternoons. The alder leaves soon follow, joining those of the cottonwoods to form a dry carpet that crackles underfoot on the paths leading down to the rivers. In the rivers themselves the trout grow restless as they recognize the signs of the changing season.

Each morning is a little cooler and each night a little longer than the last, and constellations not seen for many months begin rising once more in the east. And then one morning there is a touch of frost on the meadows, a certain sign that autum has arrived. The farmers take in their last harvests from the fields and cut the cornstalks down to stubble; the deer that foraged so boldly in summer blend suddenly into the autumn foliage and are seldom seen again; the geese fly south in ragged formations against a pale blue autumn sky.

At first fall rests upon the land as lightly as the morning frost, but then its grip tightens. The settled weather of late summer gives way to a succession of uncertain days, with sun following rain and sudden gusts dislodging the last tenacious leaves. Every creature feels the quickening pace and makes its preparations for the coming winter, and when those preparations are complete it will be time for most to rest.

But there is no rest for the trout. Fall is spawning time for the brown trout, char and Atlantic salmon; time for the cutthroat to enter the streams and wait with the summer steelhead for their own winter spawning, time for highcountry rainbows to feed avidly in anticipation of their own breeding rites in the cold runoff of the spring. And far at sea the winter steelhead have heard the ancient call of instinct to turn toward home.

All this makes autumn a golden time of year for trout fishermen, and though the time is short the opportunities are many. The hazy afternoons of late October offer a last chance for fat rainbow feeding in the lakes, for cutthroat cruising in the estuaries, for a late summer steelhead still bright from the sea. But the days pass swiftly, and soon the last October caddis has lifted off the water and the last fisherman has waded from the stream.

Fall is the final movement in the great symphony of seasons, the grand climax to the fullness of the year, fading quickly to a last long dying note. And in the hush that follows, winter comes.

Lahontans

Fall had come to the mountains and the leaves formed a vivid patchwork quilt of color as we headed down the Cascades' eastern slopes from Stevens Pass. Deer hunters were camped in clearings along the highway, the meadows still were wet with dew in the mountain shadows, and everywhere there was color—fiery orange vine maples, butter-yellow aspens and bright golden big-leaf maples, their leaves all consumed in the glory of dying.

We entered Tumwater Canyon, the great conduit through which the Wenatchee River makes its way down from the mountains, sliding through a stairstep series of emerald pools and silver riffles on its journey to meet the mighty Columbia. Then we drove past the fruit orchards of the lower valley with their endless regiments of trees lined up in even ranks, and the air was sweet with the heavy scent of ripening apples.

We crossed the Columbia itself and began the long climb up onto the interior plateau, the heartland of the state, with its rolling fields of wheat that look like frozen waves in a golden sea. At the sleepy little farming town of Mansfield we left the wheat behind and started out across the rocky, broken sagebrush country bordering Moses Coulee, a great channel carved by an ancient flood. Randy was with me and we were bound for a lake nestled in the north end of the coulee—a lake containing Lahontan cutthroat trout.

The Lahontan cutthroat is a newcomer to Northwest waters, but it is one of the oldest of western trout and once may have reached a larger size than any other trout that spends its life in fresh water. Its story is one of triumph and tragedy, a saga of nature at its best and man at his shortsighted worst.

That story begins at least 70,000 years ago, perhaps much earlier, when an ancestral stock of cutthroats somehow found its way south into the waters of the Great Basin in the country now called Utah and Nevada. The Great Basin is largely desert now, but at that time the climate was cool and wet and two great lakes, Bonneville and Lahontan, filled the basin. The cutthroat became residents of these lakes and their numerous tributaries.

Lake Lahontan, southernmost of the two, was larger than modern-day Lake Erie and the invading cutthroat found it well stocked with a natural population of minnows and suckers. The cutthroat soon learned to prey on these fish and once the predatory habit was established it continued for many thousands of years. It was a pattern that favored natural selection of larger and longer-lived cutthroat, an evolutionary trend which continued for millenia, and eventually the Lahontan cutthroat emerged as a super race of predatory trout, perhaps without parallel in the long history of the trout family.

But then, about 10,000 years ago, the climate of the Great Basin began its change to the one we know today. Without the usual rainfall and rivers to feed it, Lake Lahontan began to evaporate and shrink, its water level falling lower each year. Within a thousand years it had all but vanished and most of its trout had been forced to seek refuge in mountain streams and lakes, including some we know today—the Carson River and Independence, Summit and Tahoe Lakes. Of Lake Lahontan itself, only two sump lakes remained— Pyramid and Walker lakes.

But of these two, only Pyramid Lake was able to maintain continuity and retain its original variety of Lahontan fishes until modern times—which meant that only in Pyramid Lake was the Lahontan cutthroat able to continue on the evolutionary course that had made it what it was. Elsewhere, the fugitive trout from Lake Lahontan were forced to adapt to the more limited diets available in the mountain streams and lakes where they found themselves, and in such surroundings their predatory habits were not necessarily an advantage. Though even today they still bear a close physical resemblance to the Pyramid Lake fish and are classified as members of the same subspecies, their evolutionary path over the last 10,000 years has been quite different from the trout of Pyramid Lake. The fish in Pyramid Lake were unique, the last survivors of an ancient race of super trout.

The cutthroat were well known to the Indians who lived first on the shores of Lake Lahontan and later on Pyramid Lake, and their modern descendants, the Paiutes, became skilled fishermen. The first white men to see Pyramid Lake, John C. Fremont and his famous scout, Kit Carson, were greeted by friendly Paiutes who brought them fresh trout which they had caught in the lake. "Their flavor was excellent—superior, in fact, to that of any fish I have ever known," Fremont wrote. "They were of extraordinary size, about as large as the Columbia River salmon, generally from two to four feet in length."

Fremont and Carson and their party camped near the mouth of the Truckee River, Pyramid Lake's largest tributary and the only one in which the cutthroat trout could spawn. But during the 1860s, less than 20 years after Fremont's discovery of the lake, logging began in the Truckee watershed, causing serious erosion and siltation. Numerous sawmills also began dumping sawdust into the river, and in 1869 a Reno newspaper reported that "millions" of spawning trout had been killed by sawdust pollution. The pollution was so bad that sometimes sawdust drifts blocked the mouth of the river and kept trout from entering. By 1875 dams also had blocked the river near Reno, cutting off as much as three-quarters of the original spawning habitat of the Lahontan trout.

But dams and pollution weren't the only problem. Completion of a railroad line made it possible to ship fresh fish to market and and an intensive commercial fishery began in Pyramid Lake, involving such techniques as netting, snagging, spearing, clubbing and explosives. In 1899, a paper mill began dumping toxic wastes into the Truckee River, killing all the fish for a considerable distance downstream. Even when trout were able to overcome all these obstacles and spawn, there was no assurance their offspring would survive; each year, millions of trout fry disappeared into the growing numbers of unscreened irrigation ditches that took water from the river.

Despite all these threats, the trout still somehow managed to survive. As late as the 1880s, long after most of the upstream spawning and nursery areas were blocked or polluted, commercial rail shipments of Pyramid Lake trout ranged from 200,000 to 250,000 pounds a year, and the total annual catch was estimated at about 500,000 pounds.

The Lahontan cutthroat, including the Pyramid Lake fish, did not even have a scientific name until 1878. In that year, the second edition of David Starr Jordan's *Manual of the Vertebrates* identified the Lahontan as *Salmo clarki henshawi* in honor of H.W. Henshaw, a naturalist who had sent Jordan a specimen of the trout from Lake Tahoe. By this time the large size of the Pyramid Lake fish also had caught the eye of fish culturists, and trout removed from the Truckee River were being raised in hatcheries by the California Acclimatization Society.

The maximum size attained by the Pyramid Lake trout will never be known, but the official world-record cutthroat trout was caught in the lake by John Skimmerhorn, a Paiute Indian, in 1925. It weighed 41 pounds. Big as that was, there are reports of even larger fish having been taken in the Indian commercial fishery; Fred Cosby, a tribal fishery agent, claimed to have seen one in 1916 that weighed 62 pounds. If true, this would mean the Pyramid Lake cutthroat reached sizes even larger than the 56-pound Kamloops trout reported from Jewel Lake, British Columbia, in 1932 (but also never completely verified).

In 1938, the year of the last spawning run of native cutthroat in the Truckee River, a U.S. Fish and Wildlife Service biologist checked 195 trout taken in the Indian fishery and reported their *average* weight was 20 pounds. The 1938 run was an unusual one, however; it was the first successful spawning run in 11 years, which meant that most of the fish in it were at least that old themselves. An 11-year-old trout is bound to be large, and it is difficult to say what the average weight of the Pyramid Lake cutthroat may have been under normal circumstances. But there is no doubt that the Pyramid Lake cutthroat was capable of reaching very large size, and nothing quite like them has been seen before or since.

The fate of the Pyramid Lake cutthroat was sealed on June 7, 1905, when the gates were closed on Derby Dam, the first project of a new federal agency called the Reclamation Service, now the Bureau of Reclamation. The dam diverted the Truckee River for irrigation, and though it was built with a fish ladder, the ladder never worked as intended. It's hard to see how it ever could have worked properly, considering there often was not enough water below the dam for fish to swim upstream. A sand delta also had formed at the mouth of the river, making it difficult for fish to enter except during periods of high water.

Still, in the first few years of the project's existence there usually was enough surplus water to allow at least some cutthroat trout to spawn, and occasionally a few fish even were able to ascend the fish ladder. But then the Bureau of Reclamation increased the amount of water being diverted from the river and also began using water to generate electricity. After that spawning became more and more infrequent.

The last major spawning run was in 1927. The water that year was very high, and some trout were able to get above Derby Dam and go all the way to Reno. By then it had been so long since people in Reno had seen Pyramid Lake trout they had forgotten what they were, and when the mayor proclaimed a day of celebration in their honor he mistakenly called it "Rainbow Day."

Survivors from the offspring of the 1927 spawning formed the run of 20-pounders that returned to the Truckee River in the very last spawning run 11 years later. There might have been another, but the Bureau of Reclamation shut off the flow of the river while the trout were spawning and left them and their precious eggs to die in shrinking, stagnant pools below the dam. It was the end for the largest cutthroat the world has ever known, and two years later, in 1940, the Pyramid Lake strain of Lahontan cutthroat trout was officially declared extinct.

At the time no one fully understood just what had been lost; after all, there were still Lahontan cutthroat in other lakes and rivers. No one realized that for 10,000 years these other fish had followed a different evolutionary path; they were no longer quite the same as the long-lived, large-growing predatory trout of Pyramid Lake.

In 1950, the state of Nevada began experimental plants of trout in Pyramid Lake in an effort to replace the fishery that had been destroyed by the Bureau of Reclamation. At first they tried rainbow trout, but it was soon discovered that Lahontan cutthroat from Summit Lake and from Heenan Lake, California (where native stock from the Carson River had been introduced), displayed much better survival and growth—probably because they, like the original Pyramid Lake fish, had developed a tolerance for highly alkaline water such as that in Pyramid Lake.

But although these fish did well and succeeded in re-establishing a popular sport fishery in Pyramid Lake, they never have reached the monumental size of the lake's original inhabitants. The introduced trout have a maximum life span of seven years, compared to at least 11 for the original stock, and although they have managed to attain an average weight of eight pounds, that is still far short of the 20-pound figure recorded for the native fish in the 1938 spawning run—the only reliable record available. From this came the slow realization that the original strain of Pyramid Lake trout was so finely tuned to its environment that no other fish, not even another variety of Lahontan cutthroat, could replace it.

But there was one more strange chapter to be written in the story of the vanished trout of Pyramid Lake. In 1976, a Brigham Young University graduate student named Terry Hickman began work on a study of the Bonneville cutthroat, a rare subspecies thought to be the surviving remnant of the original cutthroat population of Lake Bonneville, which also had disappeared when the climate changed in the Great Basin. While trying to track down isolated populations of the Bonneville trout, Hickman was told that a Utah state biologist had found what appeared to be a pure strain of cutthroat in a small, unnamed creek on Pilot Peak, a 10,700-foot mountain on the western edge of the Bonneville Salt Flats. The stream wasn't even on the map, but in June 1977 Hickman set out to find it.

Packing electroshocking equipment on his back, he hiked to the reported location of the stream and found it was actually the headwaters of a creek that had been diverted to provide a municipal water supply for the town of Wendover, Utah. Above the diversion point the stream was barely two miles long, half of it in Utah and the other half in Nevada. Hickman later named it Donner Creek because it once had drained into Donner Springs, the first source of fresh water found by the famous Donner Party after it crossed the Bonneville Salt Flats in 1846.

Using his electroshocking gear, Hickman sampled the stream above the diversion and captured several fish. They were clearly some kind of cutthroat, but they were much different in appearance and conformation from the Bonneville cutthroat he was seeking.

Dr. Robert J. Behnke of Colorado State University, the foremost authority on cutthroat trout, was Hickman's thesis advisor and it was to Behnke's published works on cutthroat that Hickman turned in an effort to identify the strange fish. Of all the cutthroat subspecies described in Behnke's writings, he could find only one which appeared to match the spot pattern and physiological features of the trout from Donner Creek—*Salmo clarki henshawi*, the Lahontan cutthroat. But it seemed impossible that Lahontan cutthroat could be living in a stream on Pilot Peak, far from the ancient site of Lake Lahontan, unless they had been put there by man.

Behnke confirmed the identification of the fish as Lahontan cutthroat and a search was begun to try to find out where they had come from. No record of stocking could be found, but Behnke and Hickman were able to establish that the fish had been in the stream for a long time. A Utah conservation officer reported he had been told in 1957 by an elderly rancher that the creek "always had native trout," and the retired master of the Wendover water works confirmed that cutthroat were in the stream when he went to work there in 1952. That was before the state of Nevada began its hatchery program using Lahontan cutthroat from Heenan Lake, so the Pilot Peak cutthroat could not have come from that source.

The Nevada and Utah Fishing and Game departments reported that no Lahontan cutthroat had been stocked in either state between 1930 and 1949, so the fish in Donner Creek must have been put there even earlier than that. Further confirmation came from a retired game warden who told Hickman that during the late 1940s he had stocked rainbow trout in many local streams, but never had put them in the creek on Pilot Peak because it already held trout.

So Behnke and Hickman looked back even further. Finally they discovered that in 1910 a shipment of more than a million Lahontan cutthroat eggs had been sent to several counties in eastern Nevada, near the Utah border. Other shipments apparently followed from time to time, possibly as late as 1930. It seemed probable that Donner Creek had been stocked with fry hatched from one of these shipments; there did not seem to be any other likely explanation.

But it was the source of the eggs that created the most excitement: All of them had come from Pyramid Lake. Here, suddenly and unexpectedly, was strong evidence that the fish in the little two-mile-long creek on Pilot Peak were members of the unique Pyramid Lake cutthroat strain believed extinct since 1940.

The dramatic announcement by Hickman and Behnke of their findings created quite a stir within the biological community, and the rediscovery of the Pyramid Lake fish also soon became the subject of a widely read article in *Sports Illustrated* magazine. As a result of the publicity, the Fish & Wildlife Service made plans to collect fertilized eggs from Donner Creek and transfer them to a hatchery where it was hoped they could be developed into a breeding stock. There was even talk of reintroducing the stock to Pyramid Lake, or planting it in reservoirs full of scrap fish where presumably it would revert to its old ways and grow to old age and large size.

But unfortunately that's not the way things turned out. In a recent letter to the author, Behnke explained what happened:

"The fate of the Donner Creek cutthroat trout is an excellent example of a basic problem of fishery management with state and federal agencies—lethargy and apathy in regard to trying something new and innovative," he said. "The small population in Donner Creek has been expanded and made more secure by a transplant in a neighboring stream, but no action has been taken to utilize this resource for fisheries management. Some fertilized eggs were taken to the Hotch-kiss, Colorado, federal fish hatchery in 1980, after the publicity in the *Sports Illustrated* article. As would be predicted with a wild stock handled at a facility geared to raise domesticated trout, all fish died at hatching.

"As the publicity died down, and there was no outside agitation to do anything more, nothing more was done."

And so the original Pyramid Lake strain of Lahontan cutthroat trout, once thought lost forever only to be miracu-lously rediscovered, now has been largely forgotten again in its remote transplanted home on Pilot Peak. One can only hope that someday men will find a way to atone for their treatment of this unique fish, largest and most unusual of all western trouts, and restore it to a habitat resembling the one that made it what it was.

But while there is yet no happy ending to the tragic story of the Pyramid Lake cutthroat, other strains of Lahontan cutthroat have fared better. Their tolerance for high levels of alkalinity has made them a valuable fish in western states where there are many alkaline lakes, and Lahontan trout have been planted in many of these waters. Most of these fish have come from the Carson River-Heenan Lake strain, including the majority of Lahontan cutthroat planted in Northwest lakes.

One of these was Lake Lenore, a shallow, 1,700-acre lake located in spectacular surroundings at the lower end of Grand Coulee in Washington state. For years the Washington Department of Game had been keeping an eye on Lake Lenore, a rich water fed by underground seepage and a small creek that flowed in from Alkali Lake. Lenore always had been too alkaline to support fish of any kind, but over the years its alkalinity had slowly decreased and in 1977 the department decided to try again to see if it could find a fish that could live in Lake Lenore.

Mindful of the Lahontan cutthroat's tolerance for alkalinity, the department obtained 30 Lahontan, put them in live boxes along with a control group of rainbow trout and placed the boxes in Lake Lenore. Within 48 hours all the rainbow trout had died, but all the Lahontans were still alive. They remained alive, and though still confined to the live boxes, after a while some of them even began to grow and put on weight. Finally the 30 fish were set free in the lake and the department began searching for a reliable source of more Lahontan cutthroat trout.

Nevada was the obvious source, but its hatchery stocks had been afflicted by an outbreak of disease. No other source could be found, so for the next couple of years Lake Lenore remained barren except for the original 30 trout used in the survival experiment.

Then, in May 1979, Bill Zook, a Game Department biologist, found a pair of 19-inch cutthroat—survivors of the original 30—trying to spawn in the little stream that flows into the northern end of Lake Lenore. Struck by the possibility that a self-sustaining cutthroat population might be established in Lake Lenore, Zook commissioned a renewed search for a source of eggs. This time Nevada was able to provide 100,000 Lahontan cutthroat eggs certified free of disease. These were delivered to a pair of Washington state hatcheries where they were incubated, hatched and reared into fry. Mortality at one hatchery was very high, but 35,000 fry survived at the other and in October 1979 these were planted in Lake Lenore.

Utilizing the rich and virtually untouched food stocks in the lake, these fish—which averaged two inches in length when they were planted—grew to an average length of 10 inches by the following June. That summer the department obtained another 200,000 eggs from Nevada which produced another 135,000 fry, and these were stocked in October 1980. The lake was opened to fishing on a year-round basis with a one-fish limit, except during the spring spawning season when only catch-and-release fishing was allowed. Only artificial flies or lures with single barbless hooks were allowed.

During the winter of 1980-81, another one of the original 30 fish was caught by an angler. It measured 25 inches and weighed 6½ pounds. By that time the fry planted in 1979 had grown to an average length of 18 inches.

As Zook and other biologists had hoped, the Lahontan cutthroat soon developed spawning runs to the inlet stream at Lake Lenore. The stream is far too small to permit natural reproduction on anything but the smallest scale, so the Game Department began trapping the returning fish and spawning them artificially—a process which has now become an annual ritual. By managing the run in this way, the department has obtained enough eggs to restock Lake Lenore annually with enough left over to begin stocking other lakes.

One of the first other lakes to be stocked was Grimes Lake in the northern end of Moses Coulee, and it was there Randy and I were headed. Grimes is another highly alkaline water that never had been able to support fish until Lahontans were introduced. It is managed under the same regulations as Lake Lenore, except that it is open to fishing only from July 1 to September 30 each year because of its importance as a waterfowl-management area. That was why we had chosen to go there late in September, when the water would be cooling down just before the season's end.

We parked the truck in a dusty clearing near the lake and made a quick inspection of its shoreline, where we found hordes of little scuds hiding under rocks and noted the empty shucks of hatched-out midges floating in the surface film. Farther out we could see spent *Callibaetis* mayfly spinners resting on the surface and adult damselflies buzzing lazily overhead. Obviously Grimes Lake was rich in food for trout.

Having confirmed that to our satisfaction, we muscled the little cartop pram down to the water's edge, loaded it with our rods and other tackle and rowed up a long, narrow channel leading to the main lake. There was little sign of surface activity, but we had not really expected any; in keeping with its long predatory heritage, the Lahontan is not known as a free-rising fish. So we began fishing with a sinking line and a scud pattern.

The lake was a brilliant dark blue in the early afternoon sunlight and appeared incongruous in the dry country that surrounded it. Bitterbrush and sage grew around the shoreline and the coulee walls rose up sharply in a series of basalt terraces baked by the sun. In such warm, dry country I had expected to find the lake filled with a bloom of algae or at least a heavy growth of weed, but there was little of either; the water was surprisingly clear. I put in my thermometer and it registered an even 60 degrees at the surface—surprisingly cool for a lake in such notoriously hot country, especially at the end of a long summer.

We found a shallow bay and eased the anchor down, then started reaching out with long casts and a slow retrieve. When nothing moved to the little scud pattern, I changed it for a larger Carey Special, the staple fly of Northwest lakes. But it too went untouched, though we moved around a bit to try it in untested waters.

Then I noticed backswimmers were beginning to dart to the surface as they came up to replenish the little bubbles of air they carry with them under water, so I clipped off the Carey, put on a backswimmer imitation and began to fish it with a quick, darting retrieve to match the motion of the naturals. But the trout ignored it too.

It seemed obvious that some drastic change of tactics was in order, and I began searching through my fly boxes, hoping for an inspiration. Suddenly my eye fell upon the silver tinsel body and peacock sword wing of an Alexander, an old English pattern I had last fished many years before in British Columbia. If it caught my eye, I thought, perhaps it would catch a cutthroat's eye as well. So I removed the backswimmer imitation and replaced it with an Alexander.

The very first cast rewarded us with the sight of a large bronze shape that followed the fly as I retrieved it to the boat, but the fish turned away at the last moment. The next dozen casts brought three or four more follows, but in each case the fish finally turned away, so I tried varying the speed of the retrieve to see if that would induce a fish to strike.

At last one did; it took the fly hard and fought stubbornly in a series of short, strong rushes, never showing itself until it was thoroughly tired and I was able to lead it to the boat. It was a stout fish, all burnished bronze in color except for crimson splashes on its gill plates and a pair of prominent red-orange cutthroat slashes beneath its lower jaw. Large black spots were spaced evenly over its body, and altogether it was quite unlike any other trout I'd ever seen. It was about 18 inches long and weighed around three pounds.

A little later Randy landed another trout, nearly a twin of the first but not quite as heavy. Five or six others were hooked briefly and lost, and many more followed our flies without taking; it was obvious we had yet to find a fly that was exactly right, one they would take without hesitation. We tried other patterns, but none proved any better than the Alexander, and I regretted not having brought along a box of sea-run cutthroat flies; it would have been interesting to see if these landlocked fish would take patterns tied for their sea-run cousins.

By then it was growing dark, so we loaded up the boat and drove to nearby Jameson Lake to make our camp and spend the night. Next day we returned to Grimes Lake and fished again in hot still weather. The fishing was similar, and although again we missed many fish, we succeeded in landing trout from 2½ to three pounds, which fought in the same stubborn way. A couple of them also later proved to be excellent fish on the table.

I was glad for the chance to meet the Lahontan. It is not as spectacular as the free-spirited rainbow trout that inhabits most Northwest lakes, but its potential for reaching large sizes and its long and interesting history make it a welcome addition to the local angling menu. Not only that, but it has provided fishing in waters where formerly there was none.

I, for one, plan to take advantage of those new opportunities.

Notes from New Zealand

When a trout fisherman visits the South Island of New Zealand he is obliged to try his luck on the Mataura River. The Mataura is probably the South Island's most famous stream, an amazingly productive river that can be wonderfully generous in yielding fat brown trout to a skillfully fished dry fly or nymph. But when I arrived on the South Island early in the Southern Hemisphere autumn, the Mataura was high and dirty from a long summer of heavy rain. One glimpse and I knew it would be unfishable for days to come.

In search of an alternative, I asked around in the friendly little town of Gore, which straddles the Mataura where it makes a nearly right-angle turn and flows from east to south. A helpful clerk in the local sport shop referred me to the Pomahaka River. It was a stream I'd never heard of, but he assured me it was fine dry-fly water with a fall run of seagoing brown trout that came up from the much larger Clutha River, of which the Pomahaka was a tributary. It sounded tempting, so I thanked the clerk, bought some flies he recommended, and set out early the next morning to find the Pomahaka.

It wasn't an easy river to find, but after exploring several back roads around the village of Kelso in the hills north of Gore we came at last to a small sign that said "Anglers' Access." Beyond it was a dirt track leading across a sheep paddock to a row of willows. We followed the track beyond the willows and found the river, next to a grassy clearing that was such a perfect natural campsite that we decided to spend the night even before I sampled the fishing.

Once camp was set up I assembled a rod and explored downstream for half a mile or more. The Pomahaka turned out to be an utterly delightful stream, small, moderately clear, easily wadable and almost every inch of it fishable. But in that half-mile of water I didn't see a single rise, and though I fished with dry flies, wet flies and an upstream nymph, I hadn't had a single strike by the time I returned to camp for lunch, wondering if the river really did hold trout.

During lunch I noticed the stiff breeze which had been blowing all morning was beginning to subside. I glanced upstream and saw a trout rise in a stretch of slow, deep water. That rise was quickly followed by a second, then a third, and within moments the river was dotted with rising fish. I finished my sandwich in a hurry, picked up my rod and began wading upstream to a point where I could reach the nearest rises with a cast.

Then the breeze picked up again, riffling the surface of the stream, and the rise stopped as quickly as if someone had thrown a switch. I put my dry fly over water where moments earlier a dozen trout had risen, but not a single fish would come up to greet it.

That was my first lesson in the finicky habits of the Pomahaka's trout.

Later that afternoon I hiked upstream and found the water got better and better the farther up I went. It was classic dry-fly water, with deep riffled runs cutting under clay banks and willow roots along the river's edge, forming all kinds of sheltered holts for trout. I fished two pools bordered by spectacular sandstone cliffs, both showing marks of fresh erosion by the wind. Even while I fished, a sudden gust of wind dislodged a volley of rocks from the top of one cliff and sent them showering into the pool, frightening any trout that might have been lurking there.

Where there were no cliffs the river was bordered by rolling paddocks full of docile sheep or willows full of brightly colored birds. In one willow-bordered pool I found a fat, beautifully marked brown trout of at least three pounds that had found a good feeding station off the tip of a protruding willow root. I did all the right things, or at least all the things I thought were right, creeping cautiously through the brush to a spot well below the fish, then casting carefully upstream so that my little fly would float down over him. At first the trout was tolerant of this, but its patience finally waned and it moved off slowly into deeper water without once rising to the fly. And if ever a trout conveyed contempt by its posture or movement, this one did.

A little while later I found another, rising periodically in the center of a riffle, and this one took my fly and I landed it easily. It wasn't large—not big enough to mount, but still large enough to count—and it was my first-ever brown from a South Island stream.

That night I looked in my dictionary of the native Maori

language for the meaning of the name Pomahaka. As nearly as I could determine, "death chant" was a reasonable translation—a grim-sounding name for what seemed such a pleasant river.

Next morning there was another fine rise of trout in the big slow pool above our campsite. Small mayflies were coming off the water and tiny cinnamon-colored ants were falling into it. I waded across the river and climbed a hill on the far side, and from that vantage point I could see a winding channel through the center of the pool, a foot or two deeper than the surrounding water. About a dozen trout were cruising up and down the channel, rising occasionally either to the mayflies or the ants, or perhaps to both. They were big fish; the smallest was at least two pounds, the average maybe three or four, and there was one brute that looked as if it might weigh as much as ten pounds—almost certainly a sea-run fish.

I left the hill and made a careful approach to within casting range, and for the next two hours tried nearly every fly I had. Once or twice a fish tilted up to take a look, but none even came close to taking. By then I had decided they were feeding selectively on ants, but I had not brought any ant patterns with me from the States and had seen none among the flies in the tackle shop at Gore. (Later, after examining fly selections in many other shops, I concluded there probably was not a single size 18 cinnamon ant in all of New Zealand.)

Later that day, after the frustrating rise had ended, I met some of the people who live and fish along the Pomahaka. First was a remarkable fisherwoman named Irene Kennedy, who paused in her pursuit of trout long enough to share a cup of tea and tell us about a nine-pounder she had taken from the river a week before. Though that was our only meeting, Irene became a faithful correspondent and we still keep in touch years later. Such are the friendships made along rivers.

Next was Bill White, another local angler. He had taken

a five-pounder that very morning, but only after showing it 21 different fly patterns—something I could easily believe. When he opened the fish he had found its stomach stuffed with the tiny ants I had seen upon the water. The fish finally had taken a Greenwell's Glory—White didn't have any ant patterns either.

Then we had a visit from Bill Thomson, owner of "Camperdown," the farm on which we were camped. We asked his permission to spend another night on the river. "It's God's river," he said, "and you have as much right to be here as I have." Like our other visitors, he was warm, generous, and friendly, and we soon learned that is the natural way of the rural New Zealander.

Later I resumed fishing and came upon a freshly fallen tree lying across the river. The foliage was still attached and three large trout were lined up below it, sipping tiny insects that seemed to be falling from the leaves. I couldn't tell what they were, and had nothing that small anyway, so for lack of something better I put on a size 16 pale yellow mayfly pattern which resembled some naturals I had seen hatching earlier. I dropped the fly close to the fallen trunk and immediately a trout came up and sucked it in. But when I lifted the rod there was no answering pull—somehow the trout had escaped being hooked. The disturbance of its rise put down the others, and as it turned out that was as close as I would come to taking one of the Pomahaka's larger browns.

But I did not feel as if my fishing had been without reward. The Pomahaka is a beautiful and charming river, even though its fish are difficult, and I remember it fondly and think of it often. And one day I hope to return.

When we left the Pomahaka and drove down the hills we found the Mataura still dirty with runoff from a thousand farms and fields. So we followed the highway that parallels the Mataura west of Gore and turned off at one of its tributaries, the little Otamita, in hopes of finding fishing there. The road followed the stream and the stream led it into a narrow little valley where there was scarcely room enough for both. At the far end of the valley the sky was dark and fat with the promise of more rain.

The Otamita looked clear, but it seemed a limpid little stream without much spirit or vitality. Its banks also were lined with brush so thick that we could see the water only now and then, and it seemed there was no place that offered casting room. But then we rounded a curve and came to a point where the valley widened and the river formed a broad, magnificent pool. Its far side was bounded by a nearly vertical slope, but next to the road it was just a short drop down a grassy bank to the edge of the stream.

I parked our rented van on the roadside and got out to survey the pool, just in time to glimpse a slowly spreading circle of water where a trout had risen. Small mayflies were riding down on the slow current and as I watched I could see trout rising in at least half a dozen locations in the pool.

But there was something else in the pool: Sheep were grazing on the impossibly steep hillside across the stream, and three of them apparently had lost their footing and tumbled down to the river; now their woolly corpses were half submerged in the pool. One trout, which appeared larger than any of the others, had taken up station next to one of the sheep. Even as I watched the trout tipped up and took a fly, leaving a heavy bulge of water that lapped against the flank of its dead companion.

The flyfisher encounters countless problems on the stream. The pages of angling literature offer good advice on how to deal with most of these, and if you read enough you will find the correct answer to almost any conceivable set of circumstances. But I had never read or heard of a proper way to float a dry fly past the far side of a dead sheep in the middle of a pool. This was definitely a problem that called for some sort of innovative tactic.

I studied the situation and decided the best approach—indeed, the only one—would be from upstream. A careful slack-line cast just might succeed in a drag-free float past the half-submerged sheep. But there would be only a single chance, and the odds seemed long against success.

With rod in hand, I worked my way slowly and cautiously down through the deep grass until I dared go no closer to the stream. The trout rose again next to the dead sheep and I mentally calculated the distance, then rose to a half crouch and began working out line in a quick series of false casts. Finally I let the fly go, without much confidence in the result.

But the cast fell right on target, just a few feet above the fish, and the current carried the fly slowly downstream in a perfect natural float. I could see it getting closer and closer to the sheep, and just when it seemed inevitable that the fly would catch in the water-soaked wool, the trout rolled up and took it cleanly. I lifted the rod, felt an instant's weight, then nothing. The fish was gone.

When I inspected the fly I found the hook was broken at the bend. It was then I realized that my backcast must have ticked the fly against a concrete utility pole behind me on the roadside. New Zealand has few trees suitable for making poles, so concrete is often used instead.

Dead sheep and concrete utility poles—two unexpected hazards of angling in New Zealand. Slowly I was learning that fishing in this far-off land was not quite the same as it is at home.

A fisherman in New Zealand, or anyone who spends very much time outdoors in that lovely country, can hardly fail to notice the wonderful variety of birds. Birds colonized New

Zealand long before men and for eons had the place nearly to themselves (New Zealand's only native mammal is a bat). In the absence of any land-based predators, some birds evolved into flightless varieties, such as the giant moa, now extinct, and the shy, noctural kiwi, which has survived to become the national emblem. Others evolved in myriad different ways and brought a wealth of beauty, sound and movement to the skies and forests of their adopted land. Since the arrival of European settlers, many foreign species have been introduced, but none is quite so colorful or interesting as the native forms, and it is impossible to go anywhere in New Zealand without being in range of a host of chiming, chattering, musical birds.

Some New Zealand birds, like the kiwi, are so reclusive they are seldom seen, but others are so intensely curious one can scarcely fail to notice them. The bush robin is one of these.

I met the bush robin one morning while prospecting for trout along the margins of the South Mavoran Lake. It was a gray autumn morning and the season's first snow had left a gleaming white mantle on the beech forests that cover the crests of the surrounding hills. The light was poor, but with polaroid glasses I could catch an occasional glimpse of large trout patrolling close to shore. I was staring intently after one of these when I felt a tap on the shoulder. Turning, I found myself eyeball-to-eyeball with a female bush robin.

As New Zealand birds go, the bush robin is far from the most attractive. It has a head that looks too large for its body and a body that seems too large for the long, spindly legs that hold it up, and the female's feathers are mostly a dull, nondescript shade of brown. But its very homeliness, plus its uninhibited friendliness and curiosity, make it a strangely appealing little bird.

This particular robin had settled on my shoulder as if it had been invited there. We stared at one another for a few moments until I decided I rather liked having it there. And it stayed with me as I went on fishing, its solemn little eyes watching intently everything I did. Finally it flew away but stayed close by and followed when I started back for camp, and when I found a piece of candy it came quickly to take it from my hand.

Later, while fishing the upper Eglinton River, I made acquaintance with another bush robin. This one came from the woods and perched on my fly rod, remaining there until I began to cast. It was just one attraction in a day filled with many, for the upper Eglinton is one of the most beautiful streams I have ever fished. It flows out of the stillness of Lake Gunn into a narrow channel of golden gravel that cuts through a dense forest of native bush, giant ferns and big old mountain beeches. The water is as clear as breath, and though at this point the stream is too small to hold very many trout, it is worth fishing if only just to see. The beeches along the Eglinton are home to clusters of wild parakeets, as bright and vivid as Christmas-tree ornaments, and it is a marvelous thing to see them and hear their songs.

Beyond Lake Gunn a narrow, twisting road leads tnrough the mountains to Milford Sound, a spectacular fjord that opens to the Tasman Sea. En route the road passes through a long, one-way tunnel bored laboriously through a granite massif. Traffic halts outside at either end to await a green-light signal to proceed, and the waiting areas are favorite spots for the kea, New Zealand's mountain parrot.

The kea, named after the sound of its call, is a large and handsome bird. It appears mostly green while at rest, but in flight the undersides of its wings flash with iridescent crimson. It also is a curious bird—at least that is true of those which hang around the tunnel portals—and will take food from your hand, though it is a bit more cautious than the bush robin in doing so. But the most curious habit of the kea is its appetite for rubber; if you have nothing else to offer, it will begin chewing on your car's windshield-wiper blades or rubber window gaskets.

The lovely paradise duck is a common sight on the lakes and larger rivers of the South Island, and back in the bush you will see the cheerful fantail, which the Maoris imitate in dance. And there are many others—the tui, or parson bird, so named for its white collar; the bellbird, famous for its ringing song; the tiny little rifleman, and the pukeko, an improbable swamp hen that looks like a big blue chicken—to mention just a few. A fisherman is never far from one or more of these, and their company is just one of the many attractions of fishing in New Zealand.

The Clutha is one of the mightiest of South Island rivers, perhaps the mightiest of all. A full-fledged river at its birth, it flows out of Lake Wanaka, one of the great interior lakes of the South Island, and winds southeastward to the sea. In its lower reaches the Clutha and its tributaries host runs of seagoing brown trout and quinnat salmon and in its upper portions there is good fishing for large resident rainbow trout and browns. But perhaps the best fishing of all is just at the point where the Clutha first becomes a river, spilling from the lake in a rush of water several hundred yards wide to start its long fall toward the sea. I camped on the shoulder of a dry hill just above the outlet, and it was there that I found some of the most exciting fishing I experienced in New Zealand.

I reached the river late in the afternoon of a fine sunny day and found a hatch of unbelievable proportions under way. Mayflies, countless thousands of them, were hatching in the lake and drifting down on an accelerating current that carried them into the river. There were whole fleets and flotillas of them, dark blue in color, some almost black, and yet their wings somehow caught the sunshine and reflected it so that the river seemed full of shining sparks. Waiting to receive them were hundreds of trout of all sizes, rolling and porpoising in the current as they captured fly after fly.

Feeling the familiar surge of excitement that comes from such a sight, I waded out quickly within casting distance of the nearest rising fish. Among the flies I'd brought were some size 16 Blue Uprights that had served me well back home; they seemed too small to imitate the naturals that were hatching here, but they were the best I had, so I knotted one to the end of my leader and began casting. The little fly floated down on the current and quickly became lost among dozens of naturals, and I realized there was little chance a fish would find it among all the real ones on the water. But surprisingly one did: After several casts, my fly disappeared in a splashy rise and suddenly I was fast to a running fish.

I headed for shore, rod held high and reel singing as the fish sought out the strongest part of the flow and used it to advantage. It fought like a small steelhead, taking the line down into the backing and once running the leader around a large rock so that I had to wade out again, reach down and pull it free. But at last the trout tired and I forced it to the beach; it was a fine rainbow, nickel-bright and in perfect condition with a small head and a thick body. It weighed about 2½ pounds and I judged it was probably one of the smaller fish I had seen rising.

I rose two other fish but missed them both before the hatch began to fail at the onset of the early autumn twilight. For a while there was a lull, but then a hatch of sedges came. Like the mayflies, most of the sedges emerged in the quiet waters of the lake and were carried down by the current to the river, and soon the infant Clutha's surface was covered with fluttering, ungainly insects. I captured one and found it was about the size of a No. 10 fly pattern, with a green body and dark wings, and this time my fly box yielded a perfect match in size and shape and color. But for some reason the trout seemed less interested in the sedges than they had been in the mayflies, and only now and then did a fish rise within casting reach.

Far out in the center of the flow, well beyond the reach of any caster, it was a different story; there I could see fish rising steadily, and most of them were very large. Their rises were violent, the sounds of them audible above the sounds of the river, and they pushed water out in awesome rings. But soon it was too dark to see anything at all, and I reeled in and began the long climb up the hillside to the level spot where we had camped.

The next day was cool and overcast and the mayfly hatch did not repeat itself. Rises came occasionally and sporadically, but I fished patiently and eventually rose a fish to a local dry-fly pattern I had bought in a tackle shop in the little town of Wanaka. At first the fish ran strongly, but then it settled down to fight in a series of short rushes, never showing itself, and from this behavior I deduced it was a brown. And so it proved to be when I beached it, a handsome male of about four pounds, all freckled and speckled and tawny-gold in color, with a prominent kype on its lower jaw.

Toward evening the sedge hatch came on again, as thickly as before, and in the brief frenzied moments before darkness I rose and hooked another good fish, but held it only briefly before the fly came away.

That night was cold and clear with a brilliant display of all the southern constellations, but the following morning was overcast and cool. Gradually the monolithic clouds broke themselves up into fragments and the fragments went their separate ways and by noon the autumn sun was shining and a gentle breeze was riffling the surface of the river. Again there were no mayflies, but every now and then a solitary sedge came drifting down from the lake and disappeared in a heavy rise far out in the center of the flow. I went exploring, and at length I found a convoluted course over which I could wade out farther than I had ever gone before. The current was strong and the water lapped dangerously close to my wader tops, but I was out far enough to reach some of the rising fish with a long throw.

The fish were wary and selective in the clear water and when nothing came to a fly fished at the end of a four-pound-test tippet I switched to one whose breaking test was only three. Things began to happen then: A trout rose twice and I covered it with a long cast; the sedge imitation floated over the fish and it rose and took the fly confidently. I tightened and felt a heavy weight, but only for a moment. Inspection showed the fish had snapped the three-pound tippet with scarcely any effort. It was not a case of knot failure; the tippet was broken cleanly, halfway up.

I put on a new tippet and another fly and resumed casting. The fly soon disappeared in a large bubble surrounded by a swirl. I set the hook and the fish started off on a long downstream run, and I began the long, difficult wade back toward shore—a move that quickly proved to be a bad mistake. I was going one way and the fish another and the backing peeled off the reel at an alarming rate. The line formed a giant belly stretching far across the river, all at the mercy of the current; finally the pressure was too much, the leader parted and the fish was gone.

I began to despair then of ever holding a fish in the heavy current on such a light leader. Nevertheless, I waded out to try again and quickly rose another fish but missed the strike. A few casts later came another rise, the most spectacular of all, from a large fish that lunged at the fly and threw up a fountain of spray. Like the others, it started immediately on a downstream run that went swiftly into the backing and brought joyous sounds from my old Hardy St. John reel.

Remembering what had happened earlier, I resolved this

time that I would stay where I was instead of trying to wade ashore. And when the trout's initial run was over, I was able to lead it slowly back upstream until I had it on a short line and everything seemed under control. But then the fish began to jump, revealing itself as a big rainbow. It jumped eight times in succession, throwing itself far out of the water each time, and on the eighth jump the fly came away.

After a few more casts it was time to go, for we were due back in Christchurch to catch a plane to the North Island. My score for the day was not impressive—four fish risen, three hooked, two broken and one lost. But it had been wildly exciting fishing and I had thoroughly enjoyed every moment of it. I also took comfort from the thought that success, like beauty, is measured in the eye of the beholder, and one standard of success in fly fishing is the ability to fool large and difficult fish with a floating fly. By that measure it had been a most successful day.

An American fly fisherman in New Zealand has certain advantages over local anglers, particularly if he is well equipped and knows the double haul. By well equipped, I mean that he should have his own pair of chest waders, which will allow him to gain access to water seldom fished by local fishermen. Chest waders are very expensive in New Zealand, where so many such things must be imported, and as a consequence not very many anglers have them—particularly on the South Island. They use hip boots instead, and while this does not penalize them on the smaller streams, it certainly does on big rivers like the Clutha. While fishing there I was able to wade out far beyond the local fishermen, all of whom were wearing hip boots.

The long-distance casting technique known as the double haul also is rarely seen in New Zealand, despite the fact that most anglers there use long rods and many use shooting-head fly lines designed for use with the double haul. A visiting angler who knows this casting method can easily reach water well beyond the range of the best New Zealand single-haul caster. Again this advantage holds true only on large rivers and lakes, but there are many of both in New Zealand and it is a mystery to me why the double haul never has caught on there. Among all the fishermen I met during two long visits to that country, I encountered only one who was a good double-haul caster.

Many of New Zealand's best waters are reserved for fly fishing only, a happy circumstance that stems from the angling preferences of those who settled the country and developed its early trout fisheries. There is probably some abuse of these regulations, but generally they seem to be well respected by those who fish with other methods. Perhaps other anglers realize that fly fishing is the method most consistent with preservation of the resource, which is a matter of great self-interest to New Zealanders—not just because trout fishing is an important part of their local way of life, but also because it provides a significant source of foreign exchange for their country.

The classic kind of fly fishing, with dry flies and nymphs, is mostly in the beautiful streams of the South Island. North Island fishing is mostly done with sinking lines and large wet flies, or "lures" as the Kiwis call them. The fishing is not as good as the tourist promotions would have you believe—it never is, anywhere—but it is still very good indeed. It is seldom fast but is nearly always interesting, entertaining and rewarding, and the average New Zealand trout is much larger than its counterpart in most stateside lakes and streams. It also would be difficult to conceive of surroundings more lovely than those awaiting the angler in New Zealand.

Using British traditions as their base and making imaginative use of local materials, New Zealanders have developed their own distinctive school of fly-tying theory. This is especially true on the North Island, where tyers have created many unique feathered "lures" for trout in Lake Taupo or the Rotorua lakes. Some of these, such as the Matuka and the Hamill's Killer, now are becoming popular on North American waters and others probably will follow suit. They are, for the most part, large, colorful flies combining clever blends of feathers, fur, and tinsel. Most are what we would call "attractor" flies, many designed for use at night. Relatively few of these patterns were conceived as imitations, and if New Zealand fly tyers lag in any one respect it is probably in the science of exact imitation.

That first became clear to me when I was fishing Lake Taupo during the "smelting" season, a time when schools of smelt move into the shallows and large rainbows and browns come in to feed on them. It is a wonderfully exciting kind of fishing, with the large trout usually visible in the clear water so that you can watch them follow the fly right up to the moment of the take. But though I fished a wide variety of local patterns tied to imitate the smelt, none succeeded in matching it very well, and a truly consistent or effective pattern seemed to be lacking. In part, this may be due to the difficulty and expanse of obtaining synthetic materials in New Zealand; I think a local tyer with access to the same variety of synthetics that North Americans take for granted could soon fashion a smelt imitation that would be deadly.

But the lack of good imitations also extends to the dry flies used on South Island streams. Here again, exact imitations are few and most patterns are tied according to traditional formulas now considered out of date in most other parts of the world. The small selection of dry flies that I brought from home served me much better than the local patterns I was able to obtain, although that may have been due partly to the fact that I fished them with more confidence.

New Zealand now frowns upon visiting anglers who bring their own flies or fly-tying materials and will not allow them past customs without fumigation—a regulation intended to protect trout from diseases prevalent in other lands. But I do not think this ban would apply to synthetic materials still in the package, and if I return to New Zealand—as I sincerely hope to do—I will take along some of these together with some basic fly-tying tools, then rely upon the local shops to furnish whatever else I need.

For a country of small population with a trout-fishing tradition that goes back scarcely a hundred years, New Zealand has developed a remarkably rich body of angling literature. Some of it is known in North America and more of it probably ought to be.

One of the best-known New Zealand titles is O. S. "Budge" Hintz' *Trout at Taupo*. Lesser known, but just as much worth reading, is his later work, *Fisherman's Paradise*. Hintz, a retired editor of *The New Zealand Herald*, is a gifted writer with a fluid style that vividly captures the moods familiar to fishermen everywhere. His favorite stream, celebrated often in his writing, is the little Waitahanui, a tributary of Lake Taupo. If you should see it from the highway bridge on the eastern side of the lake you might easily wonder how someone could find so much to say about such a limpid little river. But if you explore upstream you will soon find out: The Waitahanui in its middle reaches is deceptively swift and deep, a captivating little stream that hurries down through hills covered with brush thickets and criss-crossed by anglers' trails. A rainbow hooked in its swift current is twice the fish that you expect, as I learned to my satisfaction. The Waitahanui may be small, but it is a river that fully deserves a great writer to sing its praises.

By North Island standards, the Tongariro is a giant river, one whose fame has spread across the globe. It too is a river that deserves a heritage in print and it has found one in Tony

Jensen's *Trout of the Tongariro*. Jensen lacks the practiced literary style of Hintz, but his book is a fine, straightforward, pool-by-pool account of the Tongariro, the very model of what a fishing guidebook ought to be. Although now retired from his guiding days, Tony Jensen had a remarkable knowledge of the river, which he demonstrated one day when we fished together on the Duchess Pool. Tony pointed toward a little wrinkle down toward the tail of the pool and well on the far side, and said that if I would wade to a certain point and cast so that my fly would swing through the wrinkle at a certain angle, I would hook a trout. He didn't say I *might* hook a trout; he said positively that I would. I did as he said and hooked a trout exactly where he said it would be. An autographed copy of his book now occupies an honored spot in my library, and I have read it many times.

John Parsons' little book, *Parsons' Glory*, is another excellent New Zealand title, a collection of the author's newspaper columns filled with Kiwi fishing lore and legend. Yet another is *The Flies in My Hat* by Greg Kelly, which receives my nomination for a prize as one of the best-titled fishing books in any language.

Keith Draper's *Trout Flies in New Zealand* is the most exhaustive work in print on that subject, and Rex Forrester's *Trout Fishing in New Zealand* is the most useful all-around guide a visiting angler could wish to have. And there are many other titles that could be mentioned.

New Zealand's cities and towns have many bookstores—more than you would find in any North American city of comparable size—and it is worth a fisherman's while to spend time in as many of them as he can. There he will find some treasures worth as much as the fishing itself.

Nearly every river flowing into Lake Taupo has a "picket fence." That is the term New Zealanders have coined to describe the fishermen who line up shoulder-to-shoulder off the river mouths to cast into the rips where the current from the river mingles with the quiet water of the lake. Most of this fishing is done at night, and most of the rivers have their own faithful cadres of fishermen who return to them night after night. Off the mouth of the Waitahanui, scene of the most famous picket fence, there is often a lineup of wading anglers in the daytime as well.

It is not the sort of fishing that interests most visiting American anglers. Indeed, the very term "picket fence" conjures up images of the kind of fishing mob scenes that are becoming all too common on many North American trout streams, and when an angler travels 6,000 miles to fish in New Zealand a mob scene is the last thing he expects. More than once I've heard American anglers say they would never be caught standing in a picket fence, and I suppose I once felt that way myself. But that was before I tried it.

I remember thinking that the picket fence was, after all, a part of Taupo angling tradition, and I had read many warm tales about such fishing in the books of Hintz and other New Zealand writers. I decided that as long as I had the opportunity, it might be something worth trying once, just for the experience. Besides, my stay in New Zealand was drawing to an end, and joining a picket fence for an evening's fishing seemed an ideal way to extend the angling day.

I was staying at an inn not far from the mouth of the Tauranga Taupo River, which had its own picket fence like nearly all the others. But the lake off the mouth of the Taurango Taupo is too deep to wade, so its picket-fence fishermen come in boats each evening and anchor parallel to one another in a line at the farthest reach of the river's current. The inn's proprietor had a rowboat which he offered to let me use, so I made plans to join the Tauranga Taupo picket line.

It was late in the afternoon when I set out on the short

row to the river's mouth. The sun was headed down toward the blunt, broken shape of Mount Tongariro on Lake Taupo's western shore and the great lake was absolutely still, stretching away like a vast plain of glass to distant horizons. Looking over the side of the boat I could see the volcanic sand of the bottom at great depth; I had fished Taupo years before but had forgotten how marvelously clear it is.

Two boats already were anchored in position off the river's mouth as I approached. They were parallel to one another at close quarters with a single angler casting from one and a pair fishing from the other. Being somewhat uncertain about the etiquette of such fishing—especially what was considered the minimum acceptable distance between boats— I eased my craft next to one of the others and waited for somebody to say something. But the other fishermen merely nodded in greeting, so I nodded back, dropped anchor and began to fish.

From the reading I had done I knew the usual technique was to make a long cast, let the fly sink and then retrieve it slowly. It's far from the kind of fishing I most like to do, but it's the way most Taupo trout are taken, and I soon got into the long, leisurely rhythm of it.

More boats began to arrive and get in line as the afternoon wore on toward evening. But there was no scrambling for positional advantage; the newcomers merely extended the line and were welcomed cordially by the others. Most seemed to know one another and soon they were all involved in a lively conversation with much good humor. Some of their questions and comments were directed my way and I realized I was being invited to join the conversation— even though my Yankee accent clearly marked me as a stranger. But I did join in and quickly found myself thoroughly enjoying the conversation and the company, and soon I did not feel like a stranger any more.

The sun gleamed off the still water until about 5:30 p.m. when it set behind the high western hills. The twilight seemed only seconds long; one moment the sun was shining brightly and the next there was only a milky-blue glow to mark the place where it had set. A little onshore breeze came up and suddenly it was much colder.

I had been fishing a smelt pattern without response—none of us had even had a strike—but with the sudden change in temperature and light I stopped fishing long enough to put on a heavy sweater. It also seemed a good time to change flies, so I replaced the smelt imitation with a Red Setter, one of the most famous and colorful of local patterns.

It had been dark only a few moments when one of the others announced he'd felt a fish's touch. Then another fisherman's rod bent and bucked and his reel began to talk as a trout took out line. The others offered verbal encouragement as the fight progressed, and after a few minutes a fat rainbow was writhing in the lucky angler's landing net.

Then it was my turn. Suddenly the line was snatched from my fingers and a strong fish was running with it. After the initial run we traded line back and forth a while, but the fish never showed itself and I began to wonder if it might be a brown trout. But the strength of its rushes soon convinced me otherwise.

Eventually the fish tired and the others cheered when they saw the fight was coming to an end. I had no net, but when the trout came alongside I seized it by the lower jaw and lifted it into the boat. It was a rainbow, about 22 inches long, steel-bright and almost obscenely fat—a typical Taupo trout. There were warm words of congratulations from the others.

I caught nothing after that, although one or two more fish were taken by the others. Finally it was late, and time to go.

I rowed slowly away from the others until they faded from

sight in the darkness and I was alone on the still surface of the great lake. The lights of Taupo town twinkled far across the water, 30 miles away, and overhead the sky was ablaze with stars whose light was old long before it reached my eyes. The stately Southern Cross was there, and the curious luminescent patches of the Magellanic Clouds, and by their faint light I could still see the silver volcanic sand on the bottom far below. Here and there a trout ripped the surface as it fed, but there was no other sound.

Suddenly a spectacular meteor flashed overhead, leaving a glowing trail that was visible for 30 seconds after it had passed. I marveled at the sight and thought how ironic it was that an object that may have drifted aimlessly through space since all the worlds were young should suddenly encounter the atmosphere of this small, out-of-the-way planet and die in such a momentary blaze of light.

I gazed up at the heavens from which the meteor had come and at all the legions of stars still shining there, reflected also in the still water around my drifting boat, and in the silence I wondered if another fisherman could be adrift on some dark and distant lake out there—a fisherman who even now might be looking up and thinking thoughts that were similar to mine.

Such are the feelings that Taupo inspires on a still, clear autumn evening.

I returned to the Tauranga Taupo picket fence several times after that, and by watching and listening to my new friends I learned many of the subtleties and secrets of rivermouth fishing—and there are more of these than meet the eye. Later I joined a picket fence of wading anglers off the mouth of the little Waimarino River, which has its own group of regulars. They were as friendly as the others and just as generous in sharing their knowledge, and one night when they were late arriving I discovered that I greatly missed their company.

I caught more fish, though the fishing never was especially fast, and after a time it became clear to me that for the local anglers the fishing was almost a secondary thing; it merely offered an excuse for them to get together, to talk and laugh and share their friendship—even with a stranger from across the sea. I think of them often now, casting their large feathered lures far out over the still surface of the lake, then chuckling softly to one another in the autumn dusk, and I wish I were back among them.

Someday, with a little fisherman's luck, perhaps I will be.

Fall Favorite

The sea-run cutthroat is known as a blue-collar fish, a tough, no-nonsense trout that hangs out on the waterfront, down around the docks or in the brackish lower reaches of short-run coastal streams. Those are tough neighborhoods, and maybe that's why the cutthroat seldom travels alone; it almost always has a few buddies along. Considering its wrong-side-of-the-tracks reputation, you might think the best bait for cutthroat would be a shot and a beer. But despite its plebeian image, the sea-run responds willingly to flies; in fact, it's a much better fly-rod fish than most anglers suppose. And it is one of my favorite fish in the fall.

The sea-run cutthroat bears scant resemblance to its landlocked cousins of the interior basins. After a summer of feeding in the estuaries its sides are typically as bright as a switchblade and its back is a cold blue-green. It wears a buckshot pattern of fine black spots and the cutthroat slashes that are the badges of its breed are faint like a pair of faded scars. When hooked on a fly it fights stubbornly, usually in a series of short rushes, but it sometimes jumps well and always displays surprising endurance, no matter what its size.

Those cutthroat destined to spawn in winter enter the rivers in the fall, and that is where most anglers seek them. But there are always bright fish remaining in the estuaries, fish that feed through the fall and winter and well into the following year, and a small clannish band of anglers searches for them there. These estuary anglers bring a certain amount of fanaticism to their task; they must be prepared to fish in rain from cold gray dawn to bitter dusk, to endure freezing fogs or bone-chilling winds or even squalls of snow. That's the kind of weather cutthroat like.

A Puget Sound cutthroat fisherman follows a familiar set of tactics developed over many years. He patrols the beaches, sometimes on foot but more often in a boat, and casts out among pilings or over oyster beds where cutthroat like to feed. He uses a sinking line and bright, gaudy flies, and when he sees the swirl of a feeding cutthroat he covers it quickly and strips in his fly with a rapid retrieve. Sometimes, if he is lucky, a cutthroat will take the fly; more often it will not.

Those also were the tactics I followed when I first began fishing for sea-runs. I caught fish now and then, which seemed to be about as often as anyone caught them, but before very long I realized there was a great deal more to estuary fishing than merely catching fish. I had fallen under the spell that seems to capture every sea-run angler sooner or later—a strong feeling of attraction for the great open spaces and gray-blue vistas of the estuary, for the sight of the rushing tide under a layer of morning mist, for the sound of a chattering kingfisher or the wistful cry of a lonely gull. There is something primitive and powerful about an estuary; it is a place of indistinct shapes and indefinite boundaries, a place of indefinable charms. It my be a tough neighborhood for a cutthroat, but for a fisherman an estuary is always an interesting place to be.

Still, it was the cutthroat that interested me most of all. The sea-run cutthroat is perhaps the most enigmatic of all trout; it comes and goes according to its own timetable and its own instincts, which are not for us to know. It is a neglected and little-studied fish, and what little study has been done has revealed only the barest details of its life. We know where and when it spawns and when its offspring go to sea, but we know little of what they do when they get there—except that they appear content to remain in the estuaries and feed on whatever they find there.

In time I decided to try to learn more about them—a quest motivated partly by the frequent failure of the tradition-al fishing tactics I had learned. It was hard enough to spend most of a day searching for a school of feeding cutthroat, but to finally find one, cover the rising fish and then have them repeatedly ignore the fly—as they very often did—made the whole effort seem an exercise in futility. So, in hopes of learning something that might improve my chances for success, I began to study the organisms that formed the bulk of the sea-run's diet and to record observations of its feeding patterns at various stages of the tide.

The first and most obvious thing to suggest itself from these studies was a change in the type of flies I have been using. After all, there seemed little reason other than popular tradition for using bright patterns like the old Skykomish Sunrise, the Dead Chicken or the Spruce. Such flies bore little resemblance to the sea-run's actual food and it seemed reasonable to think that imitations ought to work much better. The aquatic sowbug, probably the most common item

in the cutthroat diet, was too small to offer much hope of
successful imitation, but that still left such larger organisms as
the shrimp, the candlefish, or the stickleback. I began to
experiment with flies tied to imitate these things and found
they worked better than the traditional patterns, but still not
quite as well as I thought they should. My ratio of fish hooked
to rises covered improved somewhat, but it was still not close
to where I thought it ought to be. There had to be some other
answer.

Thinking long and hard about the problem, I was struck
suddenly by the incongruity of what I and other sea-run
anglers had been doing for so long: We had always searched
for signs of rising fish, which usually signaled the presence of a
school, and when we finally saw a rise we unfailingly covered
it with a wet fly and a sinking line. But even in salt water a
rise means only one thing: that a trout is feeding on the
surface, or just below. When you stop to think about it, there's
very little logic in covering a rising fish with a sinking fly.
Could a dry fly conceivably be the answer?

It was a radical thought. When a trout rises in fresh water
it nearly always does so in order to take an insect on the
surface, but in salt water there is rarely anything on the
surface for a fish to take. Very few species of insects live in salt
water and few of those are capable of producing anything that
could be considered comparable to a freshwater hatch. True,
an offshore breeze occasionally carries flying ants or mayflies
out over the estuaries, but only rarely had I ever seen this
happen. If natural insects were absent from the estuaries,
there seemed little chance that cutthroat would rise to a
floating artificial fly. Not only that, but the idea seemed
contrary to everything I knew—or thought I knew—about the
character of the cutthroat in salt water. It was supposed to be a
rough-and-tumble, meat-and-potatoes kind of fish, one not
given to the least form of subtlety. It lived in slimy places and

ate slimy things and the very notion of fishing for it with fine tackle and a dry fly seemed entirely out of place.

But the fact remained that cutthroat *do* rise in saltwater, for whatever reason. Perhaps it was a manifestation of their natural curiosity, or more likely a holdover habit from their early years in fresh water. A cutthroat spends two or three years in the river of its birth before making its first migration to the sea, and in that time it must surely learn to rise and take insects from the surface of the stream; rising also is a habit that a cutthroat resumes quickly when it re-enters fresh water on its spawning run. So perhaps it wasn't completely farfetched to think that a cutthroat would not forget the rising habit during the time it was at sea. Also, I remembered all the times I had teased trout into taking dry flies on streams and lakes when there were no natural insects on the water; maybe the same thing would be possible in estuaries.

I thought about the idea a long time before I finally decided to try it. To give the experiment a reasonable chance for success, I waited for a day with optimal conditions—a good tide, reasonably calm weather and a solid overcast to make the cutthroat less cautious. In the event, the first two conditions were present but the third was lacking; there had been thick fog early in the morning, but it had given way quickly to a rare day of bright sunshine by the time I arrived at a favorite spot on Hood Canal, a giant natural saltwater arm that separates the Olympic and Kitsap peninsulas.

I wasn't optimistic; it seemed likely the sunlight would put down any self-respecting cutthroat in the vicinity. Nevertheless, I rigged up with a floating line and knotted a No. 12 dry fly to the light leader. The fly was tied with a deerhair overlay and a deerhair wing to give it maximum flotation; that was important because I wanted a fly that not only would float sitting still, but one that could be skated across the surface without sinking. Skating was a method I had used often to stimulate the interest of trout in fresh water when there were no insects on the surface.

The tide was just beginning to ebb, withdrawing smoothly and almost imperceptibly from the beach, leaving behind a layer of dark wet gravel and sagging ranks of saltwort, still dripping from the tide. The surface was flat calm and a column of woodsmoke rose lazily from a cabin on the shore, dissolving slowly in the crisp morning air. I chose a favorite spot along the beach and began casting, allowing the fly to float briefly without movement after each cast, then stripping it in rapidly so that it kicked up a little V-shaped wake as it skated over the surface.

Nothing happened for the first little while. Then suddenly a bright cutthroat leaped high out of the water near the fly. Whether its unexpected appearance had been in some response to the fly, or whether it merely had chosen that time and place to jump, I could not tell. But I took it as a sign of encouragement and cast to the spot where the fish had been.

The fly floated there untouched and I began to strip it in. Halfway through the retrieve I caught a glimpse of a brownish trout shape in hot pursuit of the moving fly; even as I saw it, the fish made a quick lunge through the surface and took the fly in its mouth. Excited, I struck too quickly and pulled the fly away. Immediately I cast again to the same spot, but the trout—if it was still there—would not come up a second time.

More confident now, I resumed casting. Soon I saw the characteristic swirl of a rising cutthroat nearby and covered it. The little deerhair pattern dropped gently inside the expanding ring of water from the rise and I twitched it once, twice, three times. There was a flash of bright silver, the fly disappeared and the rod tip dipped obediently to the pull of a fat cutthroat. After a typically stubborn fight, I landed the fish, photographed it with the dry fly still stuck in its jaw, then turned it loose.

It took a few moments for the full realization to sink in: I

had taken a trout on a dry fly in saltwater, something I had
never done before, perhaps even something that no one had
ever done before. But whether I was the first to do so mattered
less than the fact that I had done it, and now I was anxious to
prove to myself that it wasn't just a fluke.

It wasn't. I caught several more fish on dry flies that day,
including some that took the floating artificial dead-drift on
the surface with classic head-and-tail rises like trout feeding in
a limestone stream. The whole day was a revelation to me,
and a display of hitherto unsuspected behavior on the part of
the cutthroat.

In the years since that day I've experimented with the dry
fly in estuaries from Puget Sound to the Alaska Panhandle and
have found that cutthroat respond to it enthusiastically in all
kinds of weather. The largest sea-run cutthroat I ever landed,
a handsome four-pounder, fell to a dry fly, and the same day
brought me another fish only a little smaller. Now nearly all
my estuary fishing is with a dry fly, and I am thoroughly
convinced that it is a much more effective method than the
wet fly—even the very best wet-fly imitations I have been able
to devise.

I still use the same basic deer-hair pattern that took the
very first fish, although now I fish it in a larger size. But
friends who have tried the dry fly in saltwater have experienced equal success on standard highfloating flies such as the
Humpy, the Goofus Bug or any of the Wulff patterns. Size and
color do not seem to matter so much as the ability to keep the
fly afloat and moving—since the moving fly seems much more
effective than a dead float.

Much to my delight, I have found that the cutthroat is
not the only species willing to rise to a dry fly in saltwater.
One day a heavy steelhead took my floating fly, then headed
quickly for Japan. The steelhead won that bout, but the first
coho salmon I hooked on a dry fly did not: It sucked in the fly
with delicate grace, then fought in a succession of spectacular

leaps until it had worn itself out and I was able to lead it to a net. At various times I have also hooked sea-run Dolly Varden and chinook salmon on dry flies and on a couple of rare occasions even succeeded in raising striped sea perch, which usually are dedicated bottom feeders. But the cutthroat is by far the most dependable riser, and most of these other fish came unexpectedly to my fly while I was fishing for cutthroat.

I still do not know for certain why the cutthroat rises to a dry fly in salt water, or why any other fish does so. But given the opportunity, I would rather take fish on a dry fly than in any other way, and the discovery that it is possible to do so in the estuaries has added immeasurably to my fishing pleasure. It also has proven that even a trout from a tough neighborhood can rise to a dry fly as delicately as the most sophisticated brown. And now, for that reason more than any other, the sea-run cutthroat has become one of my favorite fish of the fall.

A Fish to Remember

The steelheader's day begins in the early half-light of the dawn. The river is hidden under a rising mist that muffles the water's utterance, a gentle whisper that will grow louder with the day. The sun is only a robin's-egg glow of promise in the eastern sky behind the sawtoothed peaks of the North Cascades. The air is cool and quiet; even the birds are still. Somewhere, out in the river, beneath those rippling boils of current that glow briefly in the reflected silver light, the steelhead are waiting. They will not come to you; you must go to them.

And so you wade out into the dark river, sucking in

breath at the first feel of its chill against your waders. It is still too dark to see the river bottom, but you have made the crossing many times and you follow the familiar route, planting your feet carefully, sliding them cautiously over the slick, algae-covered rocks.

Finally you are in position, at the head of a long, languid pool, and you peer through the rising mist in the hope of seeing a rolling fish, down at the foot of the pool where they always lie. None shows, but that does not mean that none are there.

The sound the reel makes as you strip off line seems extra loud, a harsh, discordant note against the gentle morning sounds of the wakening river. Casting muscles, grown stiff from a night spent in camp on a bed that was not quite long enough, quickly limber up as the long green line works farther and farther out with each sweep of the powerful rod. The fly, a dark pattern with the inelegant name of Skunk, still is fixed to the leader point where you knotted it carefully in the dusk before the last few casts of yesterday.

Ready at last. The line rolls far out across the pool and carries the fly to the deep water rippling along the high rock bank on the far side. A mend upstream, and then another. The current accepts the fly, carries it along for brief inspection and then decides to swallow it. It is gone, invisible to you now, swinging in a long slow arc through the depths. Perhaps a steelhead sees it even now, is moving to meet it, following its passage as it tumbles in the flow. But nothing happens, and when the arc has reached its end and the line is parallel to the flow, you draw it slowly back, remembering all the times you have hooked steelhead on the retrieve at the end of such a cast. But that does not happen either, so you cast again. And again and again.

So many casts. So many mornings. So many times you have returned to camp, empty-handed, with the sun well up and the day warming, your stomach as empty as your creel, ready to trade in all your hopes for a single cup of coffee. The rest of the day is made to loaf, cut wood, drink coffee, talk or tie flies, and build back the morning's faded hopes until the eagerness returns by evening. Then you go back, back down to the pool, back to the silver chute of water that feeds it, back to the bouldery stretch where the current clutches at your heels and tries to dig the gravel out from under them. Maybe the evening will bring a bright steelhead, and if it does not, then a good night's sleep will again restore the shattered hopes.

It is late in the year and the river is low. Months have passed since the sun washed the last snow from the mountain slopes, and the dry days of Indian summer have caused the flow from the headwater springs to ebb. If only it would rain, you think. Not a lot; a lot would be too much. Just enough to quicken the current a little, to inject an element of freshness to a river gone stale, to awaken the steelhead and get them moving.

But the only fall so far has been of leaves from the limbs along the river. With each afternoon breeze there are more of them, old-rose and pumpkin-colored leaves from the vine maples and smaller yellow alder leaves with spots of brown rot already on them. The river collects them, as if they were colored postage stamps in an album, and plays with them in its current, turning them so that their sides flash briefly in the light. Sometimes you think the flash is from a fish and you stare long and hard to see if it will come again. The river has had its little joke on you.

You fish through the long evening twilight and watch the surface of the shallows boil as next year's smolts dash to feed upon tiny hatching flies. An old bruised salmon rolls out in the middle of the pool with power enough to send waves lapping against its farthest edges. Downstream a heron fishes in an eddy, standing as stark and still as a bronze sculpture. Light and color ebb from the evening sky and the first stars

twinkle tentatively. Now there are bats feeding on the evening hatch, and off in the woods the owls are waking. It is
time to go.

Through the scrub alders that have grown up near the
river's edge, along the open gravel bars, on the well-traveled
trail through the spike-grass and Indian potato near the river,
other anglers are returning from the day's fishing. One who
has been lucky goes before you, wading cautiously out into the
river's dark flow to make the crossing back to camp. One arm
is held high and from it hangs the broad silver shape of a
steelhead he has kept, and you feel a pang of envy at the sight.
Others are waiting as the angler exits the river on the far side
and they gather around him to pay compliments, admire the
bright catch and ask what fly and by what manner he managed
to take it. You wade across and up to them; the successful
angler is grinning and pleased and you know how he feels
because you have sometimes been in the center of such
attention. His is the only catch among the group, perhaps the
only steelhead taken on the river that day. Alas, the steelhead
no longer are as numerous as they once were.

Afterward there is a late dinner and a cold beer or two
and a roaring good campfire and some talk. The flame dies
away slowly and the talk goes with it as those with whom you
have shared the fire become transfixed by it, watching the
changing light and shapes of the glowing coals. I don't know
what it is about campfires, why they are as hypnotic as they
are, but when it grows quiet and the fire is the only light in
the darkness along the river, people stare into it as if the fire
held a message of the future, like tea leaves in the bottom of a
cup.

Finally weariness wins out and even the thought of that
too-short bed seems welcome. As you stand up from the fire
there is a quick little gust of wind that rattles the alder
branches and sends a new crop of leaves spiraling to the
ground. The stars have vanished, a layer of cloud has crept in.

As the wind freshens, there is a hint in it of the changing season. Perhaps tomorrow will bring rain. And long after you have fallen asleep, the rain begins drumming on the cabin roof.

The next morning is dark and chill. The night's rain has subsided to a nasty drizzle, and low-lying clouds, gray and ugly, have erased the mountains. They have settled into the valley as if they intended to stay all winter, as perhaps they do, dropping their cold sweat into the river. The river itself is as dark as the clouds that fill its valley. So far the rain has brought no visible rise to the water, but the current seems a trifle quicker, the temperature a little colder. Or is it just imagination?

You cross and start in at the head of the pool, finding the stiffness lasts longer on a cold, damp morning. But it is gone soon enough, and the long casts are falling on the familiar water, the fly searching through the reaches you have often searched before.

The river is quiet under rain. No flies hatch, there are no rises in the shallows. The kingfishers have yet to come awake, the water ousels have yet to come to feed and play along the margins of the river, and it seems as if you alone are awake in a sleeping world. The gentle river charms your thoughts, and you fish down the long pool by reflex, by habit, while your mind turns to memories of other mornings, other rivers. You think how long it has been since the first fish of summer, since the June days when the rivers ran high and swift with runoff and the first bright fish headed into them; how long since the morning when your fly found a bright 10-pounder in a sheltered stretch behind a boulder and you landed it after a long, hard fight in the swollen flow. You remember the late August afternoon when the retreating sun threw long shadows on the far side of a favorite pool, and a steelhead lying in the shadow seized your swinging fly, ran to the center of the river and leaped. Forever in your mind you will see its image there, a crescent silver shape poised for a long moment high above the pool. In another moment it had found a tangled root and broken you, but the memory remains as bright as the fish itself had been.

You think again of all the rivers you have fished, of how the very names of them evoke the excited sound of water rushing over stone: Stillaguamish, Toutle, Klickitat, Wind, and many more. Each river has its own personality, its own moods, its own peculiar color, sound and strength. Some are openly friendly, always bright and clear and eager to share their secrets, their currents cool enough to make the warmest summer day seem pleasant. Others are sullen and secretive, cold and dark and strong, their broken boulders waiting like submerged, spring-loaded traps to sweep an unwary angler off his feet. Such rivers are hard to know and hard to like, and yet their rewards are often great.

And there are some rivers that never let you know exactly where you stand. On bright days they seem sparkling and friendly in the sunshine, but when a misty summer rain settles down on them they turn cold and gray and vaguely hostile. They may be generous one day and totally unyielding the next, and just when you think you have come to know them they suddenly reveal a hitherto hidden aspect of themselves. In many ways they are the most interesting rivers of all. Fishermen will tell you it is the steelhead that draws them to the rivers, but much of the appeal is the rivers themselves, each with its own challenge, problems and personality.

The bright days of summer are a pleasant time to fish, but they are but a prelude to the fishing of the fall. The earth's colors soften as the days grow shorter and the nights colder, and there is a sudden stir of movement in the forests, fields and rivers. The last of the summer fish enter from the sea and join their predecessors in the shaded pools, growing restless as they sense the nearness of their spawning ordeal. There is an urgency as the season draws swiftly to a close, and it is felt as keenly by the anglers as by the fish they seek. In the mornings and evenings and sometimes all through the day the riffles and runs are crowded by anxious anglers, their rods rising and falling as they search for one last fish before the fall rains come. In some rivers it is the time for the greased line and the sparsely dressed fly, or a riffle hitch to make the fly plow a little furrow in the surface in hopes it will lead to a sudden explosive rise or bulging surface take.

Perhaps the misty rain now falling is the beginning of the end. Perhaps it will grow heavier as the day wears on and continue for days on end. Then the rivers will quickly rise and carry the color washed from the hillsides where the trees have been cut away. A hardy few anglers still will try to pit their skill against the swollen flow in hopes the river will yield a final catch, but the odds against success are great and they increase with each day of rain. So perhaps this quiet, drizzly dawn is the last real opportunity of fall.

It comes with the sudden ferocity of a blind-side football block and an electric shock rolled into one: One instant there is only the river's weight pressing gently on the line; in the next the line has been snatched from your fingertips, the rod tip pulled viciously down to the river, and somewhere out in the long pool a steelhead is lunging violently away with your fly stuck firmly in its jaw.

It is the thing you have hoped for, the purpose for your presence at the river, the result of all your patience and preparation; but still you are never quite ready when it comes. It draws the breath out of you and almost costs you your precious balance amid the slippery boulders of the midsection of the pool. For a moment you feel utterly helpless.

Then experience takes over. A picture of the geometry of the river flashes quickly in the mind's eye and the brain swiftly calculates the best vantage point from which to fight or follow the fish. Without thinking, you dash quickly through the fast, deep stretch which earlier you had so carefully and cautiously crossed. And as you splash into the shallows with your reel running wildly, you catch your first glimpse of the fish as it leaps high above the water in a flash of silver spray.

Stumbling over the rain-glistened rocks, you follow it, running as fast as waders will allow. Out of the pool it goes, down through a short, rocky, rushing stretch and into the smaller pool below where it jumps again, twisting in the air like a mustang trying to throw a stubborn rider.

Now the fish pauses in its flight and you gain some ground. The rod tip throbs and dips obediently to the movement of the steelhead as you scramble to catch up. Then the fish is away again, down to the end of the pool with a strong run that takes all the line you had recovered. You slip on a wet rock and thrust out a hand to break your fall; the reel spins wildly, then stops, and for a horrible moment you fear the fish is lost. But then a heavy pull signals it is not.

It goes on this way, down the length of the pool, then part way back up again, with two more jumps and several strong runs, but each one shorter than the last. Finally, with the line taut and throbbing like a bowstring, the leader is visible and below it the large silver shape of the fish. And in another moment the fish is on its side in the shallows, its gill plates flaring open and closed from its exertions, its strength totally spent. You wade out until the fish is between you and the shore, a gentle beach where the boulders have been buried under silt. And then the fish is in your hands.

It is a female, still fresh from the sea although the month is late. The black fly is in the upper corner of her mouth, the barbed hook point having punched its way through the thick membrane above the maxillary bone and found a purchase there. The fish is as bright as the river under sunlight, as clean as the moist morning air, and you know from the perfection of her that she has never known a hatchery's walls. All the dawns and dusks it took to capture her are unremembered now; your only thought is that this is a child of the river, and the river is her home.

You twist the fly free and wash the silt from her silver sides, grasp the wrist of her tail gently and turn her upright, facing into the current. The gills still open and close, the rhythm steadier now, and you move her back and forth, feeling in her cold flesh the gradual return of strength. And then, with a sudden powerful sweep of her broad tail, she is free of your grip, swimming slowly back into the dark river from which she was so rudely taken.

You sit down on an old water-silvered log along the riverbank and realize you are as drained of strength as the fish. The drizzle falls upon your face and your hands tremble as you try to light the wet tobacco in your pipe. Tonight, around the campfire, when notes of the day's fishing are compared, you will say that you took a good steelhead and returned it to the river. And somehow there is more reward in that than in bringing home a fish.

The tobacco reluctantly takes light and the smoke rises in the rain. You sit back and sigh and look out on the river, shining darkly in the wet, gray light, looking placid now but already gathering strength from the rain falling in the hills. Another year will pass before you see it exactly so again.

Your waders squeak as you stand up stiffly from your perch upon the log. The sky remains dark, even though above the clouds and beyond the hidden peaks the sun is up. You take a last look at the undulating pool whose surface was so recently shattered by the leaps of the steelhead you have just released, a look to fix the memory in your mind. Then you start the long walk back to camp.

Was it worth it?

Yes, it was.

It always is.

The End of the Year

The year ebbs. The blush of autumn fades quickly from the hills and the first fall storms come sweeping in from the Pacific to drop their heavy freight of rain. The days give up their warmth and the darkness lasts well into morning and comes again before the afternoon is done. High on the hillsides the snowfields start to grow; next year they will become the rivers.

All the quick life of the long warm months of spring and summer has gone to rest and the hills and valleys turn dark and drab in the gray late-autumn light. The days flow past as swiftly as the current in the streams and the prospect of winter hovers like a darkening storm on the near horizon. The season is late; the old familiar cycle once more is drawing to an end.

The years rest easily on the earth, which has seen so many come and go, but they weigh heavily on men. Inevitably their toll is felt: The trails begin to seem a little longer, the current in the rivers feels a little stronger and a dry fly floating at the end of a long cast becomes a much harder thing to see. There is a reminder of all these things in the passage of a year, and perhaps that is one reason why a trout fisherman seems determined to take advantage of every last remaining day. He plans one final trip, and then perhaps one more, even though the harsh breath of early winter already is blowing through the land.

I remember one such late-season trip. it still seemed too early to think of winter, though it was cold and wet when Pat Kirkpatrick and I left the city in early-morning darkness and when we reached the Cascades summit the first light of dawn revealed fresh snow along the road. We agreed that was not unusual in the high country, but the snow persisted all through our long descent of the eastern slope. There was even snow around the Columbia Basin lake that was our destination, and we left the only tracks on the trail leading in. The air was as cold as the blade of a knife and the lake was dark and still as we launched our boats and began to fish alone.

After a while it grew even colder and crusts of ice began forming in our fly-rod guides. No trout took hold, nor did we even see a sign of one, and there was nothing to relieve the freezing monotony of the dark morning. The cold numbed our faces and fingers until finally we could tolerate it no longer; we went ashore, shook the snow from broken sagebrush limbs and built a reluctant fire. Its pale flame was a welcome sight, but though we huddled close we could feel little of its heat; the air was so bitter that even the fire seemed cold.

But we persevered, and early in the afternoon the air

warmed a little and at last the trout began to stir. First there was a solitary rise far out in the center of the shallow lake; it was followed by another, then several at a time. Pat hit a fish and then I had one and before the afternoon was done each of us had caught a half dozen or more—all big, bright, hard-fighting rainbows. That night we drove to town and treated ourselves to a big steak dinner in a warm restaurant and decided the day had been well spent despite the discomfort we had been through.

Another time Ed Foss and I set out on a dark late-November day to fish for sea-run cutthroat. A cold wind drove mixed rain and snow into our faces and whipped the water to a froth so that we were forced to seek shelter along a lee shore. Late in the day, when we were thoroughly wet and chilled, we returned to the boat ramp and found a game warden in a warm car, waiting to check our licenses. His greeting was abrupt: "I've been all over this county and you two are the only damn fools I could find outdoors on a day like this." But he was surprised to learn we had both caught fish despite the weather, and by the standards of estuary fishing it had been a most successful day.

Yet there have been other days that were not so successful, days when we pushed the season or the weather or our luck a little too far, when wind or rain or snow or uncooperative trout forced a quick retreat indoors. And though such days tend to be soon forgotten, I suspect there have been more of them than any other kind.

What magic quality does the trout possess that compels men to search for it in such dark and desperate weather? What virtue does it offer to command such unwavering devotion? I can answer only for myself: I love trout because they are among the most beautiful and graceful of all creatures and because they dwell in some of the most beautiful and graceful of all places. I love them because I am a fly fisherman and trout inspired the invention of my sport; without them it would be a very different sport, if indeed it existed at all.

The trout has a way of rising to a floating fly that takes your breath away, and I love it for that and for what it will do after the fly is firmly taken. I love trout because they are honest and uncompromising creatures; no man was ever cheated by a trout. I love them because they have inspired me to seek a wider knowledge of the natural world, and such knowledge brings immense satisfaction and pleasure. And I love trout because they have led me into friendships with others who feel about them as I do, and such friendships make a man's life immeasurably richer.

A trout, by its very nature, is a thing that can only be touched and briefly held; an angler can never truly capture one or call a trout his own. If a trout is killed it becomes a lump of cold flesh, bereft of all the virtues that make it worth seeking; if it is returned to the stream, then the angler who caught it is left with only his fragile memory for a keepsake. Yet those are the only choices, and in that mysterious ephemeral quality of trout is the very magic that makes it something larger than itself: For us it becomes the fleeting fulfillment of a dream, a symbol that a man's hopes are sometimes realized—if only for a moment. That is why the trout commands such devotion from so many, why catching one sometimes is a mystical experience that strikes sparks in a fisherman's soul.

The bond between men and trout runs deep, though it is not ordinarily a thing that fishermen acknowledge or discuss. But it is always there, and sometimes it is revealed in unexpected ways.

One such display remains vivid in my mind. I was fishing the North Fork of the Stillaguamish and had hiked upstream from my cabin to a point where I could see the Deer Creek Riffle was empty, with no other anglers in sight. The empty stream was inviting and I hurried forward, but I had taken only a few steps when two fishermen emerged from the woods near the top of the run; they were much closer to it than I was, and my heart sank when I saw them.

But there was something unusual about the pair. They were moving at a painfully slow pace, and as I got closer I could see that although both wore waders and fishing vests and carried fly rods, one was on crutches and the other was helping him swing his legs over the scattered boulders. I stood aside and watched their slow progress toward the stream; when they finally reached it, the lame man leaned on his friend and together they inched their way out until they were knee-deep in the river. Then the helper took a crutch away, leaving his companion with only one to lean on, and gently placed a fly rod in his free hand. With the remaining crutch tucked under one arm, the lame man began to cast.

It was a touching sight and my heart went out to the young man leaning on the single crutch while the river curled around him. I learned from his friend that a bulldozer had crushed his legs and this was his first outing after many months in the hospital. Chances were he might never walk again, but even such a tragic infirmity was not enough to keep him from returning to the pursuit he loved. As I watched him there, standing unsteadily in the pool, I could not help but admire his quiet courage, and I said a silent prayer that a steelhead soon would come and take his fly.

The great sorrow is that all men do not love the trout as much. For a creature that has given men so much pleasure, inspiration and reward, the trout has suffered grievously from the activities of man. Too often it has been the victim of human ignorance, shortsightedness, or greed; the evidence lies everywhere in ruined rivers, defoliated slopes, impassable dams, and polluting industries. The truth is that man has nothing so important or urgent to do that he needs to sacrifice the trout or its habitat in order to do it—but truth is something that often is difficult for men to see while there is yet a chance to profit from the sight.

That the trout has been able to survive at the hands of man is a tribute to the toughness of its breed and to the efforts of those who have worked to preserve it. But it is late in The Year of the Trout and the future is far from assured.

November falls from the calendar like a last lonely stubborn leaf. Along the rivers the trees stand bare and bleak and dripping from the rain. In the limbs of some the eagles sit and wait, watching for the current to bring them the last of the spawned-out salmon.

The rain clatters heavily on the dead leaves that clad the forest floor and soaks down through them to the soil; soon it will re-emerge in far-off springs. Rain fills the swamps and beaver ponds in the deep woods and collects in little brooks and rivulets that mutter on the hillsides. Day after day it rains until all the springs and swamps and rivulets and brooks begin pouring their swollen discharge into the rivers. The rivers grow fat and gray and reach out to reclaim the gravel bars and empty sloughs that have been left to dry since spring. Sometimes it rains so long and hard that the rivers cannot carry the full weight of water pressing down on them; hour by hour they edge upward until suddenly they are out of their banks and running through the fields, breaking roads and threatening the transient works of men. People curse them, but the rivers are only doing what rivers have always done.

The swollen December flow brings up the first big run of winter steelhead, though their passage may be hidden by the glut of water. But late in the month, when the weather turns colder and the rivers begin to subside, there may be a chance to fish for them.

Such fishing, when and if it comes, has an unmistakable air of finality about it. There is the certain knowledge that it is the very last fishing of the year, that the steelhead—so bright and lively now—will soon be spent from spawning as their own cycle nears an end. Even the rivers seem to grow old before our eyes: We cast into the present, which exists only for the instant it takes for it to pass; then it flows downstream, forever beyond our reach, and becomes the past. Looking downstream is like looking backward from December at all the vanished moments of the year.

Some of those moments we will long remember—good times spent in pleasant places, the company of friends around the campfire, the thrill of large trout won or lost, and all the host of happy things that only a trout fisherman can know or feel or understand. These are rewards that we alone can share.

Now the winter dusk fades into darkness and the darkness brings more rain. Soon the rain becomes snow, heavy and wet and melting at its first touch upon the soil. But then it grows colder and the snow turns thick and fine and begins to stay; it collects first upon the foothill slopes, then reaches down into the valleys and finally settles slowly on the anglers' trails and empty campfire rings along the rivers.

In the softness of the snowy night the year at last steals quietly away. But time and the rivers continue flowing—and below the surface of the silent streams, the trout are always there.